Rainbow People
Reinventing Northeast India

Attention Authors

Manas Publications is fighting a war to tell the world that India can win the battle not only by the bullet but also by pen. We are converting fighters into writers. There is no dearth of intellectuals in our country, however, their knowledge is confined to them only. No sincere effort has been made by any other publisher to channelise their knowledge, which is why the talent of every intellectual remains latent. An author always presents the raw material in the shape of a manuscript and it is the job of the publisher to convert it to a finished product. Manas has been continually motivating intellectuals and publishing their manuscripts for more than two decades and would like to publish your manuscript too. If you or your colleagues have a manuscript ready for publication or are working on it, contact us with a detailed synopsis and list of contents. Manas will also suggest you a suitable title for writing related to your area of expertise. Manas is known for its publishing quality. We take utmost care in publishing and also give wide publicity to the book and its author through our national and international distribution network.

RAINBOW PEOPLE
REINVENTING NORTHEAST INDIA

Falguni Rajkumar

Manas Publications
(We Convert Fighters into Writers)
New Delhi-110002 (INDIA)

MANAS PUBLICATIONS
(Publishers, Library Suppliers, Importers & Exporters)
4402/5-A, Ansari Road
(Opp. HDFC Bank)
Darya Ganj, New Delhi-110 002 (INDIA)
Off. © 23260783, 23265523, Res. © 23842660
Fax: 011-23272766
E-mail: manaspublications@vsnl.com
manaspublications@gmail.com
www.manaspublications.in

ISBN 978-81-7049-372-3

Rs. 795

Typeset at
Manas Publications

Printed in India at
RK Print Services, Delhi
and published by Mrs Suman Lata for
Manas Publications, 4402/5-A, Ansari Road
(Opp. HDFC Bank),
Darya Ganj, New Delhi-110 002 (INDIA)

Contents

Cover Design and Meaning

The Seven figures, each with a different colour of the rainbow (VIBGYOR) holding each other's hands forming a circle, represent the seven states constituting the Northeast Region. The configuration of the figures denoting cooperation and partnership among the states of the region for economic development and progress are placed within the wheel of the Ashok Chakra, part of the national flag.

Conceptualised by the author and executed by Manas Publications.

Dedicated to

Baba, Meme, Ima

Preface

Three types of people write on or about the Northeast of India. The first are those who write because they know what they write. The second are those who think they know the region and hence venture to write. The third are those who feel for the people and the region and hence write. I belong to the third category. Two things qualified me to undertake the task. I am a 'child' of the Northeast region, and an 'adult', nurtured by the rest of India, having spent most part of life serving across the country. Writing about the Northeast is both easy and difficult for me. Easy because, I am an 'insider', a euphuism, implying I am from the region and know the people and the region. Difficult, because being an 'insider', writing about Northeast India has its own disadvantages. Either way, I am a potential victim of solicitous opinions and views.

The obvious inference is that the views and opinions from people like me writing about the Northeast region with empathy and understanding, can be taken as biased and hence subjective. Consequently, much of the assumed advantage the 'insider' may have, therefore, instead becomes a handicap. Conversely, when objectivity requires me to give due credit to the Government of India and rest of the country for the efforts made for the region, the people of Northeast tend to consider 'insiders' like me, a turncoat or a renegade. The dilemma is obvious. In spite of these imponderables, I have tried to infuse the two backgrounds, the northeastern and the national, as best and as diligently as I can.

Appreciating and understanding the Northeasterners' mind and relating it with the thinking in the rest of the country, requires a special mindset, quite distinct and different. Given my background, exposures and experiences, I am placed at that enviable position to realise and perceive the disconnect that exists between the average Northeasterner and other Indians. In doing so, I may appear critical at times but in all these, disrespect of any kind is never intended or meant to any individual, group, institutions or the concepts analysed. The task is challenging, especially since personal prejudices and biases tend to detract one from objectivity and equanimity in the articulation of one's thoughts. I am conscious of this fact.

Within these pages, occasional streaks of raw emotions and feelings, distinctly Northeastern, different from the rest of the country will be discernible. This is because different nuances operate in the average Northeasterner in the way they think and look at life. Social, cultural and ethnological differences apart, there are subtle perceptible differences in vulnerability between a Northeasterner and others from the rest of the country. The average Northeasterners are highly emotional and sensitive, thinking with their hearts rather than subject themselves to the semantics of intellectual hyperboles and logic of the abstract. Yet hidden behind these attributes, are the invisible harsh experiences and realities of life, which also give them the added discerning ability to judge life with both sensitivity and objectivity. The Northeast Indian is an enigma for many.

Appreciation of these basic differences between the Northeasterners and other Indians in the country, which is the key to successful communication, will also provide the reasons of the Northeasterners' reluctance and inability to assimilate into the national mainstream inhibiting fraternisation. The task of overcoming these differences appear difficult but is not impossible, all it needs is an open mind, devoid of prejudices and preconceived notions about the people and the Northeast region.

These qualificatory opening remarks and amplifications are necessary because writing about the Northeast for me is not merely writing about an inanimate place or region along with all its adjective correlates, it is also writing about people with feelings, their despairs and hopes. The book is a relook and a reinterpretation of the events associated with their lives, as perceived by them. Trapped as they are in perpetual physical isolation from the rest of the country and unable to find adequate voice on the appropriate platform to express and give their views or opinions, presenting their versions of history in a book like this, are important.

In writing this book, I am also constrained by the fact that I am not writing a book of fiction, but the events in history, albeit from a perspective I consider important in understanding the region. Writing fiction is like democracy, while non-fiction is like autarchy. The former is expansive, amplifying the spirit of freedom while the latter is restrictive and circumventing. I am compelled to adhere to these restrictions and respect the verdict of the unwritten code and ethics of writing.

Within history writing itself, re-interpreting history is much more difficult and complex, since it is not only re-inventing the events in history and juxtaposing them in a different context, but is also dismantling the accepted line of thinking and interpretations. The task becomes much more arduous and challenging, especially when the past is being recontextualised to address the problems and needs of the present times. This book does precisely this, it provides new perspectives of the region's history, based on reinterpretations of the events, its stories, myths and folktales, which many in the region believe are the real history of the region. Whatever is the logic of history writing; there is an impression in the Northeast, that the histories of the region are tempered by the 'inverted' constrained logic of political expediencies and other considerations at various points of time in the past. This book is an attempt to relook at some of these and put the records straight.

The additional difficulty in writing on or about the remote region as the Northeast is that the sources of history are unclear, and their authenticity often shrouded in mystery and hence considered unreliable. Sir Edmund Gait sums the dilemma in his famous book, *A History of* Assam, in the following words. *"The stories culled from the sources cannot of course be dignified with the name history. They are at best, ancient traditions, but even this cannot be asserted with certainty, and some of them may have been interpolated by interested copyists in comparatively recent times. They do, however, contain a substratum of fact. And, in any case, they are fondly remembered by the people."* Sir Edward further adds that the conclusions drawn are essentially based on indirect deductions from the *"...indications derived from philology and ethnography."* What applies to Assam is equally applicable to most of the histories of the states in the region.

The question that will instantly come up in the beginning of this book on the Northeast is, why another, especially on identity. The question is quite pertinent. However, this book is different from others on many counts. The book is neither a disjointed or segmented study of the region from various perspectives; anthropological, social or cultural nor a reappraisal of the law and order problems normally associated with any study of the region. Instead, it relooks at and reexamines comprehensively the history of the various integrating factors, which have shaped the ethnic identity politics of the Northeast. This reexamination is undertaken to understand and establish the irrefutable connections that exist between the underdevelopment, general levels of poverty and the preoccupation with identity politics in the region.

The assumption based on which the book proceeds is that there is a close connection and inverted dynamic link between the levels of economic backwardness, poverty, the general lack of development with the disparaging preoccupation of identity politics of the people in the region. It postulates, the earlier this fact is realised and ways found on topmost priority to effectively address the pernicious preoccupation with ethnic identity politics in the Northeast, the core issues of poverty and underdevelopment are bound to persist. Simultaneously, the book also assumes that this is not possible unless the various ethnic identities in the region find ways to think and work together for developmental purposes as a region by overcoming the acrimonious existing ethnic disconnect. One aspect is clear, this avertable link between general levels of economic poverty, underdevelopment of the region and ethnic identity politics exists because of the failure of the policy makers to take cognizance and recognise the significance of this corelationship. Alternatively, if they do, they do not know how to either overcome or delink the two. The problems of the Northeast lie in not only appreciating the importance of this interlink but also finding ways and means to overcome them together simultaneously.

Understanding this aspect of the preoccupation of identity and its link with the development of the region is important, especially the politics associated with it because it has got so inextricably fused in the body-politics of the region that disregarding the interlink becomes impossible. It is the vigour and belligerence of the preoccupation, now ingrained in the psyche of the people subconsciously, which is affecting regional development. The book acknowledges and recognises the importance and significance of both, and suggests ways to integrate the aspirations of ethnic identity with the development efforts directionally at the earliest, since these are vital for the region's progress as a whole.

From this perspective, it is important to understand the history and dynamics of the complex nature of ethnic identity politics in the Northeast by all those who love the people of the region. In addition, because of inadequate information, deficit details, misinformation and inaccurate analyses that automatically follow, wrong conclusions and vilifications of the people and the region have taken place. This is also partly because studies on the region are segmented rather than holistic in their contents, either they are highly academic, scholastic and complex or most often analysed mainly from the socio-anthropological or from the law and order perspective and context primarily. More importantly, the sources based on which these analyses are made are those left behind by foreigners and others, essentially from an 'outsider' perspective and not from the view or perspective of the Northeasterners who have either been the beneficiaries or most often the victims of these analyses or critique.

Moreover, issues on development or underdevelopment of the region are analysed and examined purely from the economic and financial perspectives or in the context of development strategies forgetting the fact that in the Northeast there are very strong undercurrent divisive ethnic identity problems that permeate in every aspect of life in the region. Devoid of this understanding, a contextual discrepancy and impropriety takes place, making all policy formulations and attempts at development quite ineffective, primarily because the main cause; the issue of ethnic identity divide remains unaddressed. It is the arbitrariness of this neglect, characteristically Indian, which makes the fate and story of transformation of the Northeast to what it is at present, painful. The book attempts to simplify the understanding of the tenacious corelationship between the problems of the region's preoccupation with assertive ethnic identity with the underdevelopment and poverty of the region. I hope I will achieve this.

The book is a directional variant from the general trend of looking at identity politics in the Northeast region of the country. For instance, the book does not subscribe to the rather simplistic view that the preoccupation of the people of the region with ethnic identity is due to the persecution complex that numerically small communities and ethnic groups suffer across the world. The book is a departure also from the traditional approach of looking at the Northeast region essentially from the geo-political and security related perspectives, forgetting that the root cause of the problems of the region is poverty and underdevelopment. It is also not a book about castigating the unfortunate fate of the region to its geography, which is the normal way to explain away its present woes. The book is instead simply a holistic analysis and reexamination, an attempt to trace the causes or reasons behind the disruptive preoccupation of the region with their respective ethnic identities, which in turn has adversely affected the growth and development of the region.

In proceeding with the above premises, the book discovers that the rise of assertive ethnic identity politics in the region is interplay of several factors, political misdemeanour, the British India policies, religious, social, anthropological and the lack of appreciating the subtle nuances that differentiates the region from other parts of the country by the Government of India on many issues. The book is a sincere and honest attempt to understand the various complicities and circumstances of history, the contributory factors that has gone in the making of the belligerent Northeastern persona responsible for the rise of assertive identity politics in the region in the past, to overcome the problems of the present. I believe the book achieves this, by retracing the tentative faltering baby-steps taken by the region, and the lack of nurturing skills of the Governments then in power, in the initial stages of nationhood building.

Interestingly, in arriving at this value judgment, facts and circumstances reveal that the monomaniacal preoccupation with ethnic identity in the region are not homegrown maladies spawned in the region by the people, but infectious influences imposed on the people of the region from outside as 'implants'. The ineluctable fact, which emerge, is that the ubiquitous roles played by these exogenous influences were beyond the control of the people of the region and hence not of their making. Recognising this aspect of the region's past can restore some of the age-old affiliations, bring back understanding and foster a sense of partnership, especially through their anthropological links and connections among the various ethnic groups so that the ethnic fault lines, which have formed can re-cement over time. Once these connectivities, either anthropologically, historically or simply because fate has ordained them to be 'geographically' bound together in a region is realised, alternative models for the development and progress of the region can be evolved.

To resolve the two needs of the region, economic development and overcoming the ethnic divide simultaneously, adoption of available international models and practices of partnership among nations like the European Union and empowering existing institutions like the North Eastern Council (NEC), without in any manner diluting or disturbing the federal spirit of the Constitution by respecting the existing political dispensation in the region is suggested as one possible way out. Institution like the North Eastern Council should not only be merely allowed to perform its legitimate role of the planning and developmental authority for the region for which it is established, but also empower it to bring together the constituent states of the Northeast together and bridge the ethnic divide. The hope and desire in highlighting this approach for the Northeast is to prevent the ever-growing ethnic divide in the Northeast, which is adversely affecting the development and progress of the region. In the course of the analyses, it will emerge that the general trend and attitude to find fault with each other among the various ethnic groups in the region are paradoxical, self-effacing and detrimental given the similar acculturated anthropological, ethnic and social histories and especially because of the common geo-political disadvantages shared by all of them. The intention is to ensure that the blessings of democracy, peace and progress do not remain mere mirages for the people of the region.

The book is blunt, undiplomatic at times, but considered necessary and inevitable if the given present state of affairs of development, poverty; the casualties of the overwhelming gnawing problems of the divisive nature of inter-ethnic equations and relations in the region is to be overcome.

Arrangement and Contents of the Chapters

Several factors are responsible for the disruption of the natural acculturated process of identity formation in the Northeast from a peaceful, pluralistic and egalitarian region, to one of intolerance and rivalry. Out of the many factors, from the perspective of this book only five of them are analysed. These are, (1) the adverse affects and ramifications of the disruption of the natural corridors for movement of people, trade and commerce by the partition of the country which effectively sealed off the region from the rest of the country. (2) The British policy of the 'exclusivity' under the Bengal Frontier Regulation of 1873 and the 'Excluded Area' and the 'Partially Excluded Area'. (3) The role, influence and affect of Hinduism and Christianity, the two exogenous religions. (4) The affect and consequences of the categorisation of the upland tribal communities of the region as 'Scheduled tribes' on ethnic identity formations, and (5) other related aspects and issues which are directly and indirectly responsible for the ethnic identity divide in the region.

The first Chapter analyses the various existing concepts and theories about ethnic identity formations and relates these to the Northeast. Chapter 1 forms the backdrop to the main theme of the book.

Chapter 2 examines the importance and significance of the geography of the region; it highlights how the abrogation of the natural formations and boundaries by politically contrived ones of 'Partition' and state reorganisations create serious problems of 'communication' by disrupting lives of people and adversely affecting the economy of the region. The adverse psychological impact of the segregation of the region from the rest of the country at Independence, the negation of the plural social ethos of the region by the reorganisation of the States is analysed. The tendency, on the other hand, to deal with all the problems of the various ethnic groups of the region geographically, rather than anthropocentrically, ignoring the fact that each of these ethnic identities are different with their respective problems, creates its own adverse administrative consequences. This is critically analysed as an example of the wrong application and use of geography in dealing with the region.

Chapter 3 examines various British policies in the North Eastern Frontiers especially those directly responsible for the introduction of ethnic identity politics in the region. The professed intended 'protection' of the upland tribal communities, which was used as the main reason for introducing the various administrative orders based on the policy of 'exclusion' under the Bengal Eastern Frontier Regulation of 1873, popularly known as the 'inner line permit' and the more ambitious 'Excluded Area' and the 'Partially Excluded Area' are critically assessed in the light of the ethnic identity polarization in the region today. Concurrently, the real British intentions behind the various policies and administrative decisions like the encouragement and support provided to Christian missionaries, demarcation of boundaries between Burma, China and Tibet and British India territories and a host of similar aspects of British policies directly and indirectly related to the politics of ethnic identity in the region are analysed. The Chapter deals with important aspects of British Northeast India policies in the context of 'segregation' of people in the region as the beginning of the pernicious ethnic identity 'divide' in the Northeast.

Religion, which is one of the most important factors in ethnic identity formation in the region is analysed from Chapter 4 to Chapter 6. Hinduism and Christianity, the two main universal religions, which are primarily responsible for the introduction of the concept of religious identity, and synonymous with ethnic identity in the region, are analysed critically. The introduction of the idea of religion as distinct and separate from a person's ethnic identity, which was a new concept among many communities, affected people's way of thinking and dealing with each other in the region. The history, role and impact of Hinduism and Christianity, on some of the major ethnic groups in each of the states and their overall affect in identity formation in the region are reappraised.

Chapter 7 critically evaluates the categorisation of people and communities particularly the upland communities of the region as 'Scheduled Tribes', especially the socio-political impact on the ethnic equations and relationship between those categorised as 'Scheduled Tribes' and those who were not. The consequential polarization and hardening of attitudes, the implications and ramifications on the polity in the region are analysed.

In the history of ethnic identity in the Northeast, many assumed associations, without adequate proof, have greatly influenced and adversely affected social equations among the ethnic groups in the region. Chapter 8 analyses these issues and their impact on ethnic identity formation. As an example, the assumed claims of link of the Hindus of the two states of Assam (Pragjyotisha) and Manipur with the Indic-Hindu Aryan civilisation led to the inculcation of superiority complex among the various Hindus over their non-Hindu upland neighbours in the Northeast. This adversely affected tribal (non-Hindus) and non-tribal (Hindus) relationships and eventually polarized the two sets of people. Other important issues, the problems of language, the adverse economical impact of the reorganisation of Assam in 1972 and the politics of the Plain tribals of Assam, the autochthons, which plagued Assam and its regional ramifications and significance, are analysed.

The preceding Chapters point out clearly the irrefutable similarities in ethnic histories, social evolutions and the rise of assertive ethnic identity politics among the various ethnic groups in the Northeast. These Chapters also reveal that the history of ethnic identity formation in the region is the affect of several external influences on the people of the region and are not of their making alone. It is in effect, the infusion of various exogenous influences, which has affected and immensely harmed the plural ethos and homogeneity of the region. The consequential ethnic divide introduced in the region by these exogenous factors; byproducts of the circumstances of history, polarized ethnic relations and has in turn led to the disjointed development of the States, adversely affecting the overall progress of the region.

Given, therefore, the indispensability of anthropological, socio-cultural links, ties and history of the people in the region, and compelled by the topography of the region, which bind them together, the book postulates that all ethnic groups and communities in the region must reorient their approach to development by first understanding and appreciating their anthropological links and ties in the past. Thereafter, based on these associations confront the impending problems of a globalized economic world order together as a group rather than work at cross purposes to each other's development efforts. To achieve this, a unified collective approach to development, through regional planning without in any manner diluting the federal structure of the Constitution or the political status of the States in the region, seems the only way out of the present plight of the region and the States.

Based on these findings, Chapters 9 and 10, the penultimate Chapters, examines in detail the emerging economic environment globally and India's position in it. The likely impact of these development on the Northeast region in the future is analysed. Keeping in view the present nature of disjointed economic development in the region predominantly arising out of the prevailing ethnic divide, the chapters suggest ways out of the predicament especially in the context of the emerging globalized economic scenario. In this context and perspective, a case is made for the immediate setting up or strengthening of an existing regional body capable of preparing the region to confront the impending changes that are likely to take place sooner or later, by cordenating the planned development of the region as a whole, and also one that is simultaneously capable of bridging the ethnic divide

Chapter 9 in adition, examines the reasons behind the successful working of the European Union and critically analyses in Chapter 10 why a regional setup in India like the North Eastern Council has not succeeded. The workings of the North Eastern Council, its existing powers, equations with the Planning Commission, the Ministry for the Development of the Northeast (DoNER) and other related aspects are critically analysed. Chapter 10 prognosticates, in conclusion that any institution or organisation capable of undertaking the dual responsibilities of planning for the economic development for the entire region and simultaneously, capable of bridging the ethnic 'divide' to overcome the various problems arising from, and confronting the Northeast consequently at present, can be the North Eastern council, provided the Central Government supports and empowers the council appropriately to enable it to discharge both these responsibilities.

NOTES

Map not to scale

CHAPTER – I

Ethnic Identity and the Northeast

Something there is that doesn't love a wall...
I let my neighbour know beyond the hill...
He is all pine and I am apple orchard.
My apple trees will never get across
And eat the cones under his pines, I tell him...
Before I built a wall I'd ask to know
What I was walling in or walling out,
And to whom I was like to give offence.
Something there is that doesn't love a wall,
That wants it down'.

—Robert Frost; *'Mending Wall'*

The Northeast region of India has an identity of its own, quite distinct and separate from the mainstream national identity. This regional identity is geomorphologically endowed, and ethnically enforced. Within the framework of the sub-national regional identity, many ethnic and sub-ethnic identities exist, both in the valleys (Lowlands) and in the hills (Uplands). Many of these sub-identities share either individually or collectively anthropological connectivity, linguistic, cultural affinity, migration history, and their respective native indigenous religions and faiths. Above all, they are conjoined by the common factor of geographical and political isolation. Normally, these shared attributes, which places all of them into a single cloistered exclusive category of their own, should have brought the various ethnic identities together, creating a peaceful ambience and homogeneous ethos, conducive for economic partnership, development and progress of the region. Instead, the unique social and cultural distinctiveness characterizing each ethnic group in the region sadly and ironically, has become the symbols of assertive identity politics, hindering the economic development of the region and jeopardizing the future of generations to come.

Consequently, in this surcharged atmosphere, the implosion of ethnic identity problems, visible in the form of insurgencies as its external manifestations has relegated regional cooperation, partnership for the orderly economic developments and progress of the region to obscure slots of insignificance. In the Northeast, ethnic identity politics has introduced a situational ambivalence, altering the normative processes of development. It is important to understand this aspect and appropriately address it.

This Chapter examines the various existing definitions and meanings of ethnic identity, especially its qualificatory attributes in the context of understanding the piquant situation prevailing in the Northeast region of India, where every aspect of life among the various ethnic groups is dominated by it. This Chapter forms the background to understand the synergic co-relationship between underdevelopment and preoccupation with ethnic identity politics in the region.

Introduction

Ethnic identity is inherently contradictory; it enables and simultaneously inhibits, bringing together people and dividing them one from the other. Yet, human beings gave to themselves the concept of identity. In the beginning human beings distinguished themselves from other form of living being, and then tenaciously found ways to divide themselves by fostering upon themselves names, individual titles, clan affiliates, societal associations, official positions and a host of co-relates and appellatives, all embellishments that make them distinctive even amongst themselves. Human need for an identity arises mainly from human insecurity essentially to meet the basic human needs for security, shelter, food and work, and above these, the fulfillment of a sense of self-worth. Inherent in it as a concept, identity has positive attributes that propel humans to search and pursue higher goals and nobler objectives to enrich their self-identity. Except for a few, most human beings are prisoners of their own identity.

In all these, the self-effacing attribute of the spirit of humanity finds such identifications contradictory and self-defeating in the end, since as a principle it negates the concept of universal Brotherhood of Mankind. Robert Frost bemoans this posturing and tendency to divide one human being from another, poignantly put across in the poem 'Mending Wall', from which a few lines are cited above. In his views, *"something there is"* in nature that does not accept this divide between man and man, as it imposes 'divisions' or 'walls', either as identity or qualificatory attributes associated with it, negating the law of nature.

If geography places spatially the people of the Northeast region in a category of their own, it is the many ethnic identities of the region, which reinforces this exclusivity further and yet, under the tutelage of ethnic identity, new politically bifurcated physical spaces and contrived boundaries have been foistered dividing people in the region farther apart. In the Northeast region of India, a region now metonymical with 'insurgency', 'law and order', inter ethnic relations have degenerated into an unending vortex of mistrust and tension. All these manifestations are the visible forms of assertive ethnic identity politics, the soft underbelly of the Northeastern psyche.

The concept and definition of identity has undergone many changes. Conceptually, identity by itself is a complex sociological phenomenon. In the context of identity formation in the Northeast, there are four main determinants, which are relevant and necessary to understand the meaning and implication of ethnic identity in the region. These are; (i) the defined biological inherent attribute, which is not interchangeable. (ii) The indigenous native religion a clan or community follows, which is its metonym. (iii) The influence of universal religion, primarily Hinduism and Christianity, and lastly, (iv) the role played by the Governments, the Administration and politics of the region.

Definition of Identity

In Latin (ethnicus) and Greek (ethnikas), ethnicity denotes 'nation'. In Greek, Trimble and Dickson[1] states, *"...ethos means custom, disposition or trait. Ethnikas and ethos taken together therefore can mean a band of people (nation) living together who share and acknowledge common customs. The second part of the construct, identity, has Latin origins and is derived from the word identitas; the word is formed from idem meaning same". "Thus, the term is used to express the notion of sameness, likeness and oneness"*. Trimble and Dickson combines the meanings of both the terms, 'Ethnic' and 'Identity' and introduces the term 'Ethnic Identity' denoting and meaning *"...the sameness of a band or nation of people who share common customs, traditions, historical experiences, and in some instances geographical residence."* In the conventional sense of the term, social scientists, however, refer to both 'ethnicity' and 'identity' as an overlap, more in their conjunction rather than separately. Generally, ethnic identity is most often considered synonymous with race or racial identity and hence with ethnicity. This definition, however, tends to confine ethnicity or ethnic identity, within the conventional standard of social anthropology, and conveniently does away with the intricacies that exist in the hermeneutic polemics of its definition.

The concept of ethnic identity has however, changed over the years, it is not as simple as it was once any more. While its essential and basic definition, given by Clifford Geertz as "activated primordial consciousness" remain, denoting a psycho-social phenomenon or more simply stated, a 'feeling of togetherness', a number of recent interpretations, based on empirical studies and data have added new dimensions as well as exposed some of the limitations of the earlier assumptions and definitions. These new interpretations have broadened the perspective. For instance, the earlier assumption that there is a primordial connection between ethnic identity and culture and considered as conjuncts, and as such 'essentials', has in recent times undergone changes in perception. The core-concept of culture and ethnicity as conjuncts, proxy of one for the other and held as the sheet-anchor to each, are now considered as separate and not, descriptive of each other. In other words, culture does not define ethnicity, nor does ethnicity denote culture.

Conversely, the concept of culture once considered as impervious, unchangeable and rigidly structured; in the sense of its ability to imbibe and absorb new attributes, is now instead considered just the opposite; as assimilative and capable of constantly evolving and changing. This view of culture has become the rule rather than the exception. Culture has now a distinct place of its own, quite independent of both 'ethnicity' and 'identity'. This view of culture is similar to the view of 'tradition', held by T.S. Eliot which he believed as 'dynamic' and 'evolving' constantly, changing with the times, rather than being static or unchangeable. A majority of sociologists and anthropologists subscribe to the changed interpretations.

Similarly, ethnicity, as a concept, even though more rigidly constructed and defined, implying its organic attributes as prerequisites, is now much more flexibly defined without necessarily having any primordial attributes or organic connections. In other words, the meaning of both ethnicity and culture can include other social attributes within its meaning and definitions. This new interpretation of culture and ethnic identity has unfortunately made ethnic identity formation subalternate to political manoeuvrings and other machinations, which it was once impervious. The new definition opens out a Pandora's box in an ethnically sensitive and volatile region like the Northeast.

Based on this new definition of ethnicity and culture, 'constructivism'[2] the new concept in ethnic identity formation has emerged. 'Constructivism' departs from the existing concepts of ethnic identity formation, and expounds the theory that ethnic identity can be altered either by a process of (a) engineered formulation or (b) by personal sense of affinity. It fundamentally recognises the fact that since the attributes that goes into the making and formation of identity are subject to alterations and manipulations, there exists a constant threat to the imperviousness implied in the conceptual purity of ethnicity and identity. This new view frees and sublimates ethnicity and identity from the confines of the rigidly defined meanings by providing a new conceptual framework to define ethnicity and its conjunct, identity.

The theory of 'constructivism' holds the view, that ethnicity was always 'created' or 'constructed' and therefore, not necessarily always 'organically' evolved. It implies that both ethnicity and identity are by-products of political and extraneous considerations to derive personal or political mileage whenever the situation demands. Extending the logic further, such manipulations were politically necessary as a self-sustaining activity by a group, to perpetuate and legitimize its hold over a larger number of people or to secure physically defined space. Alternatively, a weaker ethnic group may decide voluntarily to merge with a powerful and larger ethnic group. The concept and definition of 'ethnicity' from this perspective, becomes a byproduct of manipulation, contrived socio-politically through social engineering and political one-upmanship by one ethnic group over another or others.

Abner Chohen[3], propounded the new concept of 'constructivism' based on the prevalence of a deliberate manipulation of kinship and cultural affinities among the Hausa migrants in Africa, by various institutions to gain narrow political advantages over other rivals. This interpretation has in its introduction brought in other similar concept like 'instrumentalism', another term to describe such ethnic identity formations essentially through manipulations and social engineering. The concept of 'constructivism', denoting 'manipulated ethnicity', according to Benedict Anderson[4], poses a threat and a danger to ethnic identity formations since *"imagined communities"*, can come up or 'manipulate' the formations of communities without actually being one.

Benedict Anderson, who provided the theory of 'instrumentalism', however, does not ascribe the need of any particular ethnic group as a pre-requisite to constitute a nation. Anderson[5] and many others, see the concept of 'nation' or 'state' essentially as a 'construct', capable of being built by 'imagined communities' who do not belong to any one specific community or group or having different, similar or same identities. Most countries or nations like the Philippines, Indonesia and India, which are multi-ethnic, multi-lingual, multi-religious countries, have in spite of being the home of numerous heterogeneous ethnic groups evolved into nations. These are some examples.

Ernest Gellner and Anthony D. Smith[6] raised similar issues, which were basic and fundamental but significant, of whether nations were consciously 'created' or grew 'organically' *"out of pre-existing cultural communities"* rather than based on organic ethnic connections alone. Ernest Geller and Anthony D. Smith, jointly developed an intermediate position arguing that the idea of 'nation and nationality' grew and developed from the need to consolidate a pre-existing ethnic group, but accept the assumption that the concept of 'Nation' as a modern concept and essentially a 'construct'. Ernest Gellner[7] explains this in his seminal paper, 'Nations and Nationalism, Do Nations have navels?' in 1983. He observed, *"...that nations are entirely modern creations-the progeny of industrialism and the state-which more or less fraudulently invent their past to gain a semblance of antiquity and deep roots" (sic).*

The new definition of nation in one way is similar to the new definition of 'ethnicity'. Like 'Nation', which denotes a definitive space or territory, but does not denote the exclusivity of one group or set of people over it, ethnicity similarly is a much larger and broader concept. Such views are radically different from most existing conventional concepts and views held by the exponents of the traditional anthropological primordial concepts of ethnic identity, who hold the view that ethnicity is inherently organic anthropologically, impervious to changes, alterations and are reinforced primarily by a long process of acculturation of shared cultural value systems over a period of time.

Based on the new theories it is therefore safe to assume, that ethnic identity formation is both 'contextual' and 'situational'. It is 'contextual' because it is organically endowed, determined by blood relationships and dictated by the circumstances of the events in history. It is 'situational', because a dominant group can impose its will on the weaker group and thus deliberately manipulate the formation of identity. It could also be both, 'contextual' and 'situational' since identity formation could have taken place, by either the dominant anthropological group imposing its will on the weaker group or could have been formed by the willing consent of the smaller or anthropologically weaker group volunteering to be part of a larger or stronger group. In both these situations, either way the organically endowed attribute do not by itself define or constitute ethnic identity.

Clifford Geertz[8] holds the view in this context that 'selection' is an inherent attribute prevalent in every human society. Without assigning any value judgment, Geertz states that it is intrinsic human reaction to respond to such identity formations and fall prey to indoctrination, manipulations and in some cases compulsive identifications. John Rex[9] affirms this indoctrination theory and believes that these had to happen, since ethnicity by its very definition is *"instrumentalist in their basic orientation"*. The history of ethnic identity formation in the Northeast has also gone through this process in its long acculturated history of identity formation.

Epistemologically analysed, the concept of ethnic 'constructivism' existed but was overwhelmed by the predominantly conventional concept that ethnic identity is essentially organic, a combination of both biological and cultural connectivities. What is interesting is that the prevalence of such practices and precepts of 'manipulative or constructivism' school of thought as a 'tool' at nation building has only now been formally recognised and accepted as inherent in the evolutionary histories of societies. This assumption presupposes the fact that nuclear state and societies grew out of coercion, consolidation, amalgamation, through political conquests and other manipulative machinations to ensure ethnic affiliations. Various social and cultural ethnic identity related attributes could have either preceded formations of these identities and became the instruments or facilitators to the 'construction' or developed subsequently after the process of consolidation of the ethnic identity were complete following various manipulations and machinations.

Either way, ethnic identity is a self-preservative political entrapment, which was essential and relevant at a time when human beings were much more vulnerable to the threat of being cverpowered physically or overwhelmed socio-culturally by a stronger and larger clan or group. Human beings evolved the concept and idea of ethnic identity as a defense mechanism to protect themselves and their territory in which they held their family, clan and the means to one's livelihood from their adversaries. 'Bonding' was an essential physical and psychological prerequisite for effective fraternisation as members of a group, especially in a hostile and uncertain environment. It is this 'bonding', a 'trust', achieved by inventing such appellatives as ethnicity, cultural ties and identity, which was the basis of ethnic identity formation. The term 'social contract' draws its meaning from the 'association' of human beings formed in this manner to protect them both physically and psychologically.

Even though there is a general unanimity on the logic of constructivism, Max Weber makes a subtle but basic and fundamental distinction between 'racial identity' and 'ethnic identity'. In his view, while blood relations are necessary for racial identification, however, ethnic identification need not necessarily denote only biological blood relations or connections, since ethnic identity has elements of subjective choices influenced by various other factors like similarities of physical types or customs or both, common history, shared memories etc. All these are traceable in tangibles and intangible attributes that can bind a person to one group or to another for a common cause based on some real or imagery traditional connectivity either in the past or in the present. In many respects, Max Weber's analysis, the basic distinction between 'racial identity' and 'ethnic identity' is the litmus test to determine what constitutes ethnic identity or racial identity. Understanding this distinction between the two terms can remove most of the confusions surrounding the use of the term 'ethnic identity'.

Ethnic identity is by itself, only one of the many identities in a person. Human beings have individual or personal identities, family, societal or community, a regional identity, besides the overarching national identity. While the individual has the freedom to form his or her individual personal identity, there is however no choice in the social or communal identity, which is thrust circumstantially by one's birth. They can however consider a change of their regional and national identity in life but the choice is not always easy. Amartya Sen echoes this human dilemma, *"...most importantly, we have choice over what significance to attach to our different identities. There is no escape from reasoning just because the notion of identity has been invoked"*[10]. Amartya Sen describes the exercise of the choice in the following manner. *"Should they be categorized in terms of inherited traditions, particularly the inherited religion, of the community in which they happen to be born, taking that unchosen identity to have automatic priority over other affiliations involving politics, profession, class, gender, language, literature, social involvements, and many other connections? Or should they be understood as persons with many affiliations and associations the priorities over which they themselves choose (taking the responsibility that comes from reasoned choice)?"*[11] The choice is certainly not simple or easy.

In the context of the Northeast, the various new theories as 'constructivism', 'instrumentalism' and a host of other theories of ethnic identity formation are important in today's context especially in trying to understand and decipher the reasons behind the aggressive posturing among the various ethnic groups in the region in ethnic identity formation.

Conceptual Clarity

The various analyses reveal that even though there are a number of concepts and interpretations on ethnic identity, which vary one from the other, the consensus is that the theory of 'constructivism', seem to be the most credible and acceptable. What this implies is that many essential qualificatory attributes in identity formation once considered intrinsic and prerequisites are not necessarily so. The process of identity formations, which is 'consolidation' of people into ethnicities without the need for its organic perquisites, also means that ethnic identities are essentially political constructs, subject to manipulations. Since the process are not free of 'manipulations', coercions and inducements, identity formation is fallible and not free from inerrancies. In such a situation, the claim to any conceptual purity by any ethnic identity therefore is open to debate.

Seen from this perspective, the demand for defined territories and physical spaces based on ethnic purity and exclusivity, often marked by intense animosity, anger and violence, dividing and polarizing societies and communities in the Northeast appear ironical especially as these involve disputes over small territories or for inclusion of a few extra numbers of people. The present acrimonious relationships and tensions between ethnic groups and between states in the region, as such appears preponderous and self-defeating, particularly when the real issue for the people of the region is clearly the problems of underdevelopment and poverty. In such a situation, it is best to avoid the misdirected use of energy and effort, to establish the supremacy of one ethnic group over another, especially when the definition of ethnic identity clearly sets at rest of what constitutes ethnic purity.

A number of examples of ethnic identity formations in the Northeast, which conform to the 'constructivism' theory, are available. One of these is the history of the identity formation of the Mizos; a process that began around 1780 in what is now Mizoram, much before the British stepped into the state in 1844. Mizo ethnic identity formation is a classic example of consensual consolidation after an intense process of rivalry and conflicts for supremacy and dominance among the various chiefs belonging to different groups, sub-groups and sub-sub-groups of the Mizos who migrated to the present areas of Mizoram from Burma. It was the Sailos, who eventually overcame the other clans and established their supremacy[12].

The process of consolidation among the various Mizo sub-tribes started in 1780, when the Pawis, Fanais and the Lakhers moved northward, displacing in the process the Hrangkhawls, Biates, Thadous and other tribes classified as the old Kukis groups[13] who were pushed up North into Manipur, Cachar and West Tripura. The establishment of supremacy in the north compelled the Sailo chiefs to fight the Thangurs, Rivungs, Palians, Rokhums and the Zadengs. This internecine conflicts and fights resulted in the battle for supremacy between the North and South, at around 1856. A massive peoples' uprising known in Mizo history as *Lal Sawi*[14] took place around this time against the various Chiefs especially against the Sailo Chiefs, for their autocratic and whimsical rule.

Many disputes and skirmishes were common. One of these was the dispute between the two Chiefs of the East and the West, Liankhama and Kalkhama, which arose on a petty issue over the winning of the affection of one girl called Thali. Such disputes and intense rivalry dominated the period from 1826 to 1844 among different clans under different Chiefs. The incessant fights, marginalisation of people and consequential consolidation process rendered tremendous pressures on the psychological well-being of the people of Mizoram as a whole. Socially and politically, the Mizo people were a divided race. As these turbulences continued, the British sent Captain Blackwood in 1844 to intervene and punish Chief Lalsuaka who had led an attack on a Manipuri village of Kochabari on April 16, 1844[15]. The last of the tribes driven out by the Lushais were the Thadous. However, the Sylhet Light Infantry under the command of Lt. Col. Lister burnt down the recalcitrant Lushai village in January 1850. Attacks on the Chittagong Hill tract fort, the attack of the Kukis of Tripura in 1860 and many other expeditions are some of the many eventful occurrences of the period. The process of consolidation of Mizos was on.

The turning point came in 1871 on January 23, when Bengkhuaia, a Haulawng Chief attacked the Alexandrapur Tea Garden in Cachar and killed one planter named Winchester and also took his six-year-old daughter Mary Winchester as a captive. Mary Winchester was eventually freed but not without British retribution. This retribution opened up the Lushai Hills, which led the Christian missionaries into the Lushai Hills and Mizo society. All these events were serious enough for the British to launch the Chin-Lushai expedition of 1889-90. Taking the overall situation into considerations, the British administratively divided erstwhile Lushai Hills into two halves and stationed four garrisons, two each at Fort Lunglei for the Southern half and the remaining two at Fort Aizawl for the Northern half. However, on 1 April 1898, the north and south halves combined to form into one single administrative unit with Captain Shakespeare in charge. Erstwhile Lushai Hills came under the overall control of the Assam Administration with Aizawl as the Headquarters. The Lushai Hills came under British rule. Peace and calm descended after a long time marking the end of the traumatic phase of Mizo history, which covered most part of the second half of the 19th and the beginning of the 20th century.

The term Mizo today, according to P. Lalnithanga, *"...consists of several clans such as Lusei, Hmar, Paihte, Ralte and Pawi"*. Further, these groups comprise of several sub-groups, for instance, *"...the term Lushei comes several clans such as Sailo, Hauhnar, Pachuau, Chhakchhuak, Rokhum, Rivung etc. Likewise under the terms, Hmar, Paihte and Pawi, there are Lakhers and Chakmas also inhabiting the southernmost parts of Mizoram and western areas bordering Bangladesh respectively"*.(sic) It is the process of the coming together of the various tribes and sub-tribes, which is fascinating both socio-anthropologically and ethno-politically. In due course in addition to Christianity, which was the main cementing force of the various groups, the inherent native Mizo "code of conduct", known as *'Tlawmngaihna'*, brought the various sub-groups together. The philosophy of 'Tlawmngaihna' is explained by P. Lalnithanga as *"...an untranslatable term requiring on the part of the people or everyone to be hospitable, kind, unselfish and helpful to other, 'Tlawmngaihna', to a Mizo stands for that compelling moral force which finds expression in self-sacrifice for the service of others."*[16] Nothing could embody the human spirit better than the principle enshrined in *Tlawmngaihna*.

Mizos today are one unified monogenetic ethnic group, which in spite of its turbulent past has evolved into one of the most peaceful and progressive ethnic groups in the country. The process of consolidation in Mizoram provides one of the best examples of 'constructivism'. Today, if the term 'Mizo' denotes a monogenetic group comprising various subgroups of the major tribes, signifying the consolidation of sub-tribes into one single identifiable group, the history of the consolidation process has its own story to tell both long, painful but irrefutably conclusive.

Unlike the Mizos, the identity issue of the Nagas remains inconclusive and unfortunately elusive. While the Mizo 'consolidation' process was definitive and 'concluded' much before the trauma of Partition had set in, the Naga identity problems somehow linger on. The question of whether the term Naga is an ethnic identity 'construct' to fit people into an 'imagined community'; a by-product of political machination to maximize political mileage, or whether the ethnic identity of the Nagas is inherently organic, primordial, which evolved over a number of years remain unresolved. Epistemologically analysed, the problem of resolving the Naga identity issue lies in reconciling the two concepts of 'racial identification' process with the 'ethnic identification' process, which Max Weber wrote and spoke. In this effort, many unforeseen factors and issues have come in the way, since the whole attempt has come rather late in the day. The process of reconciling the two concepts of 'racial' and 'ethnic identity', acceptable to the various Naga groups, is not going to be easy. Part of the problem is the fact that each tribe consider themselves first as a member of their tribe and thereafter as members of other categorizations.

There are several versions and theories about their origins and how the nomenclature, Naga has come into usage. The various versions of origin of the Nagas itself is fascinating ranging from the Makhel tradition, the Khezakenoma tradition of the beginnings of the Lothas or of the Aos told in the famous Lungterok legends. In addition, another versions made by R.R. Shimray observes that the term Naga came from the word Na Ka, which translated means 'pierce-ears'. Shimray bases his theory in his book the "Origin and Culture of the Nagas" where there is a belief among a group of people in Chiang Mai in Thailand that one of their groups known as 'Nakari' migrated to Burma.

It was clear to the British that reconciling these different theories and versions were extremely difficult because each tribe see themselves as exclusive, identifiable by their distinctive attributes, both social and historical. Bringing all these different tribes, each one proud of their past, to be part of a single ethnologically and socio-politically definable group was certainly not easy. In a typical style of an imperial power, the British it appears, to overcome the problems of the various theories and versions available, originally introduced the term Naga as an administrative terminology to denote a physical space occupied by various groups of similar people of comparative backwardness living in a contiguous area having similar degree of primitivism. James C. Scott refers to the term Naga Hills as denoting *"a non-state space"*[17]. S. E. Peal in the nineteenth century observed that the collective *"...term 'Naga' has a definite geographical limit"* and that *"the race so designated is sub-divided into literally innumerable independent tribes, who are constantly at war with each other"*[18]. Various authoritative experts in the field, John Henry Hutton in his introduction to J. P. Mills classic ethnographic discourse of the Lotha Nagas, made in 1922, introduces the term Naga as a geographical construct rather than as a definition of ethnic or racial categorisation. He uses the term Naga, as descriptive of the geomorphological context of the vast inaccessible geographic spread areas occupied by the various tribes now forming Nagaland. For instance, according to Professor Gangmumei Kamei, R.B. Pemberton writings were responsible for identification of the tribes in Manipur as Nagas. Gangmumei wrote in his well-known compilation of his speeches and talks 'Ethnicity and Social Change', "*Whatever the British officials applied to the Naga Hills was applied also to the Manipur tribes*".

Edmund Leach and Frederick Barth had a much more liberal view in drawing the distinctions between the various tribal groups as compared to the views held by J.H. Hutton, J.P. Mills or Parry among the Nagas. Edmund Leach did not subscribe to the categorisations made by Hutton, Mills, Parry and others about the manner in which many of the 'segregation' of the sub-tribes have taken place in the Northeast merely because *"...the group which speaks a distinct language or dialect is, by definition, a separate tribe or a tribal chapter. Each such chapter is then treated as a distinct cultural and ethnographic entity with a distinct history and separate continuity in time...The Sema and the Angami (Nagas) are geographically adjacent, but they are not represented as interacting in any institutional sense. This whole approach seems to me to rest on false premises."*[19] Frederick Barth on the other hand, who also professed similar liberal views, saw the 'boundaries' to be drawn between two or more such groups or clans only if *"...they imply marked differences in behaviour, i.e., persisting cultural difference"*[20]. Both these views are not tenable anymore.

The ascribed premises by the former (Leach) that merely because the Sema and the Angami *"are geographically adjacent"* must necessarily result in *"interacting"* in the *"institutional sense"*, belies the fact that each of these two groups have dissimilar legacies and a long history of acculturated customs and habits which differ. Given the constraints and difficulties of movement and communication due to the topography in the erstwhile Naga Hills, interactions at the "institutional sense" between the Semas and the Angamis, appear most unlikely if not impossible. Even anthropologically speaking, for instance even though both the Semas and the Angamis link their origins to the legend of the magic stone of Khezakhenoma, simultaneously J.H. Hutton also wrote of the beginnings of the Sema's with areas near Mount Japvo or Tukabo. More importantly, since the distinctions between 'racial identity' and 'ethnic identity' made by Max Weber remain in defining who is a Naga, the ambiguity of the definition of the term Naga continues. This is important since the former, 'racial identity' denotes biological blood relations and connections, the latter, 'ethnic identity' does not involve any biological blood relationship. Ethnic identity is a much more amorphous, substantially broader in concept encompassing several attributes than it ever was. Today, blood connections do not alone constitute or determine ethnic identity.

In all these confabulations, one aspect of Naga life remains constant, which is that in the world-view of each Naga tribe or clan; their respective village and their clan is the centre of their world order. Furer-Haimendorf (1909-1995) who studied the Konyak Nagas, describes aptly the state of affairs. According to Haimendorf, the Nagas view a world-order in which 'mankind' was divided between a small inner circle of co-villagers, clansmen and the allied villages, on whose support he could depend and to whom he owed assistance in emergencies. The entire world, consisting not only of people belonging to other tribes, but even Konyaks living in other villages, were all potential enemies and legitimate targets for head-hunting. It is important to appreciate this aspect of Naga society or for that matter almost any tribe or community in the Northeast, because establishing a correct history of this unique trait can elucidate a 'racial' connection, which may not necessarily be 'ethnic' connection or identity. Understanding this aspect may provide a way out for resolving the vexed problems of bringing the various Naga tribes together as one single group.

Part of the complexity to the Naga identity arises because most of the writings, monograms based on which present analysis and critique are made, are documents that were written quite some time back, when Naga society was at its most primitive stage of development devoid of any exposure to the world outside and without present day embellishments. Given the Nagas' love of 'exclusivity', assimilating the many divergent tribes and sub-tribes with their respective divergent anthropological, social and other attributes, into one single homogeneous group make the task of consolidation extremely difficult. In their hearts of hearts, each tribe remains essentially unique, self-determinant, proud of their pasts and conscious of their individual identity in the present.

The 'ethnicisation' of all the various tribes of Nagas into one single group under a single nomenclature is the result of Western scholarship and British administrative ingenuity and thinking, whose instinctive response to such varied groups was to ethnicise the non-Western peoples of the world wherever they went. Similar ethnicisation process took place with almost all tribal groups of the Northeast. Sociologists the world over accept this preoccupation as disruptive and as the reflection of the incorrigible Western habit, of putting their stamp of superiority over other races. This transgression by Western 'habit' of fitting indigenous communities of the developing world into an ethnocentric perspective exposes these communities to the vagaries of *"...conscious manipulation of kinship and cultural symbols by political entrepreneurs seeking political gain"*[21].

Sanjib Baruah quoting Julian Jacob, Alan Macfarlane, Sarah Harrison and Anita Herle sums the apparent dilemma posed by the various Naga tribes. He observes *"...to make sense of the ethnographic chaos they perceived around them; hundreds if not thousands, of small villages seemed to be somewhat similar to each other but also very different, by no means sharing the same customs, political system, art or even language"*[22]. Things have changed since then, with better communications; the restrictive and limited village-world view of the Nagas has now changed encompassing a broader definition that includes the sub-tribes and closely related tribes not always biologically linked to their own. In fact, the 'inclusion' process now implies other sub-groups and in many cases, other tribes not biologically connected under the reconstructed definition of Naga identity.

Naga history is now at the cross-road, where convergence of the many diverse groups is being sought, not so much on 'racial' affiliations or organic linkages and connectivities of 'shared ancestry', but essentially to 'consolidate' and 'construct' an elusive collective ethnic identity, which was administratively conceptualised by the British. Irrespective of the inconclusive verdict on the generalised definition of the generic term Naga, its spirit, willingness to accept each other and be part of a larger group, the same impulse that once led the Mizos form themselves into a homogeneous group, which is evident, should wisely prompt all the diverse Naga groups to decide their own future. The concept of 'constructivism' discussed earlier will certainly come handy in resolving the situation.

The question of difference between the definitions of 'racial identity' and 'ethnic identity', which Max Weber spoke of, certainly comes in the way of unification, creating enormous problems in bringing the diverse tribes, sub-tribes and the sub-sub-tribes, with different social, cultural backgrounds, speaking several different dialects and occupying different parts of the vast region together. However, if in spite of the fact that each tribe among the Nagas are racially different and distinct, separate one from the other, having their respective tribe identities, is recognised and acknowledged, yet based on a consensus, can still agree to constitute into a single 'ethnic identity', as distinct from 'racial identity', the collective Naga identity can then take its rightful place in history. However, whether this unification process can become one single political physical unit, which is politically acceptable to all concerned or not, is contingent and impinges on a number of factors, which given the geo-political dynamics prevalent in the region will not be easy.

Evolution of ethnic identity; a study

The confused matrix of identity in a region like the Northeast can be numerous; however, the transformation of the Meiteis of Manipur from a tribal community to their present non-tribal ethnic identity is one of the most interesting. The Meiteis form two third of the population of the State and occupy Imphal valley, which is one fourth of the total physical area of the state. The upland tribal communities who are approximately one third of the population occupy the remaining two third physical areas. The Meiteis are predominantly Hindus, while the various upland tribal populations are Christians or follow their respective indigenous religions and faiths.

The beginnings and ancestory of the Meiteis is a popular subject among British administrators, sociologists and other scholars. Sir Edmund Gait, B.H. Hodgson, T.C. Hudson and a host of sociologists and anthropologists have written about the Meitei's tribal ancestory. Even though there is no unanimity on the origins, one aspect which is clearly established, is that the Meiteis of Manipur are Tibeto-Burmans or Indo-Mongoloid group, linguistically and racially. The Indian Historical Records Commission of the Government of India, in a paper prepared by A.F.M. Abdul Ali in its fifth meeting in Calcutta in 1923 refers to Pamheiba (1709-1748) also called by his Hindunised name of Garib Niwaz, the ruler of Manipur as being a Naga. Many popular folklore of Manipur back this theory. According to one version, King Charai Rongba (1697-1709), the father of Pamheiba was closely associated with the various upland tribes of erstwhile Manipur. Charai Rongba fearing the life of his infant son

Pamheiba brought up his son under the care and protection of a Kabui or Tangkhul Naga chief. The other version is that Pamheiba was a Kabui tribal chief who came down to the valley as the margin of the waters in the Imphal valley, once filled with water, shrank. The remnants of this big lake, which covered the entire valley, are the numerous water bodies and lakes including the Loktak Lake in the Imphal valley. The other version given by Dr. Brown, quoted by Mc Culloch tells the story of a Naga boy Pamheiba whom King Charai Rongba adopted in 1714, but who accidentally shot his adopted father King Charai Rongba while hunting. T.C. Hudson in his well documented anthropological book, 'The Meitheis' provides another version. According to this version, Pamheiba was the son of King Charai Rongba, born of one of the Meitei queens.

Based on these versions it is evident that king Pamheiba had either, a tribal ancestory or tribal upbringing. Since the tradition among the Meiteis was to protect only the life of the heir apparent to the throne and eliminate the other male children, the mother hid Pamheiba among the Quiron Tribe of Nagas in the Tangal hills in North Manipur. Pamheiba was later found and brought to succeed his father but accidentally killed his father. The village associated with the story is the Naga village of Maikel or Makhel, a village, which Gangmumei Kamei refers as the place from where all the *"ancestors of the"* southern Nagas *"emerged from the earth and refer to Khezkhenoma as the centre of migration"*. Even today, because of this association, the Nagas of Maikel gets precedence over all other tribes in the annual royal boat race, known as 'Hiyang tanaba' held in the palace in Imphal. Further, the Meiteis' ancestral connections and links with the upland tribal communities can be seen and observed during the coronation ceremony of the Meitei Kings, 'Phumban Kaba', where both the King and the Queen dress as members of the upland tribal community. Further, the principal residence of the Meitei king called 'Yum Chaou', or the 'Great house' are always made in tribal design and architecture.

Based on the Meitei oral history, T. C. Hudson also support the version held by both Colonel Mc Culloch and Captain Pemberton that the Meiteis are an assimilation and amalgamation of various tribal communities who converged into the Imphal valley from all directions over a period. Hudson wrote, *"Traditions bring the Moirang Tribes, from the south, the direction of the Kookies, the Koomal from the east, the directions of the Murrings and the Meitei and*

Looang from north-east, the direction of the Koupooees"[23]. Meitei language for instance is an assimilation of the Murrings Kukis, and Kabuis dialects. Colonel Mc Culloch wrote of the possible formation of Meitei society as follows: *"From the most credible traditions, the valley originally seems to have been occupied by several tribes, the principal of which were named Koomul, Looang, Moirang and Meithei, all of them came from different directions. For a time the Koomul appears to have been the most powerful, and after its decline, the Moirang tribe. But by degrees the Meitheis subdued the whole, and the name Meithei has been applicable to all. Since their conversion to Hindooism, the Meitheis have claimed for themselves Hindoo descent."*[24] Captain Pemberton in his report on the Eastern Frontier outrightly rejects the Meitei claim that they are of Hindu origin and descent. All evidences, both oral traditions and historical references point out that a merger of seven Salais or clans formed the Meiteis into a social group in the pre-Pakhangba and pre-Vaishnava periods. The Ningthouja, Angom, Luwang, Khaba, Khuman, Moirang and a number of other clans got absorbed eventually to form the present day Meitei community.

Prof. Nirmal Kumar Bose[25] in a memorial Lecture—'Ethnic Identities in the North-east India' provides the necessary broad theoretical as well as empirical basis of the ethnic identic connections of the Meitei community with the various upland tribal communities of the state. *"The 'tribe' had never been a fixed or static category in those early times and there were many instances of change from tribal to non-tribal status. Contrary to popular notion, the numerous culturally and politically discrete communities of later times lived in a situation of contact and communication with their respective neighbouring populations".*

These analyses indicate that the Meitei community was one of the many separate small kingdoms in Manipur who trace their origin from various upland tribes and known by their respective clan names as Meitei, Khuman, Luwang, and Moirang and who came from different directions. The Meiteis or Ningthouja ruler over time dominated all the other clans and subsequently subjugated all of them to become part of the Meitei clan. The Meiteis followed their respective indigenous pagan religions and faiths, many among whom still follow ensuring in the process, a link with their ancestral pasts. Times change, associations and memories do not, they persist tenaciously. Subsequently, all these changed with the coming of

Hinduism during the 18th century, destroying and modifying the traditional Meitei lifestyle, social and cultural history irrevocably.

The tribal origin of the Meiteis becomes significant in the analysis of ethnic identity formation in the present context of the social polarization and disconnect between the various tribal groups and the non-tribal communities of Manipur. The origin of the Meiteis points at the irrevocable fact of the anthropological connections and links of the various upland tribal communities and the Meiteis. This fact dispels many doubts about the origin of the Meiteis, which remain largely vague, unclear and unfortunately suppressed for various reasons. Additionally, the ethnic identity history of the Meiteis also opens out the uncomfortable larger issue of who are the various upland tribal communities of the state, and how are they to be categorised. For example in the Census of India on Manipur, the Tangkhuls are categorised as 'Tangkhuls' and not as Nagas. The classifications of other tribes like the Kabuis are by the name of their respective tribes, without prefixing or suffixing the generic nomenclature Naga. On the other hand, in Nagaland the qualificatory term Naga is suffixed on to both the Tangkhuls and the Kabuis. This is easily explained because anthropologically the Meiteis who were once tribes themselves were known as Meiteis or as Moirangs, Khuman, Lois etc without any prefixes or suffixes, and in the same tenor all other tribes in the state are known by the names of their respective clan identities rather than by any other qualificatory generic categorization or classification. Moreover, in Manipur both the Tangkhuls and the Kabuis have their own standing and esteem being an integral part of Manipur's social and cultural history.

In perhaps one of the most poignant social events among the Meiteis in Manipur, and one of the best examples that preserve the history of the Meitei's ancestral links to the upland tribal communities is the festival known as 'Mera Haou Chogba' (The Dance of the Tribes in Mera). The festival goes back into ancient times when the Meitei community in Manipur celebrates the festival in the month of Mera (October-November), the most beautiful time of the year in Manipur when the sky is free of the last monsoon clouds and the moon is at its brightest and best. During these festivities, various tribal communities come down to the valley from the hills and upland areas to celebrate in an annual gathering by offering gifts to the Meitei rulers. The event was marked with solemnity, joy and camaraderie. In the evening, every Meitei household would light a lamp and raise it on a tall bamboo pole in their respective courtyards of their homes so that these lights were visible from the hills surrounding the Imphal valley. Tradition believes that the lights from these lamps are signals sent by the Meiteis, considered as the younger brother, to the various tribal communities in the hills who are the elder brother, that they (Meiteis) were safe and happy in the valley. The exchanges of the greetings and the lighting of the lamps today are still celebrated and symbolises the old association of the Meiteis with the upland tribal communities in the state.

The significance of the festivities reinforces the belief among the Meiteis that they are actually upland tribal communities from the hills and mountains, who over the years came down to the Imphal valley. The inference drawn is that the Meiteis consider themselves as the younger brother because they evolved subsequently from the upland tribal communities to their present identity. Since, the Meiteis are as such a comparatively new ethnic identic group, branching off from their tribal origins, euphemistically the upland tribal communities becomes the elder brother. As this association reflects the evolutionary history of the Meitei community's pagan and tribal past, it has a lot of significance. The appellative of the 'younger brother' given to the Meiteis sums up in part, the evolutionary history of Manipuri Meiteis. It is the irony of the present acrimonious equation and relationship between the tribal and non-tribal ethnic groups in Manipur, which is disturbing.

An interesting aspect of the Meitei connections to the tribals is the associated origins of the Tangkhul Nagas of Manipur. One of the legends of the Tangkhuls is that they are associated with Makhel and in another version with Samsok (Thungdut) in the Kabaw valley (now in Myanmar), which was once part of Manipur. Both Makhel and Kabaw valley are closely associated to Manipur's history, the former locationally and socio-anthropologically, while the latter with Manipur's political history. However, what is pertinent is the traditional belief among the Tangkhuls that they migrated from Samsok to the Imphal valley but left it due to the unsuitability of the valley, implying that they left a few of them in the valley, who eventually formed a branch of the Meitei community. The inference is that the younger brother remained behind in the valley while the elder brother left for the hills; greener pastures. This version of the origins of the Tangkhul and the belief among the Meiteis that they consider themselves as the younger brothers to the upland tribal community in Manipur, epitomised in the Mera Haou Chogba' (The Dance of the Tribes in Mera) and other celebrations among the Meiteis lend credence and reinforces the versions of the tribal origins of the Meiteis.

Ethnicity and Identity; the difference

One of the best example in illustrating the subtle distinctions and difference between ethnicity and identity in the Northeast is the debate surrounding the identity of the Bishnupriya Manipuris vis-a-vis the Meitei Manipuris. The analysis is also particularly interesting because as against the present trend of consolidation and assimilation among the various ethnic and sub-ethnic groups into the larger main group in the Northeast, in contrast, the trend among the Manipuri Meiteis seem to be working in the opposite direction.

Who are the Bishnupriya Manipuris? The Bishnupriya Manipuri Meiteis are historically Manipuris settled in various parts of the Northeastern region, especially in the Surma Valley, South-Western Assam, in Sylhet, Moulvibazar, Habibganj, Sunamganj and Dhaka in Bangladesh. There are many theories about their origin. The generally accepted version is that the Bishnupriya Manipuris are Meiteis from Manipur who fled when Manipur was under Burmese occupation for seven years from 1819 to 1826, popularly known as the 'Chahi Teret Khuntaba' or 'The Seven years Exile' in Manipur's history. The King along with most of the population fled to the Surma Valley in Assam and present day north and western Bangladesh to avoid Burmese persecution. During the 'seven years' exile, many of them assimilated the socio-cultural traits and influences of the places they took shelter. The exile of the Manipur rulers ended after the British defeated the Burmese in the First Anglo-Burmese War, marked by the signing of the Yandawoo Treaty in 1826. However, many of them did not return from exile. Much later during the period of war of succession in Manipur among King Chourajit Singh, his brothers Marjit and Gambhir Singh similarly, another group of Meiteis fled Manipur and settled in Sylhet in Bangladesh. The princes built the Manipur palace in Mirzajangal in Bangladesh.

Due to the overpowering local influences in their lifestyles and habits in the places of their new domicile, many of the Meiteis lost most of the native Meitei traits and attributes. They also began to speak a new form of colloquial language that had elements and influences of Meitei, Bengali and Assamese. In spite of these changes most of them, however, continued to consider themselves as

Manipuri Meiteis and asserted their rights to be so. Since assimilation into their adopted societies was difficult because of their predominant Kuki-Chin features, which made them stand apart from the rest of the local population, these Meitei Manipuris who settled in Bishnupur[26] in Bangladesh came to be known as Bishnupriyas, literally 'worshipper of Vishnu'.

The controversy about the Bishnupriyas Manipuris' started when the Meiteis in Manipur refused to recognise and accept them as Meiteis. Given the extent of transformation and changes in the Bishnupriya Manipuris' personality over the years ever since they left Manipur, this was bound to happen. Largely threatened by ever-increasing influx of people and other dilatory influences on Meitei society, the Meiteis in Manipur had themselves become highly insular, self-protective, inward looking and hence in their anxiety to retain the ethnic, social and cultural purity, the Meiteis in Manipur discouraged any claims of ethnic or identic connections or associations with them. In the process, the Bishnupriya Manipuris became a group of people of unclear ancestry and origin.

The problem of identity of the Bishnupriyas got further complicated due to differences among the various groups of Manipuri Bishnupriyas themselves, comprising essentially of those who settled in Bangladesh and those who settled in Assam. The former group comprise mainly of those who went and settled in Sylhet in Bangladesh with strong Bengali influence on them. The second group comprises of Bishnupriya Manipuris settled in the Cachar region of Assam, speaking a mixed form of Bengali, Assamese with a mix of Meitei language. The two dialects used by these two groups were distinct and different roughly corresponding to the geographical locations of their settlements. The Rajar Gang (Kings village), phonetically is akin to Bengali and Assamese languages, while the Madai Gang (Queens village), is more akin to Assamese and Meitei languages[27].

However, both the predominant Bengali and the predominant Assamese versions, have very little or no link with the Meitei language. To cite an example, 'what is your name', in Meitei 'lon' or language is 'Nangi ming karikoui'. While in the Bishnupriya dialect it is, 'Tor nanghan kihan'; 'Tor' being either or both Assamese or Bengali, 'nanghan' or name a derivative from 'nam' which could be both Assamese or Bengali and 'kihan' or what, a derivative from the word 'ki', of either Assamese or Bengali suffixes. In Assamese it will be 'Tor nam ki', while in Bengali it is 'Tomar nam ki'. 'He will come', in Meitei will be 'Mahak lakani' becomes 'Ta ahitoi' in Bishnupriya, while in Assamese it will be 'Tehete ahibo' and in Bengali it is 'te aasbo'[28]. The dissimilarities with the Manipuri Meitei language are obvious and conspicuous.

The attempts to reconcile and resolve the difference in 1934 by the Nikil Hindu Manipuri Mahasabha failed due to internal bickerings. One of the primary reasons for the failure was the irreconcilable differences between the Surma Valley Manipuri Society (later changed to an Association) and the Bishnupriyas of Bangladesh, speaking entirely different languages and who over the years became racially distinctive and different from each other. However, later on the ostensible reason is attributed to the reluctance of the Bishnupriyas Manipuris settled in Assam, who did not want to get themselves entangled in the larger controversy of identification with either those from Bangladesh or with the Meiteis of Manipur as it would dilute and jeopardize their claim as a 'backward' community in Assam.

In the present context, problems of accepting Bishnupriya Manipuris as Meiteis by the Meiteis of Manipur, impinges on the fundamental distinction that exists between ethnicity and identity. There is a very subtle distinction and a fine line between the two concepts, but the difference is nevertheless significant. Etymologically speaking, the ethnicity of the Bishnupriya Manipuris do not conform to the classical definition of ethnic identity but fits more into its liberal definition, which has emerged in the last thirty years. The definition given by the classical schools on ethnic identity is anthropological and biological in content, laying stress on the organic and anthropological connections and less on the acculturated attributes like culture, language and other social attributes. From this view, the *"close overlap between culture and ethnicity or even culture and nationhood was generally taken as granted"*. However, as already indicated earlier, in the Chapter, others including Fredrik Barth[29] since 1969, in his seminal text, gives a complete new meaning and interpretation to ethnicity and culture, which is distinct and different from the classical view. It holds *"...that cultural differences cut across ethnic boundaries, and ethnic identity is based on socially sanctioned notions of cultural differences, not real ones. While ethnic identity should be taken to refer to a notion of shared ancestry (a kind of fictive kinship), culture refers to shared representations, norms and practices. One can have deep ethnic differences without correspondingly important cultural differences (as in the Bosnian example below); and one can have cultural variations without ethnic boundaries (as, for example, between the English middle class and the English working class)"*[30].

In short, modern concepts and interpretations of ethnicity delink the need for an overlap or connectivity between ethnicity and culture. The two can be mutually exclusive and not necessarily conjuncts. One can have a common culture but not necessarily belong to the same ethnic group having the same organic or anthropological connectivities. The converse also works, in which one can belong to the same ethnic group but need not share or adhere to the same culture or cultural value system. This is in contrast to the classical point of view, which denotes that ethnic identity must have both the organic and inherent attributes of 'shared ancestry' of language and native indigenous religion. In addition, it must have the additional associated affiliates of the acculturated attributes of social and cultural value system of the ethnic group to which they profess or claim to belong. In the classical view the organic anthropological continuum and the socio-cultural connectivity must prevail.

Seen in this perspective, the contention of the Meiteis of Manipur is that the Manipuri Bishnupriyas have lost their inherent organic connection, due to the prolonged intermixing of various racial groups organically or biologically over a period, subjected themselves to extreme forms of reorientations in language, behaviour, sensibilities, in short relegated all Meitei attributes, which entitled them to claim their 'shared ancestry' as Meiteis. Thus, even though the Bishnupriya Manipuris retain traces of cultural affiliations, a few social attribute and practices, they have 'lost' both their organic link with the Meiteis by extensive infusion of other ethnic groups through marriages diluting the quintessence of Meitei organic and biological attributes over time. In other words, while the organic connections of 'shared ancestry' or primordial attributes of the Meiteis of Manipur have disappeared completely or predominantly, the socio-cultural attributes, the visible façade of Meitei ethos and culture, like dance, festivals and celebrations are preserved and retained by the Manipuri Bishnupriyas. The traditionalists Manipuri Meiteis refuse to accept this ambivalent position and mix, which delinks the primordial organic connectivity from the socio-culture attributes.

According to the Meiteis in Manipur, the preposition that the elements of socio-cultural affinities alone are sufficient to establish one's ethnic identity is unacceptable. They hold the ineluctable view that while one can have cultural differences in a fast changing world of multiculturalism, it is impossible to dispense the ethnic cognitive attributes in defining a person's ethnic identity. The irreconcilable differences remain. In short, the differences between the Meiteis of Manipur and the Bishnupriya Manipuris are the subtle distinction that exists between ethnicity and identity. The former marked by specificity of blood and organic connections, while the later by definition, is much broader in connotation and in its application, which does not insist on organic purity as the cognitive attribute as long as there is adherence and continuity of socio-cultural practices.

The only way out of the piquant situation is for the Meiteis in Manipur to accept the fact that Bishnupriya Manipuris have evolved due to the peculiar circumstances of history to which the Bishnupriya Meiteis were exposed and hence organically and anthropologically different. Simultaneously, recognise that the sociocultural attributes retained by the Bishnupriya Manipuris are part of the larger ethos and cultural milieu of the Manipuri Meitei society. This categorisation is perhaps the most apt ethnologically as things stand, since 'Meitei' denotes specificity and organic distinctiveness, denoting both racial and sociocultural purity, while the term 'Manipuri' denotes the larger plural connotation of a Pan-Manipuri identity having 'some' connections or 'links' either socially, culturally, politically or historically with present-day Manipur. As things stand, the Bishnupriya Manipuris remain at best, Aryanised people of Manipuri Meitei origins and not Manipuri Meiteis of Manipur.

The Northeastern Identity

Shri. P.A. Sangma[31] ex-Speaker of the Lok Sabha and a well-known political figure in Indian politics hailing from the Northeast region sums up the average Northeast Indian's preoccupation with their identity in the form of a parable. When God created Indians, he gave them four boxes, containing gifts to each of the four regions of India, east, west, north and the south. Curious to know God's gift, the people of India opened the first box that contained the gift given to the people of North India. In it, they found a large plaque with the word inscribed, "Beauty" on it. God had given the people of North India, beautiful and handsome looking people and place like Kashmir, monuments like the Taj Mahal and a host of other beautiful things and places. Other people of other regions were a little dejected that God had given away 'Beauty'. Next, they opened the gift box of South India and found in it the plaque with the word

"Intelligence" inscribed. The South Indians were happy. The people of India then opened the gift box meant for Western India. In it, they found that God had given them "Wealth". People of Western India, particularly the Gujaratis, Maharashtrians, Rajasthanis and others were very happy. Lastly, the Indians opened the last gift box meant for the people of Eastern India. Strangely, they found in it another smaller box, inscribed on it "For the people of Northeast India". Curious, the Indians opened the smaller box and found a smaller plaque with the words inscribed in huge, bold capital letters "EGO" (Identity). The preoccupation of the Northeastern Indian with their identity; I am a Meitei, I am a Naga, I am a Mizo, I am an Ahomiya or I am a Bodo and so on, is God's gift to the people of the region. This preoccupation epitomizes the calamitous obsession of the Northeastner with their ethnic identity and which has unfortunately overtaken the lives of people in the Northeast. This is reflected and visible in everything they do.

The concept of ethnic identity has many facets in the Northeast, the religious, the morphological ethnic divide between the upland and lowland communities, the socio-anthropological tribal and non-tribal divide and in many other forms. These differences make the study of ethnic identity of the Northeast extremely complex. One aspect common in all these is that the preoccupation of the region with ethnic identity politics is the byproduct of circumstances of history and an indirect 'reaction' against the general despondency and lackluster response of the country to the various problems confronting the region. The primacy of the school of thought that identity politics of the Northeast region in India emerged, as a consequence of the major disconnect between the conceptual precepts of nationhood-building propounded by the founding fathers of the Indian nation, and the disappointing reality of the actual efforts undertaken at national identity formation in India, remains relevant in this connection.

The complex nature of the politics of identity in the Northeast region, which is so overwhelming and dominant, therefore does not conform to the simple notion that it is the manifestation of the basic insecurities to their identities, which numerically small groups of indigenous communities suffer across the world. It has more to do with the heterogeneous nature of the composition and mix of various ethnicities confined within a very small physical area, living in close physical proximity to each other in an extremely inhospitable region of the country. The 'ethnoscape'[32] of the Northeastern region is unique and different from other regions in India, extremely complex and difficult.

Further, badgered over time by various forms of exogenous influences beyond their control, the simple lives of the people have changed beyond their own imaginations. This is natural. What is disconcerting however, is that the politics of ethnic identity has acquired a sinister dimension and notoriety in recent times by turning it into the politics of symbols and punctuated by violence and bloodshed. Besides, assertive identity politics has become a rallying point for various political parties and vested groups to garner support for improving their electoral prospects. This poses a serious threat to democracy and its ideals in the region, besides disrupting the ethnic and social equilibrium among the various ethnicities and communities of the region. More dangerous in implication is that the misuse of identity, as a political weapon circumvents the most fundamental freedom in democracy; the ability to choose and elect one's leader, free of fear, threats and inducements. It is a silent cancer, which weakens democratic institutions in an inaccessible far-flung region of the largest democracy in the world.

Part of the preoccupation of the average Northeastern Indian with their identity and behaviour pattern is also the byproduct of the insecurities and threat to their livelihood and properties. The unabated inflow of immigrants, both legally and illegally into the region, which has put tremendous pressures on the people to part with the little pieces of arable lands available to them is one of the most important factor that has influenced the rise of the general xenophobia persona of the people of the region. The economic exploitation, especially by the petty traders and business-persons who come to the region as traders from outside is also responsible for people of the region to consider these contacts detrimental and a direct threat on their well-being, economy, and importantly on their social and cultural identities.

These factors compel the average Northeasterner to either retract into the security of their clan and community, or react violently in the confusion and uncertainty. This type of response also occurs because they are used to a much simpler form of human relationships and social equations in their uncluttered lives.

Communication under these circumstances is bound to break down and social interactions instead become points of social frictions and acrimonious exchanges. These exposures have therefore, instead of helping the Northeasterners to pave the way for better inter-communitarian communications, developed and morphed into intense form of xenophobia and parochialism. The average Indian is unable to understand and comprehend these peculiar behaviour response patterns. The psychological inhibitions and ambivalent attitude of the Northeasterner not only make them an extremely complex set of people, an enigma of sorts, but also get unfortunately dubbed as antinational and considered as generally reluctant to assimilate into the national mainstream. People in the Northeast are not only an enigma to the rest of the country and the world at large, but also an enigma even among themselves. The reasons are apparent.

Part of the behaviour pattern and response, is the confusion that the multiplicity of identities within a Northeasterner creates. The Northeasterner has four basic identities, (a) the individual identity, (b) the ethnic clan or communitarian identity, (c) the composite sub-national or regional identity and lastly (d) the national identity. All these identities coexist simultaneously within each of them and manifests sub-consciously in every inter-personal communications. The complexity and dilemma of choice from these identities however, is complex as Amartya Sen describes this dilemma of choice. *"Choices over identities do involve constraints and connections, but the choice that exist and have to be made are real, not illusory. In particular, the choice of the priorities between different identities, including what relative weight to attach to their respective demands, cannot only be a matter of discovery. They are inescapably decisional, and demand reason-not just recognition"*[33] (sic). The complexity of choice before a Northeasterner manifests in their distinctive responses to people from outside and inside the region, euphemistically termed as 'outsider' and 'insider'.

These arise due to two factors. The first due to the inability of the average Northeasterner to invoke the appropriate identity in the transactional puzzle at the appropriate time with the person involved. The second arises because identity for the average Northeasterner means essentially the self and the clan to which they belong. All other identities, including the larger sub-national regional identity or the national identity are 'intrusive' and hence nonexistent. This restrictive view of identity, limits their ability to see themselves beyond their 'self' and their identities as members of the clan or community. This in the process, inhibit their ability to understand the subtle nuances associated in interpersonal communication and interactions with other persons not belonging to their clan, tribe or community. The 'outsiders' find it difficult to understand them bcth as individuals and as members of a group. To say it is difficult is an understatement.

An interesting aspect of the interpersonal transaction, the response and behaviour pattern between two Northeasterners of different ethnic identic groups among themselves vary when they are within the region and when they are outside the Northeast. In their interaction outside the region, the response is often cordial and marked by camaraderie. For instance, within the student community belonging to various ethnic groups from the region studying in various cities outside, when confronted with threat or danger, affecting any one single ethnic group from the region, all the various ethnic groups of students are most likely to respond together as one group against the threat. However, within the Northeast the same cordiality and camaraderie is missing.

Social scientists explain this response and phenomenon in many ways but the interpretations given by Georg Simmel and reinforced by Thomas Hylland Eriksen[34] known as "Simmel's Rule" is the most interesting. The "Simmel's Rule," is a 'sociological principle', which simply states *"...that the inherent cohesion of a group is contingent on the strength of external pressure. This principle may explain why group integration generally is so much stronger in small groups, especially if they are oppressed, than in larger ones-why, for example, Scots seem to have fewer difficulties in defining who they are than the English." (sic)*. Eriksen illustrates this point by explaining the principle behind the functioning of the household refrigerator. *"The integration of persons into the groups can be described as the work of an inverted refrigerator: The function of a refrigerator is to generate inward coldness, but in order to do so, it more or less inadvertently, as a side-effect, creates outward warmth. Conversely, groups form to create warmth for their members, but they necessarily create some outward coldness in order to be able to do so."*[34] Because of the 'external pressure', an 'inherent cohesion' among the people of the region exists.

Similar in concept is the "Segmentary logic"[35], already referred to earlier in the Chapter. The pattern of response occurs between feuding tribal groups who are intermittently involved in dispute and acrimonious relationships but unite temporarily to prevent an external threat or enemy, which endanger both these groups. The 'logic' derives its conceptual position from a study of a tribal group in Somali in Africa in the 1940s. The 'contraction' and 'expansion' of 'partnership' among tribes is referred to earlier in the Chapter by Evans-Pritchard as "segmentary logic". *"It's me against my brother, my brother and I against our cousins, and our cousins, my brothers and I against everybody else."*[36] Such responses by groups in similar given situations take place everywhere within the Northeast.

The ability of the principles enunciated in the 'segmentary logic' to guarantee political cohesion and homogeneity irrespective of the nature of threat or denial of recognition to any ethnic identity is however, doubtful. *"This does not however, mean that segmentary identification does not exist, and one of the causes of oppositional identity politics in modern nation-states is caused by their not providing substantial identity groups appropriate political arenas, thereby encouraging counter reactions in the form of identity politics directed against the state."*[37] However, based on this logic, the possibilities of somehow bringing the warring and disputing ethnic groups in the Northeast to work together by forgetting their acrimonious past and instead focus on the common threat of perennial underdevelopment and economic poverty is by itself an attractive option.

Within this complicated matrix of response patterns, which divide people, the other interesting aspect that affects social interaction within the region is the relative innocuous use of the two appellatives; the 'plain-people' and the 'hill-people', essentially denoting geographically, people of the region based on the areas of their domicile. However, quite innocuously hidden behind the categorisation, the two terms denote a sinister connotation of social segregation of people, between the people from the valley areas who are non-tribals, mostly Hindus and the upland tribal communities who are predominantly Christians. These two terms, in the Northeastern lexicon, have played havoc in the history of ethnic identity relations in the region.

For instance, an Uplander or 'hill-people', may deal with the Lowlander or 'plain people' belligerently and differently, as compared to how he would deal with another Uplander. Conversely, a Lowlander may deal with another Lowlander quite differently from how he would deal with the Uplander. The transactional web is complicated. These attitudinal differences in interpersonal transactions of the average Northeasterner are legacies of prejudices of history, which has somehow tenaciously embedded in the social psyche of people and communities in the region.

Northeast and National identity

First impressions matters in life, it has a lasting impact. This is true also of the first impressions of the Northeast by people from the rest of India, and conversely the impressions of the Northeasterner about other Indians from other parts of the country. The first Indians whom the Northeasterners encountered in the region were mostly petty traders, small business-persons and low-level Government functionaries. They were predominantly from Bengal, Bihar and from the Marwar regions of Western India, generically and euphemistically referred to as 'Marwaris', and coincidentally almost all of whom were Hindus by religion. Historically the first contacts were made in the valleys of Assam.

These people from various regions of the country came with the British as labourers, business-persons and entrepreneurs as part of the entourage of British administrative machinery. They stood out distinct and different from their white skinned masters in the region. As traders, they took advantage of the general simplicity and ignorance of the people of the region and exploited them. Several stories of exploitations are part of the popular folk tales and stories across the region. Various negative attributes combined to present the first Indian in the Northeast; petty, exploitative Hindu businesspersons and an 'outsider', all combined into one. It was not the benevolent positive image, the Northeasteners would want to meet or see. Indianism meant 'petty', 'exploitative' and epitomized by 'Hindu India', an image that did not conjure well as first impressions. Unfortunately, there was no one to disprove or deny that these few people did not represent the 'real' or 'true' India or Indianism. The adverse ramification was that this silence proved highly detrimental in fostering and building the bond that the 'new' India after independence needed. Instead of projecting the positive image of the large-hearted India, benevolent and caring country, the more conspicuous vilificatory adages instead got more prominence. Unfortunately, it is this image of the 'other Indian', which somehow was etched in the memories and minds of the people in the region. In due course, this impression eventually morphed into anti-Indian feelings. In such a hostile environment of mistrust and suspicion, both Indianism and Hinduism suffered. Times did not help in changing the first impressions either.

The general attitude and behaviour of the first representative Indians working in the region also did not show empathy, behaving as irksome patronizing adversaries who treated the people in the region more as denizens rather than as fellow citizens from the same country. Sardar Patel, the person responsible for India's integration and political consolidation after India's independence when informed that the Maharaja of Manipur, who was 'confined' in the Manipur Rajbari in Laitumkrah in Shillong, because he refused to sign the Merger Agreement in 1949, is supposed to have made the famous remark, *"...is there not a Brigadier in Shillong?"* Did Sardar Patel's remark hurt the inner pride of the Manipuri people? The remark had the propensity to provoke, rather than solve problems. The post independent history of Manipur, speaks for itself.

The significance of the now famous remark lies in the fact that the process of denization through aggressive posturing may not have been difficult given the country of India's size at that given point of time in history; it is however, the damage caused to national integration by this remark, which gives to it its vilificatory importance. The Indian Government demonstrated this prowess most appropriately, effectively and evocatively in the Hyderabad episode at around this time in India's history, when it used force to make the Nizam accept his fate and destiny. However, what mattered most at that time in the context of the northeast region of the country, was to win hearts and inspire loyalty, which was no doubt difficult but not impossible. The time immediately following the independence of the country was certainly not the opportune time for remonstration of India's audacious intent. It was an avoidable episode, at least in the sensitive Northeastern region of India. The remark, needless to say, changed the whole attitude of the Manipuri Meiteis towards the Government of India and in fact changed the whole history of modern Manipur. From a situationally advantagous position of winning the loyalty and the willing support of the proud Meiteis, the Government of India forfeited and relinquished its right to consolidate and win hearts. The echoes of the remark continue to resonate even today.

There may have been diplomatic imponderables but then if the situation is correctly assessed all imponderables need not necessarily end in disasters. Demonstrations of such successful and well thought-over diplomatic manoeuvrings were the cases of Goa and Sikkim later on in history, when aggressive posturing and firmness of decision worked, and worked well. These were possible, because the timings and the executions of the 'process' were right and achieved with due diligence and tact. Was it the overconfidence or the desperation, which compelled the aggressive posturing in the Northeast in the case of Manipur in 1949 or was it the ineluctable arrogance and belief of what a few thousand semi-tribals and tribals could do against the Indian war-machine? Alternatively, was the remark the consequence of a salacious advice rendered to the Sardar by someone who did not know the sentiment or the temperament of the Manipuri Meiteis, one would never know? One has not conjured to speculate or draw any epistemological inference on this aspect in this book. Whatever might have been the reasons, the episode emphatically subsumed by the famous remark was a defining moment in Manipur's history. Assimilation of the people of Manipur into national mainstream remained a mirage for a long time.

The policy of aggrandizement initiated by the Government of India so early in the history of independent India, in a strategically important region and on a highly emotional and sensitive people, appears quite a serious error of judgment. In this connection, I have an uncomfortable feeling that a wrong turn was taken in the beginning of our journey to nationhood building, especially in the Northeast in the past. But what worries me more, is the realization that having taken a left turn in the beginning of the journey, one is always perceptibly made to feel, irrespective of all the right turns one takes subsequently in the journey, that one is always on the left side; the wrong side of the journey. Let both the people of India at large and the people of the Northeast prove me wrong. I wish to be proved wrong.

Northeast and Globalization

The concept of the ethno-centric world has evolved perceptibly. The world is today humanity's collective domain where ingression into another man's territory is increasingly considered quite impossible and in a way inconsequential. This is because given the new parameters governing international relations, which is veering more towards economic 'integration' through commerce and trade, a world of sharing and adjustments, in spite of a few diehards who persists on the perpetuation of the concept of politically imposed boundaries, is emerging. The conceptual framework of confining human activities within the politically defined territory, for self-preservation and protection, compelled by the fears and anxieties of being overpowered and exploited still remain important; but the possibilities of physical incursions into another's territory is getting less and less circumstantially improbable. The world of today is becoming a melting pot of cultures and social values where existing conventional beliefs are yielding place to emerging new ones or are being constantly revalidated and re-conceptualised.

In such a volatile situation, conceptual purity of existing interpretations of state and nations is bound to undergo shifts and changes. The concept of geo-politically 'confining' people within a physical space has lost much of its importance as large non-state multi-national enterprises have usurped and imposed their respective value systems not necessarily bound by the traditional notions of political boundaries, across the world. These emerging multi-cultural, multi-ethical groups are a natural corollary, inescapable reality of the emerging economic world order. The possibilities of these institutions affecting existing social and cultural edifices and bringing changes much beyond the present generation's imaginations are real. In the near future, retaining the immaculate ethnic, cultural or social purity of the various communities and nations across the world will be extremely difficult. It will be a changed sad world, but certainly not unimaginable. In this new emerging world the idea and concept of ethnic identity has lost much of its significance and relevance.

At this point of time in history, where do the people of the Northeast India then stand? Should they rigidly stick on to their own notions of self-imposed isolation and ways of thinking, confined within the unclear definition of ethnicities and identities, reinforced by their self-centered view of the world? Alternatively, do they take the courage to forge ahead head-on into the changing world where opportunities abound? The answers to these questions have to come from every Northeastern Indian. This need not be achieved by abjectly surrendering one's ethnic identity because the option to choose are foreclosed, but they can ensure that their respective ethnicity survives by making it adaptable and accommodative enough to adjust to live through the changing times. They need to seriously consider, introspect and recontextualise their monomaniacal preoccupation with their ethnic identities, perpetrated at the cost of everything else.

The prognosis to remedy the historical preoccupation with identity in the Northeast region therefore, lies in neither effacing the self nor the clan or communitarian identity. Instead, they should be able to think of themselves as part of the over arching national identity and simultaneously be part of the larger sub-national regional identity. The sequencing of the integrative process and assimilation into the various identities, from the state to the regional and ultimately the national identity, must take place seamlessly.

Summary on Ethnic Identity

In arriving at these conclusions, the preponderance of many of the existing schools of thoughts on identity formations as articulations of different views made from different perspectives are recognised, as essentially elucidating the concept of identity in dissimilar contexts. The efficacy of each of these schools of thought and scholarships are duly recognised and acknowledged for having established and proved empirically their hypothetical assumptions. It is evident from the studies and interpretations that the evolution of ethnic identity is not a simple natural acculturation process, but interplay of several factors, both natural and the circumstances of history, which social scientists refer to as 'constructivism'. The views and interpretations in the beginning of the Chapter provide the essential backdrop required to elucidate and understand the concept of ethnic identity in the context of the Northeast. These definitions and amplifications unravel some of the mystery hidden behind the reasons for the monomaniacal preoccupation of the people of the region with their ethnic identities.

From these definitions and interpretations and from the region's ethnic histories as a background, one fact is certain, that ethnic identity of the Northeast is essentially a 'construct', evolved through a series of processes. In this process of evolution almost all the ethnic groups in the Northeast, imbibed some anthropological or socio-cultural connections or links at some time from one another in their long acculturated histories. In addition, the present geographical and geo-political isolation of the region from the rest of the country bind them down to a common destiny in one form or the other. Seen from this perspective, the present acrimonious relationships among the various ethnic groups in the Northeast appear incongruous and ironical. Unfortunately, instead of reifying these ancient links and connectivity, and using them for pursuing a common agenda for the economic development and progress of the people and region together collectively, they are all involved in rearticulating the dissimilarities that differentiate one ethnic group from the other. It is the blatant effort to deny and negate their shared ancestral legacies and common destinies, especially given the common locational disadvantages of the region, which in some strange way is self-effacing.

The reification of these age-old ties and connections, reinforced by sheer compulsions of geography and the geo-political realities, can provide the much-needed cementing factor and direction to the economic development efforts in the region. This is possible, if the meaning and purpose for reifying the age-old connections and links is taken in the right spirit and in earnest. Such an idea of a regional identity bound by geography exists sub-consciously among people in all the regions and communities across the country and in the world; the Northeast is not an exception. What is required is to make use of this link and age-old bonds with the single-minded objective to overcome economic poverty, underdevelopment and backwardness, the common enemy for the people, and not to see themselves merely by their respective ethnic identic appellatives or the state they belong. It is in this context that a paradigm shift in ethnic relationship in the Northeast is necessary.

To be a part of this regional identity, all the diverse ethnic groups in the region need to realise that each of them need not necessarily think of themselves geographically only within their respective politically demarcated area alone, because physical spaces are incapable of confining ethnic identity attributes. Ethnic identities in today's world denote a much broader and larger concept than it ever was before, expansive and accommodative, far greater than the geographical space it is associated or linked. This broad view of ethnic identity is possible because in any case each ethnic group is entrenched much more strongly and cohesively today than ever before in the form of their respective home bases or states to be threatened by any ethnic group. In one-way, ethnic identity defies even the restrictions imposed by national boundaries not to mention or talk of state or regional borders. Poetically paraphrased, like the fragrance of the flowers, which transcends the defined boundaries of one's garden, the reach of the qualitative merits of every ethnic identity must transcend the defined physical and political boundaries.

Viewed from this perspective, attempts at further physical consolidation, expansions and additions beyond the already demarcated political spaces, really has very little meaning or serve any purpose. What is already available should as such suffice. The continued persistence to add more territories in the form of larger physical spaces in the present geo-political scenario also appears difficult, improbable and hence avoidable. This is because the task of reallocation and reorganisation of the existing physical spaces becomes extremely difficult given the complexity involved, especially when many other similarly placed ethnic identities are also demanding exclusive physical spaces for themselves within the available areas in the region. The task of reworking the boundaries to accommodate all aspirations and demands once again by consensus among the various states appears most formidable and largely impossible.

The idea of a regional approach to planning and development by reifying the concept of a regional identity is not new, since every community in the Northeast have lived and live inter-changeable lives, moving as they did in the past and as they still do today, from the valleys below up into the hills and vice versa. However, the suggestion of evolving a regional partnership among the various ethnic groups in the Northeast is bound to raise heckles of the policy-makers in New Delhi. This is unfortunate, since a certain section of people in New Delhi is still preoccupied with the notion that all Northeasterners are anti-national and consider such an idea as preposterous. Consequently, even suggestions meant for economic development purposes exclusively, can be construed as fermenting secessionist tendencies, forgetting that there are equal number of patriotic Northeastern Indians if not more in the region, in percentage terms, as anywhere in the country. This preposterous concern of New Delhi brings into focus the question of why the capitulation of the national identity among the people failed in the Northeast in the past. The people of the Northeast are citizens of this country, and are as good, bad or as indifferent as any other Indian in the rest of the country. Let there be no doubt about it. It is time that New Delhi starts to trust the people of the region.

Further amplification of this observation against the thinking in New Delhi is necessary, because the general impression in the Northeast is that the kind of posturing New Delhi took immediately following independence was more in the nature of an imperial power imposing its will and diktat over the natives, rather than that of a democratic government. It is this impression, less pronounced but subterraneously prevalent, which in one way is responsible for fermenting the assertive Northeastern persona. Somewhere in our eagerness and anxiety to foster the concept of Indian nationalism and patriotism to all Indian citizens, attempts were made to superimpose the concept of nationhood and national identity, rather crudely without appreciating and understanding the Northeasterner social psyche. The process appears was pressed on a little too aggressively and obtrusively. The fact that there ought to have been an intermediary phase or stage at identity formation, before fostering the concept of national identity upon the people of the Northeastern region of the country, particularly the upland communities of the region, was a costly omission. Consequently, the aggressive posturing, involuntarily unleashed a negative reaction, which was not at all conducive to the process of national reconciliation and consolidation that was required in the early stage of nationhood building. Psychologically, the aggressive posturing left an avoidable negative imprint in the minds of the Northeasterners; the fear of being overwhelmed and losing their respective clan or communitarian ethnic identities. Part of the present chaos in the region is the legacy of this apprehension.

In effect, the present attempt is to rectify this fundamental mistake made by the country in our attempt at imposing the concept and idea of national identity on a region and people who did not know any other identity beyond themselves, their clans and communities. The attempt in the past at coercing these communities into accepting the straightjacketed concept of national identity failed, because New Delhi did not try to understand the mental make-up of the people of the region adequately. The post-independence situation of the region were such that people had to accept the idea of national identity apart from their respective clan identities without subjecting them to go through the natural acculturation process of first assimilating them into the intermediary 'regional identity'. To the average Northeasterner, 'imposing' the 'national identity' over their 'self' and 'clan or communitarian' identities is akin to asking them to become 'someone else', a perplexing proposition quite incomprehensible and impossible to be complied. This inherent flaw in imposing the idea of the national identity in our anxiety to integrate the various people in the country lies in the fact that the notion of national identity never existed in the region until independence. Seen from this historical perspective, fostering the idea and concept of a regional identity, the intermediary stage before enforcing the idea of nationhood, becomes not only important but also desirable.

In the course of the analyses, two aspects are apparent. First, that the present state of affairs in the region is not of the making of the people of the region alone, but thrust upon them by various circumstances of history. From this point of view, people in the region can discard the subconscious psychological burden of the guilt of being solely responsible for the ethnic divide in the region and instead focus on making a new beginning in their relationship. The possibilities augur well for the region. Second, based on available studies, analyses and views on identity formation taking place elsewhere across the world, ethnic identity formation in the Northeast is in the intermittent stages, which will eventually settle down and find their respective niche. The prevailing situation of flux and uncertainty in the Northeast is the churning process at its peak and hence cannot last forever. To hasten this process of consolidation of their respective ethnic identities, understanding and appreciating the history of ethnic identity formation in the region in the correct perspective is essential.

Is there than, a major perceptible departure in the formation of ethnic identity of the Northeasterners from the rest of the country? Alternatively, are the varying degrees of assertive dalliance with identity politics, which the Northeast is intensely preoccupied, part of the national phenomenon and part of the larger natural process of selection and affiliations, a common aspiration among all communities and regions in the country? Conversely, is the natural evolutionary history of multi-ethnicism and multi-culturalism in the northeastern region, which seemingly appears breaking down, the result of a manipulative contraption being deliberately singled out *"...by political entrepreneurs seeking political gains?"* Many social scientists like Clifford Geertz[38] are of the view that it is intrinsic human reaction to respond to identity formation, indoctrination and compulsive identification. In fact, such a churning process has to happen since ethnicity by its very concept is *"...instrumentalist; in their basic orientation"*, a view which John Rex[39] held.

Ethnic identity is as such quintessentially human and should therefore, normally contribute and facilitate development of the individual and progress of both the society and the community. Unfortunately, in the Northeast, this preoccupation has subsumed other larger and important interests, including economic development and progress. This monomaniacal preoccupation and dalliance over the years has taken its toll on the Northeastern psyche. In short, this preoccupation is pinning down the whole region into a possible historical disaster and driving the region into irrelevance. The stakes involved are extremely high for the tens of thousands of innocent seemingly voiceless people who are the unfortunate silent sufferers trapped both in time and in space. The only way out of this entrapment for the people of the region is to relook into their past, understand it (which Chapters 2 to 8 do) and thereafter articulate the future course of action.

Endnotes

1. Joseph E. Trimble and Ryan Dickson, *Ethnic Identity*, Western Washington University.
2. Abner Chohen. *Custom and Politics in Urban Africa: A Study of Hausa Migrants in a Yaruba Town*, 1969. Abner revealed the existence of a deliberate manipulation of kinship and cultural affinities by political institutions for narrow political advantages.
3. Abner Chohen, ibid.
4. Benedict Anderson, *Imagined Communities: Reflection on the origin and the Spread of Nationalism*, 1983.
5. Benedict Anderson, ibid.
6. Ernest Gellner, *Nation and Nationalism* 1983 and also *Nationalism*, 1997, published after his death under the heading "*Do nations have navels?*"
7. Ernest Gelner, ibid,
8. Clifford Geertz, *Third World*, 1973,
9. Thomas Hylland Eriksen, *The nature of Ethnicity in the Project of Migration* by who refers to John Rex, 1995.
10. Amartya Sen, *The Argumentative Indian*.
11. Amartya Sen, *Identity and Violence: The Illusion of Destiny*. p-150.
12. P. Lalnithanga, *Emergence of Mizoram*, 2004, p.4-5.
13. P. Lalnithanga, ibid; p.4-5.
14. P. Lalnithanga, ibid; p.4-5.
15. Dr. Sangkima; Chapter 10, *Essays on the History of the Mizos*, 2002, p-97 to 102, titled 'The Mizo Uprising: A significant event in the History of Chieftainship in Mizoram'.

16. P. Lalnithanga, *Emergence of Mizoram*, ibid, p-20-21.
17. James C. Scott, 'Hill and Valley in Southeast Asia', quoted by Sanjib Baruah, Confronting Constructionism: Ending India's Naga war, in the *Journal of Peace Research* of The International Peace Research Institute, Oslo, Vol. 40 (3) May 2003, pp321-338.
18. S. E. Peal, 'The Nagas and the Neighbouring Tribes' in the *Journal of the Asiatic Society of Bengal*, 1874, vol. iii, quoted by S. K. Chaube in '*Hill politics in Northeast India*', p-35.
19. E.R. Leach, *Political Systems of Highland Burma*, p-291, ibid, Chaube, P 34.
20. Fredrick Barth, *Ethnic Groups and Boundaries: The Social Organization of Cultural Difference*. London, 1969.
21. Abner Cohen, 1969, ibid.
22. Sanjib Baruah quoted by him, *The Nagas: The Hill People of Northeast India; Society, Culture and the Colonial Encounter*, London.
23. T.C. Hudson, *The Meitheis*, p 5-6.
24. T. C. Hudson, *ibid*, p-5&6.
25. Ex-Commissioner for Scheduled Caste and Scheduled Tribes, Govt. of India, Gandhian Scholar and Private Secretary to Mahatma Gandhiji during his tour in riot torn Bengal during 1946-47.
26. Not to be mixed with the Bishnupur town in Manipur, which came up much later in history.
27. Manipuri: An Aryan Culture under Threat; 'The Bishnupriya Manipuris', http://manipuri.iwarp.com.
28. All Bishnupriya words and sentences taken from 'Learn Indian language: Languageshome.com'.
29. Fredrik Barth, ibid.
30. Fredrik Barth, ibid.
31. As the Chief Guest of the valedictory function of the Meet on 'Centre State Relations' conducted by the The Interstate Council, Government of India. The two days Meet at Shillong on September 30th and the 1st of October 2008 Meet was attended by all the state Governments from the Northeast, important members of the civil societies, NGOs along with an array of prominent and well-known intellectuals from the Northeast including Sikkim.
32. A term used by Arjun Appadurai, *Modernity at Large: Cultural Dimensions of Globalisation*, 1997.

33. Amartya Sen, *The Argumentative Indian*.
34. Thomas Hylland Eriksen, ibid.
35. Meyer Fortes and E.E. Evans-Pritchard, *African Political Systems*. London, Oxford University Press eds.1940.
36. E.E. Evans-Pritchard, *The Nuer*, 1940 Oxford: Clarendon, quoted by Eriksen, ibid. A proverb often used to describe the Somali Civil War.
37. Thomas Hylland Eriksen, ibid.
38. Clifford Geertz, ibid.
39. Refered to by Thomas Hylland Eriksen on John Rex's; *The nature of Ethnicity in the Project of migration*, 1995.

CHAPTER - 2

GEOGRAPHY OF THE REGION

Topographically, the Northeast Region of India comprising the states of Arunachal Pradesh, Assam, Manipur, Meghalaya, Mizoram, Nagaland and Tripura is a compact geographical entity. The region is tectonically and morphologically part of East Asia, but politically it is part of South Asia. The geography, topography and climate have played an important and significant role in identity formation in the region. The compact geographical entity, however was super-imposed by many different kinds of 'man-made' political boundaries and divisions in the course of the region's political history particularly at the time of India's independence. This not only isolated the people and the region from the rest of the country, but also changed the character of the once physically accessible and homogeneous region. The disruptions of lives of people following these political divisions are some of the main causes for the rise of assertive ethnic identity politics in the Northeast.

Further, the general tendency to oversimplify the problems and issues of the region by dealing geomorphologically, rather than anthropocentrically, tends to view and deal with the region from a predominantly tribal perspective, underplaying in the process the problems of the non-tribal communities living in the lowland areas. This creates another set of ethnic identity related problems in the region. The Chapter looks at the importance and role of geography in the ethnic identity formations in the Northeast region.

Introduction: Form and Content

Form determines content. However, contents do not always necessarily determine form. The complexity multiplies when the form is a compact physical entity, but apportioned for political and historical reasons affecting the contents. Every twist and turn of the 'man-made line', which cleavages through inaccessible terrain matters, and much histrionics are made even for minor non-consensual alterations. Confined within these defined physical spaces; the threshold of which are called international boundaries that demarcate one country from another, are further 'imaginary lines' that demarcate sub-territorial political physical spaces called by various names as States, Provinces, Presidencies, Union Territories, Regions and a host of other appellatives signifying more or less the same thing. It is within this politically demarcated territory that life is regulated and contoured by a set of legislated and legalised principles of 'Dos' and 'Don'ts' called by various generic terms as Laws and Statutes. Quintessentially, it determines and influences the entire gamut of life, which includes social, cultural, economical, political and a host of other factors that determine and shape human lives.

However, in a region like the Northeast life is often determined by the elements of nature, which superimposes its rule. Man may propose, but often it is the raw writ of the topography and the physical features of the region, which shape human destinies in the region. Often this fact is forgotten. Anthropologically the pattern of migration of the various ethnic groups into the region is closely associated with the geography and topography of the region. In fact, the anthropological history of the Northeast is a metonymical extension of its rugged terrain and geography. The qualificatory observations are necessary since understanding the problems of the Northeast without appreciating its geo-anthropology is like a mirage; it exists but can prove deceptive and misleading.

The behemoth political and administrative edifices called country, states, districts and other politically contrived setups, imposed by us on our lives, ostensibly with our consent, however undermines and relegates these non-descriptive, un-defined natural physical features, the rivers, hills, mountains into insignificance by a process of reductionism, forgetting that these often shape our lives and determine our destinies. In the Northeast, through given sets of historical coincidences, byproduct of circumstances of history but mostly 'man-made', the naturally formed geographical spaces and corridors were disbanded at the time of partition of the country, changing the course of history of the people of the region.

The Geography of Northeast; its importance

There are four aspects to understand the importance and role of geography in the context of the Northeast. These four aspects are, (i) the unique geography, topography and climate of the region, (ii) the impact of the imposition of the various 'man-made' divisions particularly at the time of India's independence, (iii) the tendency to oversimplify the problems of the various groups of people and ethnicities, without according adequate considerations to individual ethnicities. (iv) And lastly, the tendency to deal with the problems of the region essentially from a geomorphological perspective, rather than ethnocentrically. All these four are discussed.

I. The Geographical Determinants

Geographically, the northeast region is analysed from two distinct and different ways. The first is purely from the geo-physical perspective devoid of politically demarcated boundaries and the second, is to view exclusively from within the confines of the politically demarcated territories of India. The general tendency is to take the second view. The second perspective is inward looking and focuses more on the geo-political aspects and problems confronting the region devoid of its economic potentials as part of the Southeast Asian sub-continent.

Examined from the first 'perspective', the purely geographical, the whole of the Northeast region of India forms a contiguous part of the South East Asian tectonic physical features. This geographical region comprises of all the northeastern States of India, Myanmar (Burma), Southern China, Bhutan, Bangladesh, Eastern Nepal and includes Thailand, Cambodia, Laos etc, and further east. All the people inhabiting the Northeast region, essentially referred in histories as Assam[1], comprises of different ethnic groups but essentially comprising of Mongoloid, Tibeto-Burman, Tibeto-Mongoloid, Australoid and Caucasoid stock. Linguistically most of them fall into the Tibeto-Burman and Sino-Tibetan family based on the Linguistic Survey of India made by G.A. Gierson. The Indo-Aryan civilizational influence ends in the Northeast region and Southeast Asian culture and ethos begin.

Anthropologically and historically, the region is important since a number of migrating ethnic groups, both indigenous and of foreign origins, from the East and the West converged, creating unique civilizations, distinct from the rest of the country. In the process, cross-fertilization and fusion of several religious, social and cultural influences of the East, Southeast Asia with Indo-Aryan influences from the West of the region, took place. For instance, *"The Tribes of Meghalaya form a distinctive genetic cluster, differentiated from other tribes of the northeast India."*[2] and considered part of *"...the first inhabitants of India..."* along with the *"...Munda, Santhal, Dravidians and the Aryans"* and who came through the land route through Central India before reaching the Northeast.

The region is divided into four Zones based on the geography and physical features. Three of these are mountainous and hilly zones, while one comprises of rivers and their basins.

Zone (i): This Zone comprises of the Northern Himalayan ranges forming part of the Greater Himalayas, running from west to east, encompassing Eastern Nepal, Bhutan, Sikkim and Arunachal Pradesh. The Himalayan ranges then runs southwards encircling Arunachal Pradesh. These are snow-peaked mountains whose height ranges an average of 4000 to 5000 meters above sea level and beyond. Mount Kangto on the northern border with Tibet is 7090 meters. There are a number of mountain Passes like Lusha Pass (5248 meters), Kaya Pass (4755 meters) and other important Passes. Because of its relatively sparse population, these mountains act as sentinels and do not affect or interfere in human activities. The eastern Himalayas form a ridge, which segregates the Chinese Province of Kumming and the Provinces of Kachin and Northern Sagaing of Myanmar from India.

Zone (ii): The Eastern Himalayan range then tapers southwards and links to the Patkoi Bum ranges, the Naga Hills (The two highest peaks are the Sramati 3887 meters and Mol Len 3104 meters). It then runs into Manipur (Siruhi Kashong 2568 meters in Ukhrul district), into the south merging into the East and West Manipur Hills, including the Laimatol Range (Loiching 2015 meters). The Manipur Hills lent up (Thangjing 2109 meters) to the Chaifil Tlang, and the Uiphum Tlang ranges in Mizoram before tapering off into the Chin and Arakan provinces of Myanmar as it loops up with the Arakan Yoma. This zone, comprising of the many mountainous ranges, forms the main habitation areas of the Upland people of the Northeast comprising the states of Arunachal Pradesh, Nagaland, Manipur and Mizoram. In these ranges, which 'spill-over' into both India, Myanmar and China, especially in the provinces of Kachin, Sagaing, Chin and Arakan of Myanmar, members of the same ethnic communities are found on either side of the internationally demarcated boundaries. The Nagas, Kukis, Mizos, Manipuris, and a host of other indigenous people live across the political divide some as Indian nationals while some as Myanmarese citizens.

Zone (iii): This zone comprises of the Barail mountain ranges (Sherpal 1057 meters) which begin west of Manipur up to the south of the Brahmaputra valley, sandwiched between Mymensingh and Sylhet in Bangladesh. The mountain ranges comprise Jaintia Hills (North Cachar Hills), Khasi Hills (Cherapunji 1358 meters) and the Garo Hills (Kylas 1026 meters). All these form the state of Meghalaya. Many rivers originate on these highlands and almost equal numbers of them flow both south into Bangladesh and north into the Brahmaputra. On both sides of this ridge, which runs east and west, the land slopes down on both sides. On the southern slopes, which fall into Bangladesh, substantially large settlements of Khasis, Jaintias and Garos are 'spilt-over' into the lowlands of Mymensingh and Sylhet districts of Bangladesh. The Jaintia hills slope eastward into the Cachar plains, which is part of the Barak valley. Just north east of the Jaintia hills across the river valley formed by the rivers Jamuna and the Kalang, is the Rengma Hills (1363 meters) forming the Mikir Hills, rising like a plateau overlooking the Brahmaputra Valley, all around.

Zone (iv): The last zone, the rivers and their basins comprise the three river basins. This is the most populated zone in the region and mostly occupied by non-tribal lowland communities. The great Brahmaputra river basin stretches down from the lower-reaches of the lesser Himalayas in Arunachal Pradesh, in which the mighty Brahmaputra meanders from the east to the west and includes the confluence of the three rivers Dibang, Adzon and the Lohit, known as the 'Eastern Sangam'. The Surma valley, the second riverine valley, located in the southwestern part of Assam covering the district of Cachar and the state of Tripura, falls in this zone and merges into the great estuary in Bangladesh formed by the three greatest rivers, the Ganga, Brahmaputra, Padma or Meghna, which eventually flow into the Bay of Bengal. The third river valley is the Imphal or Manipur valley, formed by the river of the same name, which joins as a tributary to the Chindwin in Myanmar. It then joins the great river Irrawaddy in Myanmar on its way to the Bay of Bengal, above the Indian islands of Andaman and Nicobar Islands.

The four zones of the Northeastern region of India geomorphologically distinguishes East Asia from South Asia by the Patkoi Bum range, Naga Hills, East Manipur Hills, Mizo Hills and the Arakan Yoma which runs north to south as mountain ranges starting with the Himalayas and stretches up to the Bay of Bengal. Physically and climatically, the northeast region of the country forms part of the tropical climatic Zone of Southeast Asia. Further, the Northeast is divided into two distinct physical features, the valleys or riverine areas, and the uplands or the mountainous or hilly areas.

(a) The 'river-view' of the region

The two most significant features, which determine and form the ethnoscape of the region, are the Rivers and the Mountain ranges. Two distinct sets of ethnic groups of people migrated into the region through these rivers and mountains. The Indo-Aryans came from the west through the riverine routes from the Great Bengal Plains while the Asiatic Mongoloids comprising of the Tibeto-Burmese and Sino-Tibetan ethnic groups came from South East Asia, Southern China through the mountain-passes from the north and east.

The rivers of eastern and northeastern India form part of the Great East Asian river system. The three River systems in the Northeast are, (I) the System of the Brahmaputra comprise of numerous major tributaries, which flow from Arunachal Pradesh, Nagaland and Meghalaya hills and join the estuaries in the Great Bengal plains in Bangladesh as the Jamuna. The Brahmaputra originates as the Tsangpo in the Tibetan plateau before flowing into Arunachal Pradesh. The Brahmaputra has three other names, as the Yamuna, the Padma after the Ganges joins it in Bangladesh, and just before flowing into the Bay of Bengal as the Meghna. The confluences of these mighty rivers, the Brahmaputra, the Ganges and Meghna form part of the greater river system of Asia, and constitute one of the most fascinating river basins of the world. (II) The Surma and the Kusiyara, with their tributaries the Barak and the Irang originate from within the Northeast and flow into the Bay of Bengal through the Cachar Plains popularly known as the Surma Valley in Assam. (III) The river Manipur and other east-flowing smaller rivers form the third major scheme. These rivers join the Irrawaddy in western Myanmar in the east and eventually flow into the Bay of Bengal in the south.

These rivers provide a fascinating way of looking at the Northeast, a 'water-view of the world', a phrase used by David Ludden[3]. In many ways, they are the 'history' of the kingdoms of Assam, Manipur, the Kacharis and a host of other smaller civilizations in the plain areas and valleys of the region. This reconstructed 'water-view' of the northeast region transcends its political borders and forms part of the composite Asian Drainage systems, which sits, *"...astride a watershed that divides the western trajectory of the Brahmaputra (east flowing) by the Patkoi Range from the major drainages of Southeast Asia and Southern China (South and south-east flowing). Five huge rivers define the major corridors of settlement and mobility running from the Ganga basin across China, Vietnam, Thailand and Burma. The Brahmaputra (or Jamuna in Bangladesh) is the eastern most river of South Asia, but it is also the western most river in East Asia"*. This is because rivers have no boundaries, they refuse to have one. These rivers form important migratory routes for people from various parts of Asia by bringing the Aryan and Asiatic civilizations, cultures and social systems together.

The Western migratory route into the Northeast region from the great Indo-Gangetic Plains of Central India, came along the rivers Ganges, the Jamuna or Meghna (as the Brahmaputra is known in Bangladesh) and along other river estuaries and deltas of the Great Bengal river system. The Brahmaputra or Jamuna, which runs north to south, divides the Great Bengal plains into the eastern and the western halves. Migration into the Northeast from the rest of India across the Bengal plains was possible only through the riverine routes as the land routes were extremely hazardous and difficult if not altogether impossible. In addition, during the monsoon season a number of rivers like the Meghna, the Kalni in the Surma River valley in the Cachar Plains of Assam become insurmountable obstacles because of their spread. Inspite of these inhibiting factors, the rivers of Northeast India were the only major routes through which migration and movement of people were possible.

Many well-known and famous Hindu temples found on the banks of these rivers especially the Brahmaputra are testimonies of the role played by these rivers in the history of the region. The famous temple at Malinithan at Likabali in West Siang district of Arunachal Pradesh[4] built by the Palas of Kamrupa during the 11th and 12th century A.D, is located just half a mile away from the Ghagara river and the Gai river, both tributaries of the Brahmaputra. The temple has Orissan art and architectural influence. Studies indicate that *"the finished products were brought"* from the quarry site in Orissa or made by Oriya architects and artists who brought the stones and came along the riverine route up the Brahmaputra via what is now Bangladesh[5]. Interestingly this fact reinforces Ravi J. Deka's[6] claim and assumption of why most of the important Hindu temples in Assam are located all along the rivers of Assam and not in the interior areas away from the river valleys.

People migrated in groups for various parts of Southeast Asian region and Southern China into the Northeast of India along the Red River basin in Vietnam through the mountain passes. The Ahoms of Assam is one of the most prominent ethnic groups who came to the region in the 13th century ADE under their leader Sukhapa and established his kingdom in Chairaideo. The Mizos, Kukis moved up from the Irrawaddy basin in Burma and then into the Lushai hills. Similarly, the Meiteis of Manipur, various Naga groups came into the region from the east and the northwestern borders of China along the Irrawaddy river basin across Burma.

The Naga migratory history in this context is fascinating. There are two routes supposedly taken by the various Naga tribes. One version is that the Nagas came from the Yunnan Province of China along the Mekong River, a part of this group of Nagas then moved into the Southern Sea areas in Vietnam before taking the western route to Northeast India. The other route supposedly taken by the Nagas is along the river Salween in eastern Myanmar, thereafter migrating westwards, through the confluence of the Irrawaddy in Loi-Kaw with other rivers, and then moving towards present day Nagaland. The use of shells, cowries and conches by some of the Nagas as their ceremonial ornaments even today, explains their links with the sea at some time of their history. The accepted version is that this group of Nagas migrated from a place close to the Moulmein Sea (Myanmar) or close to the Southern Seas in Vietnam. The route taken by the Nagas have a lot in common with the routes taken by the Dyaks and Konyans, tribal people of Indonesia and the Philippines[7]. Similarly, the Kirats, another name for Mongoloid people in ancient India, came from Western China speaking Sino-Tibetan language. The Bodos, Garos, Rabha, Deuries, Misings, Morans, Sutias, Dimasas and Koches (Rajbonshi), Lalung, Hajong and few others evolved from within the Indo-Mongoloid groups in the region.

Rivers therefore hold a special place in the history of civilisation in the Northeastern region of India, especially in the valley areas. More significantly, the rivers are synonym of the life of people in the valleys. The mighty river Brahmaputra, known and admiringly called locally by the Bodos, the autochthons in Assam, as the "Tilao", (ti=river, lao=long) before it was rechristened into its Hindunised name as the Brahmaputra or the 'Son of Brahma', distinguishing it as the only male river in India is the most important. People of the Northeast, particularly those from Assam ascribe to it the same status and reverence as much as the Ganges, the holy river of India, has for the rest of India.

In a touching tribute Ravi J. Deka[8] with his immense interests in the archaeology of Assam, writing on the influences of the rivers of Assam on the state's history in a fascinating profile titled, *River of Faith*, describe the 'power of the rivers' as cyclic, creating, destroying and resurrecting. *"Studying the remnants of the hundred of ancient temples which dots the Assamese landscape, there is a possibility that there may have been a regular riverine traffic of pilgrims who came on boats from the other parts of the subcontinent during the early medieval period. An assumption also supported by the Tantric opus Kalika Purana, the oldest remaining text dealing with India's eastern region believed to have been compiled in the 9-10th century CE".* Deka is not far from the truth. It is the co-relation between the rivers and the civilizations in the region, proved by the large number of temples on the banks of these rivers, which stand testimony to this fact.

The 'Curse' of the rivers; Famine and Migration

The problems created by the rivers of Northeast India are not India specific, transcending across political boundaries, making the problem of one country the problem of the other, and endowing them a trans-Asian character. These rivers, particularly the Brahmaputra, cause extensive damages, creating havoc in Bangladesh as much as it does to Assam. Amartya Sen in 'Famine in Bangladesh' of 1974 describes succinctly the kind of endemic problems the rivers from the Northeast causes in Bangladesh particularly by the Brahmaputra. Sen sums the endemic problem, *"First the floods; then the famine. So runs the capsule story of the Bangladesh famine of 1974"*[9]. Sen made this observation citing Gilbert Etienne, who had earlier summed the floods in Bangladesh preceding the famine as the handiwork of the Brahmaputra, which overran its banks encroaching extensive arable lands and areas by flooding, not once or twice but almost throughout the agricultural year of 1973-74. Sen tacitly subscribes this role of the havoc caused by the Brahamaputra as one of the main causes of the famine, recurring as an annual phenomenon in Bangladesh. The consequential havoc the floods cause results in shortage of food grains and dramatic increases in the price of rice, the staple diet of the people in Bangladesh, eventually leading to famine.

The most affected districts, in terms of people affected and numbers who depended on the *langarkhanas* during the famine in 1974 in Bangladesh[10] were Rangpur, Mymensingh, Dinajpur and Sylhet, all districts of East Pakistan (Bangladesh) adjoining areas to West Bengal (Koochbihar), Meghalaya, Tripura and Assam in India. The consequential pressure on these adjoining Indian states has been nothing less than extraordinary. Similarly, in the chapter on the Great Famine of 1943 in Bengal[11], which recorded between 1.5 million to 3 million deaths, the most affected district was Faridpur, located on the banks of the Padma close to the district of Tippera in Bangladesh and adjoining the state of Tripura in India. The catastrophe that followed is understandable. The impact of the famine broke the supply chain leading to shortage of rice in East Pakistan. The subsequent differences between the prices of rice in undivided Bengal, by end of 1942 were Rs. 13.88 (assumed per maund) as against the price of Rs. 8.81 in Assam, Rs. 8.00 in Bihar and Rs. 6.19 in Orissa. The fact that the seasonal floods in erstwhile East Pakistan the main cause of the famine in East Pakistan were caused by the rivers of northeast India is a well-known fact.

In turn, the large affected population of these annual ravages of the floods and famines in Bangladesh; move eastwards into the higher plains and fertile terrains of Assam and other Northeastern states illegally. The indirect affect of the havoc caused by the river Brahmaputra annually on Bangladesh's economy, therefore affects the demographic composition of the Northeast region of India, particularly Assam. The fact, in short is that the rivers of the Northeast are largely responsible for both the Great Bengal Famines of 1943 and of 1974 in Bangladesh, substantiating the irrefutable fact that climate and physical features of the Northeast play an important role in the entire region beyond India's boundaries.

What these means to the Northeastern states, particularly in Assam, can be gauged from the report given by the then Governor of Assam to the President of India. In the report on the illegal immigration into Assam, the then Governor of Assam, General S.K. Sinha, reported the differential decadal growth of population of Hindus and Muslims in Assam. The figures are respectively; 33.7 per cent and 38.3 per cent during 1951-1961; 37.2 per cent and

31 per cent during 1961-1971; and an estimated 41.9 per cent and 77.4 per cent during 1981-1991. The report also further brought out the fact that as per the 1991 Census of India, the districts of Dhubri, Goalpara, Barpeta and Hailakandi have become Muslim majority districts with Naogaon, Karimganj and Morgaon closely following the trend. Most of these districts have common borders with Bangladesh, while the other districts having to bear the consequential 'spilt-over' effect. As per the Census of India 2001[12] the growth of population by religion from 1991 to 2001 shows that, the Muslim population in the Northeast has grown substantially. In Arunachal Pradesh, it has grown by 73.41 percent, in Assam by 29.3 percent, in Manipur by 42.98 percent, in Meghalaya by 61.35 percent, Mizoram by 122.54 percent, in Nagaland by 69.58 percent, in Sikkim by 99.87 percent and in Tripura by 29.49 percent. The political impact of all these is the constant acrimonious accusations and counter-charges traded between India and Bangladesh on one hand and the constant criticism of the Governments at the Centre and the states by the local Assamese population on the other.

(b) Mountain Passes

If the rivers of the Northeast largely determine the demography and the ethnoscape of the lowland areas, it is the mountain Passes, which shape the ethnoscape of the upland and mountainous areas. The number of Passes and trading points all along the international borders in these mountains and hills are examples to illustrate this point. These Passes exist in the north and the east of the region at comparatively low altitudes in Arunachal Pradesh, Sikkim and Bhutan and through the Patkoi ranges of the hilly tracks of Nagaland and Manipur. The Chinese travellers, the ambitious Burmese kings, the Japanese imperial forces and the American and British allied forces during Second World War, all used these routes and Passes from Yunnan and Kachin provinces of Burma into the Northeast region. The Stilwell road built in 1943, links North Western Myanmar (Burma), South Western China through Ledo in the Brahmaputra valley, while the Indo-Burmah (Moreh and Tamu) road from Manipur valley (Imphal river Basin) with Western Myanmar (Burma).

As a supplement to the trade and migratory routes on the rivers, the mountain Passes was an important means, which shaped the ethnoscape of the region. Access to international waters in the

Bay of Bengal is also possible from the region. The recently signed agreement between the Government of India and the Government of Myanmar, to link the state of Mizoram by an intermodal transport system, partially by road and partly through the river Kalladan by linking the port of Akyab (Sitwe) in the Bay of Bengal in Myanmar would provide the much needed alternative route for the entire Northeast to the rest of the country. In fact, this route will be an additional trade corridor for the Northeast to West Bengal and vice-versa, through Bangladesh, which India has been negotiating with the Government of Bangladesh for some time. Both of these are in addition to the existing circuitous land route through the 'Siliguri corridor', popularly called the 'chicken's neck'.

The irony of the geography of the Northeast is that even though many condemn it as the main cause for the region's backwardness and underdevelopment, in reality, it is the political divisions imposed over these natural features, which are the main obstacles to the development of the region. In fact, historically, immigrations, trade and commerce within and beyond the region have been going on in spite of these physical features for generations. In fact, in many border areas even today, people depend on barter trade and exchanges on a regular basis, albeit surreptitiously and unabashedly. In one way, many socio-anthropologists consider the physical features of the region as the mainstay and factor responsible for preserving the unique social and cultural ethos of the region and hence a positive aspect of the Northeast.

The fact is, but for the political machinations, which 'artificially divided' the country, isolating the Northeast from the rest of the country, commercially and economically, the physical features of the region is not the cause for the underdevelopment of the region. There is a general tendency to attribute the failures to develop the region on its geography and climate, which even though accepted as an important factor, is certainly not the sole reason for the region's underdevelopment and levels of poverty.

Today, officially, trading and exchanges of large volumes of goods take place at Moreh in Manipur and Tamu in Myanmar. Similarly, cement, fish are brought every day from Bangladesh into Agartala, the capital of Tripura (the boundaries between Bangladesh and India falls on the outskirts of Agartala), or betel nuts, betel pepper-leaves, areca nuts and a host of produce and products are exchanged at Dawki in Meghalaya. Also today, close to the checkpoint at Dawki, hordes of boats on the Bangladesh side of the border come not to fish from the rivers, but come to 'fish' stone and pebble that roll down from Meghalaya hills under the rivers, since stones are a rare commodity in these border areas within Bangladesh.

All these legalised and illegal trade taking place inspite of the physical features of the region, only proves that the obstacles to development and progress of the region is not geography of the region but the problems lie somewhere else. Obviously, there is a basic mistake in blaming the physical features of the Northeast as hindrances to its progress and development. If today rice, kerosene and other food items are illegally exchanging hands and sustain a large population in the border areas of Manipur and Myanmar, it is because in the expeditious enforcement of the division of the country, we in the rest of India forgot the fate and consequences the political division would have on our fellow citizens in the Northeast. What geography provided to the people of the region, politically we deprived it.

In fact, geographically, the location of the Northeast region has several advantages. The Northeast is the only region in the country, surrounded by five countries, Bhutan, Nepal, China, Myanmar and Bangladesh. The region has approximately 96 percent of its international borders, except for a narrow strip of land slightly less than thirty km-wide, linking the region with the rest of the country through the Siliguri corridor. The conclusion from all these is that the primary causes of the problems of development of the Northeast region is not the natural features but the unfortunate abrogation of the locational advantages, which the geography of the region has, by a more political expedient dispensation at the time of India's independence. The region occupies an ideal location to launch the Look East Policy (LEP) of the Government.

II. The 'Imperfect' Partition

From the geo-political perspective, it is clear that one of the primary causes for the law and order situation, economic poverty, underdevelopment and other problems in the Northeast region is the political isolation of the region from the rest of the country at the time of the Partition of the country. This had a profound psychological impact on the people of the region especially the insensitive manner in which the naturally formed trade routes and clusters of human habitations were disbanded and bifurcated at Partition.

From the historical perspective, two disruptions and dislocations of human habitations took place in the northeastern region of India. The first was during the British regime and the second was at the time of India's independence. The first disruption took place on the eastern side of the Northeast region when the present boundaries of Northeast India with Ava in Burma (Myanmar) was drawn immediately following the end of the First Anglo-Burmese War, marked by the signing of the Yandawoo Treaty on 24 February 1826. This 'partition' divided many Naga, Kuki, Mizo, Manipuri Meitei and a host of other minor ethnic groups on either side of the borders in Sagaing, Kachin and Chin Divisions of Burma and Northeast India. The British demarcated the boundaries to create a safe buffer zone to protect their growing economic interests in the region and to prevent Burmese interferences. This is apparent from the fact that the British Government selected the highest points of the peaks and ridges of these mountain ranges and hills, while demarcating the lines between them and the Burmese, unmindful of the fate of people living on either side. Besides disrupting human settlements of the various indigenous ethnic groups, formed over generations conforming to the topography of the region, the demarcation of political boundaries left many disgruntled people on both sides of the international borders.

For instance, the boundary drawn between Burma and India in the Eastern Frontier Agency or North Eastern Frontier Agency or NEFA[13], was across the crest of the Hkakaborazi peak (5881 meters) dividing British India, Tibet and China. The Saramati peak (3826 meters) in the Patkoi Range dissected Manipur from the Kabaw Valley. Similarly, dissection of the Naga Hills (Naga Land) or the Naga dominated areas in a north-south divide cut off a large number of Naga tribes and sub-tribes settled in Burma from those in India across the Patkoi Ranges. Lushai hills (Mizoram), was dissected near the Blue mountain peak (2157 meters) cutting the Arakan Yoma into two parts, in a North–South direction dividing British India from the Burmese kingdom.

The random destruction of the ethnic human settlements made mobility between the same ethnic groups across these destinations difficult but not impossible. The division not only became a logistic nightmare for the British but also for the Indian Government after independence. The British policy to checkmate Burmese expansionist manoeuvres into Assam and Manipur, therefore, came at a heavy price for the people in the region. It left a large group of disgruntled ethnic indigenous populations all along the sensitive Indo-Burmese-Chinese border, inciting dissention, fissiparous tendencies, leading to political unrest in the region.

In 1947, when India was divided creating East Pakistan at independence the second 'division' of the Northeast took place. The Northeast region was completely isolated from the rest of India geo-politically. Given the fact that the Great Bengal plains formed the main natural corridors for movement of people, trade and commerce for the entire Northeast, the partition, in a way, condemned the people of the Northeast to a state of perpetual economic, political isolation. It was a quarantine of the most disastrous kind economically for the region and particularly for the many Khasi and Jaintias families in India and those living in Sylhet and Mymensingh in erstwhile East Pakistan, now Bangladesh. The Meiteis, Garos, Mizos and the Kacharis living along these borders also suffered the same fate. Even though these events lie buried somewhere in an unknown chapter of Indian history, the pain and the anguish of these 'divisions' and 'partitions' remain encapsulated in the memories of the people in the northeast region.

There is therefore, a lingering feeling among the Northeasterners that even though the partition was a foregone conclusion, ever since the failure of the Cabinet Mission to bring about a consensus between the Muslim League and the Indian National Congress, the international boundaries drawn for creation of East Pakistan, could have been much more diligently and sensitively demarcated for the sake of the people of the Northeast. The inherent fallacy enunciated in the 'two nation theory', even though acknowledged by the founding fathers of India, by finally accepting it, besides damming every right-thinking person, also carried with it unfortunately, the stigma of completely sealing the fate and future of the people of the Northeastern region of India. It is because of this fact that people in the Northeast region think that the rest of the country looks at them and the region as a picturesque 'blotch' of inanimate beautiful hills and placid valleys, rather than a geographical region and 'space' where people with feelings and wants, live. This feeling somehow lingers on.

Critically analysed from the Northeasterners' point of view, the demarcations of the national boundaries at Partition, even though procured legitimacy of the independence of the country, has become a painful reminder that the problems of underdevelopment faced by the region is the consequence of a 'man-made' problem that could have been averted. Additionally, what also hurt the people of the region most was the indifference shown to the plight of the displaced people in the eastern half of the same country at partition, unlike the concern and preoccupation the partition of Punjab in the western half created. Many Northeast Indians feel that for most Indians, the story of Partition in the eastern half remains a forgotten episode in the by-lanes of Indian history, and for most people in the country, an untold story. One needs to assuage this feeling.

Unfortunately, the 'dispensability' syndrome by segregating the region from the rest of India denotes 'insignificance'. This feeling of 'neglect' continues to haunt the region, making the people believe that the country has not been fair and equitable, more poignantly they feel betrayed. This feeling vitiate the relationship between the Northeast and rest of India. Given these feelings many of the ethnic groups have either been led astray or fallen victims to the propagandas of the proponents of assertive ethnic identity and the politics of hate.

In addition, the various problems created by the Reorganisation of the States in the region from 1963 and again in 1972-73, when Nagaland was formed (1963) and subsequently when the States of Mizoram, Nagaland and Meghalaya were formed in 1972-73, are discussed in the last two Chapters when the question of economic viability of the region is discussed.

III. Oversimplification and Generalisation

The 'region', formed by political expediencies and compulsions, known as the 'Northeast', is an euphuism to denote physical entrapment, remoteness, backwardness along with a host of negative attributes. These adjectives describe the 'region' and works at two levels. The first is the tendency to deprecate the whole of the Northeast into a single inaccessible geographical bloc; populated by indescribable ethnic groups of people. From this perspective the people and the region is seen geomorphologically as one single large group of faceless people rather than anthropo-centrically comprising of separate distinct ethnicities with their unique set of value systems, social ethos, sensibilities and unique problems.

Second, closely linked to the first, is the use and application of a common administrative solution to the various problems, which each of the various ethnic groups across the region have.

While superficially the clubbing of the various ethnicities is administratively convenient, however, the approach has its own disadvantages. This overarching view of all the ethnic entities as a single bloc, by a process of reductionism gives an impression of undermining the need and importance of the problems of each of the various ethnic groups separately. This tendency to deal with the region as a single geographical entity ends up in over-simplified and generalisation of the issues and problems. This generalised approach to problem solving only complicate matters even further.

The case of clubbing all Naga tribes by the British for administrative reasons, which has more than forty different tribes spread across the Northeast India and in Myanmar, in spite of being fully aware of the distinctive features of each of these tribes is an example. This is in spite of the fact that innumerable studies by Sir James Johnstone, J.P. Mills, J.P. Hutton, Wood Thrope, H.H. Godwin Austin, Mackensie, Damant, and a host of social scientists both British and Europeans were available to the British. Yet, in spite of the volumes of literature available on most of the major Naga tribes, the issues and problems are dealt, as a common problem of the Nagas as a group, without addressing the individual and different needs of each tribe. While administratively, it simplifies enforcements of government rules and procedures, the usage of the common term Naga euphemistically, for example in reality distorts the needs and requirements of each tribe who are otherwise distinct and separate.

In post-independent India, the projects and schemes in the Northeast, for instance have the same generalised contents adopted for the whole country. In the process, since the issues and problems of the Northeast are unique and peculiar, the general prescription meant for the whole country does not specifically address the problems of development of the region. Consequently, these schemes and projects prove quite ineffective and out of tune with the general needs and requirements of the region. The result is that the intended solutions themselves become the problems, which are more complex than the earlier efforts, complicating the problems instead of solving them.

The use of one single poverty measurement indices for the entire Northeast region is one example of administrative oversimplification. All the states in the region base their studies and analyses of poverty, on the index of Assam, surveyed by the National Sample Survey fixed many years ago before the states were formed. Consequently, poverty index measurements of the states in the Northeast are essentially guestimates and do not reflect the true levels of poverty in these states or pertaining to the region. The state of Tripura, which alone has its own poverty index indices formulated in 1974, however, does not have the authoritative seal of approval of the Government of India yet.

Closely linked to oversimplification in administrative related matters is the trend to see the Northeast essentially as an anthropological and geographical preserve, a legacy left behind by the British that independent India has unwittingly followed. The tendency to see the region from this perspective dramatically changes the approach in resolving the issues and problems of the region. Implicit in this observation, is the fact that there is a vast difference in dealing with the problems of the region, from the anthropological and geographical perspective with the more desirable anthropocentric one.

The anthropocentric perspective impinges on the moral question and the fundamental assumption that 'human beings' have feelings and sensitivities. Approach to development from this perspective is much more purposeful, meaningful and carries with it a flavour of sensitivity and moral obligation. Devoid of these human sentiments and concerns, reflected in the anthropocentric perspective, approach to problem solving in the Northeast can be, tedious and challenging, making the entire efforts mere routine generalised application of governmental dosages of doling out largesse. Consequently, these programmes end up becoming ineffective and wasteful expenditure for the country. Appreciating and understanding the importance of the anthropocentric view in solving the problems and issues of the Northeast, is fundamental to the success of any programme undertaken either by government or by other private or voluntary agencies in the region. In short, the manner of looking at the people and the region by clubbing all the problems of the ethnic groups as one large bloc dehumanizes the people of the Northeast region by making them feel that their needs are inconsequential and trivial.

Compromises notwithstanding, the inference is that somewhere at some time in the administrative history of the region, many basic and fundamental aspects of administrative diligence required for the region, has somehow been omitted and given a go-by, thereby forfeiting the moral high ground to placate the feelings of neglect among the people of the region, a sentiment which often reverberates in the region from time to time. The fact that the problems and the issues of the region are dealt anthropologically and morphologically on a regional basis; devoid of addressing the specific concerns of different ethnicities, sensitivities, histories with divergent religious beliefs, has cost the goodwill of the people and has given the Central Government the vilificatory adage of insensitivity.

In addition, the traditional view of dealing with the various problems of the Northeast, merely from the security perspective, devoid of its economic and developmental potentials as a region, deprives the region of a new approach in dealing with the region. Because by dealing with the region essentially from the security point of view and relegating all other approaches to inconsequential slots, a too simplistic and rather naïve, and to some extent insensitive, approach in dealing with the problems of the region is being taken. Had this approach been more sensitively analysed and appropriately handled, perhaps some of the problems of the region might not have arisen. This preoccupation with 'security' disorients the approach to the development problems by ignoring the 'human' aspects involved. The only redeeming feature is that this tendency has seen some changes in recent times, where a more anthropocentric perspective and approach to problem solving has begun.

The problems and issues involved in the Northeast are many, but however, trivial it may seem or appear, each of these need dealing separately without generalizing or oversimplifying. In many ways than one, the answer to the problem of dealing with the Northeast lies in what Samuel Johnson (1709-1784) when once asked, who was greater, man or woman after a little thought replied by asking back a counter question, 'Which man? Which woman?' The sum and substance of Johnson's famous remark is that 'Greatness' in the context of man and woman cannot be made gender specific, implying that 'Greatness' is an individual attribute depending entirely on the individual's calibre or capability.

The counter-question of Johnson addresses the inherent danger and limitations that the tendency to generalize have. In the Northeast, each ethnic group, community, tribe are unique in themselves and the efficacy or appropriateness of policies and programmes meant for them must reflect the specific needs of each of these groups, instead of cataloging all the problems as common issues that can be resolved by a single common solution. This approach can provide the elusive required political dividend, which the Government has been looking for if appropriately addressed in the end. Many of the problems of the region remain unresolved because matters that need to be dealt with separately as specific ethnic identity and communities related problems, has instead been dealt in a generalised manner as a common problem for the whole region, essentially as an issue-related problem. Conversely, what should have been dealt in a generalised manner as issue-related problems, for the whole region, irrespective of the ethnicities or identities involved, has instead been dealt with as if it was meant for a specific ethnic group. Obviously, the outcome is quite easily predictable.

IV. Dilemma of the 'Lowlanders'

Closely linked and arising out of the inability to distinguish between problems to be dealt as specific ethnic identity related issues from those that need to be addressed as general or common issues as a region, is the trend to see and treat the whole of the Northeast region essentially as a tribal region. This tendency to treat the region from the 'tribal centric' perspective has affected the understanding of the problems and issues pertaining to the non-tribal lowland communities of the region, creating a sense of antipathy, an aversion of the upland tribal communities by the majority non-tribal population in the region. There is an impression that the problems of the majority non-tribal population in the region, which are also essentially economical and developmental, a common problem shared with the tribal communities, do not get the kind of attention these deserve. From the point of view of the non-tribal population, the Government at the Centre is so preoccupied with the issues and problems involving the tribal communities in the Northeast that the problems of the non-tribal communities in the region become mere subterfuges in the labyrinth of governance and administration.

Statistically, in financial terms, this may not be correct, but the general perceptions in the far-flung areas in the region, especially among the economically poorer sections of the non-tribal communities, the politically fashionable tendency to espouse the cause of the underprivileged weaker section of the society, particularly the Scheduled Tribe and Scheduled Caste communities in Indian politics generate these feelings. There is nothing wrong in this approach, except that when the 'concern' of a large number of economically vulnerable non-tribal population in a region like the Northeast, in a limited geographical area, living side by side along with the upland tribal communities is neglected, antipathy and anger against the 'favoured' group arises subconsciously. The large illiterate poor non-tribal population sees the special dispensations and economic largesse given to the tribal community in the region by the government as "reverse discrimination".

Further, the generalisation and oversimplification of the problems of the non-tribal population of the Northeast lead to the clubbing of their problems with other non-tribal communities from across the country, forgetting the fact that the non-tribal communities of the Northeast encounter and face different set of problems unlike their counterparts elsewhere in the country. In fact, the problems of the poorer sections of the non-tribals of the Northeast are almost similar, if not identical to the problems of the tribal communities of the region. A more holistic and comprehensive view of addressing the problems of both the economically disadvantage tribal community and the non-tribals people of the Northeast as a special category or group seems definitely desirable. In other words, while categorisation of the upland tribal communities as a distinct group of people is constitutionally mandated, the ground rules for extending economic support and development should factor in the prevailing levels of poverty in the Northeast as a common problem of the region rather than as ethnic identity related problems.

Verrier Elwin[14] once wrote, *"The essence and art of anthropology is love. Without it, nothing is fertile, nothing is true"*. It means that the best way to deal with the problems of the various tribal communities of the Northeast is understanding and empathy, above all with respect. However, sociologists and administrators have taken Elwin's observation too literally, instead of adopting it metaphorically. What Elwin meant was that the 'essence' and 'art', of dealing with any anthropoid is love, which means understanding and providing the specific needs of each community and people in the region. Elwin did not mean or imply that love be given only to one set of people at the cost of the other. It simply means that the many non-tribal people, similarly placed in the same level of poverty and having similar 'wants', sharing the same geographical disadvantages of land-locked economies developmentally, should also be treated with the same 'love' as is meted out to the upland tribal communities. The problem of poverty and underdevelopment is a common problem cutting across the ethnic divide in the region, irrespective of whether they are tribals or non-tribals. Given this fact, a generalised regional approach in dealing with the problems of poverty and underdevelopment as a general issue for the region, rather than a problem of any one group of people seems desirable. The tendency to look at the Northeast only from the tribal-centric approach belies the hope and expectations of the poor and the needy among the non-tribal population of the Northeast as much as it harms the cause of the members of the upland tribal communities.

Conclusion

I began this Chapter asserting that form determines contents but qualified it further by saying that it is not necessarily the other way round. Much of what has been analysed indicates that the history of the Northeast is essentially a byproduct of its geography and topography; its form. The region, in its pure 'natural state', devoid of its politically demarcated international boundaries, is not physically isolated, land-locked or inaccessible. Subsumed in this statement is the fact that its isolation economically and politically, is the legacy of 'man-made' history, super-imposed on its geography.

Most communities and ethnic groups in the region realize the irreversible nature of the political divide imposed on them by history, but there are also others who still unfortunately feel that the 'form' can be altered and 'should-be-altered' by force. This festering anger directed inward within the region, create tensions between the ethnic communities of the region and vilify the fair name of many of them. The direct fallout of this posturing is the internalization of the anger and frustration reflected in the self-inflicted problems of divide and acrimony among the constituent ethnic groups. This in turn, affects adversely the required conducive ambient environment necessary for possible cooperation and partnership among the constituent states so essential for the progress and development of the region. The paradox is the fact that by a quirk of history, quite beyond their making, what should have been essentially a problem of international territorial and border adjustment has instead become an internal problem of the people of the region and the country.

Development in a region like the Northeast encompasses cooperation and partnership amongst the various stakeholders, especially to overcome the problems of physical isolation of the region, created by history. Unfortunately, given the present propensity to assertive ethnic identity politics among the constituent states, the ability to see and think clearly beyond the boundaries and interests of their respective states appears elusive. There is an overwhelming need to downplay the preoccupation with identity politics in a region, which is otherwise geographically so homogeneous and compact and make way instead for economic cooperation and partnership by consensus among the people and states for development of the region.

This inescapable fact of interdependence among the states, imposed on them by the geography of the region needs to be realised. The fact is that what affects one affects all the other constituent states, situated as they do, literally side-by-side in a remote and inaccessible region of the country. More importantly, the fact that none of them can develop or prosper at the cost of the other, given the common handicaps of distance and isolation from the rest of the country, should make all the aggressive posturing appear ironical and preponderous. Unless this fundamental fact is realised by the constituent Governments and the people in the region, the advantages that the geography of the region possesses, as the potential 'arrow-head' of the country for trade and commerce into the East Asia and beyond, will remain a mere pipe dream.

For the Government at the Centre it is essential to discard the tendency to deal with the region only from within the context of the political boundaries of India by detaching itself with its preoccupation with security, and address the issues confronting the region from its South Asiatic geographical configuration and connections. To be specific, the fact that the Northeast is part of the South-East-Asian physical configuration sharing largely the geography, social and cultural ethos and therefore, have a favourable predilection to exploit its natural and economic potential better in conjunction and in partnership with the countries of Southeast Asia need to be part of the comprehensive policy evolved for the region by the Government. The existing fixation of always attempting to study the issues and problems of the Northeast region essentially from the security centric point of view, must give way to the fact that there is an economic dimension associated with the geography of the region, which must be put to good use.

The restricted view of dealing with the region, only from within the political boundaries only perpetuates a historical wrong perpetrated on the people of the region at independence. This will only be what David Ludden[15] describes as the *"...freezing of blocks of space inside nations"* with nothing in sight beyond this limited 'blocks of space'. It is a process that *"...had already begun by 1776 'when Adam Smith published The Wealth of Nations', with the assumption that every nation's wealth belonged inside its boundaries and under the control of its national government".*

By therefore, confining the scope and limiting the region politically, devoid of its economic potential, which the geography provides, the country might be losing a rare opportunity to put to good use what geography of the region provides to the country. What is therefore required, is a change in approach by recognizing the Northeast as a part of the Asian economic grouping comprising of what the South Asia Foundation, describes as an economic region comprising of, *"...the Eastern States of India, Bangladesh, Bhutan and Nepal - which has a definable population, GNP, land area and trade history. This relationship alone allows us to move our perspective around and to reconfigure Assam's geographical location."*

From the foregoing facts, it is abundantly clear that it is not the geography of the Northeast, which is the cause of its underdevelopment and poverty; instead, it is the politically expedient demarcation of the country's borders at the time of its independence and the subsequent containarisation of people within ethnically composed states within the region, which is largely responsible for its present plight. Appreciating and putting to effective use the economic potential that the geography of the region provides, would not only negate the effects of the historical blunder of imposing a man-made restriction on the economic potential of the Northeast region but can help in unleashing the country's economic strength and prowess in the elusive East Asian region. In turn, this can also resolve many of the major problems confronting the region.

Endnotes

1. According to S.K. Chatterji, the Brahmaputra river basin and valley qualifies Assam historically as the gateway to the Northeast, being both the 'arrival' and center for 'dispersal' to other parts of the region and to the rest of the country because of its location. *"Assam was thus to meet all the tribal movements from the East, involving the advent into India of the Tibeto-Chinese speaking Mongoloids".*

2. Glenn C. Kharkongor, Indigenous peoples: Identity and protection, *The Shillong Times*, Shillong of 12 Nov, 2008. The Northeast, including Assam witnessed the convergence of various races like the Mongoloids, Negritos, the Austro-Asiatics, the Dravidians and Aryans.

3. David Ludden, Where is Assam. *Himal South Asia*, Nov-Dec 2005
4. J.C. Dutta, *Malinithan—A study on Iconography*, Directorate of Research, Government of Arunachal Pradesh.
5. J.C. Dutta, ibid.
6. Ravi J. Deka, '*River of Faith*', http://oasis.fortunecity.com.
7. W.C. Smith, *Ao Naga Tribe of Assam*, 1925, as quoted by Chandrika Singh: *Naga Politics, A Critical Account*, pp-5.
8. Ravi J. Deka, '*River of Faith*', ibid.
9. Amartya Sen, *Poverty and Famines*, Famine in Bangladesh, Chapter 9; pp-131.
10. Amartya Sen, ibid.
11. Amartya Sen, ibid, Chapter 6; pp-52-85.
12. *Census of India, 2001*. Table-1-1: Socio-religious composition of population.
13. Comprising at present the state of Arunachal Pradesh excluding Tuensang, since transferred to Nagaland in 1963 when it became a State.
14. Nari Rustomji, edited *Selected Writings*; Verrier Elwin: Philanthropologist, Philanthropology: *The Tribal World of Verrier Elwin*-1964, Chapter-2, pp-19. Elwin is well remembered for his work on the Konyak tribe of the Nagas written in the 1930s.
15. David Ludden (ibid), Where is Assam. *Himal South Asia*, Nov-Dec 2005.

CHAPTER - 3

British Policy of the Northeast and Identity Formation

British India policy in the Northeast is conspicuous by its ambivalence. Largely contrived to suit its administrative needs for a strategically, economically and ethnically important region, it adopted a policy of convergence, by addressing all the three issues, together. To achieve these objectives, various administrative mechanisms were introduced to segregate the areas occupied by the upland tribal communities by preventing the free entry of non-tribal population and foreigners into these exclusive tribal areas. The British evolved this policy to win the confidence and establish friendly relationship with the upland tribal communities. They did this to secure and create an effective 'human shield' to protect their territorial interests in the Northeast frontier under the guise of protecting these communities and their way of life from outside interference and influence.

From the perspective of ethnic identity politics, however, the administrative containerisation of people into specific areas by means of a permit system and another known as 'Excluded Area' and the 'Partially Excluded Area' under the Government of India Act, 1935 proved highly contagious. The legally enforceable administrative segregation of the upland tribal communities from the non-tribal communities in the region by physically segregating one set of people from others from within the Northeast region based on ethnicity and areas of their domicile became the precursor of ethnic identity politics in the region.

These policies worked extremely well and served their intended purpose, as long as the British were in India. However, once they left India, the policy, because of its ambiguity, came to mean different things to different ethnic groups. Many ethnic groups misconstrued the policy as the first step towards achieving provincial or political autonomy and for some, political independence from India. The intentions behind the 'inner line regulation' and the 'excluded areas' policies, their real purpose and motives, especially the adverse ramifications on the polity of the region is analysed.

British[1] Northeast India policy; Commercial, strategic interests and ethnic identity

If one single historical event changed the course of the ethnic identity history of North East of India, it is the signing of the Yandawoo Treaty on 24 February 1826, between Britain and the Burmese rulers. It marked the formal beginning of British colonial rule in North East India when Assam, Manipur were formally annexed as part of the British Indian Empire and the Burmese made to relinquish its claim over these two kingdoms. The period following the signing of the Treaty changed and affected various aspects of the polity, social and general life of people in Northeast India; in short, it changed the ethnic equations and ethnoscape[2].

There are three distinct policy decisions of the British, which are responsible for these changes. (1) The first is the decision to bring large number of people from other parts and regions of India into Assam[3] to meet the labour requirements of the tea, hydrocarbon and mining industries, which changed the demographic composition of Assam and subsequently the entire region. (2) The introduction of the "Excluded Area" and "Partially Excluded Area" under the Government of India Act of 1935 and Order of 1936 over and above the Bengal Eastern Frontier Regulation of 1873. This Regulation of 1873, also known as the 'Inner Line Regulation' restricted the entry of all non-tribals, British Indian citizens and foreigners into these areas except by a permit. (3) By a skullduggery of sorts and through complicity, Christian Missionaries were allowed to enter and undertake religious conversions anywhere within the region including areas falling within the 'inner line' and the 'Excluded Area' and 'Partially Excluded Area' except where specifically prohibited.

The history of British association with erstwhile Assam, began in 1786 when the ruler of Ahom (Assam); Gaurinath Singha (1780-1796) sought British aid to overcome internal strife and dissensions. Lord Cornwallis sent a small expeditious force under the command of Captain Welsh, who subdued the rebels and helped Gaurinath regain the throne. British commercial interests in Assam shortly followed when in 1793 Dr. John Peter Bawdy and Geiger Ensaiswood emissaries of the British officer Captain Wales, came as traders of the East India Company and entered into an agreement with Gaurinath Singha. The agreement was purely for commercial and business purposes and not an agreement between two sovereign powers. In 1823, Robert Bruce discovered tea in the wild in Assam and discovered that the quality suited British taste better than the Chinese tea. *"In 1834 the Governor General set up a Committee to explore the possibility of tea growing in India."* The history of tea industry in Assam began when, *"...the Assam Company formed in 1839 and the Jorehaut Tea Company formed in 1859."*[4]

Simultaneously a few years earlier in 1826, J.Berry White, Civil Surgeon, of Upper Assam, discovered traces of coal and hydrocarbon in areas near Lido in Assam. *"One of the earliest discoveries was near Safarai, and as early as 1826 a quantity had actually been raised by a party of hundred men...sent there for that purpose by the Commissioner of the North-East frontier. Five thousand maunds were quarried..."*. Berry White later set up the first medical school, named as 'Berry White Medical School' in Dibrugarh, Assam, which remained as the first medical college in the whole of the Northeast region for a long time. The credit of setting up and pioneering the industrialisation process in Assam goes to Berry White[5]. *"In 1848, the East India Company provided steamers to ply between Calcutta and Gauhati."* Even though C.A. Bruce actually found economical quantities of oil or hydrocarbon as far back as 1828 while prospecting coal it was only in 1867 that, *"Oil was struck in 1867 in Makum area, south of Dehing River, during operations by Mr. Goodenough."*[6]. *"The first rail route from Calcutta towards Assam was the single line to Poradaha in 1862, the extension to Goalundo being completed in 1864."* Based on these commercially important developments, the Assam Railways and Trading Company Limited formally incorporated as a company on 30 July 1881.

In keeping with increasing British commercial interests in the region, in 1858 the British Government adopted the 'Better Government of India' Act, which effectively established the authority of the British crown over all territories in India so far administered by the East India Company from Calcutta. Many land tenure policy was introduced to consolidate British interests and extend its holdings by expanding the areas of entitlements over lands in the region to meet the growing demand of the tea and other industries. In view of the past records, the British India Government set up appropriate administrative structures to keep the Burmese rulers in check.

The next measure to consolidate its commercial interests was to encourage the migrations of large number of labourers from Orissa, Santhal Praganas and Bihar into Assam for the expanding tea and mining industries. Under this policy, large numbers of people from other regions of India came as labourers for the tea industry and settled in Assam. Similarly, the British brought many unskilled Bengali and Bihari Muslim labourers for agriculture farming, and sponsored many Nepali labourers for the mining industry. The ostensible reason given by the British in preferring workers from outside Assam was that the local Assamese considered these works as menial and hence avoidable, and considering the arduous nature of the work involved, it was felt more suited to the hardworking non-Assamese. Subsequently, many non-Assamese labourers who had no connection with the tea or mining industry surreptitiously migrated unchecked into Assam. Among them were large groups of flood-affected and land-starved Bengali immigrants from the Bengal estuary, who occupied large tracts of arable fertile lands in the Assam valley. In spite of British attempts to segregate the genuine workers and labourers from the non-labourer migrants, it was almost impossible to segregate the two types of people because of the similarities of the immigrants. The ethnic and demographic composition of Assam and the region thereafter underwent a total transformation.

In addition, the British also inducted a large number of Bengali speaking officials and supporting staff from Bengal to meet the requirement of skilled white-coloured workers to help them administer the region. This is understandable, because the British were already well acquainted with the Bengali bureaucracy in Calcutta. In fact in 1836 Bengali became the administrative language in addition to English in Assam. The induction of the Bengali bureaucracy into Assam and imposition of Bengali over Assamese as the second official language in addition to English hurt Assamese sentiments. The preference shown to the Bengalis over the Assamese by the British, besides deprecating British administration and institutions as being highly untrustworthy and biased, also made all Bengalis vulnerable to Assamese anger. In addition, the growing menace of illegal Bengali immigrants surreptitiously occupying large tracts of fertile lands from the Assamese, contributed in making all Bengalis the main adversary in the region. It is the relative disregard and the relegation of the local Assamese population and language, and the inability to prevent the occupation of fertile lands by the illegal immigrants which were primarily responsible for the rise of strong anti-British sentiment among the Assamese population.

Compounding the resentment of the Assamese against the British was the introduction of the "Waste Land Regulation". The British East India Company introduced this regulation to acquire additional lands for the expanding tea trade and industry at the cost of the local farmers and landowners. This Regulation deprived the local Assamese farmers and landowners of large tracts of cultivable lands by imposing higher land revenues on them in comparison to the amounts levied on the British tea planters. Based on this Regulation, the East India Company also acquired rights to lands for the mining industry in Upper Assam.

It is evident that the commercial interests in tea, hydrocarbon, coal and other minerals in the region, was one of the primary reason and motive behind British Northeast frontier policy. To achieve a firm hold on the region and protect their commercial interests the paramount concern of the British was to find a way out to keep the Burmese and the Chinese from entering British India territories. It was not intended, in spite of all the professed sociological pretensions to protect the vulnerable upland tribal communities in the region.

This concern is understandable. Prasenjit Chowdhury sums the prevailing situation on the borders at that time as precarious, because *"...the fundamental problem has been that before the British came, there had been no precise frontiers; each State's power extended only as far as it could march an army. The British then pushed their armies as far as civilizations settled in the mountains, which meant along the foothills. Finally, McMahon, being a tidy-minded British cartographer, drew his line along the crest of the mountains. China rejected this extension of the British territory, which the British never policed, and insisted that the frontier should remain in the foothills"*[7]. Thus when the British eventually left India, they left the country not only with *"...other liabilities to unravel"* but also the tenacious boundary problems particularly with the Chinese in the form of *"...tangled skein of obfuscation"*[8].

Since the British commercial interests at that time were more at stake with the Burmese, than with the Chinese, the emphasis was more on finding a way out of the problems in the frontiers with the Burmese than with the Chinese. Accordingly, the border issue with the Burmese was dealt much more expeditiously and definitively, while the problem with the Chinese, which was strategic, was left vague and unclear. To overcome these problems with the Burmese, the British evolved the ingenious idea of converting the Northeast into an effective buffer zone or region between the British occupied territories and the territories held by the Burmese and the Chinese. All other developments, which followed, including the Bengal Eastern Frontier Regulation of 1873, are instruments to enforce its strategic hold to protect Britain's economic and commercial interests in the region.

The Policy of 'Exclusion'

The process of industrialisation and commercialization of the tea, mining and related activities became extremely important for the British and protecting these interests became a cause for concern for the British administration. However, the increased activities and the employment opportunities provided by these developments also attracted large alien population into Assam. Some entered legally while most entered illegally. This exposed the vulnerable local Assamese and more particularly the tribal population to various forms of exploitations. The movement of people from other regions made the task of ensuring security much more difficult for the British in the border areas of Assam, the North East Frontier Agency, and importantly in the sensitive border areas abutting the Burmese territories.

To prevent the free movement of 'undesirable persons' into these strategically important areas and distinguish the upland communities, the British introduced the 'inner line permit system' under the Bengal Frontier Regulation of 1873 and the policy of 'Excluded Area' and 'Partially Excluded Area' under the Government of India Act of 1935. The idea of the Regulation of 1873 was to prevent the free entry of non-tribal populations, British Indian citizens, foreigners and members of other communities, (literally everyone and anyone), except the inhabitant upland tribal communities settled and domiciled in these areas. It was an ingenious way to 'containerize' or 'quarantine' the tribal population within the areas of their domicile by creating exclusive zones where they alone could move freely. More importantly, the 'exclusion' was to keep away undesirable and inquisitive foreigners from the commercially important areas close to the sensitive borders with Burma. Constrained by the availability of the limited armed forces, especially British officers and soldiers whom they could rely upon, the policy of 'exclusion' by an administrative dispensation ensured the security of the areas of their interests.

It is interesting to note that the policy of 'exclusion' was so designed as not to provoke or arouse the suspicions of either the Burmese or the Chinese who were against British expansionists' policies in the sub-continent. The Regulation of 1873 was very cleverly projected as creating an anthropological preserve to protect the lifestyles of the upland tribal communities to the world at large. The views and support of the British and Western anthropologists, social scientists and scholars who advocated preserving the life-styles of the tribal communities, came quite handy in dealing with world opinion. The Regulation is analysed in detail from this perspective.

The Regulation of 1873

The Bengal Eastern Frontier Regulation of 1873, Section 2 of the Regulation empowered the British authorities *"to prescribe from time to time, alter by notification, a line to be called the Inner Line and to prohibit any subject living outside the area from living or moving therein"*. The Regulation introduced the concept of 'exclusion' for the first time by dividing the region into two distinct areas, the 'excluded' and the 'non-excluded' areas. Ramtanu Maitra and Susan Maitra[9] sums what the policy really meant to the British and bemoans the role of the Government of India for its *"...failure to recognize that the British raj had converted Northeast India into a human zoo, where each tribe was allowed to roam free within its 'own territory', but was not allowed to cross the boundaries set forth by their British masters and establish contact with the rest of India."*

The British introduced the Regulation in Assam first in the two tribal areas of Lakhimpur Districts in September 1875 and in Darrang District in March 1876. Subsequently, in 1880, they enacted the Frontier Tract Regulation. The British expressed policy of these enactments and regulations was *"...to provide for the removal of certain frontier tracts in Assam inhabited or frequented by barbarous or semi-civilized tribes from operation of enactments in force therein"*. Further a number of other Acts were enacted and introduced under the provision of the Government of India Act, 1919 (Montagu-Chelmsford Reforms), supplementing the regulation, which gave the Governor General power to 'exclude' any tract of a backward area from the application of any normative provincial legislation in such of these declared areas. The Garo Hills, the Khasi and the Jaintia Hills, the Mikir Hills, the North Cachar Hills, the Naga Hills and the Lushai Hills, all districts of erstwhile Assam, were declared as 'Backward Tracts' along with the Balipara, Lakhimpur and Sadiya Frontier Tracts. The "Excluded Area" and the "Partially Excluded Area" are the 'lineal descendent' of the 'Backward Tracts'.

Subsequently two types of provinces (i) the All India federation comprising of the Governor's Provinces, the Chief Commissioners' Provinces and the Federating Indian States, and (ii) the Provinces having provincial autonomy with a Government of elected representatives in every Governor's Province were formed. Further two types of areas were categorised areas within the two sets of Provinces, (a) the "Excluded Area" and (b) the "Partially Excluded Area" by the Government of India Act of 1935 and Order of 1936. Enforcement of these provisions in the Northeast further defined the concept of exclusivity in addition to the restrictions imposed over and above those laid by the Bengal Frontier Regulation of 1873. The 'excluded areas' were geographically defined territories, where neither the regulation of the British India Government meant for the rest of British India nor that of the Provincial Government was applicable. These areas were separate identifiable administrative units directly administered by the Governor General through the Governors or the Chief Commissionors in the Provinces as the cases may be on behalf of the Parliament in England. It covered the areas dominated by the autochthones upland tribal communities in the hilly parts of the region. In other words, the upland communities living within these areas were allowed to practice and live, characteristically, as per their traditional customs and rules, peacefully within the British India domain.

The areas coming within the "Partially Excluded Area" were in administrative parlance, areas that enjoyed franchise to elect members to the Legislature. Under this dispensation, the Khasi and Jaintia Hills district, excluding Shillong, had the right to complete franchise, while in the Garo Hills and the Mikir Hills only the *Nokmas* and the Headmen respectively could vote and elect Members of the Legislature. All the other Hill areas of Assam, the Balipara and the Sadiya Frontier Tracts, (Northeast Frontier Agency or NEFA), the Naga Hills district, the Lushai Hills district and the North Cachar Hills sub-division were classified as "Excluded Area', and were to be left unrepresented in the Legislature.

The Governor directly administered the 'Excluded Area' while the 'Partially Excluded Area' even though administered by the Governor could be administered with ministerial advice if considered necessary. The rationale behind the administrative model was explained by the Simon Commission as designed to sympathetically administer and handle the communities of these notified regions, to be protected and prevent them from being economically exploited by the 'neighbours', meaning the non-tribal communities from the plains.

An interesting and important feature of the "Excluded Area" is that the Naga Hills district of Assam, now Nagaland was categorised accordingly after the representative Nagas met the Simon Commission in January 1929 in Shillong before passing the Act of 1935. The various Naga groups gave their representation in the form of a memorandum to the Commission. Out of the "27 *memoranda by various groups and associations in Assam*"[10] there were only two main groups representing the Nagas, the Naga Club of Kohima and the Nagas of Mokokchung. The twenty Nagas comprising the Naga Club of Kohima claimed themselves to be the representatives of the Angami, Katcha Nagas, Kukis, Sema, Lotha and Rengma Nagas. The memorandum contained various other demands seeking essentially exclusion from the proposed provisions of the enactment. These groups according to Prof. Sanjib Baruah, "*...asked that the Nagas not be included in any reform scheme because they were not unified as a group, educational level were poor, and because given the small numbers, in any electoral system based on numbers their interests were sure to be overwhelmed*"[11]. According to B.G. Verghese, the ostensible reason given by the representative Naga group to the Simon Commission was clearly stated. The Commission observed, "*They do not ask for self-determination, but for the security of land tenure and freedom in the pursuit of their ancestral customs...and on protection from economic subjugation by their neighbours.*"[12]. Analyses of the Naga representatives reveal that they did not ask the British for political autonomy, which the British were not keen to give. The subsequent argument that political autonomy was one of the demands, which the Simon Commission was inclined to consider appears not substantiated by facts or by other evidences.

An analyses: The Real motive

An in-depth analysis of the policy will reveal the real British intentions behind the introduction of the exclusion policies. The

"Excluded Area" covered the predominantly hill districts of Assam immediately abutting and adjoining Burma, its most troublesome neighbour at that time, and close to the areas of its economic and commercial interests as compared to the Chinese or Tibetans. On the other hand, the "Partially Excluded Area" covered the hill areas of Assam, and comprised of areas, which did not have a common boundary with Burma, China or Tibet where there were no British commercial and economic interests. These areas as such were categorised differently and separately.

Further, there were several exceptions in the application of the provisions even though the policies were to be uniformly enforced. For instance, the areas occupied by the various upland tribal communities of Manipur, bordering Burmese territories, constituting one of the most vulnerable areas from the security point of view, were deliberately left out from the purview and jurisdiction of the provisions of the 'Excluded Area', or the 'Partially Excluded Area'. Analyses reveal that this was deliberate, since the rulers of Manipur and the British had entered into a Defensive pact under the treaties of 1762 and 1833 against the Burmese. Historically, the Manipuris played a major role in all the Anglo-Burmese Wars, but most significantly, when Maharaja Gambhir Singh joined forces with the British and drove the Burmese from Manipur. Manipur as an ally provided an effective security shield and cordon to the British from the Burmese threat, thereby substituting for the provisions of the Regulation and also the administrative jurisdiction of the "Excluded Area" and the "Partially Excluded Area". In any case, the nature of belligerence professed by the Manipuri Kings against the Burmese is as old as its history, which guaranteed the required security and 'buffer zone' the British wanted. Since the Meitei rulers of Manipur adequately sub-served British interests, the areas occupied by the upland tribal communities of Manipur, even though were similar in character with the areas covered under the 'Excluded Area' and 'Partially Excluded Area' in Assam, were cleverly left out of the purview of the policy of 'exclusion'. The primacy of British intent and purpose in introducing the policy reveal itself quite unabashedly in this one single instance alone.

In contrast to the exclusion of Manipur from the purview of the 'Excluded Area' and 'Partially Excluded Area' and the Regulations, the Naga Hills, the Lushai Hills, the Balipara and the Sadiya Frontier Tracts (NEFA), which divide British India from Burma, with large mountainous and hilly ranges were all brought under the 'Excluded Area'. On the other hand, the Khasi and the Jaintia Hills, the Garo Hills or the Mikir Hills, which were physically not contiguous to Burma or China, came under the comparatively less rigidly structured 'Partially Excluded Area'. The upland tribal communities living in the 'Partially Excluded Area', had considerable freedom, autonomy and right to exercise franchise, covering as it did, the less strategic areas requiring lesser supervision.

It is apparent from the foregoing facts that the ostensible reason for introducing the policy of "Excluded Area" and the "Partially Excluded Area' over and above the provisions provided by the Regulation of 1873 selectively were many. Four of these are analysed.

1) Security concerns

It is evident that it was the growing economic and commercial importance of the region, particularly Upper Assam and adjoining areas, now part of Arunachal Pradesh, which compelled the formulation of a policy initiative to protect these areas from the Burmese and the Chinese. The policies of 'exclusion' was a dexterous mix of British administrative ingenuity, cleverly camouflaged under diplomatic niceties designed to effectively secure and establish direct control of the upland communities to form a security cordon around its borders, which was largely a *"tangled skein of obfuscation"*.

The nature of the location of these tribal settlements, which were highly dispersed, made these areas highly vulnerable and susceptible to incursions from across the international borders. These areas therefore needed constant supervision. With the constraints of manpower shortages, difficulties posed by the topography and inaccessibility, the only way out for the British was therefore to somehow create a security buffer zone, effectively sealing these areas from outside intrusion and interference. Simultaneously, they wanted to build friendly relationship with the various tribal groups by winning over their loyalties, rather than have completely hostile groups of indigenous people and communities constantly working against the British interests in the region.

It is obvious that this policy was to effectively administer the region, particularly the border areas, which the British found was extremely difficult during their initial days and experiences in the region while dealing with the various upland tribal uprisings. The shortages of British officers and men and primarily the difficulties encountered in finding loyal Indian footman were a perennial problem in effectively controlling the region. Moreover, the British were simultaneously not too keen to commit too many of its officers and men in the administration of this remote region when they were needed elsewhere in India. They had to depend mainly on the rulers of Assam and Manipur to subdue the uprisings and upheavals. However, since these assistance and support did not come free of encumbrances and conditionalities, which were not always easy to agree or concede, the desire to reduce their dependency on these rulers compelled them to find an alternative way to overcome the problem. These concerns and the need to form a security barrier between British interests and the Burmese rulers and the Chinese, subsumed its Northeast India policy.

These British strategic considerations and intentions had to be however, camouflaged and couched in diplomatic niceties given the strategic nature of the areas involved. The concept of the "excluded areas" from the arsenal of British administrative ingenuity became the means to meet these requirements; of diligently ensuring the protection of British interests territorially and simultaneously, win the gratitude of the upland tribal communities to their side. The 'exclusion' policy was accordingly projected to the world as providing an administrative 'shield' to the various upland communities, which greatly appealed to the Western sense of fair play and equity. The policy would earn accolades internationally for the British for addressing the socio-anthropological concerns of the indigenous people whose cultures and way of life was seen as largely threatened by other communities.

2) Divide and Rule

The other discernable reason behind the policy of administratively segregating the upland tribal communities from other non-tribal communities in the region was to ensure that the two set of communities in the sensitive region remain 'divided'. The logic and argument behind this approach is the British view of the "irreconcilable culture" differences that exist between the Upland communities and the Lowland communities. In the process, the policy instrument of "divide and rule", most effectively used by the British in the rest of the country to keep the Hindus and the Muslims apart, was parrallely adopted in the Northeast to keep the upland tribal communities and the non-tribal communities apart. This is apparent from the fact that there are innumerable instances in history of the region, when the local Rajas and rulers from the region and various tribal chiefs have joined forces and acted against the British as allies. The British were keen to prevent such alliances, as the threat from the combined forces of the various rulers and the Chiefs of the upland clans and tribes, would have been formidable opponents to the British. The British were aware of this threat and hence were determined on keeping both the two groups of people apart. From the British point of view the policy of 'seclusion' or 'exclusion' in one sense was a clever disguise of the infamous 'divide and rule' policy in the Northeast in a limited but formal way, to safeguard British interests, by keeping the Upland communities and the Lowland communities apart.

3) Demarcation of international boundaries

The expressed concern of the British government for the Upland tribal communities as the primary motive in enacting the policy of 'exclusion' appear blatantly misleading and mischivious by the nature of the demarcations of the international boundaries between British Indian territories with Burma, China and Tibet. For instance, even though, the British were fully aware that a large number of tribal communities, whose protection was of paramount concern to the British, were living across the two sides of the proposed international boundaries between British territories and Burma, China and Tibet, yet, the international boundaries were drawn on the highest points of the various peaks. While this ensured the protection of British territories and interests, which made crossing over the highest points extremely difficult and in most cases impossible, the method completely dislocated and divided the various upland tribal communities on either side of the international borders. The British very conveniently forgot the expressed sentiments of protecting and safeguarding the life-styles of thc Upland tribal communities, which they had pursued so assiduously and had made it ostensibly the main reason behind their policy in the Northeast frontier.

In fact, it was much later on, only at the time of British departure from India that the British began to express much more openly and freely their views on 'what ought to have been done' rather than what they 'had done' for the region. It was by then too late for any meaningful resolutions to the problems arising out of the irrational demarcations of boundaries, and mainly because by then, the British had lost interest in the security of the region and saw the problems as problem for the new Government of India rather than for the British crown.

4) Christianity and 'Exclusion'

Reinforcing the British Northeastern frontier policy of protecting its various interests in the Northeast is the tacit encouragement accorded to the Christian missionaries to convert the upland communities to Christianity in these areas. Henry John Temple, the third Lord Palmerston[13] (1784-1865), the British Prime Minister, in a cleverly worded statement observed in the British Parliament that, *"It is not only our duty...but in our interest to promote the diffusion of Christianity as far as possible throughout the length and breathe of India"*. Echoing similar sentiments later, Lord Halifax, the Secretary of State reinforced the obvious intentions behind the British policy when he observed, *"Every additional Indian Christian is an additional bond of union and a source of strength to the British Empire"*. Sir Mac Worth Young put the emphasis more precisely and categorically by stating, *"They are worth far more to the British Empire than all those civil servants, soldiers, judges, and governors of India"*.

The fact is that even though ever since 1813 Christian missionaries were allowed to undertake conversions of Indians, no person other than the upland tribal population from within these areas, including Christian missionaries was allowed to enter into the 'excluded areas'. The Christian missionaries were allowed to undertake conversion of the members of various tribes in spite of the fact that the British were aware that the conversions of these upland tribal communities into Christians would completely change and transform their way of life, a concern based on which the policy of 'exclusion' was introduced in the region.

Haimendorf, one of the pioneers in the field of socio-anthropological studies of the Nagas in his famous book, *Naked Nagas*, was very critical of the tacit encouragement accorded by the British to the Christian missionaries to convert the tribal communities. He felt that these sudden influx of Christian and western value-systems greatly affected adversely the Naga cultural traditions and practices, especially the long-term damages it caused to the basic tribal ethos and sensibilities. Haimendorf cites the impact of preventing the Nagas from participating in the Naga 'Feasts of Merit', or stopping the practice of Mourngs or dormitories, the serving of traditional drinks associated with festivities and life-styles by the Christian missionaries. Haimendorf, observed, *"Government policy has been to avoid disruption of Naga culture, respect tribal customs, wherever it does not prejudice the maintenance of law and order and tamper as little as possible with the old village organization...".* This is however belied by the fact *"...that the American Baptist Mission has little sympathy with the aims of the Government and even less appreciation of the valuable elements of Naga culture"*[14]. While appreciating the great work the Missionaries were doing in the *"...medical field and making thousands of Naga children literate"*, Haimendorf defines the deficiencies in the approach. He observes, *"...but with little understanding and sympathy for Naga culture, they might have brought more happiness to their flock and avoided many of the more unfortunate results of a sudden clash of cultures"*. This sentiment is reflected by Sir Robert Reid, a former British Governor of Assam (1937-1942) who wrote in 1944 in the *Geographical Journal*, *"The rather iconoclastic zeal of the earlier missionaries who saw evil in anything that savoured of heathenism has in modern times given away...to a more sensible policy, which is prepared to retain all that is good in the old customs so long as it is not inconsistence with the Christian message"*[15]. The American Missionaries adopted a much more cautious and subdued approach later. S.K. Barpujari[16], describes the impact of Christianity in the Northeast, particularly the work done by the American Baptist among the Nagas. *"Whatever services rendered to the Nagas by the American Baptist, the earlier missionaries condemned the Naga food, festivals, dress, ornaments, religious beliefs, communal institutions and mode of living as primitive. They insisted on the convert's teetotalism, he had to restrict himself to one wife and was discouraged from eating the meat of Mithun sacrified with appropriate invocations of the spirit."*. The observation sums up sardonically the adverse effect of the Christianisation process in the region.

The adverse impact of Christianity on the life of the upland tribal communities, which the British tacitly encouraged, as such contradicts the professed 'protectionism' projected by the British in every forum and situation. Critically evaluated, the combined effect of both the segregation of the tribal communities under the 'excluded areas' along with the aggressive proselytisation pursued by the Christian missionaries progressively destroyed tribal lifestyles and way of living. Thus while the process of Christianisation, which inherently had its intrinsic merits, however, also systematically destroyed and dismantled all that was considered hedonic, tribal and pagan in the life of the tribal communities in the Northeast by the British, albeit indirectly, by infusing large scale Christian and Western values and beliefs.

It is therefore apparent that British intentions in tacitly allowing free movement of Christian missionaries in the 'restricted' areas of the Northeast were not purely ecumenical but part of its overall Northeastern strategic and commercial policy. The tacit understanding with the Christian missionaries to selectively allow them free access, in spite of being 'outsiders' into the 'excluded areas' only reinforces the suspicion that the real motive behind the British policy of 'exclusion' was not 'protection' of the tribal communities, but to ensure as Lord Halifax, the Secretary of State observed, *"Every additional Indian Christian is an additional bond of union and a source of strength to the British Empire"*. It was British ingenuity at work to secure and protect its territorial hold through friendly Christianized upland tribal communities with the minimal costs in money and in manpower.

British Policy and Political autonomy

It is evident that from whichever or whatever perspective one looks from, the introduction of the 'Excluded Area' and the 'Partially 'Excluded Area' under the Government of India Act of 1935, in addition to the Regulation of 1873 in the Northeast was a clever British ploy intended to achieve two objectives. First, it was to create a 'buffer-zone' between British territories and the Burmese, the Chinese and the Tibetans. Second, it was to placate the feelings of the upland tribal communities so that they remain friendly, if not loyal to the British crown, in the hope and expectation that friendly and cooperative tribal communities in an inadministrable, inaccessible and extremely difficult area is much more desirable than an unfriendly lot.

Sardonically viewed, the idea of giving special status to the tribal population by excluding them from the purview of the provincial autonomy being given to others under the Government of India Act of 1935 was to placate the feelings and ensure the continued interests of the tribal communities in supporting the British administration. This is evident from the belated observations made by Lord Wavel the Viceroy in a dispatch on the 27th of July, 1944 to the then Secretary of State for India Leo Amery, about Reginald Dorman-Smith, former Governor of Burma's idea of *"...the Tribal Areas of Burma, Assam and possibly Bengal, should be formed into a separate unit and administered directly either by the Governor-General or by the Governor of Burma"*[17] when it became clear that

Britain had to give independence to India. The fact that this was under the knowledge and consideration of the British, is evident from the assertions made by Lord Wavell when in the same dispatch he asserts, *"The tribal experts in Assam have for many years taken the view that the tribes need an entirely separate administration and treatment ...one of the schemes put forward in a general way was for the establishment of a North East Frontier Province rather on the lines now being suggested by Dorman-Smith"*[18] (Own emphasis).

It is reasonably certain that this issue was debated and discussed, but was not implemented due to the reasons given by Lord Wavell. *"Constitutionally, it would, I suppose, have been easy to make a separate province when the Act of 1935 was being drafted...however, a change now would not now be at all easy...I do not think we can make any progress with the idea now"*[19]. Similar in intent, but reflecting the same thoughts, was the concept of the Crown Colony, a suggestion made by N.E. Parry. Other concepts that was examined was the "Coupland Plan" an idea conceived by Prof. Reginald Coupland in 1947 suggesting more or less the need for a separate segregated tribal belt in the region, a Colony comprising of one single administrative unit of all the contiguous tribal areas in Assam and Burma.

Various ideas were under consideration but abandoned for various reasons. One of the ostensible reasons was that the creation of large numbers of small 'independent', autonomous political entities, or semi-autonomous entities in the tri-junction of India, Burma and China would have been too alluring and irresistible to its rapacious neighbours. The British gave up the idea also because it would be extremely difficult with its limited armed forces and manpower at its disposal in the region to defend and protect these small autonomous political entities. The idea would have been more of a problem rather than a solution. Therefore, instead of giving provincial autonomy to these communities, the more administratively prudent and manageable idea and concept of the "Excluded Area" and the "Partially Excluded Area", were introduced. This in effect meant retaining a 'buffer zone' of friendly upland tribal communities who could act not only as the 'protective human shield' and be the first line of defence for the British, also ensure control over communities of people whom they could closly monitor.

From this perspective, continuing the policy of assuaging the sentiments and feelings of the upland tribal communities occupying the strategic areas in the region, especially to engage and keep the various tribal clans and groups favourably disposed to British India policies was of paramount importance to the British administration. One of the methods adopted by the British to sustain the continued loyalty and interest of the tribal communities was by openly and continuously debating and discussing the subject of autonomy for these upland tribal communities.

However, once it was realised that the independence of India was imminent and the burden of securing the security of the border region and firm hold on these communities were not required, the idea of autonomy and various issues relating to it were given an undignified burial. This left behind not only totally disgruntled and upset upland tribal communities but also the ambiguous nature of the provisions of the 'Excluded Area' and 'Partially Excluded Area' intact. The administrative problems raised by these expectations and hope of autonomy among the many upland tribal communities and the problem of ethnic polarization, arising out of the problems of exclusivity symdrome are the consequences and affect of the British policies, which independent India is compelled to bear and resolve.

More significantly seen in hindsight, it is obvious that the policy of 'exclusion' was cleverly used by British political strategists to keep the more vociferous and cantankerous elements among the tribal communities from openly challenging British authority and intent. This 'bait' of a policy for Dominion status was nothing but political aggrandizement of the most mischievious kind, which only whetted the appetite and aroused the expectations among the upland tribal communities. This is apparent and evident from the fact that even though various British policy makers dealt the issue of autonomy and other related issues at various levels, the subject matter remained more on paper, among academic circles and mostly confined to debates and discussions in the British Parliament. It was more in the nature of a speculation rather than a reality intended to make it happen.

The unkindest cut of all, is that this allurement was essentially prompted by British strategic needs of the time rather than spurred on by the love of the upland tribal comminutes in the Northeast. No doubt, the introduction of the 'excluded' areas in perspective, was a mischievous piece of British ingenious legislation, which divided the people of the region irreconcilably. It was also 'mischievous' because the policy which gave a taste of 'autonomy' to the expectant upland tribal communities could never be fulfilled given the strategic nature of the location these communities occupy, the tri-junction of Burma, China and India. The effect of the policy of 'excluded area' inherited by independent India, is that it unwittingly has given rise to the notion of 'independence' and 'freedom' among the various ethnic groups in the region. B.G. Verghese, bemoans this fact when he observes, *"The term 'excluded' area has mistakenly been interpreted to suggest that these areas were excluded from British India of which they were a part."*[20].

The policy of exclusivity indirectly provided the theoretical basis and idea of independent national territories based on ethnic identities in the Northeast. It was the subsequent persistent demand based on this expectations roused by the British during their tenure that eventually, a compromise had to be made with each of these ethnic groups, by granting States and Union Territories within the Union of India in partial fulfillment of this aspiration. It is another matter that inspite of this compromise, dissatisfaction remain and the problems continue to fester the body politics of the region. The dilatory British administrative policy in the Northeast, and the subsequent interpretations given by the Government of India to British policy of 'exclusion', continue to be one of the main causes of the continued disengagement between the Nagas and the Central government. British policy of 'excluded areas', remains confabulated in controversy even today long after the British left the shores of India.

It appears therefore, that the underlying policy for creating an effective security barrier against the Burmese rulers and the Chinese in the Northeast frontier provinces prompted the British to adopt the policy of 'exclusion', to effectively administer and control the sensitive Northeastern Region and thereby prevent 'outsiders' into these strategic areas. This policy of 'excluding' physically the sensitive border areas peopled by the tribal communities served British purposes extremely well. Seen from this angle, the policy of 'exclusion' was merely a clever British ploy to cover up their true strategic and commercial intentions by overtly projecting them as acts of socio-anthropological empathy and considerations, advocated by British and European socio-anthologists.

British policy and identity formation

The British Northeastern India policies, especially the policies of 'exclusivity' by means of the Regulation of 1873 and the provisions of the 'Excluded Area' and the 'Partially Excluded Area', were administrative policy decisions where obviously the emphasis was not people (upland tribal communities) but the areas these people and communities occupied. The British, it transpires, were keener to closely protect and control the areas belonging to the upland tribal communities by any means only to protect their geo-political and economic interests without attracting too much international attention.

While ostensibly there is nothing wrong in the approach, it is the inadvertent introduction of the politics of identity into the region, where there was none, which was the most damaging aspect of the policy. By ruthlessly segregating and categorising people and communities in the region based on the areas of the domicile, abrogating all anthropological and socio-cultural connections and ties, the policy transformed ethnic equations and relationships in the northeast beyond recognition. By an insensitive and inconsiderate dispensation of administrative decision, the British introduced not only the concept of ethnic identity politics, but by highlighting differences and distinctions between the upland tribal communities from the lowland non-tribal communities, sowed the seeds of misunderstandings and acrimony.

The concept of 'exclusion' also had serious long-term adverse impact on the normative development of the tribal communities as a group of people. The policy retarded their personal development and growth as individuals. By introducing a legislation, which quarantined the upland tribal people, the British entrapped these people into the pages of anthropological preserve and history for their limited selfish interests. In one way, therefore the policy of segregation and 'exclusion' condemned the upland population to perpetual backwardness and ignorance. Ramtanu and Susan Maitra aptly term the policy as the 'apartheid' of the upland tribal communities of the Northeast by the British, and confining them in a time zone of perpetual underdevelopment and despondency.

It is obvious that the history and politics of identity formation and the politics of ethnic identity itself in the region, would have been quite different from what it is now, had the British adopted and followed a much more positive and affirmative people oriented approach to tribal welfare in the Northeast, instead of adopting a negative approach, which was more 'area' oriented rather than 'people' oriented. Prof. Nirmal Kumar Bose in a memorial Lecture 'Ethnic Identities in the North-east India' echoes this sentiment when he observed, *"The British policies and the activities of the Christian missionaries who came to the region contributed significantly in creating a freeze effect on the communities and social formations"*.

Seen from the socio-political history of the Northeast, the physical isolation of the various upland tribal groups from the non-tribal plain communities from within the region under the 'excluded' areas policy certainly protected the vulnerable upland tribal communities from exploitations and prevented dilution of their lifestyles. However, in the process the segregation not only defied age-old traditional social interactions between the various communities of the region, but also kept these communities far away from the realities of the fast changing world. It is not that such interactions and relationships are entirely free from any blemish, given the innumerable stories of exploitations of the tribal communities by the non-tribals in the region. But merely because these instances occur once in a while, sheltering and preventing the future generations of young hopeful tribal youths to explore their full potentials as mature and self-confident individuals is also not being fair to them. Isolation is often a state of mind, and not always necessarily guaranteed by mere physical segregation and protection.

Put in perspective and appropriately contextualised, the policy of 'exclusion' ingeniously prevented the two sets of people of the region, tribals and non-tribals, from developing healthy attitudes and equations by learning to adapt to the needs of the other. This policy in retrospect has become a major hindrance and obstacle in the process of normalizing social fraternisation among the various communities and people of the region. In effect it changes the very premises on which human societies are supposed to interact and develop, *"...where flux, movement and Change"* should have been *"the rule and not the exception in social life."*[21]. It is in effect the disruption of the normative Durkheiman process of identity formation.

Historically and socio-anthropologically, the idea of physically segregating tribal communities from the non-tribals from within the region also goes against the normative acculturated process of ethnic identity evolution in the Northeast. In the Northeast, there is very little difference between the tribal and the non-tribal anthropologically and ethnologically, as they belong to the pan Indo-Tibeto and Indo-Mongoloid race tracing their origins from East Asia including South China. Many non-tribal communities like Assamese, Manipuri Meiteis even though are not legally classified as tribes today in the Constitution of India nevertheless, all belong to the pan Mongoloid racial stock to which tribal communities like Nagas, Mizos, Kukis, Bodos, Kacharis also belong. For example, the Assamese[22] are of Indo-Mongoloid lineage originating from Southwestern China and Burma. The term Assamese[23] for instance is a colonial derivative; comprising of all people who speak the Assamese language bound by a common language for social interactions. The Ahoms themselves are immigrants from Mungrimungram, the original homeland of the Tai people in South East Asia whose linkages go back into South East Asia and not to Aryan origins[24]. It is evident that the Assamese people were not mere morphed Ahoms, but carry with them a long legacy of traditions and customs with connection to the Tai community in South East Asia. The All-Assam Ahom Association, founded in 1893 by the descendents of the Tai-Shan tribal groups in South East Asia from whom the Ahoms trace their ancestry keep the link alive[25]. Similarly, the Meiteis of Manipur may not be categorised as tribals, but belong to the same ethnic groups in the region. The segregation therefore of people by the British by drawing a distinction between tribals and the non-tribals in the Northeast, based on the areas of their domicile is not only mischievous but also morally and ethnically wrong.

The compartmentalisation of people into two physical areas, inconsiderately pronounced by the policy of 'exclusion', in furtherance of their Northeast strategic policies the British in effect created not only a situational ambivalence but also created an anthropological void in the sociological history of the people of the Northeast by disrupting and destroying social, cultural and historical ties and bonds between the upland and the lowland communities. It is a blatant disruption of the socio-anthropological history of the region. Quite unabashedly, the British has left behind a historical verdict, a legacy, which has destroyed the camaraderie and age-old ties of the various communities and people, and in the process, incapacitating and preventing them from taking a constructive collective approach to development and progress as a region. The policy of 'exclusion' was clearly a retrogative step and a disservice by the British to all the people of the Northeastern region of India.

It is not as if the British with all the scholarships and learnings at their command and disposal were not aware of the historical and anthropological links and connections. Because, if the various monographs left behind by British administrators in the Northeast to which references have been made earlier, is indicative of the level of knowledge, based on which the policy of 'exclusion' was formulated, than one can reasonably be sure that the British's approach to the Northeast was deliberately miscued by security and commercial considerations. It is this inconsiderate manner of pursuing single-mindedly their security objectives and commercial interests at the cost of the future of the various ethnic groups of the Northeast, which is the most inconsiderate aspect of the policy. This belies the much hyped charitable and 'benevolent' predilection accorded to British intentions in introducing the Regulation of 1873 and the 'Excluded Area' and the 'Partially Excluded Area' in the Government of India Act of 1935, as intending to 'protect' the upland tribal populations of the Northeast. Segregation, according to many in British India was protectionism at its best, a way out of the impending obliteration of the way of life and culture of the various tribal populations. This socio-anthropological approach appealed equally well to the tribal sense of fair play and equity, which was largely a biased Western predilection based on Western notion of the 'noble savage'. The people of the Northeast never knew what had hit them.

From these perspectives, it is apparent that the socio-politically illogical tenure of the British policy of 'exclusion' was more positively hyped than it really was. Ethnic identity per-se is a fusion of assimilated attributes of acculturated social and cultural inputs, as well as biologically inherited attributes and as such, mere physical segregation could not have changed the inherent attributes. The biologically inherited attributes are not easily erasable by mere social interactions with other people from other communities and much less from mere associations or contacts. Further, all traditions are dynamic, constantly evolving and changing and infusing such dynamism into the lifestyle and way of thinking of the upland tribal communities should have been the basis on which the principle of 'protectionism' so assiduously pursued by the British should have been formulated. British policy should not have been 'exclusion', but a gradual 'modulated assimilation' of the upland communities with other communities in the Northeast, by a deliberate and consciously calibrated process of gradual integration.

In the ultimate, the British could have achieved the same objectives of preventing undesirable people from entering freely into the strategic and sensitive region if they had only made a distinction between non-tribal communities from within the region and those coming from outside the Northeast. This approach would have facilitated the two sets of people from within the region to mix freely, a continuation of the age-old socio-anthropological history of the region. It would have been ethical, constructive, and positive and ensured the healthy growth and development of relations among the people of the region. This would have prevented the ethnic identity conflict, which has polarized the Northeast with no end in sight. From the perspective of ethnic identity relationship in the Northeast the main drawback of the policy lay in the generalisation of people, which was based purely on physical spaces occupied, rather than based on 'which' people (non-tribal communities) to be debarred from entering into these 'excluded areas'. The mandate to treat all non-tribal communities alike irrespective of their origins categorically introduced the politics of ethnic divide in the Northeast. In short, the Regulation of 1873 and the policy of 'Excluded Area' and the 'Partially Excluded Area' under the Government of India Act of 1935 together introduced the politics of ethnic identity in the region.

Assertive identity politics is human, and hence the 'actualisation' process of identity is a natural corollary and not inherently wrong, but when such aspiration divide people living side by side for generations, the consequences and ramifications are obvious, it can only end in communal rift, animosity and disunity of purpose. In addition, because identity entails physical and geographical demarcated 'real estates', subsequent creations, changes and alterations of existing politically acknowledged physical spaces and entities, adds a new meaning and dimension to ethnic identity politics. Consequently, the reorganization of Assam in 1963, when Nagaland was formed, and again in 1972 when other ethnically formulated states were carved out, it literally opened a Pandora Box dividing people, their minds and the region.

These problems of assertive ethnic identity politics, social polarization based on ethnicity, the problems of territorial adjustments and realignments among the states, are the legacies of the vaxactious British policies of 'excusivity', which were in the nature of shenanigams. They continue to trouble the region. The creation of ethno-politically based desirable states by disbanding the composite economically viable state of Assam is the result with neither signs of peace nor much development in sight. More appropriately, the evils of ethnic divide, the "legacy" of the British policies, was independent India's "inheritance". Thus sadly, while the British accomplished their strategic and economic interests well under the various policies of 'exclusion' and 'exclusivity', they forever 'quarantined' not only the upland tribal communities physically and psychologically by denying them their legitimate right to grow much faster and bring about *"radical change in the trajectory of their lives"* as Thomas L. Friedman observed in another context in *The New York Times News Service',* 2009, but also left behind a 'divided' family. British India Northeast Frontier policies sheperded the people of the region into deifferent and distictive slots of identities for their own selfish requirments and needs.

Endnotes

1. There are three sources based on which British policy in the Northeast can be analysed. The first is to examine the British policy based on the written records left by the British themselves, left either by British political officers-turned-sociologists-ethnographers or imperial historians or official writers supported by other European powers at that time. The second source is to take recourse to various versions of native oral histories, traditions and beliefs. Alternatively, take recourse to a third option, to ensemble a mix of both these views and perspectives, and draw one's conclusions. All the three sources and views are important, but reliability and dependability largely impinges on the manner of interpreting objectively these sources.

    The first way to view the British policy is to base on their own records and sources, substantiated and corroborated by the voluminous records and documentations left by the British administration or more specifically by the political officers cum ethnographers, official writers and scholars, which is the generally accepted approach. British record keeping traditions and inerrant reputation being the main determining factor in relying on these sources. However, relying on this source alone, especially pertaining to a remote, inaccessible region like the Northeast and considered one of the most difficult areas to administer, may not be without its blemish. In fact, the reports on and records about a region like the Northeast frontiers tend to be highly subjective, dangerously distorted, because of the absence or ineffectiveness of the counter-checking mechanism to verify the accuracies and factual position of these reports. Even for the British administration, it was quite an impossible task, given the terrain and efforts required to verify many of these reports. Given these factors and the other preoccupations of the British, the local administrators determined the nature and content of reporting. It is not surprising therefore why many historians, scholars question the veracity and facts, interpretations of some of the records of events left behind by the British. Seen from this perspective, the second source, the local versions, even though unauthenticated, largely oral and available in the traditional histories and folklores become important sources essentially as counterbalances.

The second sources, available are local historical versions, folktales and stories, as people from the region saw and still believe in. These are important sources from the Northeasterners point of view; residual impressions passed down the generations and etched in their minds as perceptions. While many of these records, folktales and local histories are used as secondary sources to trace the histories pertaining to periods before the British came into the scene, most local versions pertaining to the periods covering British rule in the region, are neither recognised, reported nor given the attention they deserve by present historians. This is because the local versions of history lacks the formatted documented evidences, which historians insist upon before putting their scholastic seal of approval. These versions were unacceptable simply because as the British found, quite at variance with their views and could undermine their reports.

The only other sources are the monographs, studies etc left behind by sociologists, anthropologists and foreign scholars, important academically and anthropologically but not anthropocentrically. To be fair and charitable to the British and other European anthropologists, sociologists and ethnographers, in terms of their academic contents and values these records from the point of view of the respective disciplines are often beyond compare. Given the emphasis and background, however, these studies are not adequate to substantiate the facts of the events in history or capable to act as a counter balance to the administrative versions of reports left behind by the British administrators, both official and private. Even the versions left behind by British officers turned ethnographers are anthropologically unbiased and objectively recorded, it is however, the interpretations of the events and sequences, essentially in their roles as political agents and administrators representing an imperial power, where doubts and inaccuracies arise. The objectivity and balance required in reporting the events or sequences is missing in some of the official versions of their report or records.

Seen from the Northeastern perspective, the traditions of writing history and record keeping on the Northeast by the British Administrators and foreigners are as such highly sanitized, often deviations with the wrong emphasis on the events, as people of the region believe they know. In their perception, there is much more in what remains unwritten or untold than what is written and left behind as records. In one way, therefore, the so-called history of the Northeast, is replete with 'wrong emphasis', often biased and based solely on the versions and interpretations of the British as they saw and want the world to see and perceive. The assumption is that many events and happenings that were detrimental and against British interests went unreported or underreported. From the Northeastern perspective or view, what this means is that the British administration in the region gave detailed reports of many events and incidents, which sub-served their interests, but those which could be critical or question their decisions later were cleverly either sugar-coated or not reported at all. This is because there was no local tradition of history writing except for the few records maintained by rulers of Assam and Manipur, which were incomparable to the record keeping traditions of the British officials. In addition, verification of the facts recorded by the British administration was not possible as these were not easily accessible at that time. The records of the British in India, more particularly of the Northeast in short, are British versions of the history of the Northeast and not necessarily the 'true' version history of the region written objectively and dispassionately.

Such a sartorial blemish on the histories of the northeastern region of India arises for many reasons. First, the remoteness and the backwardness of the region made it almost impossible for anyone to refute or challenge the British version of events given the reputation of inerrancy attributed to British record-keeping traditions. Second, the restrictions imposed on entry into the region of people, including other Indians, prevented unbiased and objective reporting. The only records and reports made available to people were the only ones given as official communications and official versions. Thirdly, there were no local versions of history or vernacular literatures of that time to dispel inaccuracies if any, because such literature did not exist or even if they did, did not have the wherewithal to contradict the available British versions.

2. 'Ethnoscape', a term used by Arjun Appadurai, *Modernity at Large: Cultural Dimensions of Globalisation*, 1997.

3. Assam then included all northeastern States and Union Territories, the North Eastern Frontier Agency now Arunachal Pradesh and Sylhet in Bangladesh, which was part of erstwhile British Assam, except Manipur and Tripura, which were Princely states.

4. *The story of the Assam Railway and Trading Company Limited, 1881-1951*, C.F. Birney, Chairman, p-5.

5. ibid.

6. ibid.

7. Prasenjit Chowdhury, Bordering Skullduggery, *Hardnews*, August 2008, p-37.

8. ibid, Prasenjit Chowdhury.

9. Ramtanu Maitra and Susan Maitra, Northeast India: Target of British apartheid, *Executive Intelligence Review*, October 13, 1995.

10. B. G. Verghese, *India's Northeast Resurgent, Ethnicity, Insurgency, Governance, Development*. p-30.

11. Prof. Sanjib Baruah, *Confronting Constructionism: Ending India's Naga War*, May 2003.

12. B.G. Verghese. *India's Northeast Resurgent, Legacy of the Raj;* p-31.

13. Arun Shourie, *Missionaries in India* ibid, p-109.

14. Haimendorf C. *Naked Nagas*, pp. 56-57.

15. Reid, Sir Robert, The Excluded Areas of Assam; see *Geographical journal*, 1944, Vol. CIII, Nos. 1-2, Jan.-Feb.pp.18-29. Sir Robert Reid, was a former British Governor of Assam (1937-1942.

16. S.K. Barpujari, *Christianity and its impact on the Nagas; An assessment of the work of the American Baptist Mission*, University of Guwahati, pp. 120-121, compiled and edited by Sebastian Karotemprel SDB, PhD, from his book, '*The Tribes of Northeast India*'

17. B. G. Verghese, *India's Northeast Resurgent, Ethnicity, Insurgency, Governance, Development*, p-31.

18. Verghese, ibid, pp-29-31.

19. Verghese, ibid, p-29.

20. Verghese, ibid pp 119-120.

21. Thomas Hylland Eriksen, *Ethnic Identity, national identity and intergroup conflict: The significance of personal experiences*. In Ashmore, Justin, Wilder (eds.): Social identity, intergroup conflict, and conflict reduction, pp 42-70, Oxford University Press, 2001.

22. S. K. Chaube, *Hill Politics in the Northeast India*.

23. Moffat Mills, *Report on the Province of Assam*, Calcutta gazette office, Calcutta, 1854, described the Assamese as 'unattractive', 'degenerated' and 'stupid'.

24. Padmanath Borooah, *Buranji-Bodh*, 1900.

25. Yasmin Saikia, *The Tai-Ahom Connection*. Yasmin holds the view that the Assamese retain their old traditional beliefs and faiths until they embraced Hinduism. As late as 1967, the 'Ahom-Tai Mongolia Parishad' demanded a separate state in Upper Assam. Prominent ritual experts like late Domboru Deodhai Phukan from Assam were recognised as the last of the great ritual experts of the Tai-Ahoms the world over.

CHAPTER - 4

Religious Dimensions of Ethnicity in the Northeast

Of all the influences in identity formation in the Northeast region, religion has been one of the most important, powerful and potent means of social engineering. Religion intoxicates like no other aphrodisiac, it mesmerizes. There are no simple adjectives to define the profundity of religion. It is multifaceted, implying different things to different people. Religion is space and time specific, having flourished in different parts of the world, at different times in the history of human civilisation.

Religion, especially indigenous religion, in the Northeast region is synonymous with clan or ethnic identity, implying thereby, the ubiquitous connection between religion and identity. Understanding, religion epistemologically in the context of the Northeast region of India, is to understand the socio-political dimensions of identity formation in the region. Religious beliefs by themselves are harmless; it is however, its unbridled pursuit and the methods used to 'impose' it on communities and societies, especially on innocent and vulnerable communities like those in the Northeast, which are controversial. Exaggerated narrations, romanticised incidences, events, and use of pecuniary inducements are therefore common.

Starting with indigenous religion, which has left their indelible mark in the region for hundreds of years, the two universal religions, Hinduism and Christianity exerted their influence and imposed their stamp of influence in the region. Yet, the influences and the roles played by the two in identity formation in the region, completely transforming people's way of thinking and dealing with each other in the region, has not been looked into with the seriousness and attention the subject deserves.

This and the following Chapters examine the important role of religion in ethnic identity formation, the changes and the influences these religions brought in the lives of the people in the Northeast, especially in transforming their ways of thinking and dealing with each other. In the course of the analyses, it emerges that the two universal religions instead of being mere appellatives to ethnic identity formation became the change agents themselves. In the subsequent Chapters, the impact of Hinduism and Christianity on people in general and in some of the States is analysed.

Religion: The enemy within

Salman Rushdie in one of his articles; 'Imagine No Heaven' published in '*The Guardian*' in October 1999, observed, *"The real wars of religion are the wars religions unleash against ordinary citizens within their 'sphere of influences'"*. Given Rushdie's predilection in all his writings, to espouse his concern and central theme of *"...the idea of overcoming, or breaking down, the boundaries that hold us in and surpassing the limits of our own boundaries"* reflect the inherent contradiction which every religion carries within themselves[1]. The inherent contradiction in every religion is visible; between the views held by believers on one hand and the vilificatory and sarcastic opinions of the non-believers on the other. It is this inherent contradiction in religion, which make its unbridled acceptance difficult. One can sardonically see human history as a theocratic civilisational progression of conferring religious identities on people and nations under the guise of piety and holiness, with the sole intention and preoccupation to espouse one's religion, both numerically and spatially[2]. The segmentation of the world based on religious affiliations in the name of the unseen silent Gods, is unfortunate. From this perspective, religion deprecates humanity and makes human beings insignificant.

The desire to encapsulate the whole world neatly into the fold of one's religious beliefs undermines religion's otherwise inherent inerrancy and infallibility. This assumption has the ubiquitous implication that all other religious beliefs, except the religion one professes are subservient, suffering from many conceptual infirmities and inadequacies and hence unworthy of any affiliation. This assumption further compounds the misconstrued belief and interpretation that proselytisation and 'winning' people for one's faith and religion endows divine forgiveness and hence does not have any consequential divine retribution. This belief makes proselytisation and any form of conversion unacceptable to many.

Religion by itself is neither disruptive nor capricious, expansivity being its essence, yet the preoccupation to convert the human race and bring it within the fold of a particular religion, countermanding in most cases the inherent freedom of choice available to human beings, is disturbing. Histories of religious conversions in the Northeast region of India where conversions have taken place without soliciting personal conviction or consent of the converts suffer similar criticism. The implication is ominous; it vilifies religion and the sanctity associated with religious beliefs. This restriction imposed in the choice of one's religion takes away the moral sagacity that religion should possess, to carry conviction and command loyalty from its followers and respect from the non-believers.

In another sense, the benefits of religion can be reciprocally mutual to the 'proponents' and the 'converts', provided the converts accepts the religion based on 'convictions'. The word 'conviction', has however dubious and portentous connotations, since such reciprocity is not free of inducements or pressures. Moreover, theologically speaking, one has not yet come across any hermeneutical exposition of what constitute inducements, or the permissible degree and extent of 'persuasions'. In the context of the Northeast, these are important aspects of religion, which has socio-political ramifications. Historically, both Hinduism and Christianity in the Northeastern region of India are subjects of criticism on this account, partly because of the vulnerability and simplicity of the converts at the time when these religions made their inroads into the region. The fact that religion can incarcerate freedom of choice because of its inherent preoccupation with conversion, in one way, proves the premises that each religion carries within itself the seeds of its own destruction.

The other problem that religion in a vast country like India, with a large ignorant and innocent population entails is the preponderance and overwhelming emphasis on the visible rituals and ceremonies, the external embellishments, which is the façade of religion and not the essence. This emphasis to adhere and observe these mundane rituals, shifting the focus of religion as it does from the essence and meaning of religion to the less sublime aspects, overwhelms the illiterate converts. This focus on the superficial elements of religion makes the semantics of what are 'convictions' and 'beliefs' highly ambivalent, debatable and open to various interpretations.

The crucial aspect of religion therefore, is whether the initial superficial attachment to the external embellishments can gradually change into genuine acceptance, or whether one remains preoccupied with the initial impressions of the façade, never to transcend beyond the association with the superficialities of religious rituals and ceremonies. However, in a country of India's size, with its large illiterate and vulnerable population, the continued preponderance towards the superficial, the externalities of religious practices initially imbibed, continue to have in most cases a stranglehold on people. The same is true of the Northeast. In this respect, religion remains a charade, lacking the depth and understanding it should normally inculcate.

Religion and religiosity are powerful instruments of social engineering and categorisation of people. Religious affiliations and associations is 'inherited', a legacy of one's birth, ancestory, biologically and defined by the specific ethnic group or community one belongs or circumstantially endowed. However, this 'affiliations', can be 'engineered' and 'tutored' by means of manipulations by contriving situations, juxtapositioning of events and by external stimulants, which may not be within the control of the individual. Conversely, religious affiliations and beliefs need not necessarily be permanent; it is subject to evolve, change and be selected or discarded, depending upon the individual's belief and choice. However, in actual practice since many factors both social and personal come in the way, exercising such changes are easier said than done.

It is in this situational predicament of sorts; the inherited stamp of association of a person to a religion by the circumstances of their birth, which restricts the freedom to choose one's religion freely. In addition, all religions find themselves in a precarious situation today, between the dictates of the growing scientific temperament of the world on one hand, and the burden of the association imposed on the individual as member of a particular ethnic or social group to which each one is born into, on the other. Religion survives today by compromise, a mix of religiosity tempered by the temporal needs of human rationalism and logic. It is precariously placed without the wherewithal to carry conviction against the ever-increasing number of questioning literate population. Religion in the Northeast is also in the same vulnerable situation.

Religious Dimension of Ethnic Identity

Religion in the Northeast of India is one of the main causes of the endemic problem of ethnic identic conflicts, serious law and order problems affecting psychologically the people and in the process hampering the general economic development of the region. While postulating this premise, the assumption is that religion by itself is not bad, provided it does not interfere with the normative acculturation processes of identity formation and progression of human life. Unfortunately, the problem of religion in the region, like everywhere else is that it does interfere, and sometime destructively.

Historically analysed, the history of religion in the Northeast has two distinct phases of development. The first phase is the period before the coming of the exogenous or universal religions of Buddhism, Hinduism and Christianity into the region. In this phase, there was no conflict or dichotomy between the religious practices, beliefs and ethnic identity, each complimenting the other as conjuncts and sub-serving the interest of the other. The second phase begins with the coming of Buddhism followed by Hinduism, as some historians believe from the fifth century onwards in Assam. Christianity later followed during the nineteenth century.

Religion in the Northeastern region has six important attributes and characteristics with relation to the understanding of its role in ethnic identity formation.

(i) First, socio-anthropologically, before the universal religions came ethnic identity (clan or community) and religious belief were considered synonymous and conjuncts. In fact, there is a seamless non-discernible link between religion and the clan identity. This comprehensive view of religion gave the individual and the community a distinct identity, unique to the group or community. This in turn provided the much-needed sense of 'belonging' and security, which is so vital for the survival of the individual and the group. In short, in the Northeast, religion has been an intregrel and inherent part of one's ethnic identity; one is born either with it or without it, never requiring a special process of assimilation like conversion, to get into its fold. In the context of the Northeastern societies, traditionally, religion therefore precludes ethnic identity, suggesting both an organic as well as a theocratic symbiotic link between ethnic identity and religious belief.

The universal religions, particularly Christianity, without realising the implications and significance introduced a formal sanctified ceremonial process of establishing a 'connection' between religion with ethnic identity in a person. Once this process was introduced, the symbiotic organic link between religion and ethnicity endowed on a person based on one's birth, a belief in these societies for hundreds of years, got diluted and defused. This 'distinction' introduced changes in the concept and definition of ethnic identity itself. By a process of logical deduction, the concept of ethnic identity became amorphous and indefinite. The first adverse consequence of this distinction was that the respective clans and communities lost their control over the people they once held together.

(ii) Second, since in the Northeast, a person's religion or religious identity is organically endowed, ingrained and inherent in the person the moment one is born into a particular clan or community, the process of 'conversion' considered an essential prerequisite in conferring the right to membership into Christianity for instance, was therefore new to the region. Implied in this semantic, is the fact that the element of choice, considered so crucial by modern socio-anthropologists and scientists, as a fundamental right of a person in choosing one's religion, did not exist in the region. Thus proselytisation and religious conversions, especially their significance and importance were neither understood nor taken too seriously.

(iii) The third dimension of religion in the Northeast is that it has a geo-physical connotation or association. In other words, religion has a physical dimension, geomorphologically and geographically defined and associated with either the valleys or the hills and mountainous areas of the region. Consequently, Hinduism is predominantly a religion of the non-tribal communities in the valley or lowland areas of the region, while, Christianity is a religion of the upland tribal communities who dominate the hills and mountainous areas in the region.

Further, religion also has a climatic dimension. Hinduism is essentially a warm weather religion, where water is used extensively in all its rituals and ceremonies. Christianity, on the same deduction is a cold weather religion, its ceremonies adopted to suit the cold climate and weather of the West. These aspects will partly explain why Hinduism failed to attract the upland tribal communities, residing in the cold mountainous areas and climates within its fold and why Christianity succeeded instead in propagating itself in the upland and mountainous regions in the Northeast.

(iv) The fourth universally applicable general aspect of religion is that one cannot always give religion a definitive adage of time because as long as there are believers, religion tend to become 'timeless'. Religion has therefore within it a 'timelessness' quality, a state of permanence. When we talk of religion, we are not only talking of religion in the context of a given point of time in the past, nor of the present but it is always in the continuous present or future tense.

However, in the context of the indigenous traditional religions prevalent in the Northeast, social scientists are less charitable and tend to be more time specific, giving these religions a definitive time slot and contextual inference by associating them with human beings living at a particular time and place. Thus, when we discuss or speak of 'Ancient' or 'Religion of Antiquity', we are qualifying religion in its association with human history and measured in human 'age' and 'time', a sartorial definition of religion by making them both time and place specific. This concept of both time and space becomes relevant.

(v) Another aspect of religion, the fifth, which the Northeast shares with many communities in the country, is the disturbing mismatch between the intelligence of the religious missionaries and exponents on one hand, and the simplicity and ignorance of the potential converts on the other. Seen from this perspective, all religious conversion in the Northeast, tend to be an unfair proposition set by highly intelligent proponents against the simple, naïve potential converts.

In this connection, an obvious reaction against Christian aggressiveness and Hindu selectivism, where the innocent tribals and people were victims, one Jadonong[3] started an indigenous sub-structured primal religion known as *Zeliangrong* in the beginning of the 20th century in Manipur. His well-known follower 'Rani' Gaidinlui brought the 'movement' into national limelight. (The term *Zeliangrong,* is a combination of the shortened form of three Naga communities of Manipur, the Zemei, Liangmei and Rongmei Nagas, which adds up as Ze+Liang+Rong.) The Zeliangrong movement was against Hinduism and Christianity overtly, but as many believe, it was covertly a reaction against the ethnic identity conflicts between the Kabui and Kuki feuds. As a religious movement, the Zeliangrong sect exhibits elements of Hinduism, in the use of the place of worship, which is in the shape of the temple and in the use of the image of God and Goddess.

The Zeliangrong movement is important in the history of religion in Manipur, and indirectly in the Northeast because it is a manifestation of the latent anger against all forms of organised forcible religious conversions, negating all principles of ethics and morality, especially the wanton exploitation of the innocent indigenous people of the region. The movement is also significant because it stands for the preservation of indigenous ethnic beliefs, socio-cultural value systems, which many tribal communities hold dear to their hearts. In this context the universal religions, Christianity in particular, has been a threat to the cultural exclusivity and social specificity of the tribal ethos and sensibility. Many socio-anthropologists hold the view that *"Jadonong saw Christianity as destructive of the tribal customs which he wanted to uphold."* [4]

Gandhiji once wrote; *"If I had the power and could legislate, I should stop all proselytizing... It is the deadliest poison that ever sapped the fountain of truth"*, Gandhiji was amplifying the dehumanization processes of proselytisation and religious conversions. What was disturbing Gandhiji, was the circumvention and emasculation of the inherent ability of the individual to exercise the choice of one's religious beliefs, which should be an expression and manifestation of one's inner most faith arising out of conviction. Unfortunately, all proselytisation is a process, which semantically and in practice focuses more on achieving numerical 'successes', rather than in facilitating the exercise of 'choice' to the individual.

To prevent such conversions from taking place and prevent the use of inducements, a few State governments in the region have introduced laws to prevent it. In Arunachal Pradesh, the State Government has enacted the Arunachal Pradesh Freedom of Religious Act of 1978, which prohibits conversion *"...by the use of force or by inducement or by fraudulent means"*. Instead, Donyi-Polo a unified concept of all those Animistic beliefs of the people of Arunachal Pradesh comprising of the Tibetan and Thai-Burmese origins is encouraged.

(vi) The sixth and last feature of religion in the Northeast, which is of recent development, is the increased interests and efforts to revive the various indigenous faiths. Many have begun questioning the moral authority of the universal religions to subjugate the native religions and in the process their native sensibilities and ethos. This resurgence of interests has led to reassessment of the unquestioned hold and tenure of the two universal religions of Hinduism and

Christianity in the region. More importantly, this renewed interests in the indigenous 'traditional religions and beliefs', has a corresponding resonance in the increased interests in ethno-nationalistic aspirations among some of these communities.

There are three basic reasons why this affiliation to the indigenous religions and belief will increase and exert their influence. (a) Indigenous religion is community and clan specific and hence synonymous with the ethnic identity of its believers. The magico-religious cults, beliefs, associated taboos and the rituals of the indigenous religions, all have a powerful hold on these societies, ethno-identically, socio-culturally and psychologically. (b) Reification of these faiths and beliefs is symptomatic of the rising assertive ethnic identity politics in the region. (c) The increased interests in these faiths and religious beliefs are reaction formation against the exogenous universal religions for eradicating traditional socio-cultural values and indigenous way of life.

Religion in a 'Flat world'

A class of young children when once asked by their teacher to come prepared the next day to explain how they were born, in the manner that all primary school teachers ask. One of the 'young men' went home and asked his eldest brother, his mother and his grandmother of how he was born. He was told about all the wonderful stories of how the stork had brought him all wrapped in a nice blue towel, or how the fairy Godmother brought him during his mother's sleep and all the conceivable stories possible. None of his family members told him about the natural phenomenon of his birth in plain terms. The young man went back to school the next day and declared to his teacher and the class non-challantly that, in his family for the last three generations there has never been a 'normal birth'.

The truth and essence about religion and particularly in the Northeast of India, is like the story of birth told to the 'young man' by the members of his family, more in the abstract, a mystery wrapped and shrouded in hyperboles, made impossible for the people to understand when these universal religions first made their inroads into the region. Today the problem confronted by religion is different in the region from what it was once. The 'riddle' about religion in today's world cannot be explained away in abstract terms and in hyperboles as it was once done in the past, it need to be backed with reason and logic, if religion has to find its niche in a rationalist's world.

The meaning and connotations of religion in the Northeast has undergone many changes in recent times. For instance, the resurgence of the native indigenous faiths and religious beliefs is a reflection of the inadequacies of the universal religions and their long-term impact on these societies. This reaction and response, even though confined only to a few segments of each of these ethnic groups, nevertheless reveals that the universal or exogenous religions have only dented the surface of the religious beliefs of these societies over the years, leaving the core native inherent attributes and beliefs unscathed and in many cases only further fortifying them. Given this loyalties and affiliations to their respective ancient faiths and beliefs, it is evident that accepting and adopting either Hinduism or Christianity has never been easy for the people of the region even though they may not openly admit it. Many communities in a way look at the universal religions, Hinduism and Christianity, as obtrusive diversions in their social and cultural history. The conclusion is that the value-systems and norms of the universal religions, steeped in alien values, often quite diametrically opposite of the indigenous traditional religious beliefs and ways of life may not induce enough convictions to enable the people of the region to surrender the unique status and position these societies have accorded to their native indigenous faiths and religions.

Religion has the propensity to transform the lives of people, society and the nation. This is exactly what religion, more precisely Hinduism and Christianity did to the northeast region of the country. The two exogenous religions changed and transformed the whole way of life, the mind-set and psyche of the people of the region and in the process, changed the entire ethos, sensibilities and social equations among the various communities in the region. The two universal religions polarized people of the region between the upland tribal and lowland non-tribal population in the region. The heterodoxy of religious beliefs no doubt is part of life but the aggressive posturing and sometimes the clamorous unethical methods of proselytisation, visible today in the form of the religious based ethnic divide in the Northeast, has taken the 'grace and dignity' out of all religion and faith.

Bill Graham in one of his famous discourse observed that while the technological change and pace at which the world is developing are beyond our imagination, the commensurate progress towards moral rearmament is deplorably slow. Bill Graham foresaw the pace at which technology is outpacing our moral value systems, threatening the omnificence of the concept of God and the idea of religion itself. Bill Graham is no ordinary evangelist. Religion has to respond to this challenge. Hinduism and Christianity have responded to this changing perception of religion by redefining their objectives and approach. The Vatican II initiative of the Roman Catholic Church has for instance made adjustments taking into considerations the increasing concerns of a world where science is out pacing all sense perceptions by moving into the realms of spirituality and every aspect of human cognitively.

In a world, therefore constantly out paced by technology and science where does religion stand? In addition, if humanity itself is being out-moded into antiquity if not made altogether irrelevant, what is the future of religion for which humankind has fought each other for generations? Late Prof. E. Nilkanta Singh, imminent Professor of Philosophy from Manipur writing about Hinduism sums the position of what religion should do in the fast changing world. Quoting Acharya Vinoba Bhave, late Prof. Nilkanta said; *"The march of human cycle indicates that we must adopt a futuristic outlook. We can go back to the Vedas but cannot live the Vedic symbolism. All religions, even the most advanced ones, are a little off-the color now. The future belongs to a creative synthesis of science and spirituality"*[5](sic). Perhaps the answer lies in what 'The Mother' of Sri Aurobindo Ashram once said, *"One must not confuse a religious teaching and a spiritual teaching. Religious teaching belongs to the past and stops all progress. Spiritual teaching is the teaching of the future. It enlightens the consciousness and prepares it for the future realization. A spiritual teaching is above religions and strives towards a total truth. A contact with the divine"* (sic). We have entered the spiritual age, the religion of the future, the religion of the self and the religion of fairness. The polemics of religion is endless, but its purpose and ultimate meaning is the emancipation of the soul, the self within each one of us, or simply put, to make good human beings out of every one of us.

Identity formation is a long acculturated process in which religion plays an important role, but no religion has ever played such an important role as Hinduism and Christianity did in the Northeast region of the country. These two religions have changed their defined or assigned role of being a mere appellative to identity and instead transformed themselves into change-agents of identity itself. They have done precisely what they ought not to have done. In the process, the two universal religions have attracted upon themselves a vilificatory connotation and became subjects of judgment rather than be the judges themselves.

How does an average native Northeast Indian view Hinduism and Christianity? I am afraid with equal disdain and equanimity. People in the Northeast find faults with both, Hinduism for its passivity and stratification of people into social hierarchies and for excluding the upland communities from its fold. Christianity is criticized for its monomaniacal pursuit of winning 'souls for Christ' unmindful of the fact that these conversions have curtailed the freedom of choice to the individual, obliterating the traditional religions, value systems, social habits and customs of the upland people.

Primal and Indigenous religion, Definitions and the Beginning

One of the most basic features and common aspect of the Northeastern societies and communities is the prevalence and practice of indigenous religions. These native indigenous faiths and religions are synonyms of particular clans, tribes, communities and evolved over the years with them. They constitute a powerful and important institution for community moralling. Because of these factors, in spite of Hinduism and Christianity, the various ethnic groups in the Northeast inwardly remain loyal to native indigenous faiths and religions. Consequently, religious beliefs among the people in the region remain highly syncretic in form and content. Understanding some of the basic meaning, features and theoretical aspects of indigenous religion is important.

From the socio-anthropological perspective, there are many common aspects among many of these indigenous religions cutting across the ethnic divide. This is essentially because the various ethnic groups in the Northeast share similar, if not the same or common ancestory and origin. The gradual dismantling and disappearance of these indigenous religions, mainly due to the influence of Hinduism and Christianity in the region, has destroyed these anthropological linkages.

The term 'Primal Religion'[6] coined by Dr. Harod Turner, meaning the primary or basic religions, is a generic term and encompasses all the primordial sub-categorisations that goes by various nomenclatures and includes all indigenous religions. Animism, Paganism, and Totenism etc, all fall under this categorisation. What Dr. Harod Turner meant was that any religion, which believes in the existence and the prevalence of a 'primordial' god, connected with and related (i) to the indigenous people, (ii) and existed prior to or different to the universal religions, without any connectivity or necessarily linking to any special group, falls under the term of 'Primal religion'.

The other term relevant in the study of the indigenous religions of the Northeast is the concept of 'primordial monotheism'. Primordial monotheism is a belief in a 'Supreme Being', a concept propounded by the famous Scottish folklorist Andrew Lang (1844-1912). It postulates the existence of a pontific, 'Supreme Being', which lords over other lesser gods, spirits or demons. The concept of an omnipotent being superintending all others is significant for various reasons.

Further, there are two schools of interpretations of Primal religion. One school of thought believes that 'primal religion' is monotheistic, similar to the concept propounded by Andrew Lang of a single 'Supreme Being'. The second school believes that 'primal religion' is essentially polytheistic in concept and believes in the existence of many gods, spirits and demons. The former, monotheistic school believes that Polytheism is the degraded form of the primordial monotheistic religious beliefs, essentially a stage before it evolved and consolidated into monotheistic religion.

Sir Edward B.Taylor[7] (1832-1917) considered the father of social anthropology first pointed out the prevalence of animistic faith and cults in various societies. Sir Edward propounded the concept of animism, when he wrote that, *"The theory which endows the phenomenon of nature with personal life might perhaps conveniently be called 'animism"*. Sociologists like Andrew Lang, Emile Durkheim, R.R. Marret and Wilhelm Schmidt are critical of whether it would have been better to describe primitive religion as 'Spiritualism', instead of giving a somewhat derogatory meaning and connotation by the use of the term 'animism'. The controversy and debate was not about the definition of indigenous religion, but about the co-relation of 'animism' to what was further described by Taylor as a religion of the 'savages'. Many of Taylor's critic felt that this gave 'animism' not only a judgmental vilificatory qualification but also made the followers of 'animism' an implied 'primitiveness'. Further, Taylor's critics felt that the association of 'animism' as the 'Belief in the Spiritual Beings', which meant 'a belief that all natural objects have souls', thereby having attributes of 'spirituality' and the capability to establish communication with the 'dead' as highly objectionable. Most critics and admirers found this aspect of Taylor's premise unacceptable because of the associated suggestion that 'animism' was a form of necromanticism.

In the Northeast region, even though today the majority of people follow the universal religions, Animistic or Animism is the most common form of indigenous religion and belief and one that is still extensively prevalent across the region, with each community professing it in their respective unique and different ways. Seen from this perspective many scholars from the Northeast region therefore, find many of the definitions of indigenous religions given by various social scientists and scholars as derogatory and demeaning by implication. As against Sir Edward B.Taylor's view, a much more acceptable view is the one held by James Frazer in his epoch making book, 'The Golden Bough'. James Frazer, by a process of deductive logic, held the view that Animism as a religion marks a stage in the evolutionary development of all the tribal communities and therefore an essential transitory stage in societal evolution.

Common Attributes and Classifications

The various definitions, characteristics and interpretations of indigenous religions broadly provide the identifiable attributes based on which similarities between the various indigenous religions practiced in the Northeast is easily discernable. The fact is that irrespective of the stage of social transformation and development these ethnic groups and societies are today, they all inherently remain part of the larger Indo-Mongoloid grouping having moved over to the region either separately or as groups at different times in the past. This aspect also supplements the existing assumption that most of the ethnic groups in the Northeast share in many respects anthropological, social and cultural connections in some form or the other in their acculturated histories. Each of these common aspects is analysed.

The intention of analysing this aspect of the Northeast is to bring out the fact that in addition to the tendency to abrogate the socio-anthropological links among the various ethnic groups in the region, the refusal to see the obvious links that exist in the various indigenous religions practiced among various ethnic groups, are possibly signs of the growing ethnic divide and social polarization among the various ethnic groups in the region. One believes that this growing divide has to be narrowed down if any meaningful peace and prosperity is expected in the region.

The various identifiable attributes of the indigenous faiths in the Northeast fall broadly into two groups. The first category includes the natural elements like light, air, water, wind, rain and other natural phenomenon. The second category include the natural objects like the earth, hills and mountains, forests, trees, rocks, stones, rivers and streams. Further, in the second category there are two subcategories, involving inanimate deities and those involving animate deities.

In all the indigenous religions and faiths in the northeast region the underlying common principle behind the propitiation is to appease and placate the 'unknown spirits' for a peaceful and trouble free existence. The Garos call their religion as *Songsarek, Sanamahi,* among the Meiteis of Manipur, *Donyi-polo* among people of Tibetan origin, while the people of Thai-Burmese origin in Arunachal Pradesh call it *Rangfrah*. The indigenous religion of the Bodos, the original autochthones of Assam, calls it as *Bathou Borai* faith. The Ahoms of Assam who ruled over Assam for more than 600 years from the beginning of the 13th century ADE when its founder Sukhapa began his kingdom from Chairaideo, believed in many indigenous gods and goddesses. The Ahoms believed in *Phuratara* (Creator), *Lengdon* (God of heaven), *Jasingpha* (Goddess of learning), *Phai* (God of Fire), and *Kao-Kham*[8] (God of water). The Ahoms had their own traditional priests known as Deodhais, until the Brahmans replaced them. The influence continued until King Sudangpha also called as the Baamuni Kunwar (1397-1407) became interested in Hinduism. The influence continued until the actual and formal acceptance of Hinduism during the reign of king Jayadhvaj or Jayadwaj Xingha (1648-1663).

In the entire region, it is impossible not to come by a patch in the countryside where such deities are not incarcerated either in a clamp of forest or perched on a rock formation. Deification and transformation of the natural phenomenon like thunder, lightening, earthquakes and all the inexplicable fearsome countenance of nature into gods and spirits are common in all societies. Over a period, these deities became both the dispenser of justice and the social conscience keeper of the community. The fear psychoses generated by these deities helped the communities to ensure social decorum and enforce order in their respective clans and communities. Infusing and providing the much-needed elements of mystery and fear of the supernatural in the myths and folklores to captivate the believers was a common trait. Additionally, these beliefs also helped in keeping the members of the clan and community unified as a group or community.

In addition, there are five main common elements or attributes in all the indigenous religions of the region. These are (1) Belief in the existence of 'One Supreme Being', both omnipotent and omniscient. (2) All natural phenomenon and 'things' natural are endowed with supernatural powers and attributes. (3) These gods, goddesses, spirits and deities are divided into the 'outdoor' and 'indoor' spirits as well as the 'Good' and the 'Bad' spirits. (4) Ancestor Worship is generally a common aspect and feature involved in all these faiths. (5) All indigenous religions have some form of ceremonies, rituals, rites, both formal and informal, and in some cases accompanied by taboos, magic, occultism and esoteric practices.

The last two of these common attributes, (4) and (5) do not require much explanation or elaboration, as both of these are universally common aspects and hence dealt summarily. This is primarily because the fourth category, involving ancestor worship is a universally accepted and widely prevalent ceremony, which is common and prevalent all across the region and in many other societies and communities and hence may not require any explanation. As part of this belief, each community in the region set aside special days to honour and revere their ancestors. In the fifth category, there are a number of rituals and ceremonies practised across the region and a study of the subject would entail a whole book by itself. Suffice to say, the religious ceremonies and rituals associated, and observed form the external manifestation of the reverence to opiate the gods and the spirits. The first three attributes however require further amplification, because they can provide the clue to the socio-anthropological links of many of the ethnic groups in the northeast.

The concept of the omnipotent 'Supreme Being' or 'Supreme God' is prevalent among all societies and communities across the region, both in the plains and in the hills. The Garos call the great 'being as *Tatra-Rabuga*, the Khasis as *U Blei Nongthaw* or *U Blei Nongpynlong*, the Kukis know it as *Chung Pathein*, the Bodos call it *Aham Guru* or *Obonglaori*. The Hmars and the Koms call it *Panthien*. The Thadous also share similar concept but have another name. The Meiteis of Manipur in and around Shekmai, Payeng, Leimarem and Andro areas call the Great Being *Tengbanba Mapu*. The Tripuris, the autochthons of Tripura call it as *Matai-Katar*. The

Kabui Nagas refer to the Supreme Being as *Ra-Gang* (also spelt as *Ragwang*); the Tangkhul Nagas call it *Virivara*[9]. The Mizos, especially among the Lushai, Gangte and Vaiphais call the Supreme Being *Manasia*, phonetically similar to *Menashe*, the name of one of the ten Lost tribes of Israel. The similarity is significant, because some of the Mizos from Churachandpur district of Manipur and Mizoram claim their connections to this lost tribe from Israel. The Amishav; an Israeli religious group has accepted more than 600 persons from these areas and they have migrated to Israel since then.

In all these societies, the 'Supreme Being' does not necessarily conform to the concept of it being the main Pantheon, since there are a number of other lesser deities or spirits who have their own individual position in these societies independent of the 'Supreme being'. Nevertheless, all of these together constitute a hierarchical, stratified linkage. In almost all these societies, the omnipotent 'Supreme Being' stands quite apart on its own, commanding a special position of importance and significance. The 'Supreme Being' is formless and mostly exists in the 'realm of the beyond', invisible to human beings. Even though some of the communities believe it to be in human form and likeness, the 'fearsome countenance', is in most cases overshadowed by the benign and benevolent aspect of the 'Supreme Being'.

Natural objects and spirits are common and important religious symbols of the indigenous faiths and religions. Besides, they form one of the most important anthropological sources of tracing the origins of many of the ethnic groups among many of these communities. For instance, there are many legends, myths and folktales associated with these objects, which traces the beginnings of clan and communities. The stone or rock is an important natural object among many communities in the region. There is, for instance, a popular legend among the Chankhesang Nagas (earlier known as Eastern Angamis) known as the *Kheza-Kenoma* legend set in the village of the same name, which tells the story of a stone in that village that could double the paddy spread on it every morning by the end of the day. Three brothers, Angami, Sema and Lotha (three Naga tribes) would quarrel amongst themselves almost daily to have possession of it. In spite of various formulas worked out by their father and mother for sharing the stone, the quarrel among the three brothers continued. Fearing bloodshed, the parents set the stone on fire and burnt it, breaking the magic stone and irreparably damaging it. The spirit in the stone left it and as such lost its magical powers. The three brothers saddened by the outcome of their behaviour, left Kheza-Kenoma and went to their different destinations, becoming in the process the ancestors of the Angami, Sema and Lotha Nagas.

Another story, similar in nature, is the one about the ancient arrangement of six stones known as Lungterok (six stones) located on a hillock having mythological significance in a village called Chungliyimti (also spelt as Chongliemdi) located fifty-five kilometers from Tuensang town in Nagaland. The Ao[10] and the Phom Nagas believe that they originated from Chungliyimti. Incidentally, '*Lungterok* (Six stones) is phonetically almost identical and in meaning to the Manipuri Meitei language. In the Meitei language, *'Nungtaruk'* means 'six stones', *Nung*, meaning stone and *Taruk* meaning six. The coincidence and similarity is significant.

In both these legends and in other folklores of the region, the association of the rock or stone is conspicuous by references to these natural formations in the many fables and folklores. The use of stones as religious symbols, representing the 'unknown' spirits and gods, found across the Northeast form an inherent aspect of the megalith culture of the region. These are associated with religious cults, ancestor worship, for burials and other rituals. The silent stones tell many stories across the Northeast.

The issue of the 'Journal of Asiatic Society of Bengal', also in 'Man in India'[11], suggests that the use of *"stone for grave or memorials...to both Mon-Khmer and Tibeto-Burman culture of the region...with the same practice by the people of Indonesia, Philippines, Luzon, Nias and other islands in the Pacific"* are common. The use of stone and similarity in the burial rituals in Burma and South-east Asia with the practice among many of the upland communities in the Northeast provides the East Asian connection. In Khimosniang between Jowai and Jarain, Nartiang and Nartiang bazaar in the Jaintia hills of Meghalaya series of menhirs, dolmens and burial cists exists. Similarly, the Kacharis have left an impressive array of megalithic evidences at Dimapur (now in Nagaland), while existence of megalithic cultures in North Cachar in Nunglo, Bolasan, Derebora, Kobak and Karlong are established. These megalithic structures are classified into the Chessman, Y-shaped and the buffalo-horn types with figures of various animals like elephants, deer and tigers. Much of the Neolithic and Megalithic culture, even though not accurately dated, point to the importance attached to the natural objects as part of the social and religious history of many communities in the northeast.

Mountains and hills are very important deities in these religions. In Manipur among the Tangkhul Naga community, the mountain peak of *Shirui Kashong* (8421 ft) is sacred and revered. People popularly believe that many strange phenomena happen and occur all the time on the mountain. The Meiteis have a similar belief and reverence for the *Koubru* hills. The Khasis consider *U'lei Shillong* (Shillong Peak) as deity in natural formation along with the *Rableng* hill, within view of the Shillong Peak; the *Symper* hill, which is considered as the abode of *U Sympera*, a powerful deity. The list goes on. The intrinsic value and the reverence attached to these geological formations by human beings particularly by several groups in the Northeast are common features, since it is these natural formations which have protected them from enemies and given them shelter and food. There are number of fables and folklores woven around these natural objects and formations and the various communities and societies even today, among them Hindus and Christians, hold annual festivals and other ceremonies in their honour.

J.P. Mills points out the importance attached to these naturally formed objects based on the large number of pre-historic Neolithic and Megalithic formations found from various areas and sources in the region[12]. J. H. Hutton, based on his extensive tours in the Northeast region, similarly compares the similarity of the megaliths found in Dimapur (Nagaland) with those found in Malaya or Malaysia. Besides, the large numbers of megaliths found in the Khasi-Jaintia Hills (Meghalaya) even though belong to a different genre and influence, also fall into this categorisation. The associations and the similarities in the usages of these natural objects among the various ethnic groups, and their similarities with those found in other parts of Southeast Asia provides additional proof to many of the theories that the people of the Northeast trace their origins and ancestral histories with East Asia, particularly Southeast Asia.

Anthropocentricism and Indigenous Religion

An important common aspect of indigenous religion in the Northeast is the close association and affinity between human beings and the natural objects and formations, signifying the interdependence of man on nature. Thus, indigenous religions believe that human beings are an integral part of the eco-system in which these natural phenomenons discipline and shape human lives and in a way control their destinies. From this perspective, an orderly world order can prevail only if the principle of complementarities and mutual respect between man and nature is enforced. This require adherence to basic and elementary principles of ecological ethics by maintaining the delicate balance between what nature can provide and what human beings need for their sustenance. Most indigenous religions of the Northeast have this principle as the basic and fundamental intrinsic attribute, a prerequisite for its very sustenance. Sociologically, deifying the natural elements was the easiest way to conservational ethics and hence deification of natural objects was a common phenomenon in these societies.

The concept of the *'Umang Lais'* (Forest Gods) among the Meiteis of Manipur or the *'Kyantang'*, (Sacred groves) among the Khasis of Meghalaya are socially enforced environmental laws to preserve the endangered forests, especially the innumerable species of medicinal plants, herbs and trees. L. Jeetendro Singh, N.Biraj Singh and Abhik Gupta, Dept. of Ecology, University of Assam, Silchar in a study titled, 'Environment Ethics in the Culture of Meiteis from North East India' have identified in the Meitei society a number of 'Umang Lais' with a number of species of the protected plants having magico-religious importance. The study has identified at least seven of these in Manipur and one in Khorihaba, Sonai in Cachar district among the Meitei populations of Assam. According to the study[13], *"These groves...might have been established with the purely anthropocentric concept of preserving some greenery in the area, or for maintaining some trees of religious importance that are associated with the deity"*. Further, they observe, *"While these might have been initially planted and protected because of utilitarian reasons, the ethical position gradually changed with these being now considered sacred along with the deity of the grove"*. The self-preservation instinct of humans embodies itself cleverly in these indigenous religions under the guise of religious piety and reverence.

According to B.K. Tiwari, Reader and Head of Department at the Centre for Environmental Studies, North Eastern Hill University, there are as many as 79 groves, 48 in the East Khasi district, 15 in the Jaintia district, 8 each in the two districts of East and West Garo districts[14]. In the *Imperial Gazette of India* (XV, R55) of 1908, describes the Khasi hills as *"...clothed with clumps of oak, chestnut, magnolia, beech and other trees, which superstition has preserved from the axe of the woodcutter"*. The tradition and ethics involved in all these are similar in its philosophical orientations to the Shinto tradition in Japan with its shrine located in 'Himorogi', which is described as 'places where trees grow thick' [15]. The Ami Tribe of Taiwan also worships various species of trees or sacred plots of land since gods are supposed to reside in these places. The animistic cults in the Northeast of India and elsewhere in the world follow similar preservative instincts and philosophy. In effect, it is this aspect of interdependence of man and nature, which is the primary reason why the indigenous beliefs and faiths have survived in spite of the onslaught of Hinduism and Christianity in the region.

The preponderance of both Hinduism and Christianity over the years has undermined the importance of the philosophy of ecological balance in society enshrined in these native religions. Over the years, people have gone about desecrating the sacred groves and other symbols of the rich traditional religious legacies indiscriminately. Dr. N.W. Bor distinguished British Forester and Botanist bemoans this aspect, *"It has always been a matter of great regret to me that the spread of Christianity in the hills tends to involve the complete destruction of all that is most interesting in the lives and customs of primitive people"*. This view of Dr. Bor especially the religious sanctity attached to the natural vegetations is reinforced in an article by Prof. Henry Skolimowski, Professor in Engineering School at the University of Michigan, who after his visit to Shillong in 1993 wrote, *"One can capture the sense of exhilaration of the ancient people, when they entered the sacred groves, felt purified and were uplifted because their attitude was reverential"* [16].

Significance of Indigenous Religions

An interesting aspect about indigenous religions in the Northeast is that in spite of the overwhelming success of Christianity and Hinduism; they continue to survive even today. One reason ascribed is the differences that exist between the inherently polytheistic or pluralistic concept of gods prevalent in the various indigenous religions, and the monotheistic view and concept of god in Christianity. In contrast, Hinduism is essentially polytheistic, where *"The predominant emphasis is on personal salvation, a journey in which the individual is essentially alone with his karma and his god."* [17] It has easily accommodated many of the indigenous practices and religious rites. In many societies, for instance among the Hindu Meiteis of Manipur, the Sanamahi cult exists side by side with Hinduism.

The main reason is that these indigenous religions are an intrinsic part of every ethnic group and community and hence synonyms of their clan or ethnic identity. Socio-anthropologically, no other attribute of the Northeastern social ethos reinforces cognitively the unique identity of an ethnic group more poignantly and emphatically than these indigenous religions. It is in the nature of this definitiveness and the seamless link between religion and ethnic, or clan identity that in spite of changing affiliations to other religions, most ethnic identities in the region continue to survive and the people remain loyal to their ancient and traditional faiths and beliefs. The conceptual separation between ethnicity and religion, introduced by the two universal religions has not been able to severe completely the links between religion and ethnic identity.

There are several examples of the perpetuation and revivals of indigenous faiths and beliefs in the Northeast. The *Seng Khasi* movements founded in 1899, its sister organisation *Sein Raj* among the Khasis and the *Pnar-Khasi* movements in Jowai in the Jaintia areas are the three main ones, besides religious beliefs like *Kyntang* are examples from Meghalaya. The *Sanamahis* among the Meitei community of Manipur, *Donyi-Polo* in Arunachal Pradesh, the *Tatara-Rabuga, Chorabudi, Saljong, Kalkame* among the Garos are just a few examples. Many of the traditional customs and festivities have their connections with the various indigenous religious beliefs and practices and form an integral part of the social and cultural ethos of the various ethnic groups. The cataloging therefore, by such terms as 'religion of the savage', 'animism', 'paganism', 'antiquated beliefs' etc, is therefore indirectly a judgmental vilification of these societies where these religions are still practised and followed. It would therefore not be fair to use these terms by subjecting the various native indigenous religions to be judged by the standards and norms of a rationalized world, without the necessary contextualization to regions like the northeastern region of India.

Today two things are therefore very conspicuous. First, since the indigenous faiths and beliefs constitute an essential socio-cultural trait and attribute of the various ethnic groups as symbols of each ethnic group, they are much more than mere religious beliefs and practices. The universal religions have accordingly learnt to adjust and co-exist side by side with these beliefs and practices. Second, because of these factors, irrespective of the influences of Hinduism and Christianity the indigenous religious beliefs and practices known as Animism, Paganism, Nature worship etc. still prevail syncretically in these societies in some form or the other all over the Northeast.

Endnotes

1. Ravi Vyas, Rushdie's Children; an article in *Frontline*, July 13, 2007.

2. As per the Census of India 2001, the total Hindu population in the seven Northeastern States, including Sikkim is 57.27 percent of the total population, Islam with 22.82 percent is the second highest and Christianity 16.12 percent. These figures are in comparison to the National total average of 80.51 percent Hindus, 13.44 percent Muslims and 2.34 percent Christians. Christians, state-wise; Nagaland has 90.00 percent, Mizoram 87.04 percent, Meghalaya 70.46 percent and Manipur 34.06 percent. Arunachal Pradesh has 18.88 percent, Assam 3.70 percent, Sikkim 6.69 percent and Tripura 3.20 percent. Hindus constitute 85.65 percent in Tripura, 64.92 percent in Assam, 61.06 percent in Sikkim, 46.03 percent in Manipur, 34.90 percent in Arunachal Pradesh, 13.32 percent in Meghalaya, 7.70 percent in Nagaland and 3.55 percent in Mizoram.

3. Zeliangrong is an indigenous religion, which grew set against the backdrop of the Kabui and Kuki feud and animosity in Manipur. The British Administration in Manipur viewed the movement suspiciously, especially Jadonong its founder and leader. On the ostensible ground for an alleged murder of four Manipuri betel leaf traders, who lit a fire when there was a ban at that time, as part of a sacred ritual of the sect called the 'genna' by Jadonong's followers. Jadonong was arrested and hanged in Imphal jail on 29 August 1931.

4. John Parrat and Saroj N. Arambam Parrat; *'Kabui Messiah': The Jadonong Movement of Manipur.*

5. Prof. E. Nilkanta Singh: *Status of religion in Tribal areas of Manipur.*

6. Term coined by Dr. Harod Turner '*A Lion Handbook: The World Religion.* 1994, London.

7. In his paper titled 'Religion of Savages' in the *Fortnightly Review* 1866.

8. Dr. S.L. Baruah: *A Comprehensive History of Assam.*

9. P.Lalit, *The Life and Culture of the Tangkhuls of Manipur.*

10. The Meiteis call all Nagas as 'Hao' a derivative of 'Ao' with whom they probably first had some historical or anthropological connections. This is interesting since according to S.K. Chatterjee in his famous work *Kirata-jana-krit*, the Ao, Angami, Sema, Tangkhul and a few others along with the Manipuri Meiteis form a distinct group of the Tibeto-Burman language and dialects classification falling under the Assam-

Burmese group. Hem Barua in his book, the *Red River and the Blue Hills*, 1962, p-97, refers to S.K.Chatterjee.

11. *Journal of Asiatic Society of Bengal*, 1879 Vol. II, pp. 118-122, also in *Man in India*, vol.viii, pp.228f.
12. J. P. Mills; *Journal of Assam Research Society*, Vol. I. pp.3-6, p-61.
13. Refer to Syngai, D. 1999. *Sacred Groves in Meghalaya, Biodiversity-North East India Perspectives*.
14. Teresa Rehman, *India Today* website, dispatch/ 20001111/ rehman.html.
15. G. Kato. *A Historical Study of the Religious development of Shinto*. Translated by Shoyu Hanayama, *Japan Society for the promotion of Science*, 1993. Tokyo, p-182.
16. Prof. Skolimowski, Professor of Humanities in the Engineering School at the University of Michigan in his article; Early Eco-Philosophers among the Tribal People: Letter from India, Trumpeter 1993. Prof. Skolimowski also holds the first Chair for Ecophilosophy at the University of Poland. He is best known for his book, *Ecophilosophy: Designing New Tactics for living*.
17. Pavan K. Varma, *Being Indian*, p-96.

CHAPTER - 5

Hinduism

Hinduism is the second universal religion after Buddhism, which unleashed a powerful influence in Northeastern India, changing in the process the entire course of ethnic identity formation, the social and political history of the region. Pioneered by the Rulers of Assam and later by the Rulers of Manipur, Hinduism became the primer religion for the largest number of people in the Northeast. Confining its activities primarily in the more accessible lowland areas of the region; the valleys of Assam, Manipur and Tripura, Hinduism became by circumstances a discriminative religion. In the process, it not only earned the criticism of deliberately trying to exclude the upland tribal communities from its fold but also divided and polarized the entire Northeast between Hindu non-tribal ethnic groups and the tribal non-Hindus. The ethnoscape and identic equations would never be the same after its onset into the region.

Partly due to the complex nature of its philosophy and the lack of knowledge and understanding by its early converts in the region, Hinduism took many curious forms and shapes. Transposed into the region, it made many compromises and adjustments and became a highly esoteric and convoluted religion, mixing many pagan and indigenous religious practices with Hindu teachings, rituals and practices. It evolved into its own brand of Hinduism, becoming highly eclectic, quite different from the Hinduism found in other parts of the country.

The Precursor

Buddhism came to the Northeast region in two distinct phases and from two different directions as the first universal religion and left its indelible imprint. The first phase began in the twelfth century ADE during the rule of the Senas in Bengal when it made inroads into the western periphery of present day Northeast region close to the Great Bengal plain. The second phase was around the sixteenth to the eighteenth century ADE when Buddhist immigrants entered the Northeast from Kachin in Burma, South East Asia and Southern Yunnan province of China.

The teachings of Buddha and Mahavira started much earlier in eastern India in Bihar and Bengal, and by the beginning of the first century ADE, the two religions covered almost every part of India. In fact, even before the Buddhism spread into what is now Bangladesh, Jain Tirthankar Mahavira had stayed in Pundranagara (probably in a place known as Basu Vihara) and converted people to Jainism in the sixth century BCE[1]. A large number of Buddhist monuments, stupas, and edicts are found in Bihar, West Bengal, especially in places like Rajgriha, Vaishali, Nalanda, Gaya, Bodh Gaya and Magadha, signifying the spread of Buddhism. In the northeast region, however, there is no find, which is anywhere near in scale to the ones in either West Bengal or Bihar. As per the 2001 Census of India, only 1.35 percent of the total populations in the Northeast including Sikkim profess Buddhism. The States of Sikkim has 28.17 percent, Arunachal Pradesh 13.14 percent and Mizoram 7.94 percent of their population as Buddhists.

When Heuen Tsang (Xuanzang) visited different parts of Bengal, he found many followers of Vedic religion, Jains and Buddhists of almost equal numbers. The teachings of Buddhism spread as far as China. Heuen Tsang (Xuanzang) and Fa Hien, took with them many Sanskrit manuscripts and imbibed the teachings of the Buddha and various Indian philosophical thoughts and discourses. These inputs had moderating influences on both China and India. According to Amartya Sen[2], these had *"a moderating influence on China's insularity"* and simultaneously, *"helped to moderate Indian self-centeredness and sense of civilisational exclusiveness"*. In fact, Buddhism in China, in the opinions of the Chinese intellectuals, created a tendency towards displacing the Chinese-world view by an Indo-centric-world view[3]. Fu-yi, a powerful Confucian in the seventh century complained to the Tang emperor, *"The people began to shave of their heads and refused to bow their heads to the Princes and their ancestors"*[4].

The influence of Buddhism in Bengal and in eastern India changed dramatically when the Senas who were Hindus succeeded the Palas in Bengal who were Buddhists, began to incinerate the Buddhists in the twelfth century ADE. It was during this period that large number of Buddhists left Bengal and sought refuge elsewhere nearby into what is now Bangladesh and the adjoining hills and mountainous areas. The famous Paharpur Monastery, the largest Buddhist monastery in the world in terms of single monastery coverage in Bangladesh is the testimony to these influences in history. The Chittagong Hill tract region, particularly the Sylhet and Mymensingh areas of Bangladesh, the plain areas of Bengal, the western rims of the Northeast covering present day Tripura, foothills of southern Meghalaya, western half of Mizoram and the hill tracts of western Assam all came within the influence of Buddhism.

According to many historians, this phase in the history of Buddhism marks the beginning of the 'decline of Buddhism' in India[5]. However, there are also those scholars who consider this phase; the so-called 'decline phase of Buddhism', actually as the starting of the great Buddhist movement when it truly became a universal religion by spreading across the world. In fact, in the views of Indologist late Dr. N.N. Bhattacharyya *"...the so-called decline of Buddhism in India was really a gradual assimilation of Buddhism into Hinduism"*[6] in which, Buddhism *"... acquired a functional significance of religious character"* (ibid.) of its own. Because of its ability to retain many attributes and influences from Hinduism, many Hindus *"...found no difference between the worship of Visnu and Buddha, Siva and Avalokitesvara, or Parvati and Tara."*[7]. The disapproval of animal sacrifice, organisation of monastic traditions prevalent among the Hindus on the lines of the Buddhist *"Sanghas, emphasis on image worship, prayers and incantations, pompous ceremonies and rituals, incorporations of many folk-beliefs, etc"* (ibid) are few examples of the similarities. Writing about the Haihayas of Tripuris R.D. Banerji[8] observed *"...many of its elements were absorbed by the existing systems like Saivaism and Vaisnavism"*. In fact, according to D.C. Sircar[9], the so-called distinction between Hinduism and Buddhism thereafter became an 'artificial distinction'. It is these similarities between Hinduism and Buddhism, which made assimilation and acceptance of each other quite easy.

One of the distinctive contributions of Buddhism in the Northeast region is that it created the necessary conditions conducive for Hinduism to find its bearing in the region. This was possible because of the similarities in the basic tenets and concepts of Hinduism with many schools of Buddhism. These similiarities influenced and facilitated the acceptance of Hinduism in the region. An example is the influence of Sahajayana Buddhist sect on Vaishnavism, particularly on Shri Chaitanya Mahaprabhu, who has large followers in Assam, Manipur and Tripura. Similarly, Buddhism greatly influenced the Dharma cult of Bengal, which has followers in Bengal and in the adjoining areas including the western periphery of the Northeast.

In addition, many believe that Buddhism has many similar tribal attributes and characteristics[10]. Dr. R.C. Majumdar[11] observes that the basis on which the foundations of the Buddhist Sanghas are modeled are in conformity with the three principles of equality, democracy and absence of private ownership of property, the main characteristics of tribal societies. A number of tribal customs, rituals and social practices like tribal initiations of its members as a full member of the tribe, the need for sanctions by the elders of the clan on various occasions, the rituals of adoptions are similar to those practices and rituals found in the Mahavagga sect of Buddhists. The concept of the symbolic union, of Radha and Krishna reflected in Jayadev's famous Gitagovinda espoused by Chaitanya Mahaprabhu, is the influence of the Buddhist Sahajayana sect, an offshoot of Mahayana Buddhism on the Vaishnavaits. According to Dr. N. N. Bhattacharyya[12] the Buddhist Sahajayana sect has links with various Tantric systems practiced by many Hindus. Similarly, the Hindu Dharma cult widely practised in West Bengal is an amalgamation of various Hindu and Vajrayana Buddhism, which M.M. Haraprasad Shastri[13] describes as 'Living Buddhism'. There are numerous examples of the reciprocal influences between the various sects of Buddhism and Hinduism.

Many scholars find semblance between the asceticism practised by Lord Siva in Hinduism with what the Buddha practised throughout his life, of renouncing the world and going into the life of hermitage and seclusion. Similarily, Lord Siva is characterised with unkempt hair and beard, wearing the skin of animals, with snakes curled around, akin to the stage in which Buddha placed himself at the peak of his search for 'Nirvana'. Siva "*...was* *modeled on... Buddha. Siva was often identified with Buddhist Avalokiteswara. The iconic form of Buddhist Nilakantha Lokesvara is similar to that of Siva"*[14](sic). The humanization of Siva has many similarities with Buddha who sacrificed every worldly desire or object and lived a very frugal and simple life. The identification of Shiva with Buddha marks an important point of convergence between Hinduism and Buddhism. Thus, even though Buddhism is an 'offshoot' of Hinduism and hence comparatively of a later development as a religious movement it preceded Hinduism in the Northeast region of India, and facilitated the acceptance of Hinduism in the region. In fact, Buddhism was the link between the pagan indigenous religions and Hinduism in the Northeast.

In the Northeast, many scholars[15] link Buddhism with Assam, through a place called Sualkuchi near Hayagriva-Madava temple at Hajo, Nalbari District in Western Assam close to Guwahati where there is a belief that the *mahaparinirvana* of the Buddha took place there. Other legends attribute the cremation of the relics of the Buddha in Hajo. One can find a number of icons of the Buddha in many different parts and places of Assam. King Dhitika, the successor to Upagupta is responsible for the spread of Buddhism in Assam. Even though controversy still exist regarding the fact as to whether Buddhism actually found its roots in Assam[16] before Heuen Tsang (Xuanzang) visited India during the reign of the Guptas, Buddhism had established itself in Eastern Bihar, Northern Bengal, Assam and present Northeastern India.

The second phase of the influence of Buddhism in the Northeast began around the 17th to the 18th century when Buddhist followers entered the Northeast from the Southern Chinese borders, East and Southeast Asia. This phase is quite distinct and separate from the earlier phase when Buddhism came into the Northeast region in the 12th century from Bengal. These Buddhists came as immigrants through the many mountain passes in the eastern periphery of the Northeast. Some of the important passes are the Pangsau, Chaukan, Hpungan (in Changlang district), Kumjawati and Diphu (in Lohit district), Kaya Pass, Tsang Kang Pass (Augla La), Yongvap Pass, Andra Pass, all in the Dibang valley in East Siang district in the erstwhile North Eastern Frontier Province (Arunachal Pradesh).

Traces of Buddhism pertaining to the second phase are found among the Tai-Phakes community in the Eastern plains of Upper

Assam, in a village called Namphake located about six kilometers from Naharkatiya town, which is thirty-seven kilometers from Dibrugarh close to the banks of the river Burhi Dihing, a tributary of the Brahmaputra. The Buddhist monastery at Namphake village is believed to be built in 1850[17]. According to Sir Edward Gait in his book 'History of Assam', the Tai-Phakes were first residents on the banks of the Nam Turung or Turung pani in Assam. The Tai-Phake is a subsidiary group of the Tai race in the Indo-Chinese peninsula, who entered Assam in the latter half of the 18th century. The Tai-Phakes community resides in Tipamphake, Borphake, Man Mau, Nam Chai, Man Long, Nang Lai, Ning Gum and Phaneng in Assam, while in China they are found in Kwangsi, Hainan and in the interiors of Yunnan provinces. They are known as Shan in Myanmar (Burma), Siamese in Thailand, and Lao in French Indo-China and Pai in Yunnan in China. People of the Thai-Burmese origins, like Khampti, Singpho, Zekhring and Chakmas follow Buddhism, while the Theravada Buddhism sect is widely practised in Lohit, Tirap and Changlang areas in present day Arunachal Pradesh. All these three districts of Arunachal Pradesh are the eastern-most districts of the state abutting Kachin and Sagaing states of Myanmar (Burma) along the Patkaibum Ranges.

Briefly, the major impact of Buddhism in the Northeast is the conceptual affinities found between its teachings with Hinduism and the various indigeneous tribal religions of the region prevalent at that time. Buddhism played a pivotal role in preparing the arrival of Hinduism into Northeast India. In one way, therefore, Buddhism was the precursor to Hinduism in the Northeast, even though Buddhism historically is an offshoot of Hinduism.

Principles of Hinduism

Hinduism is not a religion, in the sense that it differs in many ways from the traditional classical definitions of religion. For instance, unlike all the major religions of the world, Hinduism has no founder, as there is no single founding personality or 'originator', a single source to be definitively assigned as the 'progenitor'. Islam has Mohammed, Christianity has Jesus Christ, Judaism has Moses, Buddhism has Buddha, Jainism has Mahavira, and Sikhism has Guru Nanak so on and so forth. Hinduism also does not have a specific scripture, which encompasses the philosophy and essence of Hinduism as the Christians have the Bible (The Old or the New Testament), Islam has the Koran, and Sikhism has the Guru Granth

Sahib. Further, there is no single dogma or doctrine, which all Hindus must necessarily conform to or agree with. The exponents of Hindu religion also point out that even though it is one of the oldest of religions it has never invaded another country in the name of Hinduism.

Because of the plurality and vastness of its definition and meaning, no words can define it better than the two adjectives, *Vasudhaiva Kutukbakam*, which in Sanskrit means 'tolerance and pluralism', implying that the universe is one large family where all are equal. All things large and small and all organism are manifestations of God and hence universally acceptable and lovable. The philosophical concept enshrined in Hinduism is; *Ekam sat vipraha bahudha vadanti*, the famous Sloka Swami Vivekanand recited in the World Parliament of Religions in 1893, which translated means; *"...that which exists is One; sages call It by various names"*. Hinduism is 'limitless' and 'boundless' in its outlook and has no definable boundaries as a concept. In this context, Hinduism has never assumed the role of being the only sanctimonious haven through which everyone must traverse to find salvation and peace. David Ludden sums up the concept of Hinduism: *"The idea that define Hinduism as a religion, therefore, deeply discourage the formation of collective Hindu religious identity among the believers and practitioners"*[18]. More appropriately, it makes more sense to use the term Hinduism in its generic connotation. Hinduism is too diverse, too broad based and encompasses concepts and ideas, to confine itself within the epistemic meaning of the definition of religion too rigidly.

It is this ubiquitous nature of Hinduism encompassing a much wider connotation involving both religious and secular elements in its definition, which makes it unique. Identifying it purely as a religion devoid of its multifaceted attributes is to circumvent its true character. It is all these essence and attributes that makes Hinduism truly a universal religion.

Students of comparative theology will understand that religion influences and simultaneously also imbibes many of the social and cultural attributes to which it is exposed. Any discourse on Hinduism is incomplete if only its implied generic connotations are given and explained. Because of its long history, there are many interpretations and adaptations of Hinduism, which in some respects has confused the uninitiated. However in spite of all these, Hinduism is in one way the simplest of all religions, since it has the omnificence to let its believers the freedom to interpret it the way they choose to do. The exponents of Hinduism believe in the universality of all religions and that no one religion is better than what the others are. It is this unique philosophical accommodative spirit enshrined in Hinduism, which is its greatest appeal and ironically also its weakness.

Hinduism has not taken to religious conversions in a mission-mode because of its catholicity, accommodativeness and tolerance. Many see these positive aspects and qualities as its inherent weakness. The principle that every human being has the potentiality to self-actualisation, and also to determine and chose their own faith and religious beliefs, and that each person can achieve the goal of redemption or salvation in their own unique way, distinguishes it from many other religions. It believes that there is no single path to salvation or emancipation. Hinduism with its long history, vast reservoir of knowledge and scholarship is a formidable religious institution, but how much of these attributes actually found way into the Northeastern region is what determines its success in the region.

As a religion, the term Hinduism is of comparative recent origin. The term is associated with the Sanskrit name for the river Indus in Sindu on which its history began. The Persians called the vast lands between the rivers and the people of the region as Hindu instead of Sindu. Hinduism therefore is a collative term to denote the compilation of the various social and life-styles of the people of Sindu in their geographical context. Hinduism derived its name initially denoting a race or group of people who occupied a geographical space, living their way of life and following the religion of their choice. It is much later that Hinduism as a religion spread across to many other regions and lost its geographical specificity, giving it its universal character. However, for many, especially in the Northeast, Hinduism is a religion of the great Indic Gangetic and Indus civilisation, essentially an epitome of the Aryan civilisation. It is this association to an alien-culture and life-style, quite different from theirs, which is the main inhibiting factor in accepting it in the region, especially among the upland tribal communities.

Hinduism has a number of sects but only a few of these are relevant in the context of the Northeast. Of these, the three basic divisions of Vaishnavas, Saivas and the Saktas are the most conspicuous because of their influence in the region. The Vaishnava worship Vishnu, the Saivas; Siva and the Saktas, Devi or Mother. The Chaitanya sect of Vaishnavism prominent in Bengal and Orissa founded by Chaitanya Mahaprabhu (Born in 1485) is the most dominant sect in the context of the Northeast. The Vaishnavism referred in the context of the Northeast region excludes the Sampradaya, Ramanandis, Vallabhacharins, Nimbarkas, Maghavas and other sects. The followers of Chaitanya Mahaprabhu further, through the Brahma-Madhava-Gaudiya Sampradaya introduced a particular type of Vaishnavism through succession, known as Gaudiya Vaishnavism. Both forms of Vaishnavism, particularly Gaudiya Vaishnavism under Chaitanya played important roles in both Assam and Manipur.

Assam

Hinduism in Assam

Erstwhile kingdom of Pragjyotisha now Assam embraced the whole of the present Northeast region, excluding the two kingdoms of Manipur and Tripura. It is composed of mountains, hills and a large river valley in which the mighty river Brahmaputra flows. The Ahoms who came from the east in the 13th century ADE replaced the Bodos, authochtons of the kingdom. The topography of the kingdom slopes from east to the west towards the Great Bengal Plains, through which several rivers from the Northeast flow into the Bay of Bengal. Pragjyotisha epitomizes rare civilisational legacies of influences and associations in its long acculturated social, cultural and political history. The mountains and hills are the home of the hundreds of upland tribal and various ethnic groups who have come from all directions into the kingdom, creating its own socio-cultural ethos and sensibility.

Hinduism is the first universal religion, which brought the comparatively isolated region into the main stream of Aryan Hindu civilisational history. Hinduism came to Assam through the rivers from Bengal where Hinduism was widely prevalent. It established itself through royal patronage in the 14th century ADE and in three distinct phases[19]. There are however claims of Hinduism finding its way into Pragjyotisha or Kamrupa, present day Assam, when Brahmanism or Bamons, a sub-sect of Hinduism found its way into Assam much earlier during the fourth and fifth century ADE among the members of the royal families, the caste-Hindus and few others. This school believes that the process of Hindunisation of Assam began with the Varman or Barman Dynasty of Assam who ruled Assam in two phases, and its influence was restricted in the Western half of the Brahmaputra valley among the ruling families of the Khems, the Koches and the Bhuyans in the first phase. Later, in the second phase, it spread to the Eastern Brahmaputra valley, among the 'Plain tribals'; the ruling family of the Chutiyas, Kacharis, Maras and the Barahis. The main expansion of Hinduism in Assam began only in the 16th century[20].

Dr. S.L. Baruah one of the exponents of this school of thought, who believe Hinduism, came to Assam in the fourth and fifth century ADE in her well-documented book, 'Comprehensive History of Assam', however believes there are more than two phases of its expansion. The first phase of Hinduism began with the Brahmanic influence during the Varman or Barman dynasty beginning with 350 ADE until 594 ADE, and again from 790 to 910 ADE[21]. It was during the reign of the Varman or Barman that a settlement of about 200 Brahamanas came up in a place in Pundravardhana Bhukti on a land donated by King Bhuti Barman (510-555 ADE) between 545-550 ADE. Their influence continued until the beginning of the Ahom rule in the first half of the 13th century. The Varman or Barman dynasties also setup many Agrahara settlements for Brahamanas among the non-Aryan races, but the exact locations are still not very clear. Many historians believe that Pundravardhana Bhukti is located in a place bounded by the dried river of Kausik in the east and the Ganganika in the west[22] in present North Bengal. Whether these settlements resulted in conversion of the local people to Hinduism during the Barman and early period of the Pala dynasty in Assam is unclear.

The second phase began with the reign of king Sudangpha (1397-1407 ADE) also known in history as 'Baamuni Kunwar', almost 150 years after the first Ahom ruler Sukapha entered Assam in 1228 ADE from Molung in Upper Burma and founded the Ahom kingdom in Charaideo in 1253 ADE. It was during this period that the Brahmanic influence and process of Hindunisation began extensively in Assam. It took another 250 years before another Ahom king, Jayadwaj Xingha or Jayadhvaj Singha (Bhoganiyaa Rojaa) (1648-1663 ADE), formerly embraced Hinduism essentially to propitiate the gods to atone for patricide[22]. The subsequent attrition within the Hindu religious movement took place because of the support accorded to Vaishnavism, a later entrant into Assam by the successors of Jayadhvaj. This attrition continued until the reign of Sulikphaa also known as Loraa Rojaa (1679-1681 ADE).

King Gadadhar Singha or Godhaadar Xingha (1681-1696 ADE), who succeeded Sulikphaa strongly advocated Saktism and persecuted the Vaishnava Mahantas and Gosains. Following this royal preference, Saktism became the accepted religious sect among the royalties, principal nobles and officers, while Vaishnavism became the religious sect of the common people in Assam. The rulers in Assam supported both Saktism and Vaishnavism, for political and social harmony. King Sutanpha or Xiba Xingha or Siva Singh (1714-1744) became a Shakti worshipper and joined the cult through one Krisnaram Bhattacharya, who later became the head priest of the Kamakhya temple situated on Nilachal Hills near Guwahati.

King Sutanpha known for his religious frame of mind and total dependence on astrological beliefs ruled through his wives, first by Queen Phuleswari and later after her death, through his second wife, the younger sister of Queen Phuleswari whom he married based on astrological advice. King Sutanpha built many 'mandirs' or temples including the famous Shiva mandir in Sibsagar known as Shiva Dol, Dhai Ali, Gauri sagar tank and the Sibsagar tank. Thus while Sutanpha was a Sakti worshipper, the general population followed Vaishnavism, which was popular and mass-based. In spite of being a Sakti worshipper the ruler was compelled to support Vaishnavism because it had become very popular among his subjects and also because he could not openly disagree with the Satras or monastic bodies, which administered and managed the affairs of the temples including the vast tracts of land for maintaining the temples. In addition, even though the rulers of Assam were followers of Hinduism, they were compelled to support the traditional Ahom indigenous religious rituals and ceremonies performed by the Deodhais or traditional Ahom priests to propitiate traditional religious beliefs for the benefit of the subjects. The balancing act was difficult.

Deviations

From the various evidences and records available, it is clear that the Brahmanic Hinduism began in Pragjyotisha or Kamrupa, essentially as a religion of the elite, the royal families, nobles and the upper echelons of Assamese societies. The Brahmin or Bamons, the high-class priests in the traditions of Hinduism everywhere, nurtured Hinduism and gave a niche for itself among this class of people. Because of its elitist beginnings and air of exclusivity, it remained for many years a religion of a selected class of people only, leaving out the common people. Further, by its elaborate ceremonies and rituals the importance of the religious contents shifted from the essence to the mundane. This confused the new converts.

Hinduism underwent changes and transformations in Assam, creating new sects and forms by assimilating many local indigenous religious practices and concepts eventually evolving into an esoteric religion. Many Hindu sects and sub sects like Saivaism and Saktism[23] became popular among the common people. Saivaism especially became popular based on the belief that Lord Siva is Hindu god for the poorer sections of the Hindu society, since in the annual visit of Durga to her poor parent's house, Siva stays with them sharing whatever they had. The aesticism and frugal life style of Shiva greatly appealed to the poorer sections of the society and with whom they could identify themselves easily.

Both Saivism and Saktism assimilated several aspects of the indigenous faiths, beliefs and pagan practices, making them highly complex and obfuscated religious sects. This infusion introduced elements of the cult of magic and occultism into Hindu religion making it much more alluring and appealing in Assam. For instance, Tantricism with its exotic and intensely pervasive cult attracted many followers, partly because it had assimilated many aspects of indigenous practices of animism and paganism prevalent in the region. In contrast to the very orthodox Brahmanical order, Tantiricism with its esoteric association with occultism appealed to the general psyche of the people at that time primarily because it accepted five elements, namely madya (wine), mangsa (flesh), matsya (fish), mudra (parched grain) and marihuana (sexual union) as essentials. It is believed that the Ahoms propitiated human sacrifices[24] that took place at Kamakhya, Kechai-Khati and Jayanteshwari temples.

It is evident that Vaishnavism, Saivism, Saktism and Tantricism eveloved in Assam but these differed from the mainstream beliefs and practices proliferating elsewhere in India. *"Fetishism, animism, cult of fertility, human sacrifice, ancestor worship etc. which were prevalent among the non-Aryan people of Assam, as elsewhere in India, passed on to Hinduism, and molded its character which became manifest in new local forms"*[25]. Because of these factors the region, particularly Assam got the vilificatory connotation of a land full of magic, occult and Tantricism. Unfortunately, this impression persists among many Indians even today.

As observed, Hinduism and its sub-sects took a distinctive form in Assam partly due to the apparent need of the royal families who were Siva worshippers and other Hindu deities, were also compelled to follow the esoteric forms of the traditional indigenous rites practised by the people. King Naranarayan for instance allowed his followers to worship Siva according to tribal customs and offer animal sacrifices. Many believe that this was to prevent disputes between the followers of Brahmanism and other sects like Saivaism, Saktism and other forms of Hinduism. This had its inherent merits and salutary effect since it generated interests in Hinduism among the Bodos-Kacharis, the Koch and Mech the Plain-tribal communities of Assam who eventually became the first Hindu converts among the tribals in Assam.

In its historical perspective, Assam therefore professed Brahmanism to begin with, essentially among the royalty, nobility, upper echelons and the intellectuals, but subsequently because of several factors, people began to adopt and follow other sub-sects of Hinduism. This mix of various sects and sub sects of Hinduism, combined with many aspects of indigenous faiths and religions, created a new genre of Hinduism with various esoteric formats of worship and reverence unique and sui generis to Assam. In this given situation while Hinduism, (Brahmanism) was largely practised and followed by the upper classes and intellectuals who were able to maintain most of its format by warding off the influence of extraneous indigenous religions, the brand of Hinduism followed by the masses were highly esoteric, a mix of sects and sub-sects of Hinduism with indigenous religious practices. The assortments of the various sub-sects and forms of Hinduism not only confused its followers but also in the process led to several digressions from the basic text and teachings of Hinduism. Because of the confused array of diverse influence of the various cults and sects, Hinduism over a period, became one of the main sources of social discrimination in Assam.

Hindu Religious Reforms

Mahapurusha Srimanta Sankardeva (1449-1568), a colossal figure and perhaps the greatest of the religious, cultural and social reformer of Assam was responsible for ending the confusion by rescuing Hinduism, more precisely Vaisnavism from the adverse consequences of the many divergent cults and practices that evolved in Assam. Bani Kanta Kakati described the pre-reform status of Hinduism in Assam in the following words. *"... the land was infested with itinerant teachers of the Vamacara tantric schools with the insistence on the philosophy of sex and the palate. Tantric brand of Sakta Hindu faith came to be overloaded by occult primitive practices and thereby was degenerated"*. Sankardeva changed all these. He brought about a renaissance in social and cultural ethos of Assam, and removed all the misgivings associated with Hinduism, which had affected the social and cultural fabric of Assam. Institutions like the Satras (Religious Training institutes) and the Namghar (village level common prayer halls) were set up.

Significantly, Sankardeva's idea of Neo-Vaisnavism and social reforms were quite distinct from the Bhakti movement launched in the country by Ramanuja (who died in 1137 ADE). Sankardeva, came in the scene much later only in the 16th century, yet the spirit of reform, which encompassed his entire reformist philosophy, the doctrine that accepts Bhakti as the means to realize the creator, brought a transformation in thinking and re-orientation about Hinduism and religious beliefs in general in Assam. He cleansed Assamese society of the evil and the obscurantist elements of Hinduism that had crept in over the years. Sankardeva gave character to Assamese religious sensibility and brought in refinement at par with the reformist movements in the rest of India. In the end, the Assamese's brand of Hinduism stood at par with the mainstream Aryan Hindu practices and standing.

Perhaps the greatest contribution of Sankardeva as a religious and social reformer was his role of cleansing the esoteric elements that had crept in Hinduism in pre-reform Assam. By doing this, he also indirectly removed the social stratification of the Assamese society among the Hindus by making Hinduism a religion of all categories of people irrespective of their political, social or economic status. The social stratification and religious-class divide, which was prevalent ended in the reign of Gaurinath Singh (1780-1795) towards the close of the 18th century ADE.

Sankardeva went over to the Koch kingdom, west of Assam, where king Naranarayan and his son Chillarai became his devotees. However, the Mahapurusha, an icon who brought religious and social reforms among the Assamese, in which new values and harmonization was accepted as the essence, could not himself do much to spread the Hindu religion among the tribals living in the hill areas of Assam.

Hindu Identity in Assam

The Hindu identity of Assamese society traces itself back to the history of its expansion. Hinduism came into Assam for the first time in the form of Brahmanism, assimilating and evolving latter into distinctive forms of Saivism and Saktism unique to the kingdom. Vaishnavism came into the region later as a counterbalance to Saivism and Saktism. Brahmanism as a religion was elitist confined as it did to the higher echelons of the Assamese society. In the process, it created a socio-religious divide within the Assamese society, between the followers of Brahmanism and those who were not. The exclusivity created its own aura of superiority among its followers.

While Brahmanism was essentially a religion of the nobility and the upper echelons of Assamese society Saivaism, Saktism, Vaishnavism and Tantricism, which had assimilated elements of black magic, occultism and elements of obscurantism, were popular in Assam. These evolved alongwith the needs of the masses and soon became their religion. All these sects also assimilated many indigenous religious practices, religious rites and rituals of the plain tribals like the Bodos and Kacharis. Rock carvings and stone blocks found in the state are evidence of this unique convergence of Shiva-Shakti worship with Vaishnavism and also with indigenous religions.

The associated class and social distinction introduced by Brahmanism on one side and Saivaism, Saktism, Vaishnavism and Tantricism on the other, the former for the royalty and the elite and the latter, for the common people created two distinct categories of Hindu identities in the kingdom. This aspect of Hinduism in the long run created problems in bringing the upland tribal communities of the kingdom within the fold of Hinduism, even though it succeeded extremely well in bringing the Plain-tribal communities into its fold. Hinduism in Assam in the process created two sets of ethnic identities; the Assamese, essentially confined to people of the plain areas and the excluded non-Assamese comprising of upland tribal communities who were left out of the Hindu fold. This distinction would eventually cast its ominous shadows, affect socio-ethnic equations, and give rise to ethnic identity politics in the state.

Manipur

The Beginning

Manipur comprises of a large central valley (plateau) surrounded by seven ranges of hills and mountains. The hills and mountains cover three fourth of its total area while only one third of its territory form the valley area. The highest peak is Essau Tenipu (9824 ft) in Mao close to the Nagaland borders. The boundaries of Manipur once extended much beyond its present boundaries. In the East its borders touched the Chindwin River (Myanmar), covering almost the entire Kabow valley in Burma and to the West its territories included present day Silchar and Cachar districts of Assam and parts of Sylhet and Mymensingh in Bangladesh. The west flowing rivers, Barak, Irang, Makru and Ijei, join the river Surma in Cachar district of Assam. These rivers along with the various mountain passes connect Manipur to the Bengal Plains in the west and to the east into what is Myanmar now and South East Asia. These routes provided the much needed connections and cultural corridors through which political, social, cultural and religions exchanges took place. Hinduism and Brahmanic influences came to the kingdom through the western routes.

The transformation of Manipur, especially the Meitei community from a kingdom of believers in Sanamahi, the indigenous religion into a predominant Hindu kingdom is fascinating and socio-politically significant. Many Manipuri scholars however see this transformation of the Meiteis, as denization of the Meiteis. The process of Hindunisation or Sanskritisation is a classic example of how an essentially tribal people with a strong attachment and affinity to their indigenous roots and ethos can transform itself completely because of religion. It is however the socio-political and cultural divide introduced by Hinduism in the erstwhile kingdom by polarizing the two main ethnic groups, the Meiteis and the upland tribal communities, which is important from the history of ethnic identity formation in Manipur.

In the latter half of the 17th century, the Burmese overran and occupied almost the entire Kingdom for seven years. The ruler and

Manipuri Meiteis went into exile in many parts of present day Assam, Tripura, and in Sylhet and Mymensingh in present-day Bangladesh. It was during the seven years of Burmese occupation of Manipur, locally known as 'Chahi Taret Khunthakpa' or 'Seven years exile' that the Meitei rulers met Bengali religious scholars and intellectuals, who ultimately introduced Hinduism into the Meitei society. These contacts during the 'seven years exile' would change the religious, social and cultural milieu and history of Manipur, marking the end of paganism and tribal affiliations.

King Charairongba (1697-1709) was the first ruler of Manipur who embraced the Nimandi sect of Hinduism founded by one Nimbarkacharya, a Vaishav preacher in 1703. His son Meidingu Pamheiba (1709-1748) ADE, popularly known in history by his Hindunised name as 'Garib Niwaz' was next. One Gopal Das converted King Meidingu Pamheiba to Vaisnavism in 1717. It was however one Shanti Das Goswami a Bengali religious scholar belonging to the Ramandi cult who influenced Pamheiba to transform Manipur into a Vaishnavite Hindu kingdom, a process that was completed in 1737. There is however, another version in which one Krishnacharya, a south Indian Brahman from Bengal, converted king Pamheiba to Hinduism or more precisely Vaishnavism. Many historians, however, believe that the Hindunisation process in the kingdom was complete when Gaudiya Vaishnavism of Bengal later became the main form of Hinduism during the reign of King Bharata Sai. Whatever are the roles played by Gopal Das, Shanti Das Goswami and Krishnacharya, Vaishnavism and particularly the sect founded by Chaitanya Mahaprabhu also known as Lord Gauranga, which began in Bengal during the 15th century ADE, became the adopted form of Hinduism in Manipur.

There was a dramatic transformation and attitudinal change in the Meitei community following the conversion of king Pamheiba to Hinduism. The indigenous Sanamahi religion of the Meiteis was immediately banned becoming the first casualty of Hinduism in the kingdom. Historical records, royal chronicles, manuscripts, books of antiquity and anything connected with the indigenous religious practices of the Sanamahi were destroyed indiscriminately, the followers persecuted mercilessly and whatever elements of the indigenous religious influences remained were deliberately removed by the orders of the king. Heaps of these valuable records and documents were consigned to the flames, some say in the market places for everyone to see and witness. It was a major social and cultural purge of immense significance. The episode is known as 'Puya Meithaba' or the 'burning or torching of the Puyas' (Puyas are ancient Chronicles) in the history of Manipur. The Brahmans or Bamons replaced the traditional priests known as Meitei Maichous in the Loisangs (temples).

The concept and idea of the indigenous Meitei pantheons were systematically destroyed. Similarly, there was a ban in the singing of ancient and traditional songs, including the use of the ancient Manipuri 'Meitei Mayek' or script. People were told that singing songs written in the Meitei Mayek script would transform them into owls and if they die in the night, they would turn to crows. Other versions spoke of stories where people who committed similar offences would, when they die in the day, be flown to the Makoi-nungoi-ching, a hill associated with sorcery and evil spirits. Social scientists consider these versions of stories as attempt to make people severe their links with their 'ignominious pagan past'.

Thus while the Vaishnavite Hindus consider the introduction of Hinduism a major and significant event in Manipur's history, and the role played by Pamheiba as a great social and religious reformer, many others consider his role as socio-historically cataclysmic. Understandably, the practitioners and followers of the Sanamahi religion consider Pamheiba as an iconoclast and an agnostic who deliberately severed Manipur's link with its pagan past. Since the Sanamahi religion intrinsically embodies what is truly Meitei social sensibility and ethos, its insensitive destruction in one sense, greatly harmed the egalitarian and inherent plural character of Meitei society. This mindless random destruction and severance of its ancient identity, would later affect the social and cultural equations and relations between the Meitei community and the upland tribal population of Manipur. The adoption of Hinduism by the Meitei community at the expense of their pagan and tribal ways of life therefore, ended the age-old connections and ties between the Meiteis and the upland tribal communities of the kingdom. Sir Edward Gait in his well known book, *A History of Assam*, describes Pamheiba, ruler of Manipur, as "a Naga chief", of tribal origin from the hills, who by an ironical twist of circumstances, instead of trying to retain his tribal connections and ancestory, actually destroyed it.

Following the conversion to Hinduism from a tribal society, the Meiteis became highly orthodox and conservative. A class of newly converted Hindu zealots emerged in Manipur who in their newfound enthusiasm not only destroyed their own native religion and its history but also unconsciously projected a wrong image of Hinduism as an intolerant religion to the non-Hindus in the kingdom. To make matters worse, whatever residual attributes of the traditional indigenous religious faith, social, cultural and indigenous customs remained were either reinterpreted or made to conform and accommodate Hindu religious teachings and beliefs. The Puranic gods like, Shiva, Hari, Ganesha, Laskmi, Saraswati etc. became reincarnations of the Meitei pantheons.

Similarly, the famous pagan Lai-haraoba, the dance forms of the Maibas and the Maibis, (traditional priests and priestesses) were reformatted, adapted to conform and choreographed appropriately to accommodate the Hindunised classical Raasa Lilas during Chingtam Khomba alias Bhgayachandra's reign (1764-1798). Dance became one of the most important forms of religious discourse, even though the Meiteis did not understand the songs and kirtans, since these were sung in Bengali. It was during his reign that the Gouriya form of Hindu religious life-style of Bengal was introduced into the Meitei society. It became fashionable for the people to follow this form of orthodox life-style in their daily chores.

Pamheiba, ironically was killed just as he had killed his father, in 1748 by Shyam Shai his eldest son and Ajit Shai, his son from the second queen, some say accidentally, while many others believe deliberately as a religious retribution by the followers of the Atiya Shidaba Mapu or Sanamahi. In spite of all the greatness and efforts made by king Pamheiba, it is however Chingtam Khomba alias Jai Singh also popularly known by his Hindu name as Bhaigyachandra, grandson of Pamheiba, during whose reign Vaishnavism and Hinduism truly flourished in Manipur. Many historians see him as a pacifist, who brought the people of the hills and the plains together as his name Chingtam Khomba suggests. Expanded, the meaning of the name is 'Ching'=Hills, 'Tam'=Plains or valley and 'Khomba'=Unifier, or "The unifier of hills and valleys". Many believe that this name Chingtam Khomba, therefore, to be an appropriate epithet to describe one of the greatest rulers of Manipur.

Bhaigyachandra during his reign encountered Rajeshwar Singha (1751-1769), the Assam king during his exile in Assam. The romanticised version of the 'encounter' between the two is an extremely popular theme in local folklores. Not knowing Bhaigyachandra's identity as the king of Manipur, Rajeshwar Singha wanted him to prove his bona-fides by asking Bhaigyachandra to capture a wild rogue elephant single handedly. The popular version is that Bhaigyachandra without any weapon subdued the wild rogue elephant with divine intervention of Lord Govindaji (Lord Krishna), whom Bhaigyachandra had seen in his dream the night before. The event is accepted partly as a fable and partly as history. Bhaigyachandra ascended the throne of Manipur in 1764 with Rajeshwar Singha's help. In return, Bhaigyachandra gave his daughter Kurangonayani in marriage to Rajeshwar, reinforcing through the marriage the political contact between two Hindu rulers in the region. The heirs to these Manipuris who accompanied the princess as a bride have settled in Digchai in Assam.

Bengal the Transforming Agent

The conversion of the Meiteis to Hinduism has profound implications in the social and political history of the state, which saw a complete change in the attitude of the Meiteis towards the tribal population. The upland tribal communities began to look and treat the Meiteis suspiciously as a transformed and different people from the ones they knew or were familiar. The transformation of the Meitei community from their pagan way of life, as adherents of indigenous religious faith, which had many common attributes with the tribal faiths and beliefs to the Hindu ways of life, marked by extreme conservatism and orthodoxy, only reinforced the suspicion. The upland tribal community viewed the change in attitude of the Meitei's as an affront, an abrogation of the tribal and pagan way of life. The use of Bengali script, replacing the ancient Meitei Mayek or Meitei script, adoption of Bengali etiquette and lifestyles, marked the culmination of the drift of Meiteis from their old pagan and tribal ways of life. The changeover marked the end of the fraternisation and commarderie between the upland tribal and the lowland communities in Manipur.

The impact of conversion to Hinduism affected the Meitei community in many ways. (1) The Meiteis began to disown their own indigenous ethnicity, religion and social history. (2) They slowly detached themselves from their age-old ties and bonds with the many upland communities with whom they had close associations and shared history. (3) It transformed the character of the plural social ethos and sensibility of the kingdom, by dividing the people on religious lines, between the non-Hindu tribal communities and the Hindu Meitei community. (4) Hinduism introduced the concept of the 'pure' (Chengba) and the 'impure' (Mangba), in line with the socio-religious caste systems of the Hindu societies.

The phenomenon of social polarization between the Meiteis and the tribal communities of Manipur is not what many make out it to be, a simple act of social discrimination of the tribal communities by the Meiteis based on either ethnicity or their being tribals. The reasons are much more complex. This is evident from the fact that social discrimination and ostracisation exists even among the Meitei community itself, between those who are Hindus and those who are not. For instance, the Lois, Sekmais, Yaithibis and many other Meiteis who refuse to embrace Hinduism and instead follow the ancient Meitei indigenous religion are still ostricised by the Meitei society even today. These socially ostracized Meiteis continue to eat meat, are categorised as Scheduled Castes and reside in Andro and Shekmai, peripheral areas far from the areas occupied by Hindu Meiteis in the state. In an ironic twist of fate the 'pure' became the 'impure', and the 'impure' became the 'pure'.

It is therefore evident that the basis for social ostracisation in Manipur is purely religion-based segregation, between those who are Hindus and those who are not. The upland tribal communities like the Lois, Sekmais, Yaithibis and many other Meiteis, who were not Hindus, became victims of this social ostracisation. This observation is significant since there is a tendency to believe that the upland tribal communities of Manipur are discriminated merely because they are tribals, while the main reason for the social discrimination appears is that they are not Hindus. The much-hyped tribal non-tribal divide controversy is an afterthought, which arose later. In fact, analysis reveals that the ostracisation of people had nothing to do with the community or ethnicity but primarily because the upland tribal communities and people like the few Meiteis remained defient and failed to or refused to accept Hindu religion enforced by royal edict.

The paradox of the religious history of the Meiteis is that in spite of adopting Hinduism as their religion they have not completely dissociated or severed their affiliations and links with the traditional indigenous faiths and religions. Even today, in every Hindu Meitei home there is a designated corner known as 'Sanamahi kaachin' (Sanamahi's corner), normally the Northeastern corner which is dedicated to the Metei pantheon Sanamahi, and is held sacred. A lamp is kept burning at all times of the day and night. Many indigenous religious practices and precepts are revered and observed like the famous 'Andro fire', which is believed to have been burning ever since the beginning of the indigenous religion in Manipur. Many traditional hereditary customs, dance festivals like the Lai-Haroaba festival in Moirang, dedicated to the traditional gods and goddesses like Thanging, Nongpok Ningthou, Panthoibi, Lairembi and other gods and spirits, are a few examples kept alive and observed with traditional fervour and devotion just as it was in ancient times. Participating in these essentially non-Hindu festivities by the Hindu Meiteis is not a social taboo. In fact, attempts to reify their ancient pagan faith and beliefs is considered by many as a reassertion of their age-old tribal identity especially among the younger generations of Meiteis.

Atombapu Sarma: Manipur's Agastya[26]

It is in this background that the role of many prominent Meitei scholars and intellectuals, who espoused the cause of Hinduism, has come under a lot of cloud because of their role in attempting to foster Hinduism on the Meitei society at the expense of their pagan and native ethnic identity. The role of scholars and intellectuals like Pandita-Raja Atombapu Sarma Vidyaratna (31.1.1889 - 2.8.1963) who advocated the Meitei-Indic connections is one such example.

Pandit Atombapu Sarma was born into a Brahman family at a time when Meitei society was at a religious and cultural crossroad; torn between the sentimental attachment to their pagan past and the rigorous onslaught of Hindunisation largely pioneered and enforced by royal diktat. Devoid of intellectuals of national imminence and stature, much of Manipur's rich social and cultural history, especially its fascinating religious historical legacy remained entombed in obscurity. Perhaps more than anybody from Manipur, Atombapu espoused the interests of the Meitei community of Manipur to Bengali scholars and intelligentsia. It is a fact that it was the solicitous consent, support of Bengal's intelligentsia and the efforts made by religious scholars like Atombapu, which gave respect and recognition to Manipur's socio-cultural status in India today. He won the attention and respect of the scholars and intellectuals from Bengal by his brilliant scholarly disposition and his ability to interact with them in their own branch of scholarship.

Brought up in the tradition of scholastic pursuits like his father Nikunjabihari, Atombapu showed exceptional flair for translating and interpreting the sacred Sanskrit Hindu texts into Manipuri. He was the Panditraja (Chief Priest), and was conferred the title of 'Vidyaratna' by His Highness Maharaja Sir Churachand Singhji KCSI, CBE of Manipur because of his immense scholarship and knowledge of astronomy, religion and above all as a Sanskrit scholar of great repute. He was fluent and had a special flair for Bengali language.

Single handedly he built the theoretical premises of the religious history of the Meiteis as being part of the Brahmanical traditions. In his world, Meitei Gods and Goddesses *Nongpok Ningthou* and *Panthoibi* became Shiva and Parvati. The indigenous dance forms of *Augri hangen, Ching kheirol, Kek-re-ke* and the *Lai Haraoba*, metamorphosised into the famous Rasa Lilas and gave the traditional pagan dance forms a Hindu religious orientation and connectivity through his various scholastic interpretations and narrations. Atombapu's efforts reinforced Manipur as a bastion of Vaishnavism Hindu faith in the Northeast. The intellectuals[27] and religious scholars in Bengal acknowledge this role. His greatness lay in his ability to carry the weight of his scholarship to the Bengal intellectuals with whom he could eruditely communicate.

In the context of the history of Hindunisation of the Meiteis, the pre-imminent role of Panditraja is undisputed, no doubt, but many of his critics find his attempts at harmonization of the Meitei traditions with Vedic origin factually incorrect. Similarly, quite many view his attempts at the reinterpretation of the Manipur History, as abrogating Manipur's ancient pagan ethos and traditions. Many Meiteis in Manipur, especially the followers and believers of the traditional Sanamahi and Meitei religion also consider his role as self-effacing and an iconoclast.

One has however to be fair and much more charitable to Atombapu. Given his intentions and the circumstances under which Atombapu played this pivotal role in projecting Manipur to the country as a civilisation of its own standing. His role and contribution is best remembered and judged purely as a Meitei Hindu scholar and philosopher and not as a politician or Administrator. This amplification is necessary because the Panditraja never dealt the subjects of his scholarships and interpretations circumvented by the terms and conditions of the rationalised world of political niceties or administrative conveniences.

Atombapu in his lifetime never reflected in all his writings, any animosity or prejudice against the upland communities of Manipur who were not Hindus. He kept politics out of his religious discourses. His contribution is best seen and judged therefore, as essentially what a religious scholar or intellectual would have done; to provide an erudite exposition of his world view of the Meitei society through his scholastic ingenuity, devoid of the necessary articulations of political checks and balances. There is a need to distinguish between Atombapu's contribution as a scholar of Hindu theology and the inadvertent role he might have played unconsciously as a political novice who did not understand the impact of political consternations his work would cause. A detached and objective view of this aspect seems desirable.

In hind-sight the role of Atombapu even though is seen and interpreted as politically naïve and socially paradoxical, an example of pure scholastic pursuit and study, the fact remains that the Manipuri Meitei community would not have been what it is today, an epitome of rich traditions, social and cultural legacy, had it not been for his significant contribution. Atombapu works deserve to be given their due share of credit for their own intrinsic value, content and scholarship. His position as an exponent of Brahmanical Hinduism in Manipur remains unassailable. The fact remains that irrespective of the criticism labeled against him Hinduism found in him an extremely erudite exponent and symbol of his desire to find a place for the Meitei community in it. Thus while many imminent Manipuri Meitei scholars like Prof. Nilkanta Sharma, L. Ibongohal, Dwijamani Sharma, R.K. Jhalajit Singh and others acknowledge Atombapu's role as a change-agent in the Hindunisation of Manipuri Meitei society, they also tacitly accept the immense harm this has caused to the multicultural ethos and sensibility of Manipur.

Dr. Suniti Kumar Chatterji, National Professor of India in Humanities who knew Atombapu personally during his lifetime sums the role of Atombapu as *"...attempting to harmonise the legends and the traditions of the Meitei people with the Brahmanical Puranas"* in his famous lectures on the Panditraja. Dr. Chatterji delivered two lectures at the Atombapu Sarma Memorial Lectures in Imphal in the second half of the 1960s on (1) India's Integration and Brahmanical Hindu Culture, and (2) A Present-day Rishi, an Agastya for Eastern India: Atombapu Sarma. (Quotes from both these lectures are provided in the later Sections of this book). Seen in perspective, in the context of the unabashed exercise and attempt to reinvent and re-interpretate the pagan past of Manipur to make it relevant in the Hindu-present, and without any substantial support from his compatriots, Atombapu[27] had to fall back on his own scholarship and self-cultivated knowledge while advocating his theses. The task was stupendous but accomplished it with aplomb.

In the context of the social history, works like the one accomplished by scholars and intellectuals such as Pundit Atombapu, is in a way only a stage of the continuous acculturation process and evolution of social and cultural ethos and values of every society that is forever changing and evolving. It is part of the long on-going and continuous process of tradition formation, which every society goes through without any sign of permanency.

Impact of Hindunisation

The Hindunisation of the Meiteis established the Vedic Hindunised links, predominantly through Bengal by abrogating socio-culturally Manipur's 'pagan' past. Even though this put the Meiteis in an elevated social pedestal in the social map and history of India, the assumed air of superiority over the tribal communities by the converted Hindu Meiteis had serious socio-political fallout in the kingdom. The tribal communities felt offended by the behaviour of the Hindu Meiteis. This had many adverse consequences on the social history and ethnoscape of the state. The transformation of the Meitei society destroyed the homogeneous social ethos and the multiculturalism of Manipur. Simultaneously, even among the Meiteis this led people like Naoria Phullo to start groups like the *Apokpa Marup* essentially a reaction against the Bengali Hindu influence on Meitei society by attempting to reify and revive the indigenous Sanamahi religion. This phase of the history of Manipur marks the beginning of the ethnic divide between the upland tribal communities of the state and the Meiteis.

It was the relentless pursuit of the exponents of Hinduism and Hindu scholars at that time, without hermeneutically analyzing the socio-political implication, especially of the adverse impact that Hinduism would have on the upland tribal communities, which is largely responsible for the social polarization in the state. A much more assiduously calibrated approach would have prevented the ethnic divide had the proponents of Hinduism been more discreet and circumspect.

The concept of *'amangba-achengba'* (untouchable and touchable or impure and the pure) in Manipur, which acquired importance in the wake of the Meiteis' conversion to Hindus, based on the socio-religious categorisation of people in the caste-system of Hindu societies, was a totally unknown classification of people in the region before Hinduism came. What should have been essentially a distinction of people based on their economic status and levels of poverty, instead morphed into the obnoxious caste-system of the Hindu society practiced elsewhere in India. Social segregation in Manipur like the concept of *'amangba-achengba'* (untouchable and touchable or impure and the pure) had to do more with the question of acceptability of Hinduism rather than with the community or caste of an individual. The ostracisation of the tribal communities by the Hindu Meiteis with whom the Meiteis had anthropological and historical links was most unfortunate.

In conclusion, it can be said that the solicitous nature of all religion affects human societies across the world and that the vilificatory connotation religion acquires are often due to the selfish exploitative nature of those who take advantage of the accommodative spirit of every religion. Manipur also suffered the same fate. The subsequent social ostracisation by the majority Hindu Meiteis of the upland tribal communities, who refused to convert to Hinduism is a brazen example of the damage religion can create or cause to ethnic relationship and societies without understanding or appreciating the essence of religious tolerance. Whatever the reason, the introduction of Hinduism into Manipur did immense harm to the unity, diversity of Manipur's social ethos and history.

Tripura

Geography and Demography

Geographically and physically, Tripura is the extension of the Great Bengal Plains. It comprises mainly of flatlands with the highest peak, the *Betling Sib* rising up to a height of 939 meters or approximately 3200 ft forming part of the north-south ridge in the Purbachal ranges. In the east, these hills merge with those in Mizoram, while in the west the land slopes down and merges into the river-plains of Bangladesh. Forty percent of the total area of the state comprises of valleys and the rest are uplands and hills. The state has 80 percent of its borders with Bangladesh, with only 20 percent with Assam and Mizoram in India. Demographically and ethnologically the various ethnic groups of the State spread out into a much larger area comprising the Surma valley in Assam, western fringes of Mizoram, the Sylhet region and the Chittagong Hill Tract in Bangladesh. Most of them are almost similar and identical having similar physical features, making it extremely difficult to segregate them one from the other.

Tripura has a fascinating anthropological and demographic history, which has witnessed one of the most dramatic changes in recent times. It is a melting pot of ethnic groups, comprising of those from the Bengal plains, mostly Bengali Hindus and Muslims, and the autochthons tribal groups of the state. From a predominant tribal kingdom comprising of autochthons tribes, sub-tribes and sub-sub-tribes called by the collective name as Tripuris, the kingdom became a predominant non-tribal state over a short period predominated by Bengali migrants. These indigenous autochthons were in majority until the beginning of the 20th century. The prominent tribes among them are the Tipras, Nuatia, Jamatia, Reang, Halans etc. Besides there are number of important sub-tribes like the Puratia, Koloi, Murasing, Rupinis etc. During 1901, the ratio between Tripuris, including Manipuris and a few other tribes was approximately 75 percent, while the Bengalis (both Muslims and Hindus) constituted the balance 25 percent. However, as per the Census of India 2001, the local tribal population has dwindled down to 32 percent of the population as against 68 percent of Bengalis, with the Muslim population among the Bengalis marginally coming down as compared to Bengali Hindus. At present the ethos and sensibility is essentially Bengali because of its proximity to erstwhile-undivided Bengal, now Bangladesh.

The demographic changes which took place in Tripura is closely related to what happened during the late 18th century and early 19th century in British-Indian history in Bengal. The introduction of the Permanent Settlement of 1793 in Bengal, replacing Muslim agents with British agents, combined with transfer of large estates to Hindu landowners[28] increased the tensions and animosity between the British administration and the Muslim landowners of Bengal. This affected the predominant rural agrarian economy and social order in Bengal, affecting the region all around Bengal including Tripura. The British policies led a number of Bengalis, both Hindus and Muslims to move elsewhere into other far-flung areas of the region. Tripura was one of the most convenient destinations.

The inflow of a large number of Bengali immigrants and landlords into Tripura led to the ethnic clashes between the local autochthons, the Tripuris and the Bengali immigrants to control the valuable flat fertile lands in the plain areas of Tripura. This increasing ingression of Bengalis, their social and cultural influences into the kingdom along with the increased presence of large number of illegal migrants overwhelmed and marginalised the autochthones Tripuris, their life-styles, including their indigenous religious beliefs. The various social, economic and other problems of displacement of the autochthons, the impact on their lifestyles and their way of life were unfortunately ignored.

Closely analysed, the social tensions between the local Tripuri population and the predominant Bengali immigrents from Bengal has less to do with religion, between the followers of Hinduism and Islam, but arises mainly because of the politics of land tenure and holdings. The subsequent rise of assertive ethnic identity politics among the Tripuris in the state is a reaction against the displacement of the local autochthones by Bengali immigrant land grabbers, labourers who not only deprive them of their land but whose growing numbers overwhelm their tribal way of life. The inherent contradiction and lacunae of land laws in the state, which is reflective of all tribal land tenures, which recognizes legally only individual ownership of land, without according similar legal title and ownership to the community owned lands makes it convenient for illegal immigrents to physically occupy these community lands with impunity.

Origin and name

Like all ancient civilisation, the state of Tripura has many interesting stories about its origin. Some trace its origin to a kingdom in present-day Uttarakhand in North India, then known as "Kar-Tripura" during the reign of Emperor Asoka. Some believe that it moved east into what is present-day Sikkim and was known as "Kirata desha" or "Kirata pura", and from where it moved over to its present location. However, the most fascinating one is the name derived from Hindu mythology.

In Sanskrit, according to the Hindu mythology, Tripura means the three cities (tri=three, Pura=city), which was built by the great architect Mayasura. As per the Hindu mythology, Tarakaksha, Vidyunmali and Kamalaksha, sons of Tarakara (who was killed by

Kartikaya) after severe penance obtained a boon from Lord Brahma to let them built a fortress that would be impregnable and everlasting. Lord Brahma granted the boon. However, unwilling to compromise the basic principle of the cosmic law that nothing is everlasting said that the city to be built could be destroyed by a single arrow only at one stroke. However since he knew an arrow of such immense power could be shot only by Lord Shiva and being a great devotee of Lord Shiva, Tarakara agreed to the condition given with the boon, knowing full well that Lord Shiva would never harm him. With Brahma's blessings, the great architect Mayasura was assigned to build such a fortress. Three separate cities one made of iron, another of silver and the third of gold were built and each located separately on earth, in the sky and in heaven respectively to form the impregnable city. The three cities were located in three different spatial and time zones. These cities revolved constantly in the three spheres so that the three cities could never be found at one given point of time and location except for a few moments once every thousand years.

Because of its indestructible reputation, the three cities became a popular city for the Asuras (evil) to flock around. The increased strength of the Asuras due to the fortification of the city slowly began to challenge the Devas (good). A battle between the Asuras and Devas eventually took place. In the ensuing battle, Lord Vishnu intervened and selected the precise moment both in time and space when all the three cities were aligned for a few moment in one line and at that instant fired his arrow, destroying the three cities and killing all the Asuras. Tripura carries the name of this fabled myth and story. It also carries the name of the pre-partition district of Tippera, now called Comilla in Bangladesh. Tripura was a kingdom until recently.

Unlike the two erstwhile kingdoms of Assam and Manipur where Hinduism was confined among the communities in the lowland or valley areas, leaving out the upland tribal communities in the uplands, in Tripura no such segregation took place. One of the main reasons Hinduism spread into Tripura was its close physical proximity to the Bengal plains, which surrounds the state from three sides. In less than a century, in a kingdom once predominantly tribal in character, leaving out a few areas where tribal and indigenous religion and way of life linger on, the rest of the state follows Hinduism. Hinduism has assimilated with many of the indigenous religious practices, deities, gods and goddesses quite seamlessly. This was possible because both Hinduism and the indigenous faiths and religions were polytheistic.

Non-Discriminative Hindu religion

As per the Census of India-2001, Hindus constitute 86.50 percent of the total population of the state, Muslims; 7.13 percent, Buddhists; 4.65 percent, Christians; 1.69 percent and others 0.05 percent. As against this, the ethnic breakup of the total population of the state is 32 percent comprising of Tripuris along with other local ethnic groups, while the Bengali Hindus and Muslims constitute 68 percent of the population of the state. It is evident from the statistics that Tripura is predominantly a Hindu state. What is interesting from the comparative analyses of the two statistics is that the local Tripuris and the dominant Bengali population follow Hinduism. More importantly, the statistics point out that there is no religious discrimination by the Hindus between the tribal and non-tribal population in Tripura. Second, this indicates that the ethnic animosity and tensions between the autochthonous Tripuris and the Bengalis in Tripura is not religious based but has to do more with land tenure and other issues.

Hindunisation in Tripura exist as Saktism, Saivaism and Vaishnavism, sub-sects of Hinduism and in a few places as an assimilation of the traditional indigenous religious practices with Hinduism. The Tripuris, the Reangs, Jamatia, Naotias, Kalai, Rupini and Halams have adopted Vaisnavism. The Naotias and the Halams are Sakti cult followers. The fusion between Hinduism and indigenous religious practices and customs are visible in various festivals among the Tripuris. For instance, every Tripuri household celebrates the festival of Hojagiri[29], which is synonymous with Laxmi puja among the Hindus. The Goddess Mailuma, the indigenous version of Laxmi, the Hindu goddess of wealth is transposed into Hinduism and is worshipped as one in Tripura. There is a celebration among the Reang community, a dance form celebrated throughout the night across the state which involve not only the body but also the mind and spirit, which many believe is essentially Hindu in character.

Further the Cantais (Tripuri High-priests) and Deodais, who are regarded as the custodians of the Tripuri traditional religions are accorded exalted status in social and cultural hierarchical position in the respective communities even among the Hindus. Simultaneously they also find pride of place in the Brahamanised

Hindu Tripura society. This religious tolerance and co-existence of traditional elements of indigenous religious beliefs side by side with Hinduism is a unique aspect of the history of the state. Hinduism in Tripura, like elsewhere in the Northeast region, exist in a syncretic fusion with many traditional indigenous religions to form a unique sect of Hinduism.

Buddhism came to Tripura essentially when many Buddhists migrated from Bengal to avoid persecutions in the hands of the Sena rulers of Bengal in the twelfth century. Many scholars also believe that various ethnic groups in the state came under the influence of the Arakan rulers in Burma, who converted them to Buddhism. Buddhism's influence in Tripura is substantial and important since out of over three hundred thousand (300,000) Buddhist population in the whole of the Northeast, approximately one hundred and twenty thousand (120,000) of them are in Tripura. Buddhism came to the state earlier than Hinduism in two phases and constituted 4.65 percent, the third highest religion numerically after Hinduism; 86.50 percent and Islam; 7.13 percent as per the Census of India conducted in 2001. The discovery of a few inscriptions dating back to the tenth and eleventh centuries in Tripura[30] traces the influence of Saivaism and the Mattamayura Buddhist sect. The Chakmas and Marmas from the Hill tracts of Tripura are Buddhits.

Other aspects of Hinduism

Discrimination?

One of the most significant impact of Hinduism on the three states of Assam, Manipur and Tripura, is the introduction of the concept and idea of religious identity. Hinduism by failing to embrace the upland tribal communities into its fold not only became a religion of the people and communities in the plains or valley areas of the region but also brought about the social polarization and ethnic divide between the non-Hindu tribals and the predominant Hindu non-tribals. The vilificatory adage accorded to Hinduism, as a 'discriminative' religion, a popular perception among the upland communities was the 'exclusion' of the upland tribal communities by Hinduism in the Northeast. The upland tribal communities of the region embraced Christianity with a vengeance, essentially as a reaction against their repudiation by Hinduism.

The religious 'divide', which became much more pronounced and conspicuous after Christianity was adopted by the upland tribal communities, marks the beginning of the unfortunate phase in the history of the region when religion got itself entangled with ethnic identity politics. There are various causes responsible for the 'exclusion' of the upland communities from Hinduism. However, whether the 'exclusion' of the upland tribal communities by the Hindus in the region was a deliberate act or the result of unintended collateral damage arising out of factors beyond its control needs further elaboration.

There are two schools of thought on the issue. One group, primarily the upland tribal communities, feels that their exclusion was deliberate. They feel that it was the social prejudice arising out of the inherent orthodoxy and conservatism of Hinduism, which is responsible for their exclusion from becoming Hindus. On the other hand, there are those who are more charitably disposed and believe that the 'exclusion' was due to circumstances, a byproduct of the difficult physical terrain, and inaccessibility into the areas occupied by the upland tribal communities, which prevented the Hindu missionaries from going there and converting them.

On the face of available facts, it is true that the unfortunate exclusion of the tribal and upland communities appears highly discriminative and selective. Equally significant is also the fact that the professed orthodoxy and conservatism adopted by the inadequately informed early Hindu converts who in their enthusiasm emphasised more on the superficial attributes of Hinduism rather than on its essence was greatly responsible for the 'exclusion'. The charge by the upland tribal communities of the region that their 'exclusion' as a deliberate act of discrimination by the Hindus from this perspective appears justified.

However, a dispassionate and objective analysis and conclusion is possible by factoring in and contextualizing the prevailing physical features and condition of communications in the region at that time, especially when Hinduism first made inroad between the 5th and the 15th century ADE. What emerges from this perspective is that Hinduism could not bring the upland communities of Assam into its fold primarily because of the inhospitable and inaccessible terrain in which the upland areas of the region were located. The topography and physical conditions made it impossible for the early exponents of Hinduism from entering these areas. The comparison often made in this connection, between the initiatives and role of the Christian missionaries, who brought Christianity into the Northeast in spite of the region's topography and geographical constraints, with the early exponents of Hinduism are incomparable. This is simply because Christianity came to the region in the later part of the 19th and very early part of the 20th century, whereas Hinduism came to Assam much earlier between the 5th and the 15th centuries. The conditions faced by Hinduism from those faced by Christianity were therefore very different.

Topographically analysed as such, the rivers were the only efficient and possible means of transport into the valley-areas of Assam at that time. Ravi J. Deka[31] in a paper lucidly brings out this possibility when he points out why large numbers of Hindu temples are found all along the banks of the rivers of Assam and not as much elsewhere in the state. According to Deka, the Brahmaputra and the Surma rivers connected ancient Assam to the Bengal plains, and through which Hinduism spread itself all along the banks of these rivers and their valleys. The innumerable Hindu temples found along the major riverbanks in Goalpara, Guwahati, Tezpur districts and other river-based temple towns of Assam proves this point. The famous Malinithan temple sites[32] on the rivers Ghagara and the Gai, tributaries of the Brahmaputra, which are now in Arunachal Pradesh, reinforces the riverine theory.

The discovery of the temple site in old Baitbari, a small village in West Garo hills, on the southern bank of the river Jinjiram at a distance of about three miles from Phulbari on the way to Tura is significant. The temple base has mud-cum-burnt brick with 28 terracotta figures of Hindu God and Goddesses. The temple has three components of the Garbagriha, the Enterole and the Mandapa. Within the temple, the fortification runs at least for five kilometers in north-south direction, a miniature Shiva Linga found indicates the influences of Saivism. A Buddhist Stupa is also found on the same site. Since this site[33] is located on the slopes of the Garo hills as it rises from the Assam plains close to the river Brahmaputra whether this temple was used by the upland Garos or by the lowland communities, either separately or collectively, is yet to be established.

The locations of all these temples indicate that physical contact and communication of people from the region with the outside world was possibly mainly through the riverine routes. Given this prevailing condition, contacts between the Hindus with the upland tribal communities was extremely difficult if not impossible. This physical constraint appears to be one of the most austensible reasons why the upland tribal communities had to be excluded and left out when Hinduism first made inroads into the Northeast.

In support of the premise that accessibility was the main determinent for inclusion of any upland tribal community into Hinduism, is the example of the Jaintias, Khasis and Garos who are tribal communities in the state of Meghalaya and yet embraced Hinduism. Geographically the Khasis, Jaintias and the Garos of Meghalaya, among all the tribal communities of the Northeast occupy one of the most accessible areas from the Bengal Plains. Meghalaya, erstwhile Khasi and Jaintia Hills, and the Garo Hills of Assam are natural hinterland for trade and commerce between the people living in the Bengal Plains and the various tribes because of the physical contiguity of the areas these upland tribal communities occupy. Historical evidences indicate that Khasis, Jaintias and the Garos have a long history and tradition of commercial and social contacts with the important trade centres of northern Bangladesh at Jamalpur, Sylhet and Mymensingh. William Robinson gives the account of the contacts of the Jaintias. *"A considerable trade in cotton, iron ore, wax, ivory, betel leaf and clothes, is carried on between the plains and the hills in Jaintiapur, the capital, is the great entreports in which all commercial dealings are transacted between the inhabitants of the plains and those of the hills. The articles specified, are bartered for salt, tobacco, rice and goats"*[34].

The accessibility factor also determined political relations and equations in the region. The Jaintia ruler Jasa Manik encountered Pratap Singh of Assam (1603-1641) in Phulaguri in Nowgong district of Assam. Similarly, when the Jaintia king Dhana Manik captured Dimarua a protected Chief of the Kachari kings, the Kachari king Satrudaman invaded the Jaintias in the beginning of the 17th century. The rulers of Bengal and Assam with whom the Jaintia rajas were in touch and in contact were all Hindus. This also greatly influenced and facilitated the Jaintias in accepting and embracing Hinduism.

Because of these contacts and association with the people from the plains, many Khasis, especially the Jaintias became staunch Hindus. The Jaintias, who are classified as a Khasi sub-classification called the 'Synteng', (also 'Pnar') converted to Hinduism probably in the 16th century. The famous Durga temple found in Nartiang in the Jaintia region is a proof and legacy of Hinduism among the Jaintias. Jaintia kingdom and the Jaintias derive their name from goddess

Jayanti Devi, one of the deities worshipped by the Jaintia royal family. Their capital was at Jaintiapur in the Bengal Plains now in Bangladesh. U Parbat Roy or Parvat Ray the first Jaintia king of the Sutnga lineage and dynasty, which had seven kings in all, has a Hindu Bengali name. The last of the kings of this dynasty died in 1612. Other Jaintia kings from other dynasties ruled the Jaintia hills till 1822. The various names of the Jaintia kings like Parvat Ray, Bar Gosain, Bijay Manik who ruled in the 16th century suggests strong Hindu influence and connections. The Borghat temple, named after the Jaintia Raja Borkuhain or U Bor Singh who had embraced Hinduism, and the Durga temple at Nartiang are mute testimony to these facts of history.

The influence of Hinduism on the Jaintias also extended to many social habits and costumes. For instance, the dhoti, known as *iu-slein*, the drape of a muga silk shawl over the shoulder and the turban etc, all form part of the formal custom and dress of both Jaintia and the Khasi tribes. The Khasis adopted Hindu names, one of them was the famous Tirot Singh, the legendry ruler (Syiem) of the Khasis who fought the British and died in the Dacca prison. A large number of Jaintias and Khasis have settled in the adjoining districts of Sylhet in Bangladesh. The impact of Hinduism among the Khasis and the Jaintias could be one of the reasons why the percentage of Christians in Meghalaya, compared to the Nagas or the Mizos are far less.

Even today, the Pnar Society retains their distinctiveness. For instance, disinheritance of legal heir of the youngest daughter who becomes Christians is rigorously enforced[35]. In fact, people from predominant Christian localities were not allowed social contacts with the Pnar society until very recently. The years have softened these attitudes mainly due to the weakening of family bonding as an institution in the entire region including the Jaintia hills[36].

Another example of tribal communities who are Hindus, because of accessibility, are the Bodos and the Kacharis of Assam, both of which are recognised tribal communities of Assam and euphemistically known as 'Plain Tribals'. The Bodos are the autochthones of Assam who once followed the animistic cult[37] and occupied the plains of the Brahmaputra valley before the Ahoms came to Assam from the east. Many converted Bodos have formed into separate groups known as Koch, Sarania, Sonawal, Rabha and

Deuri[38]. One of the major points of dispute between the Bodos and the Assamese is that the Bodos feel that after converting them into Hindus, they are slowly assimilated into the Assamese society, and in the process reducing the Bodo population in the state. The Bodos and the Kacharis often cite the case of the Kalitas, who were originally Koches but subsequently categorized as Assamese after converting to Hindus.

The point of interest in the present context however, is that the Bodos and the Kacharis, even though are tribals could convert to Hindus, primarily because they were living in areas and places, which were easily accessible to the Hindu priests and pundits. Similarly, various other Plains tribal communities like the Mirings in Assam embraced Hinduism because they were easily accessible and had regular interactions with Hindu communities. In erstwhile Assam, as per the Registrar General of India there were 93.63 percent Hindus among the Bodos and Kacharis, 75.11 percent of Mikirs, 99.79 percent of Dimasa in the Assam valley. In the district of Naga Hills, now Nagaland 40.67 percent Garos, 98.72 percent Mikirs, 86.67 percent Mishmi and 46.97 percent Noctes had embraced Hinduism.

The other example of a state where tribal communities embraced Hinduism is Tripura, where the majority of the tribal communities in the state are Hindus mainly because of the accessibility to the state from the Bengal plains. Among the Tripuris, the Reangs, Jamatia, Naotias, Kalai, Rupini and Halams have adopted Hindu as their religion. The Naotias and the Halams are Sakti cult followers, while the others are followers of the Vaisnavism sect of Hinduism.

It is obvious from the examples that physical accessibility was the main deterrent in converting the various upland tribal communities in the Northeast to Hinduism or for that matter to any other religion from outside the region. These examples substantiate the assumption that Hinduism did not deliberately leave out the tribal communities from becoming Hindus as is often alleged by its critics. The vilificatory adage accorded to Hinduism as ethnically selective in its propagation is not substantiated by the facts from history as such. Because wherever social contacts took place between the Hindus and non-Hindus largely determined by the factors of accessibility, irrespective of the people or community involved, Hinduism embraced them into its fold.

The doubts and suspicion raised by this 'exclusion theory' has been one of the irritants nagging the upland tribal communities, a factor responsible for the social polarization between the upland tribal communities and the lowland non-tribal communities in the region. These, and many such assumptions, which are not backed by facts have over the years damaged inter communitarian relationship and equations in the region. Unfortunately, due to the credence given to these theories, suspicion and resentment persists between the non-tribal Hindus and tribal non-Hindus which vilify the fair name of the region.

In short, the exclusion of the upland tribal communities from the fold of Hinduism, which was essentially a by-product of the constraints and restrictions imposed by the geography of the region, was quite unintentional and was not deliberate as is often made out. Besides, a number of other factors are responsible for the exclusion of the upland tribal communities from Hinduism. Some of these factors are (i) the lack of understanding of Hinduism's complex philosophical contents and teachings by its early converts, which led to misdirected emphasis in its implementations in the region. (ii) Hinduism's evocative inherent restrictive passivity and self-restraint philosophy that every person has the right to choose a religion of one's choice ironically inhibited it from undertaking an aggressive missionary role in its propagation and in the process retarded its own growth and expansion. (iii) The lack of institutional support to Hinduism as a movement, which was neccasry to propagate and expand its teachings into the remote and inaccessible areas of the region at that given point of time in history was also an important constraint.

From the foregoing facts it is evident that the rise of ethnic identity politics in the region, even though is attributable to Hinduism, indirectly there are evidences to suggest that Hinduism per se did not intentionally or deliberately leave out the upland tribal communities from its fold. From the evidences available, it appears that it was compelled to leave out the upland tribal communities from its fold mainly due to inaccessibility and the lack of institutional support to it from anybody. Somehow, in its long chequered history and association with the people of the Northeast because of the wrong impression that this unintended 'exclusion' was deliberate, many believe that the concept of religious identity in the region and idea of social discrimination was introduced by Hinduism.

Complex nature of Hinduism

Hinduism devoid of the semantics, philosophical contents and other lateral influences is a simple religion. However, being one of the oldest religions in the world, Hinduism in the course of its long history of evolution incorporated a number of concepts and ideas from various influences and associations. This aspect has been explained earlier in the Chapter. Hinduism even though theoretically considered by many as a simple religion and interpreted as a 'way of life', accommodative and expansive, willing to affect changes and make adjustments, in actual practice and application in the Northeast gave a different picture of itself. It was seen as being impervious and inflexible, besides being conservative and orthodox. It sent out a wrong message of its intent and purpose to the large number of potential converts with whom it came in contact. Even though, these were mostly the by-product of inadequate understanding and appreciations of its true essence by the new converts in their role as exponents of Hinduism, it alienated many potential converts. The introduction of concepts and interpretations based on their limited understandings, assumptions and incorrect interpretations, reinforced by interpolations with local indigenous religious rituals and ceremonies unfortunately affected adversely its image as a religion. More significantly, it was confusing.

Hinduism with several sects and esoteric ceremonies, the meaning and purpose of which were not understood or appreciated by many converts had its own adverse effects on it as a religion. The superficial understanding of Hinduism and the preoccupation of the early exponents with the rituals and ceremonial aspects of Hinduism, the pujas and bhajans, which were not its essence shifted the emphasis from the epistemological content of its teachings to the more mundane aspects of adherence and observance of format of worship, ceremonies, rituals, pujas etc. These made Hinduism appear highly ritualistic, ceremonial, and consequently expensive and time consuming. The fact that these rituals were elaborate and observed meticulously in form and much less in its contents only gave a wrong impression to the non-converts. Somehow, Hinduism failed to carry conviction of its true meaning and purpose.

Hinduism's preoccupation with ritualism, was perceived as dogmatic and too rigidly structured to provide the kind of flexibility that many tribal societies in the upland areas of the Northeast would have desired. For instance, while introducing the various rituals and ceremonies in its worship in the region, the significance and importance of the climate and seasonal conditions prevalent in the Northeast, was never considered important enough for allowing some flexibility and modifications. As observed earlier, Hinduism is a warm weather religion, which uses water extensively in all its rituals and religious ceremonies, which unfortunately was not possible or convenient in the cold mountainous terrain where the upland tribal communities lived. These aspects of the Northeast were conveniently overlooked. The fact that Hinduism as a religion is accommodative and expansive enough to adjust itself to accommodate the needs and requirements of a region, especially problems arising out of the climate, weather, topography of the region, was not adequately appreciated by the early proponents of Hinduism. Consequently, Hinduism was seen as highly ceremonial and ritualistic, and in one sense dogmatic, a highly esoteric religion with its own ways, which would not under any circumstances make overtures by adjusting to the needs of the people and the environment. This lack of sensitivity to the need of the region left its own negative imprint on the minds of the people. Hinduism became a much-misunderstood religion in the Northeast especially among the upland communities of the region.

Further, Hinduism instead of relieving the upland tribal communities from the bondages of obscurantism, introduced alien social concepts and practices such as untouchibility, caste system etc, in the otherwise casteless societies of the region. These factors combined without the necessary sensitivity to understand and appreciate the climatic, physical features and needs of the upland communities like the extensive use of water in a cold climatic zone like the Northeast as an example, only discouraged and inhibited the upland tribal communities to accept Hinduism, even if they had accessibility. These communities found adherence and acceptance of the 'new-lifestyles' difficult and quite alien to their life-styles and ways of living. In a way, this checkmated its growth and expansion. Lack of appreciating and understanding this inherent flaw in its teachings in the early period of propagation in the Northeast is important in understanding why Hinduism failed to make the kind of impact it could perhaps have made among the upland tribal communities in the Northeast. If its early proponents realized these aspects, the impact and influence of Hinduism in the region would have been entirely different.

Untouchability, the scourge within

One of the most misunderstood and misused concept attributed to Hinduism is 'untouchability' and the associated metonym the 'caste-system'. The two concepts, separately and in conjunction created considerable social turmoil in the Northeast like anywhere else in the country. In effect, it became one of the most pernicious and self-inflicting damaging aspect of Hinduism, which changed the social equation and in inter-ethnic relationship in the region. This needs elaboration in appreciating the genesis of the rise in assertive ethnic identity politics in the Northeast.

The concept of the caste system is embodied in the Manusmriti (Laws of Manu or Institutions of Manu) written around 200 ADE in India. Manusmriti forms the foundation of Hindu law, based on which ancient Hindu society evolved. The core and essence of the philosophical content of Manusmriti is 'human being', the fountainhead of humankind and forms the central theme of the Laws of Manus, or the Laws of 'Man'. They contain in short, the codes, rules and laws through which human beings, both as individual and as members of society, must conduct themselves. There are 18 Smritis of the Dharma Sastras or the Law of Righteous conduct. Unlike the Vedas, which are eternal, or of divine origin, Smritis are of human origin and hence are likely to have human flaws. The Smritis are texts which "are to be remembered", and do not come under the same classifications as the Vedas, the Indian Epics, the Puranas and other treatises.

The principles enunciated in the Smritis conform to the basic Hindu view that there exists a universal order, a cosmic discipline where all the planetary system functions each within its assigned realm. It is because of this self-imposed order in the cosmos that life is possible. If in this self-disciplined world order, even if one constituent member in this universe (order) did not adhere to the path assigned to it, there would be chaos and the universe would not have been in existence. It is this universal order or Dharma; the Universal Law of Order, which is the very essence that guarantees 'life' or 'existence' itself. Order is therefore the essence of life, without it there will be chaos and hence no life. This universal order, the principle of Dharma, superimposes itself and exists in the lives of human beings and the world. Consequently, every society must have various groups of people doing different types of jobs or activities in a coordinated fashion to sustain the orderly existence of society. The sum total of all these activities, performed within the prescribed assigned roles of each human being gives order and ensures life and continuity.

Thus, the Manusmriti divides human activities into four classifications called Varna Vyavastha (Arrangement or Structure of Colour or Coordination of Colour) purely on the nature of work assigned to each group and not on the group of community or ethnic identity. The four groups are (1) the priests and teachers, (2) The rulers and the warriors, (3) the merchants and cultivators and lastly (4) the servants who do the menial work. The further amplification implies that if a person assigned one task starts doing a task not assigned to it, the only consequences would be either the work would be very badly done or if done at all, it will be of substandard quality, since the person doing the work may not know the work or is incapable of doing it. Transgressions of the limits assigned to each class means chaos.

Life in the Hindu system is therefore, compartmentalized into castes. Each caste performs specific roles and myriad functions to sustain society. This is to restore symmetry and order where asymmetry and disorder prevail. The caste system was an instrument of governance, meant to ensure orderly existence of life and society through societal stratification of duties and functions. The whole concept however through various circumstances of history underwent a redefinition and became the main cause for social asymmetry. The fact that each category of people need to perform specific tasks and activities within a given hierarchy of functions and that this was an economic necessity for an orderly function of the state was not very adequately explained or clearly defined by the early proponents of Hinduism to the new converts in the region. Instead, it became, by processes of distortions, an instrument for deliberate stratification of people into the socio-religious concepts of 'touchables' and 'non-touchables', which unfortunately morphed into the tribal and non-tribal categorisation in the region. Social asymmetry is therefore inherent in the Hindu philosophy of life, but is not without qualificatory provisions or can be indiscriminately applied either to its followers or to believers in other religions. Much of the conceptual clarity of the caste-system was lost in the polemics of debate and dialogue, which confused people more than it could clarify.

The concept of the caste system in Hinduism as a socially formatted division of labour to manage society is therefore, theoretically unassailable, but it is the circumventing religious sanctity accorded to it by Hinduism, which in the course of time became much more diverse, wrongly applied and misinterpreted that inhibit rationalists from accepting the concept on its face value. Consequently, the negative features of the concept tend to dominate its cartographed progress in Indian social history. The system imposes with impunity the enforcement of assigned role-play of people in a society in a stratified hierarchical social order in perpetuity, without according any opportunity to the lowest stratum of the social hierarchy to redeem themselves from the clutches of the traditional job assigned to them even if they have higher potentiality. The injunctions favouring certain types of human beings of specific communities, through job stratifications and gradations as conjuncts to the 'man-made' social order without hope of redemption, is condemned and criticized especially because it is a hierarchy of human beings made by man and not by divine intervention. The only redeeming aspect of the caste-system is the fact that the Manusmriti to which it is ascribed, acknowledges that it is of human origin and liable and susceptible to human flaws.

The categorisations of human activities are not unique to the Hindu society alone. Division of labour is a sociological phenomenon and used in statecraft ever since human beings learned to live together as members of a community or society. However, it is perhaps only in the Hindu concept of society that the categorisation is formulated as a social treatise or code. However, what distinguishes the Hindu concept of the division of labour and makes it unique, is that the concept of interchangeability of labour among the members of the society does not exist in it. The problem becomes complicated when such a rigid social structure has the sanctity of Hindu religion, which enforces the corporal functions of human beings. Since there is an inherent conflict between the rights of the individual to choose one's profession but with the commensurate support from the society or group the individual belongs, the rigorous religious sanctions against the exercise of such a choice by the individual through the society itself is what gives the concept universal notoriety.

In short, in the Hindu world order, while a person 'assigned' to do or perform a particular job or task does not require to become 'clean', 'cleanse' or 'purify', after completing the assigned duty or task, any other person who undertakes the job or work not socially 'assigned' to do 'the job', especially a work lower down in the hierarchy of works categorized by the society, is expected to 'clean' themselves before resuming their normal daily chores. It is this concept of 'cleanliness', from which the concepts of 'untouchability' and 'caste system' emerged. It is the associated metaphor and implication that the actual person assigned to do or perform the lower category of work is lower in social status or heiarchy to another individual or member of the same society merely because of the duties assigned by society, which vilifies the concept. The corelation of the nature of the job and the social status and often the stigma attached to an individual for no fault of theirs, and especially without any hope of redemption is what makes the concepts dehumanizing.

Ethically analysed, the practice in reality are a set of social conditions imposed to ensure personal hygiene and cleanliness in any human activity after any physical activity, in addition to ensuring that the required social discipline and order where each member or group is required to perform the assigned job socially sanctioned is maintained. The very fact that the process of 'cleansing' exists indicates transgression into such an 'assigned activity' or 'activities' by any other not assigned by society are prohibited. In this conceptual 'rehabilitation' of people, the use of water, and water itself becomes an important prerequisite and requirement as the cleansing medium. The Gouriya cult, practised extensively in the Hindu communities of the Northeast, which came from Bengal, introduced strict regimentation of 'cleanliness'. The 'cleanliness' here implied the extensive use of water as a cleansing medium to attain both physical cleanliness from the personal hygiene point of view, and religiously in the metaphysical sense of the term. Water and its use came to play a significant role in all rituals and ceremonies of Hinduism.

Water, as we have observed earlier, is not only soothing in warm weather or temperate climatic zones, but also endows in its use a sense of sublimation and feeling of cleanliness. The Northeast is not exactly a 'warm region' climatically, and since it is most of time wet and cold almost throughout in the hill and uplands, usage of water is minimal. This limitations in the use of water, the 'purifying element' in the Hindu way of life in the daily chores among the upland communities of the Northeast imposed by the climate of the region, is antithetical to the needs of Hindu religion and runs contrary to the basic principle of 'cleanliness' as enshrined in the requirements of the caste system. However since most of the upland communities who occupy the higher reaches of the region use very little water or no water in their daily chores due to adverse seasonal and climatic condition, the upland tribal communities never conceptually understood or could establish any conceptual link with the concept of being 'clean', as a religious requirement when Hinduism first came to the region.

The use of water by the converted Hindus from the plain areas was in stark contrast to the limited usage of water by the upland communities. This seemingly innocuous difference in the life-styles and habits between the two sets of communities in the region set the tone of socially differentiating Hindus from non-Hindu upland tribal communities living in cold climatic conditions in the Northeast. Later the differences in perception degenerated into the obnoxious concept of 'untouchables'. All upland communities therefore became 'unclean' and hence categorised as 'untouchables'. In addition, while the converted Hindus became mostly vegetarians subsequent to their adoption of the Hindu faith, the upland communities remained non-vegetarians, who ate beef and pork, both prohibited by Hinduism.

Part of the problems faced by Hinduism in the Northeast, lay in the inability to constantly update the teachings of Hinduism with the changing times based on new findings and scholarships available to the rest of India, due to the region's location and isolation. The early converts and exponents of Hinduism from the region did not have the facility and opportunity to imbibe new concepts and interpretations, posing a major handicap in their understanding of Hinduism. Due to this factor, Hinduism remained confabulated within its own doubts and problems within the region. On the other hand, Hinduism acquired many self-effacing obscurantist and esoteric attributes and practices, which did more harm than good to it by becoming victim of its own unintended precepts. Because of all these factors, Hinduism presented itself as a confused array of sects and sub-sects, neutralizing its chances of finding acceptability among a much larger population like the upland communities of the region. Hinduism in the Northeast in its historical advent and progression soon became a religion for the elite and of the lowland communities only, leaving out the upland communities.

Perhaps one of the greatest handicaps of Hinduism in the Northeast therefore lay in the fact that the new exponents and converts to Hinduism, in their initial enthusiasm without adequately understanding the essence of Hinduism, have misapplied concepts like the caste-system indiscriminately without factoring in the social habits, the climatic conditions and other factors peculiar to the Northeast region. The tendency to view and judge the traditional value systems of the upland tribal communities in the Northeast through the rigid standards of Hindu social percepts, and categorise them as 'untouchables' offended the sentiments of the upland communities who lived a much more bohemian life-style. Unfortunately, due to these factors, essentially impressions from the perspective of the upland tribal communities, Hinduism and its followers were seen as ethnically prejudiced and biased against them as a social group. Hinduism in spite of its universal appeal and catholicity, therefore largely remained a religion of the lowland communities of the Northeast.

Passivity of Hinduism

A more fundamental problem in Hinduism, which prevented it from becoming a religion for all communities in the region, particularly in the upland areas and the tribal communities, is its inherent passivity enshrined in its philosophy of catholicity, tolerance towards other religions. This somehow made Hinduism a passive, complacent and status-quo religion. The evocative principles in Hinduism, however rich and profound it may be, were not conducive for its own growth and expansion. Hinduism in one way, by its own precepts and teachings was a major hindrance to itself. This lack of a 'missionary zeal', inherent within its philosophical precepts, unlike Christianity, made it a religion of sanguine passivity.

Max Muller[39], defines 'success' of a religion, in the sense of its ability for propagation and expansion, on its steadfastness and faith in itself. This attribute forms the inner urge that compels the believers to preach their faith or religion with conviction and determination. Unless a person is convinced of the religion one has voluntarily opted for, the person (believer) will not be in a position to either carry conviction or have the moral and psychological courage to be bold enough to advocate or preach that religion. Conversely, without this conviction reticence is the sanctuary of the unconvinced. Religion, Max Muller said, *"...must convince and convert...As long as there are doubts and darkness and anxiety in the soul of the inquirer, reticence may be his natural attitude."* Hinduism suffered from this prerequisite.

It is this inner urge, which infused the "missionary character" in "Buddhism, Mohammedanism, and Christianity", which Max Muller considers as being that attribute that keep these religions 'alive' and 'kicking'. Conversely, it is the inertia, the lack of initiative and drive, in comparative terms with Buddhism, Mohammedanism and Christianity that relegates Hinduism to the condemned slot of a 'dead' religion. When Max Muller therefore, declared in his now famous lecture in December 1873, "On Missions" in Westminster Abbey that Hinduism was "dying or dead" he echoed this concern about Hinduism. The sub-text meant, giving Hinduism a not too decent a burial, much to the chagrin of his admirers, even though he actually meant well for Hinduism.

Max Muller did not mean or imply, when he summarily pronounced the early dead rituals of Hinduism, that Hindus had no faith or conviction in Hinduism itself. On the other hand, what he meant was that if Hinduism is what it professes to be, the religion founded on the freedom of choice and therefore, precludes both convictions and certainty, nothing ought to have prevented it from aggressively pursuing its philosophy. It should have gone ahead with propagation and extension vigorously as other religions did in the rest of India. He felt that aggressive advocacy of Hinduism; by implication, was the best prescriptive diagnosis to counter both aspects of being misunderstood, and for countering the propagandas against it. Perhaps, it was an indirect provocative statement to solicit adequate response from the advocates and followers of the Hinduism. Max Muller may have underscored a point, which advocates of Hinduism missed out in India, especially with reference to their role among the upland tribal communities in the Northeast.

Thus by the time Christianity was aggressively trying to *"persuade...convince...and convert"* the various upland communities of the Northeast, Hindus seem to have gone into premature hibernation in the Northeast. In fact, Christianity came in only where Hinduism failed to convert and consolidate. The paradox lies in the fact that Christianity was at that time in history a religion of foreigners who trudged across the lands and sailed across the seas to bring their faith, while Hindus were on home turf. Hinduism and the process of Brahmanisation began in the Northeast through Royal patronages and primarily at the invitations and initiatives of the rulers of that time, whether it was Assam or Manipur, yet failed to take the advantages it possibly commanded. Hinduism failed to capitalize on the opportunity to bring the Northeast, especially the upland communities into its fold.

Affect of this inherent drawback is from Manipur, where primarily due to the lack of 'Missionary zeal' among the Hindus in the Imphal Valley, and because there was a prohibition to convert the Meitei population to Christianity in pursuance of an understanding between the British administration and the Maharaja of Manipur, the British tacitly encouraged the Christian missionaries to propagate Christianity to the upland communities in the Uplands. The segregation of physical spaces of sorts, between the Hindu and Christian-areas of influence was the result of the failure of Hinduism to extend its teachings to the upland tribal communities.

Organisational Support

One of the major handicaps, which affected Hinduism in the early stages of its propagation in the Northeast, was the lack of organizational support. It was one important factor, which inhibited its expansion and efforts to extend itself among the upland tribal communities residing in the remote areas of the region. This in turn led to the geographical segmentation of the region based on religious influence and ultimately ending in the spatial divide between Christianity and Hinduism, which would become the scourge of the region. All this could have perhaps been avoided had Hinduism, like the Christian missionaries, had adequate institutional support to back them up. Christianity perhaps achieved what they have in the Northeast region partly because of backup support system in its missionary efforts from other different Christian denominations and congregations, all of whom worked in tandem supporting each other, especially in times of need. Further the British administration, even though as a state policy professed administratively to be neutral in religious matters, was always available to the Christian missionaries should the need and occasions arise.

Hinduism in contrast, did not have any institutional support system to backup its efforts, leaving instead the entire process of propagation to its new converts. Moreover Hinduism did not have the support of the British administration at the time when it first entered the region. Hinduism lost out in the upland areas of the Northeast because it simply did not have the support system in the form of institutional support to backup its efforts. Further, each sect of Hinduism worked independently and most often at cross-purposes. Consequently, each group of Hindus was involved in extolling the merits and virtues of their respective sects of Hinduism within a restricted area of influence, without involving other sects or groups. Obviously, without the essential collaborative spirit or institutional support system to back them up, especially in such a dispersed, logistically difficult region as the Northeast, the efforts by the few early converts were bound to be hopelessly inadequate.

Hinduism remained therefore according to Dr. Suniti Kumar Chatterji, National Professor of India in Humanities, *"... that great body of unorganized missionaries."*[40] Hinduism had to leave out the upland tribal communities of the Northeast from its fold much against its wishes.

Endnotes

1. Gautama Buddha was born in 563 BCE while Mahavira was born in 540 BCE.
2. Amartya Sen. *The Argumentative Indian*, p-172.
3. Sen. ibid. Chapter 16, pp 352.
4. Bagchi, *India and China* p.134, referred to by Amartya Sen, ibid p-189.
5. Mitra, *Decline of Buddhism*, Visvabharati 1955; L.M.Joshi, *Studies in Buddhistic Cultures of India*, 391ff; Eliot, *Hinduism and Buddhism*, II, 6ff.
6. Dr. N.N. Bhattacharyya. Hook Swinging, *Ancient Indian Rituals and their Social Contents*, pp-238-240.
7. Dr. Bhattacharyya, ibid.
8. R.D. Banerji, *the Haihayas of Tripuris*, quoted by Dr. Bhattacharyya, ibid.
9. D.C. Sircar, *Religious Life of Ancient and Medieval India*, 1993, ibid Dr. Bhattacharyya.
10. Dr. Bhattacharyya, p-150, ibid.
11. R.C. Majumdar, *Corporate Life of Ancient India*, Calcutta, 1919, 310ff, 317-318, Quoted by Dr. Bhattacharyya, p-150-151.
12. Dr. Bhattacharyya, ibid, p-245.
13. Dr. Bhattacharyya, ibid, p-p-254.
14. Dr. Bhattacharyya, ibid, p-242.
15. Waddel, *Buddhism of Tibet*, K.L. Barua, *Studies in the Early History of Assam*.

16. Taranath, *History of Buddhism* p. 199.

17. Zafar Mudasser Nofil, Senior Sub-editor, *The Sentinel*, Guwahati.

18. David Ludden, *Making India Hindu*, p-6-7.

19. In terms of the historical period, Hinduism first entered Assam before it did in Manipur or Tripura. Assam, it must be amplified is meant to denote all the Northeastern states and Union Territories of the region, excluding Manipur and Tripura, which were princely states.

20. Dr. Mrs. S.L. Baruah.

21. Dr. Mrs. S.L. Baruah, ibid. p-95). *The Pala or Paala Dynasty in Assam* (970-1195 ADE).

22. Dr. Mrs. S.L. Baruah

23. Saivism and Saktism were immensely popular in the formative years of Hinduism in the region. Saivism reflects the concept of dualism (Dwaita) in life, the conflict of the opposites, in which Sakti brings the balance. The concept of Sakti, in simplified term is the 'medium' or 'energy force' through which link between the 'Pure and Ultimate Consciousness', personified by Shiva, and the 'Unconsciousness' representing matter or object, can be bridged. To make this understood to the simple common people, Sakti is humanized and made the consort of Shiva. The 'union' of the two 'creates' the essence or the 'formative energy' of consciousness. Thus, knowledge of Sakti (Energy Force) is the means to salvation. However, because of the highly complex nature of the contents and tenure of Saivism and Saktism the form of Saivism and Saktism practiced in Assam degenerated into various cults and occultism of the most obnoxious kind. This caused immense confusion. These aberrations eventually led people in Assam to abandon both of these and instead began to follow Vaishnavism, which was a much less complex form of Hinduism.

24. Dr. Mrs. S.L. Baruah, p-444.

25. Dr. Mrs. S.L. Baruah, pp-158.

26. Rishi Agastya was responsible for spreading the Aryan culture in the south of India.

27. Dr. Ramesh Chandra Majumdar, eminent historian, Prof. Nirmal Kumar Bose, Commissioner for Scheduled Castes and Scheduled Tribes, Government of India and well-known Gandhian scholar, Dr. Sunitikumar Chatterji, National Professor of India in Humanities all honored Atombapu by delivering some of the most fascinating lectures pertaining

to the northeast region in the Panditraj Raja Atombapu Sharma Memorial Lectures in Imphal in the mid sixties. These references and papers were presented in the November 15-16 of 1966-67 on *Expansion of the Aryan Culture in Eastern India*.

28. Hiranmay Karlekar, *Bangladesh, the Next Afghanistan*? p-27-28.

29. Reference from '*Tripura, the land of History and Legends*', www.tripura.org.in.

30. Dr. Bhattacharyya, ibid, p-241.

31. Ravi J. Deka: 2000, '*River of Faith*', Archaeology/web/ oasis.fortunecity.com.

32. C. Dutta, Directorate of Research, Arunachal Pradesh, 1997.

33. Dr. Mrs. S.L. Baruah, believes that a section of the Garos became Hindus and subsequently became Koches. ibid, p-378).

34. William Robinson: *A Descriptive Account of Assam*, Reprint 1975, p-408.

35. Sir Keith Cantlie: *Notes on Khasi Law*, Edited by A.S.Khongphai, 1974, p-57.

36. *Meghalaya District Gazetteer, Jaintia Hills*, 1995, p-34.

37. Rev. Sidney Endle; *The Kachari*, London, 1911, p33.

38. A.G. Grierson, *The Linguistic Survey of India*, Vol-III, Part ii, p-1.

39. Arun Shourie, ibid, p-140-150.

40. S.K. Chatterji. *A Present day Rishi Agastya for Eastern India: Atombapu Sarma*; Atombapu Memorial Lecture-1; delivered in Imphal on 15th of November 1966. pp-13-14cf.

CHAPTER - 6

CHRISTIANITY

Christianity came to Northeast India as a 'supplement' to British interests in the region. By a tenacious mix of Christian missionary zeal and timing, combined with British administrative opportunism, Christianity somehow found its way into the remote Northeastern region. The upland communities, left in the lurch by Hinduism, responded enthusiastically to Christianity. In the course of its proselytisation and propagation, Christianity transformed the region dramatically, socially, culturally, especially the lives of the upland tribal communities of the region.

The social impact of Christianity in the Northeastern region of India, particularly among the upland tribal communities, has been nothing less than spectacular and in many respects profound. However, hidden behind this success and profundity is the lamentable negation of the tribal-way of life and abrogation of many of the tribal traditions and value-systems by the Christian way of life. These changes has bred its own inner contradictions and infused a sense of dichotomy in most tribal societies, between the traditionalists' indigenous ways of life and the more flambuoyant western lifestyles and value-systems. This Chapter relooks at the process of Christianisation especially of the important upland tribal communities in the region and the role played by Christianity in ethnic identity formations among the various Upland tribal communities of the region.

Background and Statistics

As per the 2001 census of India out of a total population of 1028 million Indians, 24 millions have shown their religion as Christians, or accounting for approximately 2.3 per cent of the total population of India. For the sake of comparative analysis, Hindus number 828 million (80.5 per cent) while Muslims number 128 million (13.4 per cent) of the total Indian population. About 0.7 million have not stated their religion. Thus in terms of number, Christianity in India has the third largest congregation of people in terms of religious beliefs.

In Northeast India, the Christian populations in the States, in terms of percentages to the respective states total population are, Nagaland 90 per cent, Mizoram 87 per cent, Meghalaya 70.3 per cent, Manipur 34 per cent, Arunachal Pradesh 18.7 per cent, Assam 3.7 per cent, Tripura 3.2 per cent and Sikkim 6.7 per cent. In comparative terms, the major states of Rajasthan, Uttar Pradesh, West Bengal, Punjab, Orissa, Maharashtra, Gujarat, Bihar and Jammu and Kashmir each have less than 2 per cent of its population as Christians.

The number of conversions to Christianity in percentages from the years 1951 to 1981 on an all India comparative basis grew at 7.80%, 10.47%, 12.53% and 16.74% every ten years respectively in the Northeast comprising of Assam, Arunachal Pradesh, Manipur, Meghalaya, Mizoram, Nagaland, Sikkim and Tripura. These figures are based on the Christian Bishops Conference of India Survey Report dated 1 December 1993[1]. There has been, on the other hand, a regular fall in the southern region, western region, and a marginal or no increases in all the other remaining regions of the country.

As per these estimates, out of the 24 million Christians in India (constituting 2.3 per cent of the total population of the country) approximately, 60 to 65 percent of them are in the four southern states, which cover about 21 per cent of the total physical area of the country. In the Northeast region, Christians account for 14 percent of the total population of the region, occupying only 6 per cent of the country's total territory. In the remaining 20 to 21 per cent of Christian population are spread out in the remaining 73 per cent of the country covering other regions. Out of this Christian population, approximately 85 per cent are Dalits and other backward communities.

According to the Agape Bible Fellowship: Christian Charitable Trust (Regd.), headquartered in Karnataka, the literacy rate among Christians in 21 states and Union Territories in India from the age profile of 7-year old and above, is more than 75 per cent. Mizoram from Northeast India is among the five highest literate Christian States and Union Territories having more than 90 per cent. The rate of literacy among males is 84.4 per cent and 76.6 per cent Christian females.

The Way of the Cross

Christianity came to the Indian subcontinent in 52 ADE when one of the Apostles of Jesus Christ, Saint Thomas landed in the West Coast port of Cranganore near present Cochin in Kerala. From 52 ADE to about 72 ADE, St. Thomas set up seven churches in and around the Malabar Coast region. Rev. Richard Howell[2] believes that St. Thomas visited almost every part of India and observes that there is some evidence that he had visited the court of king Gondophernes, the Indo-Parthian Kingdom of Taxila.

The spread of Christianity in India, except in the Southern region proved extremely difficult for the missionaries. In the Northern and Western region in 19 years, only 19 people decided to become Christians. Resistance, were encountered in many places from well-entrenched religions like Hinduism, Islam, Buddhism etc in these regions. Moreover, Indians who were in general wary of foreigners identified the missionaries with the imperialistic powers, and hence were highly suspicious of their activities. The discouraging response in the North, the West and in the Central regions of India led the Christian missionaries to the east to Bengal, Bihar and Orissa as an alternative destination. Historically, the Jesuit missionaries, Father Anthony Vaz and Father Peter Dias in 1576 and the Augustinian Friars in 1580 had already started work in Bandel, a Dutch town in Bengal.

However, the maximum expansion and spread of Christianity took place coinciding with the growing influences and importance of the various European Powers in India with each European Power entrusting their own missionaries to spread the teachings of the gospel within the territorial jurisdictions they held or controlled. For instance, the British East India Company did not permit any other European nationals or missionary to work within British occupied and trading areas. It was only in 1813, that Christian missionaries could enter British occupied territories in India by an Act of the British Parliament. Thus by the time the missionaries decided to move eastward into Bengal, Bihar and Orissa, the British Raj had already entrenched themselves commercially and to some extent politically in the eastern region, with Calcutta as the administrative headquarters in India. The Gossner Mission Society, Berlin for instance sent a few selected men who landed in the Chotanagpur and Ranchi areas in Bihar around 1845 by diverting the group originally meant to go to Burma. The thrust of the Christian proselytisation and evangelic efforts in the east was to lay the foundations of a strong nucleus for Christian movement with Calcutta as the home base, the centre of political capital of Imperial British India.

The decisions of the European powers as well as the British suited the Christian missionaries since it was an ideal arrangement that suited both parties. For the British and the European powers, their respective Christian missionaries would supplement their efforts at imposing their rule and control over India. Conversions to Christianity of Indians were encouraged, as it would inculcate awareness of western value systems and concepts, which might indirectly induce loyalty to the European powers.

Protestant missionaries started work in three phases in Bengal between 1793 and 1857 known as the Carey and Duff's period. Alexander Duff (1806-1878) a Scottish missionary founded the Scottish Church College, as a school in Calcutta on 13 July 1830. Ram Mohan Roy warmly reciprocated Alexander Duff's efforts in setting up the Scottish Church School (later College). However, the relationship soured and ended when Duff persuaded a group of Calcutta boys to become Christians. The episode raised a great outcry and social uproar, which stirred anti-Christian feelings among the Bengalis. The Brahmo Samaj, which Ram Mohan Roy headed reacted strongly and dissociated itself from all the professed educational and social programs of the Christian missionaries, leading Ram Mohan Roy dissociating himself from the Christian missions, in spite of the excellent relationship and work done together in the field of education. Similar reactions took place elsewhere in other regions of India. Christianity suffered in Bengal consequently for a number of years due to this event. The signs were obvious and ominous; Christianity had to keep its ecumenical and missionary activities confined within acceptable social limits, confined especially to education and educational institutions only. One of the main criticisms against the Christian missionaries was that they used these educational institutions for propagating their religious beliefs and teachings instead of treating them as institutions of learning and education.

The other pioneers who brought Christianity into Bengal was English Baptist William Carey, who landed in Calcutta on 11th November 1783 and from where he immediately started work in a Danish settlement under the sanctuary of the Danish Governor of Serampore. He and his two associates Joshua Marshman (1768-1837) and William Ward (1769-1823) formed a formidable threesome known then as the 'Serampore Trio'. The Serampore Mission under William Carey became one of the most important centres for the spread of Christianity into the Northeast. It was from here that the Christian missionaries eventually for the first time entered present-day Cherapunji in Meghalaya to bring the teachings of the Gospel and Christ to the Northeast. William Carey translated the Khasi bible in Bengali script and Shella dialect, spoken around Cherapunji, from here. It was possible for William Carey to enter the Khasi and Jaintia hills primarily because of the physical proximity of the Khasi and Jaintia hills (Meghalaya), which was easily accessible from Serampore through the plains from Sylhet. A number of Christian missionaries thereafter ventured into the northeast region through the Khasi and the Jaintia Hills. These efforts combined with the British Government's decision to remove the restriction imposed on all foreign missionaries to work in British occupied territories from 1813, greatly helped the various missionaries to work in the region.

According to Rev. Richard Howell it was essential, to win over the local people to Christianity because, *"The poor and the oppressed responded to the gospel, for it promised them self worth and dignity"*[3]. The situation in Bengal however, remained largely unfulfilled as the Bengali society accepted and reciprocated to the overtures as long as the missionaries restricted their activities in the field of education and other social welfare activities. They did not accept or tolerate any dilution or interference of the Bengali ethos and the Hindu way of life in any manner. Christian missionaries therefore, had to restrict their activities outside the main stream of Bengali Society. In many cases, the missionaries were compelled to shift their activities outside Bengali dominated areas. The Baptist Mission for instance, had to shift their activities away to the peripheral localities and areas and undertook the conversion of the Kartabhajas from Barisal and Jessore around 1840. The Christian missionaries were eventually compelled to spreadout across the region and move up further east into the Northeast.

British policy and Christianity

Even though the British government's approach to Christian missionaries had considerably changed, since 1813 when foreign missionaries were given permisson to enter India, the British adopted a cautious policy towards the Christian missionaries, essentially to enforce administrative control and ensure peace in the border region of its eastern frontier province. The British Government policy towards the Christian missionaries in the Northeast of India further changed dramatically after the end of the First Anglo-Burmese war when the Yandawoo Treaty was signed between Britain and the Burmese in 1826. The British began to consider the Christian missionaries as a potential and important institution for their Northeast Frontier policy.

Thus, even though manifestly and overtly the British administration welcomed Christian missionaries' purely as Christians missionaries, covertly however, the Christian church was increasingly seen as a desirable partner to obtain the support and cooperation of the people living in the secluded border areas of the frontier regions of Eastern India. This approach would supplement the administration's efforts at consolidation of British interests in the Northeast. Consequently, the British Administration began to encourage the missionaries to undertake missions into the interiors of the region right up to the international borders.

The British did not openly support the efforts of the missionaries because of its sensitivity back in Britain. The warning was given by Reverend Tucker to the Select Committee on Indian Territories in 1853, when he observed, *"I would be very sorry to see the Government departing from its present position of strict neutrality. If the Government openly announces Christianity to be a part of the education it imparts, Christianity will immediately lose the high vantage point it now occupies".* This however, did not get the attention it deserved. With the introduction of the Wood's Education Dispatch (1854), direct and open involvement by the missionaries like the 'Zenana System' (a system of domestic instruction mostly by wives of missionaries) came into existence on the ostensible ground to emancipate women. The third Lord Palmerstone, Henry John Temple the British Prime Minister[4] from 1854 until his death in 1865, supported the role and work of the Christian missionaries in India.

Arun Shourie[5] describes the eastward policy thrust initiated by the Christian missionaries as part of a greater design where the British administration, Christian missionaries and European Indologists colluded to 'vanquish' Hinduism. From this point of view, the effort was essentially to overcome the Hindu 'scourge', by converting as many Indian souls into Christianity. They found the British administration's support in their efforts to spread the message of Christ in the remote and inaccessible region, a virtual virgin territory, as Godsend opportunity. However, situationally Shourie's observation may be true largely in the rest of India, but the situation was not the same in the Northeast, since Christian missionaries were successful in converting mainly the upland tribal communities who were in any case not Hindus. On the other hand, in the valley areas of the region dominated by Hindu population, the efforts of the Christian missionaries for all practical purposes were either ineffective or partially successful but mostly inconsequential.

The British administration, European Indologists, socio-anthropologists, other academics and the Christian church all saw the move eastward as a great opportunity for furtherance of their respective interests. The British India administration saw the opportunity as an ingenious way to consolidate their hold on the potentially rich and strategically important and sensitive region. The British and European Indologists, socio-anthropologists and other academics on the other hand, saw the situation essentially as an opportunity to understand India and its people much better, and possibly discover new aspects of the region and people. The Christian Church saw the opportunity as a tremendous opening to extend its teachings among the illiterate and backward region. In all these the European Indologists, socio-anthropologists and other academics, the Christian Church made use of the British administration's support, which the British India administration happily provided in return for similar cooperation from them. The joint collaborative effort was beneficial to all.

The Church of Rome

Even though the Roman Catholics assert that Fr. Cacella, sj, and Fr. Cabrel, sj, both Jesuits[6] the first Catholic priests passed through Assam on their way to Tibet in 1626 ADE, the first batches of Catholic immigrants, actually came much later as tea plantation workers from Bihar and Bengal to the various Tea-Estates in Assam. The real work began when the Roman Catholic Churches in Assam and Lhasa combined in 1850, and in September 1851 Fr. Krick of the Foreign Church Work of Paris reached Dibrugarh. In 1870, Assam became part of the Prefecture Apostolic of Krishnagar. Fr. Jacob Broy of the Foreign Church Work of Milan was the first Resident priest of Assam with headquarters in Guwahati supervising Dibrugarh.

It was in 1889 the Prefecture Apostolic of Assam was created with Shillong as its headquarters. In 1921, the Prefecture of Assam came under the Salesians of Don Bosco.

An interesting aspect of the history of Christianity in the Northeast is the comparative late entry of the Roman Catholic Church only in the early part of the twentieth century in the region. This is surprising, especially considering the fact that the British policy in India had changed since 1813, when all European Christian missionaries could enter British occupied territories in India including the Northeast region. The subsequent restrictions imposed by the Bengal Eastern Frontier Regulation of 1873, which introduced the concept of 'inner line permit system' came only into force in 1873.

However, the impression one gathers is that somehow unintentionally discrimination and preferential treatment appear to have taken place in dealing with the Christian Churches by the British administration in the Northeast. The professed 'neutrality' principle was given a go-by, not only in dealing with inter-religious matters, between assertive Christian dalliances viz-a viz Hinduism, but also appear to have occurred in dealing with the Christian fraternity themselves; between the Protestant and the Roman Catholic churches. For instance in the Lushai Hills, now Mizoram, the Roman Catholic Church could find official entry into the Lushai Hills only through the initiatives of individual efforts by ordinary Mizos and not by the support of the British Administration[7]. Again, in the erstwhile Khasi Jaintia Hills, now Meghalaya, the Roman Catholic Church came as late as the 1930s. In contrast, the Protestant missionaries first entered the Khasi and Jaintia Hills in 1813 when Rev. Krishna Chandra Pal of the British Baptists from the Serampore mission got in touch with a few Khasis in Pandua, a marketing centre near Cherapunji, which was under the Cherapunji Syiemship.

In fact, in the case of the Lushai hills it was the Baptist Welsh Mission itself, which hindered the effort made by the few Roman Catholic Mizo converts to bring in the Roman Catholic Church. This is evident from a letter written by one Lalhutta Sailo to Fr. Boulay, the first Catholic priest to have set foot in Mizoram in Aizawl and who was the Parish Priest of Chittagong, under the Diocese of the Bishop of Dacca, on 21 December 1925. In the letter, Sailo exhorts the unfortunate nature of controversy and debate that was prevalent between the two denominations of Christianity, since it affected local opinion and impressions about Christianity. The emergence of the Roman Catholic Church as an alternative to the Protestant Church and as a competitor is apparent in what D.E.Jones wrote to Mr. Morris on November 10, 1925. *"We have another shock lately, Seven men from a village 8 miles away, from among the Salvation Army near here, have been down to Chittagong asking the Roman Catholic fathers to come and begin work in the country..."*[8].

Because of these factors, it was only as late as 1946, when the Governor of Assam officially communicated the permission on 18.12.1946 (Order passed on 15.12.1946) to Fr. Bianchi of the Roman Catholics missionaries to officially reside and administer their belief in the Lushai Hills. The permission came only a few months before the departure of the British from India when they ceased to have any interest in Indian affairs, especially when India's fate was in the hands of Indians themselves. The delayed permission appears to be deliberate.

Hypothetically, had the British Government accorded permission to the Roman Catholics to settle and preach in Lushai Hills when it first wanted to do so in 1925[9] the scenario and history of the Christianity in Mizoram would have been quite different. Even today, in spite of Mizoram having the highest numbers of Christians among the States in the region, it still does not have a Diocese of the Roman Catholic Church, while Nagaland has one and Shillong already has an Archdiocese, which is an irony of sorts.

The British policy and approach to proselytisation in Bengal and Northeast is reflected in the official Resolution No.4 formulated by the Commissioner of Surma valley and Hill Division where it was *"Resolved that since there are Missions in any Hill District it is undesirable that any other should be allowed"* [10](sic). The communication however addressed to the Superintendents of the Division, was amplified when the resolution was sent for implementation stating, *"His Excellency is not prepared to Issue orders on this and will consider each specific case on its merits"*[11]. The most plausible explanation therefore, of restricting the entry of Roman Catholic Church into the Lushai hills, is because the British administrators wanted a clear delineation of territorial divisions and jurisdictions between the various Churches and their denominations, so that issues and problems arising out of conflicts of interests between these Churches could be avoided; at least during their tenure and regime. This fact is evident from the correspondences cited above.

Thus, in spite of the expressed policy pronouncements at convenient intervals and times of opening out the Northeast to all the Christian missionaries, the Roman Catholic Church could not enter the region along with the Protestant Church somehow. One of the possible reasons given by many observers is the fact that the British monarchy, itself being Protestants would have preferred the Protestant Church to that of the Roman Catholics. This however, appears too simplistic a view and naïve, even though on the surface the logic appears quite appealing. What appears more plausible and convincing is that logically, from the British administration's point of view and its policy of aggrandizement and consolidation this segregation was necessary. (i) To cover larger areas of the Northeastern region by the Christian missionaries in line with the British professed policy to Christianize the people of the region by deliberately preventing the duplications of efforts among the various denominations of the Christian Churches. (ii) This 'segregation' divided the activities among the Christian Churches by preventing clashes of interests, and thereby prevent both law and order situations and embarrassments within the Christian British and Europeans communities living in India and in Europe.

From this perspective, it was the political and administrative expediencies and compulsions based on the formula of 'one mission one area' that determined the British religious policy in the Northeast. From the British perspective, nothing could have been better than to have friendly converted Christian natives in these vast tracts of inhospitable mountainous uplands, than to confront hostile tribal populations. Thus, the more the coverage and hold by Christian missionaries on the region, irrespective of their denomination or congregation, the better their prepotent hold on the region. This also had the added advantage of a possible diplomatic alibi for the British who would have been accused otherwise of directly involving in the control and management of these sensitive border areas as part of its policy of expansion. Viewed from this perspective it is possible that as part of this policy, the Roman Catholic Church was compelled to work only in areas where the Protestants had not ventured into earlier or had established their hold and hence the manifest reluctance to permit conversions in the areas now forming Mizoram.

It may appear to be a case of excessive lateral thinking and perhaps out of the way but the other inhibiting factor, which might have made the British reluctant to permit the Roman Catholics to enter the sensitive border areas could be the conspicuous nature of the elaborate nature of services, dress code of the Roman Catholic clergy. Quite unlike the Protestants, the services and mass observed by the Catholics are elaborate rituals performed in a grand manner. These facts combined with the cassocks worn by the Catholic priests tended to be very conspicuous as it stood out against the rustic village settings. This may have been one of the inhibiting factors prompting the British Administration from allowing Catholic missioners going into a sensitive region like the Northeast since as a policy the British were deliberately trying to underplay their presence in the sensitive border areas close to the Chinese and Burmese borders.

The interpretation is pertinent since as already pointed out the British approach to proselytisation in the Northeast was intended to be a discreet and in a way meant to covertly achieve rather than overtly, the consolidation of the area and the aggrandizement of their position in the region. Surreptitiously, may be too strong a word to define the approach, but the nature of strategic location of the Northeast necessitated such an approach. Seen from this perspective and assumption, that the British Administrators would have found the Catholic priests in their cassocks and the nuns' habit too conspicuous for their liking in areas so close to Burma, China and Tibet seems relevant.

Seen therefore, purely from the British administration's perspective, it is quite evident that the British administration wanted a clear spatial segregation of influence between the Protestant church and the Roman Catholic Church essentially to prevent the clash of interests between the two churches and therefore, imposed an informal administrative demarcation. It is important to note that Roman Catholic Church is essentially Italian and European in character, while the Protestants are English and British in Character.

Historically, the Roman Catholic Church has made up the lost time and opportunity today. On 9 July 1934 the first Diocese at Shillong, followed by the Diocese at Dibrugarh on 12 July 1951 came up one after the other. The Diocese of Tezpur came into being on 16 January 1969. Thereafter the Archdiocese of Gauhati-

Shillong was formed on 26th June of 1969 (name changed later as Archdiocese of Shillong-Gauhati in 1970), Diocese of Kohima-Imphal on 29th January 1973, which was later split into the Diocese of Kohima and the Diocese of Imphal on 28th March 1980. The Diocese of Tura came up on 1st March 1973, the Diocese of Diphu on 5th December 1983, the Diocese of Guwahati by combining the Diocese of Tezpur and Tura on 30th March 1992. Finally, the Diocese of Shillong was elevated to an Archdiocese by creating the Dioceses of Nongstoin and of Jowai on 28 January 2006. The resume sums up the growth and expansion of the Catholic Church in the Northeast region. Recently the Archdiocese of Shillong-Gauhati (old name) split into the Archdiocese of Shillong and the Archdiocese of Guwahati[12].

Linked closely to the spatial distribution of the two types of churches in the region, interestingly, analysis shows that the two different churches have evoked two distinct socio-political responses from the people and communities they converted. For instance, it is interesting to note that the problem of insurgency, which is the metonym of political identic assertion in the region, is conspicuous much more and prevalent in the Protestant dominated areas. The two predominant Protestant groups are the Presbyterians and the Baptist Church. In comparative terms, in the Roman Catholic Church dominated areas the problem is less intense and somewhat subdued. The classic example is the insurgency problems of the Nagas and the Mizos. Both Nagaland and Mizoram not only have the highest number of Christian population, but the majority of them belong to the Protestant denomination of the Christian Church. Interestingly, insurgency in the Northeast first began from these two states. In both these States, interestingly the Roman Catholics form a very small percentage of the population.

On the other hand, the Khasis, Jaintias and Garos and various tribal communities of Arunachal, where the Roman Catholics either dominate or have a major presence, the insurgency movements have been comparatively less intense and less wide spread. While a more detailed study and analysis is necessary on the subjact, the finding can be interesting. However for the immediate, the inference is that while the protestant Churches has somehow got itself entangled in the politics of ethno-nationalistic aspirations, the Roman Catholic Church has been able to remain comparatively free from this association.

The Christian Churches in the Northeast region of India have greatly influenced the lives of the people of the region. According to Arun Shourie[13], the Churches have over the years changed (1) from calumny to expressions of empathy; (2) from the claim to being the sole possessors of Truth to ecumenism; (3) from uniformity to "contextualisation". Opinions on these vary, but the Roman Catholic Church and their tolerance of other religions in the region and in India have made adjustments and accommodations in the last few years. Christianity is much more accommodative and culturable of local traditions and social values than it ever was in the past. *The Background Paper: CBCI (Catholic Bishops Conference of India): Paths of Mission in India Today: Our Common Search*, Para-106, given at the conference in Pune, India in January 1994 under the aegis of the CBCI reflects this changing trend. The Conference observed, *"In the Vatican II the Church has opened herself to the world, to the secular realities. In earlier periods of her history, she had controlled many spheres of culture and social life. The emancipation of all these spheres from the tutelage of the Church was a painful experience...She did so not to withdraw into a purely spiritual sanctuary, but in a new way felt 'intimately linked with mankind and its history."*[14].

Christianity in the States

Christianity is predominantly prevalent in the Northeast in Meghalaya, Mizoram, Nagaland, and in the upland or hill areas of other states. Brief resume about the Christianisation process in the states of Nagaland, Mizoram, Meghalaya and Manipur is given in the following paras.

(a) Meghalaya

The first significant and important fact about Christianisation among the Khasis, the Jaintias and the Garos in the state of Meghalaya, is that even though they are the first among the Northeastern ethnic groups who came in contact with the Christian missionaries, the number of Christians among them is only about 70.3 per cent of the state's total population. The Khasis and Jaintias came in contact with the Christian missionaries because they were easily accessible from Sylhet and Mymensingh districts of erstwhile Bengal, now Bangladesh. In comparison, Nagaland and Mizoram have over 90 per cent and 87 per cent Christians respectively of the population [15] even though Christianity reached these states much later than in Meghalaya.

The Khasis or Khyriams came into contact with the Christian missionaries when William Carey from Serampore Mission in Bengal first established contact with them in 1813 through Rev. Krishna Chandra Pal of the British Baptists. In fact, Krishna Chandra Pal stayed in the Khasi and Jaintia Hills for a few months in Pandua, a marketing centre near Cherapunji, which was part of the Cherapunji Syiemship. William Carey translated the Bible (The New Testament) into Khasi in the Bengali script in 1824[16]. In 1832, Alexander B. Lish another missionary of the Serampore mission arrived in Sohra (Cherapunji) and started schools at Sohra, Mawsmai and at Mawmluh. The Calvinistic Methodists Mission led a mission in the Khasi and Jaintia hills after a shipwreck in the Bay of Bengal on 18 January 1837and accomplished pioneering work. Rev. Thomas Jones of the Welsh Presbyterian Church and his wife arrived in Sohra (Cherapunji) on June 1841. It was the missions under Thomas Jones, which adopted the Roman script to write the Khasi language[17]. Rev. Thomas Jones is considered as the 'father of Khasi Alphabet'.

The contacts with the Jaintias or Pnars or Syntengs were also circumstantial. It was only when a number of British subjects were abducted for sacrifice before Goddess Kali (at Nartiang) in 1821 that the British became first involved with the Jaintias in the Khasi and Jaintia Hills. To assess the situation and buy time to charter the future course of action David Scott, then Agent of the Governor General entered into a treaty with the Jaintia king Ram Singh for peace on the 10th of March 1824. The treaty let the British virtually run the traditional Doloi system, while the Jaintias remained in power in name. Unfortunately, the terms of the treaty were unfavourable to the Jaintias, while the Khasi chiefs on the other hand were comparatively free. However, the Jaintias including their rulers for a long time remained esentially either Hindus or Pagans, in spite of attempts to entice them to Christianity.

The Garos of Meghalaya resided close to the plains of Bengal and intermittent skirmishes between them and the Zamindars of Bengal created serious administrative problems for the British administration. These Zamindars besides being large landholders were also involved in the trade of cotton and minerals available in the Garo hills. The Garos would swamp the people in the villages in the lowlands, loot, kill, and disappear. Their reputations were formidable and vicious. The captured human heads being a special attraction for the villagers to celebrate[18]. The British were already aware of the Garos escapades in Goalpara (Assam) and Mymensingh and were only looking for an opportune moment to bring them under their control[19].

David Scott, who was the Commissioner of Koch Behar was the first to think of bringing the marauding Garos within British control. David Scot wrote to Lord Bayley, Secretary to Government in 1822, *"I am satisfied that nothing permanently good can be obtained by other means (than sending a missionary) and that, if we do not interfere on behalf of the poor Garo, they will soon become Hindu or half-Hindu".* Secretary Bayley's reply was equally consummate, indicative of his intent on the subject. He wrote back *"I do not think the favorable opportunity for making this interesting experiment should be lost".* The fate of the Garos, their indigenous religious beliefs of Songsarek was sealed. The Garos eventually embraced Christianity through the efforts of two young Christian converts of the Bapist mission Omed and Ramkhe.

The impact of Christianisation among the Garos affected the indigenous Songsarek religion, practised extensively at the time among the Garos. According to 1961 census as many as 1,42,274 (46.3%) practiced Songsarek among the Garos, which went down marginally in 1971 to 1,39,148 (34.22%). In the same period (1961-1971) Christianity went up from 87,311 (28.42 %) converts to 1,65,715 (40.75%), while Hinduism, which stood at 51,876, (16.88%) went up to 78,061 (19.19%), Islam from 17,163 (5.59%) to 21,929 (5.39%). Thus, even though Songsarek along with Christianity is the two most popular religion among the Garos, the traditional religion Songsarek was slowly losing out to Christianity.

Christianity and the challenge within

The biggest obstacle to Christianisation of the Khasis, the Jaintias and the Garos was their steadfast loyalties and adherence to their respective traditional indigenous native religions. This is essentially because like other tribal groups of the region, the Khasis, Jaintias and Garos identify themselves socially and culturally as distinct ethnic groups primarily due to the distinctive nature of their traditional indigenous faiths and religious beliefs, based on the inerrant principle that one exists because of the other. Conversely, there can be no true detachment between one's religious beliefs and faith from one's ethnic identity, culture and value systems. The traditional Khasi religious traditions, with their belief in the supreme god *U Blei* still retain its hold on the Khasi society and influence their thinking.

For instance, to counter the influences of Christianity, which was affecting their ethos and social values, a number of educated non-Christian Khasis notably late U Jeebon Roy Mairom, scholar and public servant got together other like-minded believers to form the *Seng Khasi* social movement, a powerful socio-cultural organisation in 1899. Efforts to revive the indigenous religions are going on among the Khasis, pioneered and led by the *Seng Khasi* movement, while the *Niam-tre* groups are making similar efforts to revive the *Seinraj* religious beliefs among the Jaintias. The strong revival movement among the Khasis and Jaintias or Pnars to revive their ancient traditional religion, essentially to counter the adverse influences of Christianisation has also unfortunately given birth to ethno-nationalistic aspirations among the younger generations of Khasis and Jaintias. This revival movement checkmates the process of Christianisation among the Khasis and Jaintias. Among the Jaintias, additionally the old connections with Hinduism have also affected the Christianisation process.

(b) The Mizos

The Christianisation of the people of Mizoram is a fascinating story on its own in the annals of the history of the Christian church in India. Mizoram stands out as the most intensely Christianised state in India and as one among the various Christianised communities in the World. No other ethnic group in the Northeast exhibits religiosity better than the Mizos[20]. Religiosity is part of Mizo ethos, sensibility and culture. This distinctive attribute of the Mizos is not restricted to their belief and faith in Christianity alone, but the general predilection to religiosity, piety and respect extends to all religions. The fact that this religiosity finds its manifestations in Christianity[21] is a matter of historical coincidence. One thing is certain; given this mental disposition of the average Mizo towards their religion, any other religion, which the Mizos would have embraced would have been similarly venerated by them.

One of the sociological explanations of this religiosity prevalent among the Mizos is the inherent social code of conduct, which the Mizos have given to themselves, popularly known as *'Tlawmngaihna'*. This code requires every Mizo and other human being to be 'hospitable, kind, unselfish and helpful to others'. *'Tlawmngaihna'* is considered as the moral force that govern the lives of the Mizos. The second probable explanation of the Mizos' intense religiosity is the fact of its turbulent past, which has seen and witnessed violence, skirmishes and fights among the various Mizo chiefs for supremacy and dominance. These internecine conflicts and fights led to the famous massive peoples' uprising against the various Chiefs especially of the Sailo Chiefs, for their autocratic and whimsical rule known in Mizo history as Lal Sawi[22].

These incessant fights and skirmishes had an adverse psychological impact on the mind of the people of Mizoram. Life was uncertain, often brutal and short, peace and harmony was the desire of the people. Thus, when the British placed Captain Shakespeare to take charge of the Lushai hills with Aizawl as the Headquarters and brought it under the Assam Administration in 1898, and peace returned, the Mizos welcomed it. Like elsewhere in the Northeast, the entry of the British administration opened up the Lushai Hills and Mizo society to the Christian missionaries. Petrified and disturbed by years of uncertainty, turmoil and war the Mizo community was all set to receive Christianity with a sense of relief. It is in this setting of the traumatic and turbulent years that the desire for spiritual experience and religiosity overtook the Mizo society. What the Mizos were looking for was a religion, which besides giving them mental solace and peace, one which could bind the whole Mizo community into one harmonious group so that they could forget their acrimonious past and live in peace and harmony as one ethnic group.

Although the process of Christianisation among the Mizos actually commenced subsequent to the participation of the 11 Mizos in the religious conclave at Mairang in the Khasi hills in 1906, followed by the phenomenon of 'revivalism' on their return to Mizoram, the first contacts had however, actually begun in 1891, when William Williams, a Welsh missionary traveled from the Khasi Hills to the Lushai Hills, as the first Christian missionary. Two Scottish Arthington missionaries, James H. Lorrain and Frederick W. Savidge, followed him on 11 January 1894 and stayed there for four years. Like other missionaries, they started their study of the Mizo dialect and reduced it to a written form. They translated the Gospel of Luke and John and the book of Acts into the Mizo language. They were able to convert two locals by the name of Khuma and Duma between 1894 and 1899. They both had to return since their sponsor Robert Arthington, Jr. of the Arthington Aborigines Mission decided to withdraw his support for further work among the Mizos. Before their departure, D.E. Jones of the Calvinistic Methodist Church joined them. Edwin Rawlands joined Jones later on and both of them started the Welsh Presbyterian Synod in the northern part of the Lushai Hills. In 1905, the Baptist Missionary Society entered into an agreement with the Calvinistic Methodist Church and again sent both James H. Lorrain and Frederick W. Savidge to Southern Lushai Hills. Lorrain started the Lakher Pioneer Mission among the Lakher (Mara) in 1910.

It is a pure historical coincidence that Christianity was 'lurking around' in the Khasi and Jaintia Hills close to them. Thus when Rev. D.E.Jones in Aizawl (north) and Rev. J.H. Lorrain in Lunglei (south) send an eleven member (Four each from North and South and three women) delegation to attend the Presbyterian Church gathering held in Mairang in the nearby Khasi Hills in 1906, the first formal introduction and experience of Revivalism of the Mizos took place. The ecstatic religious experiences of the eleven-member group of Mizos on their return from Mairang, described as the first experience of 'Revivalism'[23], or the 'Wave of Revival', created a great stir among the people in Mizoram. It marked the dawn of a new beginning for the Mizos.

This unique and distinctive experience of intense religious fervour of the Mizos witnessed in the popular outburst of intense joy and sense of elevation experienced by those who become involved in the experience is described by Rev. Lalsawma as 'Revival' or the awakening and reawaking of the public religious fervor. *"It is a vehement upsurge of public excitement into religious commitments, accompanied by diverse manifestations of emotional outbursts through songs, movement and transitory in nature"*. This Mizo experience has corresponding historical counterpart in the Revivalism movement in England and in Wales in the British Isles, almost a century earlier.

Psychologically, revivalism as an experience, a state of mind reached by intense personal emotive religious inspiration, a state of trance where one is in communion with one's self, where besides the moment of experience nothing else matters. The key to the igniting spark is the moment of that 'inspiration', which can come in a flash anywhere at all times. The inspirational spark that ignites the emotional intensity that propels an individual to get into a state of trance and religiosity, leading to physical manifestation like by utterances, songs, laughter and such similar pronouncements met the needs of the Mizo temperament. When a group of such individuals collectively undergoes either such an experience, individually inspired or collectively, a Revival takes place.

There were four reported instances or waves of Revivalism in Mizoram between 1906, 1913, 1919 and 1929/30. The very fact that the Mizos were capable of getting into the trance-like experience even in the first instance, which is a mental state experienced in such 'revival', speaks about the latent religiosity within the Mizo people and society. Christians around the world consider the Mizo 'revivalism' experiences as unique. 'Revivalism', has given a special and unique position to the Mizo form of life and their religiosity. Because of which they stand apart among all the Christianised communities in the region and in India.

The spirit of Revivalism is essentially emblematic of the communitarian ideals of sharing a felt need of being inspired together. This suited Mizo way of living and lifestyle. Like the Welsh in Britain, the Mizos were in search for something intense, more attuned to their temperament. No such phenomenon exists in neighbouring Nagaland, one of the highest concentrations of Christians in the country and in the entire Northeast region. This is partly because the American Baptist Church initiated the Nagas into Christianity, while in Mizoram it was the Welsh Presbyterian missions. In Wales, Howell Harris, founder of the Calvinistic Methodism or The Presbyterian Church of Wales, a schoolteacher, started it by preaching based on his inspired experience, on the other hand the Revival Movement in England was started earlier with John Wesley's Aldersgate's experience. Even though the Mizos have their own form of indigenous religion pontificated by the almighty *Pathian*, it remains largely a personal and family oriented religion and hence could not provide the catalytic role to act as the cementing force for all groups, which Christianity provided to the Mizos as a group. Because of the private and exclusive nature of the indigenous religion arising from *"this note of individualism"*, which *"...relegated religious things to the background of public life."*[24], Christianity became the religion to fill the socio-political and religious needs of the Mizos. Traces of the indigenous religion still find a place in Mizoram but in only a limited way.

The Church: The Shelter

One of the reasons for the success of Christianity in Mizoram is the result of proactive co-operation between the Scottish Baptist

Missionaries and the Welsh Presbyterian Missionaries. Both the Churches within a short span of about 50 years brought almost the entire population of Lushai Hills into the Christian fold. The 'Kristian Tlangau' (The Christian Herald in Mizo), a magazine on Christian teachings was first brought out in 1911 by the Mizoram Presbyterian Church's Synod Press. The fraternisation exhibited by the various denominations, in spite of each having to compete for converts, was a rare example of 'togetherness' among Christian missionaries, which is not only exemplary but demonstrative of Christian brotherhood among the Mizos.

The success of the Christianisation story among the Mizos is also the result of people's participation and involvement. An unique example is the case where many woman folks among the Mizos set aside every day a little amount of uncooked rice known as *'buhfai tham'* in a special vessel, for contribution to the Church so that out of the sale proceeds the Church could meet some of its expenses. One is not aware of any such practice in the region, which is as poignant as this all for the cause of the Church. Because of such reverential adherence, most missionaries in Mizoram found their missionary work extremely rewarding and rich. Combining the traditional communitarian approach and practice of participative management with Christian missionary zeal and fervour, Christianisation was bound to succeed in Mizoram.

The success of the Mizo story is reflected in the emergence of the Universal Christian Mizo. Prasan Sonwalkar, in his article *'Mizos return favor by preaching Christianity in Wales' in the Indo-Asian News Service*, Saturday, 11 March 2006, wrote that Mizos who were once converted by missionaries from Wales between 1840 and 1960 are now returning the favour. An Indian Mizo Rev. Hmar Sangkhuma, from the Diocese of Mizoram, has been preaching spiritual guidance to the local Welsh population in Maesteg, near Bridgend in Wales in the United Kingdom. Rev. John Colney, another priest from the Diocese of Mizoram, arrived in Wales in April 2006. Sonwalkar wrote, *"India...is increasingly catering to the spiritual needs of Christians in the West by conducting services for them from India-and also meeting a shortage of priests"*. There are approximately 190 Mizo missionaries and priests, not to mention other communities from India and the Northeast, who are working across the world and in surrounding neighbouring countries according to Zari Malsawma[25].

The Lesser healers

One of the interesting fallout of the intense religious predilection and Christianisation in Mizoram is the emergence of a large number of self-appointed evangelists working outside the formatted structure of the existing congregation of Churches. These "deviations", reflect the intensity and the surcharged atmosphere of religiosity prevalent in the state. To name only a few of the prominent ones are Zakaia of Aiduzawl, Sanghera of Ngopa, and Khuangtuaha of Sialsuk/ Hmawngkawn[26]. The other well-known self-professed figures are Rorelliana, a Veterinary doctor named Biakmawia, Chhunkhama of Venglui and Vanawia in the Chhimtuipui area. One Zathangvunga of Champai who had a large followers is believed to have referred to Saint Paul as being lesser than he is and hence 'behind' him. In the eyes of the Synod, these self-professed religious preachers are vexatious figures[27]. However, the fact remains these 'evangelists' command large adherents and followers within Mizo society.

(c) The Nagas

There are, according to B. G. Verghese 32 tribes, which constitute the generic classification called the Nagas. They are *"scattered within Nagaland, Manipur, Tirap in Arunachal and the North Cachar and Karbi Anglong districts of Assam"* within India. The first contact of the Nagas with the British took place in January 1832 when a British expedition under Captain Jenkins and Pemberton marching through from Manipur to Assam accidentally encountered the Angami Nagas. Later in 1870 the Assamese came into contact with the Ao Nagas when an epidemic broke out in the Ao territory in the Mokokchung district of Assam, now in Nagaland in which many Ao Nagas were forced to flee to the Assam plains to avoid the epidemic[28]. This contact was inevitable since the Ao areas in Mokokchung district were immediately abutting present Jorhat district of Assam.

It is through one such contact, purely circumstantial, that the first Christian missionaries came in contact with the Ao Nagas. Realising the importance and significance Rev. Edward Winter Clarke of the American Baptist Mission was keen to enter the Ao territory. However, since the British administration did not permit him to enter the hostile territory, he sent Godhula Rufus in October 1871 into what is the present Ao region in Mokokchung district of Nagaland along with some Molungkimong village traders. Rev. Clerk could enter the Ao territory and follow Godhula later on 17 December 1872.

The credit of converting the first Naga to Christianity goes to E.W. Clarke. *"The first nine converts were taken to Assam and were baptized by the missionary E.W. Clarke in Dikhu River on Sunday the 10th November 1872 on their profession of faith in Christ"*[29]. It was however, only when Rev. Clarke could make his first entry into the Ao Naga territory that the first baptism on Naga territory took place on 22 December 1872 when 15 Nagas embraced Christianity. Godhula worked with the Ao Nagas until 1876. The Rev. Edward Clarkes and his wife left Impur in 1911 after about 40 years of work among the Nagas. Mokokchung became thereafter an important centre for the Baptist Church. In 1960, 'The Nagaland Baptist Church Council (NBCC)', established a Home Board in Mokokchung. Later, the name was changed and known as the 'Nagaland Missionary Movement' (NMM).

There are various theories and claims of being the first Naga convert among different tribes of the Nagas. For instance, the Konyak tribe claims that they are the first to convert to Christianity in 1847, even before the Aos, when Rev. Wickstrand converted one Yongma, a Konyak Naga to Christianity on 11 December 1832. The Angami Nagas and the Lotha Nagas claim that they first spread the message of the Gospel to the Sema, Rengma, Zelieng, Chakesang, Pochuri, Zemi and the Mao Nagas[30].

The attempts at converting the Nagas to Christianity were not without problems. Christianisation imposed restrictions and insisted on changes in lifestyles, like stopping the social habit of drinking locally brewed rice beer and liquor, which were social perquisites. This interference by the Church created tensions between the Church leaders and the Naga traditionalists. The traditionalists were not only opposed to the restriction imposed on their way of life and living, but also because of the reasoning that their beliefs and lifestyles were primitive and pagan in character. In fact, the Chang tribe and the Phoom Nagas who resemble the Konyak posed many problems for the missionaries.

Christianity, in spite of these oppositions, became a metonym with reforms and social change and was accordingly accepted as a change agent. The Church setup schools wherever possible in this remote region. This impressed many Nagas. While missionaries like Clarke were busy converting the Nagas into Christians, the British administration was busy consolidating its position. The areas occupied by the Angamis, the Rengmas, and Lothas were brought under British control and consolidation of the Aos was completed.

In spite of these oppositions to these conversions, on 4th July 1920 seven Sema Nagas converted to Christianity at Semasettu village[31]. The conversion is significant because the event took place in the paddy fields where the converts were working. Following these conversions, Rev. W. F. Dowd was able to convert two more persons from the Chang Nagas in Jakpa village. It was only on 23 August 1925 that Rev. Subongwati, an Ao ordained minister administered baptism to four Sangtam Nagas from Chari village. The British administration was not in favour of these conversions undertaken by native converted Naga ministers because of the nature of these conversion tended to be numerically oriented rather than ecumenical. In fact, Dr. Bendangyabag observes that the *"British authority levied a fine of sixty rupees"*[32] from two Naga evangelist Rev. Kijungluba and Evangelist Semsaliang for baptizing 50 people who preached in a few villages among the Sangtams. Soon many more Aos, Angami, Chakhesang, Chang, Lotha, Phoom, Sangtam, Sema, occupying different parts of present Nagaland and Myanmar, became Christians. The Chakhesangs known as Eastern Angamis, a combination of the Chakri, Khezha and Sangtam sub-tribes, now split as the Pochury and claim a distinct identic group, became Christians.

Impact of Christianity

Christianity was able to breach the psychological as well as the physical barriers and divide among the myriad tribes of Nagas, sub-tribes and sub-sub-tribes. However, in spite of the success of Christianity in breaking down the initial hesitations and winning over the confidence of the various Naga tribes, the Church could not unify or forge a link and bond among the various Christianized tribes. The Church could not repeat the success story of the Mizos, of providing a unified and cohesive group even though it brought all the different groups of Nagas under its common fold as different tribes albeit under different denominations of different Churches. In 1937, the first Naga Hills Baptist Convention (NBCC) took place in Kohima. The formation of the NBCC (The Nagaland Baptist Church Council) setup in 1953 is the legacy of this attempt at religious unification among the various divergent groups of Nagas under the aegis of the Baptist Church. Later on, this indirectly contributed in the formation of the Naga identity.

Placed in the pontificated status by the Nagas, the Church became a haven for guidance and leadership destined to change Naga history. The Church could undertake this role because its strength lay in its communitarian approach to religiosity. This approach of the Church suited the Naga communitarian psyche and frame of mind. Consequently, when the Church introduced the Sunday services it became a rallying point for the members of the various tribes and communities to meet, pray and above all socialize together. These 'Sunday' gatherings soon transformed into a community council of sorts, albeit infused with religious piety and reverence for most part. It is through such interactions and gatherings, both within members of the same tribe and with other tribes at the services through the aegis of the church that the much needed political platform or institution for the various tribes to come together became a reality accidentally. The Christian Church provided the rare opportunity and the platform needed for political activities within its precincts. The role of the Church thereafter took an ominous turn, it was both the 'conscience keeper' of Christian faith and simultaneously became inadvertently a haven for 'unlawful anti-national activities'; all rolled into one. The Church forgot in the Northeast that if keeping politics out of the Church were not simple and easy, keeping the politics of ethno-nationalism away from its followers would prove much more difficult. The Church never foresaw the emerging situation.

A. Bendangyabang describes the situation succinctly, *"The church probably became a centre of identity, a platform for Naga solidarity and integrity"*[33]. Whether the church and the missionaries were aware of these developments, the political overtones that were getting associated with it is a matter of debate and speculation, but the fact that young politically ambitious Christian Nagas used the church as a political platform is an ineluctable fact of Naga history. The Government of Assam and the Government of India were always suspicious of such a situation developing and knew of this fact. The Church has as such not been able to escape from this criticism even though to be fair, most of the missionaries and other members simply did not know that such anti-national activities were taking place under their own roof. In whatever way one views these developments, the fact is that the Church unknowingly and unwittingly facilitated and helped the Nagas to come together for a common cause by providing them a ready-made platform to assert their ethnic identities.

The adverse impact of this unintended but solicitous role the Church found itself; by becoming party to the various surreptitious political activities in its precincts, placed the leaders of the various Churches under severe strain, especially because of the air of suspicion hanging above them all the time. It will however, be wrong to condemn the Christian church outright, since the church as an institution was never directly instrumental in instigating and steering anti-national or anti-Indian aspirations among the Nagas as has been made out. Simultaneously, however, a few Church leaders and foreign missionaries were indulging in anti-national activities but their numbers were insignificant, compared to the number of those who have contributed positively towards national building as well as towards the general development and welfare of the Nagas. From this perspective therefore, generalizing all Christian foreign missionaries in the region as anti-national would be too naïve and simplistic a view.

Briefly, the role and contribution of the Christian Church to the Naga should be objectively assessed devoid of any prejudice. What needs to be appreciated is the fact that in the absence of any form of governmental intervention and welfare measures at the time when Christianity first made inroads among the Nagas, it is these Christian pioneers or missionaries who provided some hope and undertook some welfare measures for the benefit of the Nagas. One has to be grateful to the Church for these acts of charity, even if these were undertaken purely for religious considerations. Perhaps it is these departures from the purely ecumenical pursuits, which in today's welfare jargon is called 'inclusive' growth and development that the role of the Church is best judged. One thing is certain; the Christian Churches infused the sense of belonging together as a group among the various Naga tribes, which in turn generated the idea and concept of a Naga ethnic identity.

(d) Manipur

As per the 2001 Census of India, around 34% of the total populations in Manipur are Christians. Geographically, Manipur comprises of three fourth hills and mountains, with only one fourth comprising of valleys. The different tribes, who constitute about one third of the population of the state and who are predominantly Christians occupy the mountainous hill-areas, while the Meiteis who are Hindus and followers of Islam who are non-tribals occupy the remaining two third valley areas. The state is surrounded by the two predominant Christian states of Mizoram in the North and Northeast and Nagaland on the South and South West.

Historically analysed the histories of the various tribes in Manipur are intermingled with those of the Meiteis. There are ample numbers of studies and scholarship to suggest that the Meiteis were once tribes. It was only after the Meiteis became Hindus that new theories denying this anthropological linkages and association began to float. Historians cite the social purge during the reign of king Pamheiba[34] after he embraced Hinduism in the 18th century as the period of change. The pagan ethnic history of Manipur thereafter became an infringement on its Hindu incarnation and thereafter the protagonists of the Hinduism conveniently debunked the anthropological links and associations of the Meiteis with the upland tribal communities of the kingdom.

On king Pamheiba's ascension to the throne in 1714, Sir Edmund Gait describes *"... Pamheiba, who is reputed to have been a Naga chief, and who subsequently became a convert to Hinduism taking the name Gharib Nawaz or 'patron of the poor"*[35](sic). Similarly most British research works and records left by Col. McCullock, Major-General Sir James Johnstone, K.C.S.I and others, suggest that the Meiteis share a common ancestry with the hill tribes, particularly with the Kabuis. The shift in religious affiliations of the Meitei community to Hinduism from their indigenous religious beliefs combined with Hindu orthodoxy and conservatism changed the social equations between the tribal uplanders and the Meiteis. The subsequent ostracisation of the non-Hindu upland tribal communities following the Hindunisation offended the people of these communities and hurt their feelings and sentiments. In fact, one of the grudge of the upland tribal communities against the Meiteis is that the Meiteis by accepting Hinduism, an alien religion, severed the ties and bonds with them. The conversion of the Meiteis to Hinduism changed the entire future course of the ethno-political history of Manipur.

The process of Christianisation in Manipur first began in the valley areas, to be precise in and around Imphal. Several missionaries followed the British officials into the erstwhile kingdom. Under the purview of the British Political Agent and with the permission of the king of Manipur many missionaries, scholars did commendable work. The role of Rev. William Pettigrew who originally joined as a missionary under the Arlington Aboriginese Mission and worked in Dhaka (Dacca) in Bangladesh, but eventually joined the American Baptist mission on 1896 in Sibsagar in Assam in this regard is significant in many respects. He started the first school in 1872[36] in Imphal and translated the Bible into local Meitei 'lon' or language. Similarly, Dr. G.H.Damant published the Meitei script for the Asiatic Society of Bengal in 1877. The Johnston Middle School started in 1885[37] at Imphal. Singularly, Pettigrew encouraged inter community marriages and worked relentlessly for the development of the Meitei language besides spreading Christianity in Manipur in the upland areas of the state. Rev. William Pettigrew[38] also changed the medium of instructions in schools from Bengali to the Meitei-language. Christians of Manipur owe much of its success to Rev. William Pettigrew alone. In spite of being a Christian Rev. Pettigrew remained loyal and faithful to the cause of all the people of the Manipur including the Hindu Meiteis. People irrespective of their ethnic affiliations remember him for this commitment to Manipur.

The Christianisation process in Manipur however, suffered immensely after 1891 when five British officers including J.W.Quinton, the Chief Commissioner of Assam and Grimwood the Political Agent were murdered. The British accused Maharajkumar Bir Tikendrajit, the Bar Senapati the son of Maharaja Chandrakirti for the murder of the British officials. The British hanged Tikendrajit for the murder publically in 1891. A strong resentment against the British and political upheaval and turmoil followed. This led to the ban of the propagation of Christianity in the Imphal valley by a royal diktat due to which missionaries like Pettigrew had to move out of the Manipur valley and divert their activities in the hills. Rev. Pettigrew moved into Ukhrul among the Tangkhuls.

Set against this backdrop and especially the social segregation of the upland tribal communities by the Meteis after they became Hindus, the upland tribal communities were psychologically ready to accept Christianity, as some people believe, more in retaliation and as a reaction to Hindu orthodoxy and selectivism. Thus when Rev. William Pettigrew moved into Ukhrul in the uplands the Tangkhuls were more than ready to accept him with open arms. Rev. Pettigrew started the first branch of the American Baptist mission on February 1896 in Ukhrul. The activities of the mission were confined to Ukhrul village and surrounding areas from 1896 to 1916. It was after seven years that the first conversion and a lone Church could be set up. By 1915, sixty-three conversions, mostly Tangkhul Nagas took place. By 1932, the numbers increased and Christianity was by then well established in this part of the region.

Earlier in 1913 Rev. Pettigrew was officially asked by the British with the permission of the Manipur Darbar (headed by the Maharaja), to visit the areas occupied by the Thadou-Kukis and the Kom Kukis in Sadar Hill district in the North and Northwest region of Manipur. He also received representatives from the Kabuis, Thadous and from the Annals in southeast region of the state for such missions. Eventually, because of the increased requests, the American Baptist Mission shifted its headquarters to Kangpokpi. The Mao Nagas living on the borders close to Nagaland also converted to Christianity.

Another young missionary responsible for the spread of Christianity in Manipur was Watkins R. Roberts, a Welshman who converted the Hmars in Churachandpur in Southern Manipur abutting Mizoram. Watkins R. Roberts left Aizawl, the headquarters in the Lushai Hills on 5th February 1910 and set up his base in Senvawn, one of the biggest Hmar villages in Tippaimukh in Manipur at the invitation of the village chief Kamkholun. Following his invitation, various Mizos settled and domiciled in Manipur. Watkins set up the North East Indian General Mission[39] in 1919 and undertook active conversion. This group spread its area of operation into neighbouring North Cachar Hills of Assam, Tripura and to the border town of Tamu in Burma.

Christianity in the Northeast: Summary and Conclusions

Christianisation has been successful in its proselytisation particularly in the Northeast as compared to any other region in India, with the exception of South India. The available statistics and trends of conversions to Christianity, in terms of numbers and percentages from the years 1951 to 1981[40] prove this point. In a matter of thirty years, while the number of Christians in the Northeastern region, comprising of Assam, Arunachal Pradesh, Manipur, Meghalaya, Mizoram, Nagaland, Sikkim and Tripura grew at the rate of 7.80%, 10.47%, 12.53% and 16.74% every ten years respectively, there has been a regular fall in all other regions including the southern and western regions of India. In the northern and central regions, there has been a marginal or no increase.

Perspectively speaking, one aspect is clear, Christianity found plenty of receptive followers in the Northeast partly because of the void created by Hinduism by its 'selectivity' and blatant exclusion of the upland tribal communities in the region. Many upland communities consider the 'exclusion' as 'deliberate', perpetuated and instigated by the lowland non-tribal communities on them because of their social habits and lifestyles. The upland communities did not take to this 'exclusion' kindly; in fact, this exclusion is one of the main causes for the social polarization between the two sets of communities, the non-Hindu upland tribal communities and the Hindu non-tribal communities from the lowland areas of the Northeast. Thus, when Christian missionaries came to the region and started converting the upland tribal communities to Christians, it was a moment of fulfillment and self-actualisation long denied to them by Hinduism and other universal religions. They embraced Christianity with vengeance. The adoption of Christianity as the main religion by most of the upland tribal population set in motion the balkanization of the Northeast on religious lines. Christianity completed the process of ethnic 'divide', which Hinduism had unwittingly introduced in the Northeast.

To state that Christianity transformed and affected the lives of the upland communities of the Northeast, is an understatement. In fact, it affected every one across the board in the region, cutting across the ethnic and political divide. In a way, it changed social equations, reconceptualised the prevailing concepts of social discrimination and prejudices by changing the thinking of people and communities in the region. For instance, it transformed the air of complacency and neutralized the assumed superiority of the majority Hindunised communities over the upland tribal communities. The Hindus were rudely shaken out of the proverbial state of stupor and contentment regarding their social position among the ethnic groups in the region. This awareness is significant not so much, because there was any perceptible threat or danger to Hinduism, but more importantly because it would change the entire course of ethnic relationship and equations in the region forever. This is most conspicuous in the impact created by the extended meaning and association of the western notion of modernity with Christian value systems in the region. The ramifications of the association and identification between Christianity and Western life-style would affect not only the Christianised upland communities but also the non-tribal non-Christian population in the region.

For the Hindus, Christianity introduced the concept of the westernized view and approach to life in the region, an entirely new prescription not anticipated. It introduced into the Northeast a life style very distinct and different from the lifestyles that most Northeastern societies were familiar with. The compelling lifestyle changes among the new Christian converts combined with the newly acquired status as 'Scheduled Tribe' conferred by the Constitution of India on the Christianised upland tribal communities transformed the outlook and ways of living. These transformations created a visible impact both on the upland tribal communities and also equally among the non-tribal Hindu communities of the region.

The associated implication and import of the connections between Christianity with Western values, and its extended meaning and notion of 'modernity' became the symbol of 'change' and hence 'forward looking'. In short, Christianity became emblematic of what was considered as modern and progressive, in contrast to Hinduism, which was seen and perceived as being orthodox and conservative. Christianity became sociologically important because it broke the age-old stranglehold and concept that religion is essentially ecumenical, restrictive, inhibiting and devoid of any temporal significance and importance. Religion, especially Christianity for once became the harbinger of change, modernity, progress and development. From this perspective Christianity, more indirectly, than directly became a change agent in the Northeast region cutting across religious and ethnic divide. Modernity was never a dirty word ever again. More dangerously, the issue veered into the debate of the merits and demerits of 'being a Hindu and an Indian' or not being one.

In addition, the fact that Christianity was a religion of the ruling elite of the world at the time of its introduction into the Northeast when Britain and European countries ruled the world left a very powerful impression in the minds of many communities everywhere and on the highly impressionistic upland tribal communities of the region. In its wake, it reinforced subconsciously the belief that becoming a Christian was 'westernisation' and in a limited sense, a reflection of 'modernity'. This assumption may be an over simplification, but the fact remains that the Christian Church became symbol of 'progress', 'change' and synonymous with 'modernism'.

Critically analysed these changes however, especially the concept of modernity created its own inner contradictions within the upland tribal fraternity, essentially a conflict between the traditional tribal way of life and the need to conform to Western notion of civility and life-style that Christianity introduced. The consternation was in the fact that the concept of modernity was wrongly understood and misinterpreted more in the superficial sense of the term, implying a bohemian, flamboyant lifestyle and imitations of Western lifestyles by the younger generations of the Christianised communities at the cost of their own traditional value systems. The idea of modernism meant permissiveness rather than inculcation of the positive aspects of life, which include religious tolerance, equanimity, development, progress and a host of other positive correlates.

The Christian Church on its part would have been happy to go without this associated embellishment, but did not openly try to delink the two concepts; Christianity and Westernisation, since the 'association' to a great extend helped it in influencing the new and potential converts in the region. In the sociological sense, while this change in attitude and adoption of Western life-styles and values transformed the lives of the tribal communities in the region, it destroyed the inherent native socio-cultural value system, which is intrinsic to the tribal-way of life. The christianisation process, for the upland communities themselves was therefore, not merely about adopting a new religious faith but also impinged upon acquiring a new identity, which sadly relinquished their native indigenous traits and traditional value systems.

The social transformation brought about by Christianity and the supposed idea of modernity as a result, were symptomatic of the danger the adaptations of Western values posed on the various traditional institutions in the region. This affected on two counts. First, it distorted the native traditional social and cultural practices by superimposing a borrowed alien social-value system in one of the poorest regions in the country, which did not have the economic or the financial capacity to sustain such a life-style. Second, it brought about a clash of value systems between the occidental way of life and oriental way of life in one of the remotest and largely inaccessible part of the country. In due course of time, the introduction of Christianity along with alien Western value systems and life-styles would erode not only the traditional socio-cultural value systems but introduce the politics of anti-national assertive identity in the region.

The contagious nature of the blind imitation of the West without the economical and financial ability to sustain these western embellishments among the younger generations of the upland Christian converts that led to the random destruction of the traditional social ethos of these communities morphed into the sensitive debate of the relevance and appropriateness of Christianity itself for the poor communities like those in the Northeast. The inverted impact was the apparent confusion in the minds of the younger generations of non-tribal non-Christian youths in the Northeast visible in their inability to reconcile the differences between the Christian ways of lifestyles, made synonymous with modernity and their seemingly conservative Hindu ways of life that their ancestors have been following. It is precisely the inability to reconcile the differences between the two lifestyles, between the Christian ways of lifestyle symbolising modernism and the Aryanised Hindu traditional lifestyle of the non-tribal communities in the region, which would create social tensions both within and between the various ethnic groups in the region.

There is nothing wrong about Christianity introducing the concept and notion of Western value systems in its wake, but it is the associated connotations and implications, namely the disparaging undertones that what is Indian is not Western and hence not 'modern', which was a misplaced distinction. The unkindest criticism against Christianity is as such that it encouraged the upland communities to doubt and question their Indianness. Even though, the Christian Church cannot be directly blamed for these developments or be made responsible for the political nature of the activities perpetuated from within its precincts, yet the fact that the initial platform for such activities was provided by it, albeit unintentionally, has put all the Christian missions in the region under a scanner.

Religion is a right and a privilege, an essential ingredient of one's right as a human being, but the conjured sense of modernity associated with Christianity is disturbing, especially when Christianity itself is against such assumptions or notions. The ubiquitous prevalence of Christianity as a religion and its transgression into the simple indigenous life of the new converts with its superficial Western value systems without actually realizing the damage to tribal traditions is what disturbs many native traditionalists. Traditionalists are up against these innuendos and are not willing to accommodate these influences, which affects and in many ways alter their native traditions, indigenous culture and social values. For them, modernity is a double-edged sword; it cuts on both sides; it is good but also destructive. It is the negative association of Christianity with modern value systems at the expense of traditional values and replacing them, without adequately understanding the meaning or import of the concepts of 'modernity' by the converts as well as the 'non-converts' (the non-tribal communities), which has given a bad name to Christianity. Conversely also the malfeasance that all alien religions pose a serious threat to the very existence of many indigenous native societies and communities is also not being realistic since many of these indigenous people and communities in the Northeast, even after accepting Christianity as their religion still live life sustained by many of these ancient traditions and values. But, more importantly, Christianity in the Northeast after its epochal descend only completed the process of 'ethnic identity' divide, which Hinduism began much earlier in the region's history.

Endnotes

1. Christian Bishops Conference of India survey report dated 1 December 1993.
2. Rev. Richard Howell: *The South Asian Scene with Special Reference to India to Celebrate Messiah 2000*. The figures are extracts as given in, org/celebrate/howell.htm.
3. Rev. Richard Howell: *The South Asian Scene*.
4. Arun Shourie, *Missionaries in India* ibid, p-109.
5. Arun Shourie, *Missionaries in India: Continuities, Changes, Dilemmas*, 1994, ibid, p-120.
6. Refer to the *Internet of the Diocese of Dibrugarh*.
7. Dr. Sangkima; *Essays on the History of the Mizos*, Chapter 20, History of the Catholic Church in Mizoram, p-207 onwards.
8. Dr. Sangkima, quoting from '*The Life and Witness of the Churches in Mizoram*' by Rev. Dr. C.L.Hminga p-155.
9. C.L. Hminga, *The Life and Witness of the Churches in Mizoram*; The Literature Committee, Baptist Church, Lunglei, 1987 p.159.
10. J.P. Mills, Secretary to the Governor of Assam addressed to the Commissioner, Surma Valley & Hill Division. *Proceedings of the Hills Officers' Conference, Memo No. 3348-50 G.S. dated Shillong, 26.7.1935*.

11. J.P. Mills, ibid.

12. Each Diocese covers approximately an average of 50,000 Catholics ranging around 3% to 4% of the total population of the population covered by the physical area of the Diocese, while each of the Archdiocese cover approximately an average of 1,50,000 to 2,50,000 Catholics. Keeping in mind that Roman Catholics constitute about 30% of the total Christian population in the Northeast region the expanding Archdioceses and the Dioceses will indicate the growing strength of the Roman citadel in the region.

13. Arun Shourie. ibid.

14. Arun Shourie - ibid. p-228.

Christianity in the States: Meghalaya

15. *Gazetteer of India, Khasi Hills* District, 1990 p-50. Also refer to Gazetteer, *Jaintia Hills*, p-31. There are substantial number of Non-Christian Khasi-Pnars (Jaintias, adherents of indigenous religion) who in 197142 census numbered approximately 127000, against 248800 Christians and 102709 Hindus out of the district's total population of 491209. Similarly among the Jaintias (Pnars), those who returned as practicing War, Pnar, Khasis, Jaintias indigenous religion was around 35,301, forming 32.6%43 out of those who declared themselves as Scheduled Tribes numbering 1,08,289.

16. Dr. Sylvanus Lamare, *Khasi Language: The beginning; "Khasi language As A Written Language"* (sic); Khasilit. Org.

17. Dr. Sylvanus Lamare, ibid.

18. Milton Sangma, *History and Culture of the Garos*, 1981, p-5.

19. *Meghalaya District Gazetteer, Garo Hills*, 1995, p-34. Also, see A. Playfair, *The Garos,* reprint 1975, p-7 to 14.

The Mizo

20. The Mizo as a single group comprises of various subgroups and clans such as Lushai, Hmar, Paihte, Ralte, Pawi and many other groups. These are further subdivided into smaller denominations. The Lushai have Sailo, Hauhnar, Pachuau, Chhakhhuak, Rokhum and Rivung as sub-clans. In spite of the multiplicity of clans and sub-clans constituting the Mizo society the level of religiosity in these groups is revelatory. 'Operation World, Asia', (*Source; Internet), categorizes Mizoram as an excellent Christian state having more than "60 denominations and

numerous independent congregations." Mizo missionaries in India and abroad number over 2,000.

21. Mizoram has more than 87% of its population as Christians.

22. ibid, p.4-5.

23. Rev. Lalsawma, *Revivals: The Mizo Way*, 1994, p-23-24. Zari Malsawma and Rev. Lalsawma details the four distinct waves of the revivalism among the Mizos. (1) The first was one that took place immediately after the initial spread of Christianity in the adjacent Khasi and Jaintia Hills in 1905-06. A group of 11 potential Mizo converts and believers went to the Khasi Hills and on their return found themselves inspired and overcome by the inspired exuberance of (2) The second wave of revival was in 1913 characterised by ecstatic dancing quite distinct from the occurrence in 1906. (3) The third wave began in 1919 and followed by the (4) fourth wave in 1929-1930.

    According to J.H. Morris, *History of Welsh Calvinistic Foreign Mission*, Revivalism historically goes back to the Reformation movement in the eighteen-century in Europe as response to the lackluster experience of the Reformation, which did not impress the Welsh sensibilities. The experiences in Wales are more relevant in the context of the Mizo experience since it is the Wales Presbyterian Church, which initiated the people of Mizoram to Christianity. The Welsh were looking for an inspirational line of religious experience quite out of the ordinary practices captured by the Traditional Churches of England. The Non-Conformists, the Baptists, the Puritans and the Quakers appealed more to their sense of religious quest and inquisitiveness.

24. P. Lalnithanga, *Emergence of Mizoram*, 2004, p-6.

25. The Mizos of Northeast India: Proclaiming the Gospel to their neighbours near and far, *Mission Frontier*, The Bulletin of the U.S. Center for World Mission, Nov/Dec. 1994.

26. Rev. Lalsawma as mentioned in his book on *Revivals: The Mizo Way*.

27. P. Lalnithanga, *Emergence of Mizoram*, 2004, p.4-5.

The Nagas

28. A. Bendangyabang Ao, *History of Christianity in Nagaland, Social Change 1872-1972*, p-67-68.

29. ibid, p-71.

30. ibid, p-170.

31. ibid, p-163-164.

32. ibid, p-167.

33. ibid, p-176.

In Manipur

34. T.C. Hudson, '*The Meitheis*', p.4-9.

35. Sir Edmund Gait, '*A History of Assam*, p-269-270.

36. Bendangyabang, ibid, p-71.

37. *History of Manipur*, Dr. Lal Dena, 1990 and *History of the Christian Missions in Manipur*: Karam Manimohan Singh, 1991.

38. Y.D.Luikham-Rev.William Pettigrew's Message of Oneness, in Rev. William Pettigrew, *A Pioneer Missionary of Manipur*, p-94, 1996.

39. Lal Dena, Christian Proselytism 1894-1946, *History of Modern Manipur 1826-1946*, ibid p-109 and 199.

40. Based on the Christian Bishops Conference of India Survey Report.

CHAPTER - 7

Identity and the Tribal Paradox

In the Northeast the term and concept of a 'tribe', as a categorisation of people is of comparatively recent introduction and usage. The British adopted it for administrative purposes by adopting the term from the definitions provided by British and European socio-anthropologists. Historically, in the Northeast, distinction between the upland tribal and lowland non-tribal communities merely denote two sets of people, living two distinct lifestyles in different geographical areas. The term 'tribal, which denotes a primitive life-style was first used by social scientists to describe the tribal way of life, as distinct from western notion of civilsation. However, in various contexts in India the term has somehow acquired a derogatory connotation. There were initial objections from the various upland communities in the Northeast when they were categorised as 'scheduled tribes' because of the juxtapositioning of the term 'Scheduled Tribe' in the Constitution along with 'Scheduled caste'. The implied equation between 'Scheduled Tribe' with the 'Scheduled caste', a socio-religious classification based on the caste systems prevalent in Hindu social hierarchy offended tribal sentiments in the Northeast.

The categorisation of the various tribal communities in the Northeast in the 'Scheduled Tribe' category, no doubt opened new opportunities for the upland communities in areas of employment, financial concessions etc. However, their inclusion, without considering the plight of the economically and disadvantageously placed lowland Hindu non-tribal communities by providing some form of concessions, unwittingly created social tensions, which affected ethnic equations and relations between the tribal and non-tribal communities in the region. Many non-tribal communities began to consider the categorization, especially from the point of the various governmental largesse and concessions given to the upland tribal communities as reverse social and economic discrimination directed against them. Consequently, the Government instead of bridging the ethnic divide and reducing the socio-economic disparities created a situation in which the ethnic divide between the upland tribal Christian and the lowland Hindu communities got further aggravated.

The Chapter examines the impact and the consequences this legislation had on the ethnic identity politics of the region.

The post Independence legacy

In a democracy, the majority make policies on behalf of the remaining minority. In this dispensation, the peripheral and numerically small communities like those in the Northeast, particularly the upland tribal communities often play no role in the decision making process, and if at all, the role is too insignificant to be taken seriously. In plain language, their problems most often are relegated into inconsequential slots. Further most often, the decisions made by the majority may not always be appropriate or commensurate with the wishes and desires of the numerically smaller groups who are at the bottom of the numerical pyramid. Unfortunately, in spite of this inherent deficiency in democracy, such decisions never the less become the law, which in turn determine the lives of all people. Democracy has its inherent limitations and weaknesses because even though such laws are well intended, they create more problems rather than solve them. In the strategically sensitive region like the Northeast, with its heterogeneous mix of ethnicities and communities, following different religions and physically confined within a small geographical space, policies formulated by the majority without due sensitivity and wisdom become problems themselves rather than the solutions.

One such decision taken in post independent India is the categorization of people and communities as 'Scheduled Castes' and 'Scheduled Tribes'. Both these legislations have a profound impact on the social and political history of Northeast India. While the categorization of people and communities as 'Scheduled Castes' did not have much impact in the Northeast, the latter, the categorization of people and communities as 'Scheduled Tribes' profoundly affected the ethnic equations and relationships in the

Northeast. The categorization of people essentially meant for the welfare of the historically neglected and downtrodden upland communities in the Northeast and in the country in general, morphed into a major ethnic identity issue, responsible largely for the ethnic divide between the upland tribal and the non-tribal lowland communities.

The *Chambers Twentieth Century Dictionary*, defines 'Tribe' as *"...a division of a nation or people for political purposes: a set of people theoretically of common descent: an aggregate of families' forming a community: a race: a breed: a class or set of people: loosely, a classificatory division"*. There is nothing demeaning or derogatory either in the definition or in implication and hence there is no scope for any ambivalence to construct any other meaning than what is given. However, somehow and most often, the term has acquired a derogatory and demeaning connotation.

The term, Tribe, is of Western origin introduced in India by social scientists to sub-categorize small, racially and anthropologically different groups of people, differing from Western models of human societal formations, levels of civilisational attributes, cultural ethos and sensibilities. The term 'tribal' is the adjective appellate of the term 'tribe', which for some inexplicable reason has come to denote and imply the negative attributes of the terminology rather than amplify the more desirable epithets. In the process, the seemingly innocuous term has come to denote primitivism, backwardness, poverty, believers in animism and a host of other negative attributes. Besides, cataloging people into pre-conceived slots of backwardness and social deprivation, it has a socio-religious conotation in India.

The affirmative constitutional categorisation of people as 'Scheduled Tribe' and 'Scheduled Caste' was reformative and intended to correct a social aberration rampant in the Hindu caste-ridden societies in India. The constitutional remedy was to accord a special status to this category of people and provide them a series of concessions and economic largesse that would enable them to assimilate into the mainstream social ethos, and importantly to discover their own potential. Unfortunately, instead of making the legislation progressive, the Constitutional enactment became in many ways a formalization of the existing social disparity and divide prevalent in the country. From this perspective, the Constitution, which intended to negate and undo the historical wrongs and social biases ingrained in Indian Hindu society, somehow unintentionally only helped in perpetuating a social aberration that was inherently inhuman and wrong.

In addition, somehow, but by a strange logic, exemplified by the subtext of the overall comparative simplicity and innocence of the members belonging to these communities, the term 'tribal' also carries with it the stereotyped geographical and other associated appellatives, including a host of inadequacies. For instance, it is a common assumption and belief, surprisingly even among many of the well educated that all people living in the hills and mountainous regions of the country, especially the Mongoloid groups are simple, 'backward', besides being economically deprived. These disparaging constructions of people based on geographically qualified notions has led to the popular national habit of bracketing all the Mongoloid Northeasterners into the predetermined slots of people belonging to the lowest stratum in the socio-religious stratum of the Hindu caste system. The categorisation of people, therefore as 'Scheduled Tribes' instead of making it an enabling provision for social amelioration, caused considerable consternation among the people in the Northeast in its wake. The categorization of the 'upland community' by segregating and differentiating them as 'Scheduled Tribes' along with a socio-religious grouping from other communities which the 'upland communities' feel they did not belong, affected the psyche of the Scheduled communities in the region.

Historically and socio-anthropologically in the Northeast such categorisation and distinction of people, based on birth and their community did not exist prior to the coming of Hinduism. Even if differences existed, it was the differences in lifestyles of people and communities in the different parts and areas of the region, largely dictated by the geography and climate in which they were living. As such if any distinctions existed, it was purely as two different sets of people living two different forms of lifestyles. The introduction of the word and concept of 'tribal' and 'tribalism' by implication, therefore introduced a new social genre having derogatory sociological connotation. Thus, when the Indian constitution formally introduced and included the various upland communities of the region as 'Scheduled Tribes' it only validated what was considered derogatory, divisive and discriminatory.

Constitutional Definition

In the Indian Constitution, there is no definition of a 'Tribe'. Article 342(1) of the Constitution, empowers the President to *"specify the tribes or tribal communities or parts of or groups within tribes or tribal communities"* as Scheduled Tribes in relation to that State or Union Territory. The Parliament is empowered to either include or exclude any tribe or tribal community from the notified lists. The President has to draw-up such a list in consultation with the Governor of each State or Union Territory. Technically, a member of a tribe in one state, need not be recognised as a tribe in another state of the Union. The other provisions in the Constitution dealing with the terminology 'Tribe' are the Fifth and the Sixth Schedules. The latter is with specific reference to the various Tribes of the North Eastern Region, enacted under Articles 244(2) and 275(1), which has Provisions for the "Administration of the Tribal Areas in the States of Assam, Meghalaya, Tripura and Mizoram". Thus while the Constitution provides the procedural charter, administrative structural arrangements and details of listing the communities covered as Scheduled Tribes, no definition of the term has been provided. In the absence of any clear definition of who is a tribal, each state gives its own definitions and interpretations, creating considerable confusion in the process.

The criterion for categorisation of 'Tribe' or 'Tribal Community' in the Indian Constitution is based on indicative primitive traits, distinctive features and cultures, geographical isolation, religious beliefs, shyness of contact with the world at large and backwardness. These indicative attributes find mention in many references and in various official Commissions, Studies and committees constituted from time to time. Compilations of the implied meaning of the term are available in various official documents. These include the 1931 Census, the reports of the First Backward Classes Commission of 1955, the Advisory Committee (Kalalkar), the Lokur Committee for Revision of SC/ST lists of 1965, the Joint Committee of Parliament on Scheduled Castes and the Scheduled Tribes orders (Amendment) Bill of 1967; also known as the Chanda Committee of 1969 and other official documents.

Reaction of Upland Tribal Communities

Lalsangkima Pachuau sums up the sentiments and feelings of the tribal communities of the Northeast with reference to the definitions and the implied meanings of the term 'tribe', 'tribal' or 'tribalism' as derogatory in connotation, which *"...are pejorative terms denoting the primitive-stage-therefore, a temporary stage-in human evolution or development"*[1]. The term has therefore, acquired a *"...denotation of primitivity and inferiority of the people for whom the name is applied"*[1]. The resentment is understandable, since by implication the upland tribal communities of the Northeast[2] fall within the typical stereotyped derogatory connotations the term is understood in the rest of India.

Critically viewed, if one examines the sequence of the arrangements of Article 341 and Article 342 in the Constitution, the response of the tribal communities is understandable. Article 342 immediately follows Article 341, implying thereby that the Scheduled castes and the Scheduled tribes fall under the similar, if not the same category of people, the underprivileged, socially outcast communities. The fact that the members of the Scheduled caste communities in India occupy the bottom of the social hierarchy of the Indic Hindu society, and the implication that all the tribal communities fall in this socio-religious categorisation was unacceptable to tribal communities in the region. Unfortunately, many of the Northeastern upland tribal communities believe that this 'equation' was deliberatly done to bring the upland communities of the Northeast into the larger Indic 'socio-religious hierarchy' of the Hindus. In short, from the perspective of the upland tribal communities of the Northeast, the placement and juxtapositioning of Article 341 and Article 342 therefore has a different connotation and meaning.

Carefully analysed however, the apprehension was unfounded. This is apparent from the fact that Article 341 defines the power available to the President of India, to declare a community or a group as a Scheduled Caste, subject to Parliament's prerogative to either include or exclude *"any caste, race or tribe or part of or group within any caste, race or tribe"*. This is significant, since by implication, it implies that any group of people can be declared as Scheduled Caste. Thus, technically and legally by this provision a tribal community can be categorised as a scheduled caste community. Conversely, however, there is no provision to classify any person, including a Schedule Caste community as Scheduled Tribes. This qualitatively differentiates by proxy the fact that a member of a tribal community does not fall into the same category as a Scheduled Caste. Because of this difference while Scheduled Tribe can become Scheduled Caste, after obtaining Presidential consent and approval,

Scheduled Caste communities cannot become a Scheduled Tribe under existing provisions.,

A reading of the provisions makes it clear that the definition of the Scheduled Caste is far more expansive because it is not a racial categorisation but a socio-religious hierarchy, which can include members of any community, including upland tribal communities into the Scheduled Caste classification. The significance of this distinction also lies in the fact, that while categorisation of people as Scheduled Caste is not organically based, on the other hand categorization as a member of the Scheduled tribe involves the prerequisite elements of an organic link either by blood or by race or of both. Scheduled Caste as a concept does not define or denote a race but is linked to the nature of job performed by an individual or a group of people as a community or social grouping. The distinction is significant.

These issues, must have been debated before enforcing the constitutional validations in post-independent India, but whether specific discussions in the context of the Northeast, especially with reference to the socio-political ramifications this would have in the Northeast, is not known. This is probably where the problems associated with the categorisation of the upland communities of the region have arisen. This 'confusion' and ambiguity in the Constitution about the character of the tribal communities of the Northeast perhaps arose because as B.B.Kumar[3] points out, that in the common Hindustani usage both 'community' and 'caste' are interchangeable and used as 'jat' and 'jati'. The usage of these two terms are not only confusing but also misleading in its implication, as these two terms do not mean the same thing. Because while the former denotes a person's 'community' (jat), the latter denotes the 'caste' (jati), each of them having two distinct and separate social and ethnic identity implications in actual application and usage. The interchangeability of the two terms in Hindustani got probably mixed up in the English version in which 'Tribe' should have denoted the 'community' (jat) of the person and not catalogued as being part of or made to appear as 'caste' (jati).

In the case of the Northeastern tribes, the term 'jat' (community) was more appropriate since this would describe or denote the community or the 'jat' of the upland people. However, while categorising the tribal communities of the Northeast the term 'jati' (caste) somehow was implied as an appellative, because of the simultaneous introduction of the constitutional enactments and juxtapositioning of the two Articles one after the other. The confusion created by categorising the Northeast tribal communities, based on their 'tribal' attributes as their caste or 'jati' was the unfortunate mistake. This is because the concept of caste or jati is non-existent in the Northeast region among the tribal communities. The apparent confusion created by the two terms, has therefore left the Northeastern tribal communities confused and agitated.

Constitutional legal experts, however, tend to hold the view that the term 'Tribe' used in the Constitution, especially the Tribal communities notified, are sub-categorisation of groups of people for administrative purposes and convenience and in a way, a recognition and statement of their distinctive way of life. According to them, nothing beyond this inference should be drawn, implied or meant. The clarification notwithstanding, the tribal communities of the northeastern region have not taken the classification kindly. The constitutional amendment initially at the time of its introduction therefore, did not generate the kind of enthusiasm, which the reservation and economic concessions have generated subsequently in recent times.

While these clarifications have removed the doubts later, the damage caused by the categorization indirectly in ethnic relationship and equations in the Northeast remains irreparable. This is the most disturbing legacy of this categorization in the region. This is analysed further.

Reaction of non-tribal communities

The non-tribal communities were skeptical and critical of the legislation. The non-tribal's contention was that majority of them live comparable lives like the upland tribal communities separated by different social conditions and value-standards with comparable economic conditions. According to them, the main criteria for according the special status to the people of the Northeast region should have been the economic status based on general levels of poverty indices and not based on social poverty. From the views of the non-tribal communities the constitutional categorisation was as such discriminatory. It was Government's failure to recognise the economic plight of the large number of economically poor sections of the non-tribal communities in the region, which was not much different from the tribal people, which was the main cause of the anger and resentment against the categorization.

The criterion adopted by the Government of India in providing special financial and administrative support and concessions to the upland communities' consequent to their categorization as members of the scheduled tribes became a highly contentious issue in the region. Given the fact that the only source of employment in the region was Government and semi-Government jobs, as private employment for all practical purposes were non-existent, the extension of the special concessions and reservation policies on jobs, including financial assistance only to one set of community only intensified the rising social animosity between the two communities in the region. Consequently, in an ironical twist of circumstances what was to bring social cohesion and equality, instead further divided the people of the region much more than it was before the Constitutional categorization took place.

The problem in the Northeast was created mainly because the categorisation of people as Scheduled Tribes was undertaken on an all India basis. In the Northeast, both the tribal and non-tribal communities literally live side by side, interacting closely, confined as they do within a very small geographical area unlike in the larger states in the country where the tribal population is confined within small well-defined isolated pockets. Consequently, in the Northeast, each group is aware of the economic plight and conditions of living of the other. This awareness creates its own unique and distinctive problems. In other words in the Northeast the ethnic spread and dispersal of people are physically restricted by the topography of the region compelling both sets of people, the tribal and majority of the non-tribal population to live almost in similar economic conditions. This complicates the task for any Government to provide special packages' and government programs or financial largesse to one group without providing similar packages or developmental programs to the other group. Such action is bound to create a sense of discrimination.

Consequently, the special dispensation as per the Constitutional provisions to one section of the population in the region, without providing any compensatory administrative dispensations or other Government's largesse to the non-tribal communities was bound to create unnecessary social tensions between the two groups. The excluded non-tribal communities felt discriminated. A strong resentment against the tribal policy of the Government of India was inevitable. This adversely affected the implementations of various

Government programmes and schemes meant for the upland tribal communities mainly due to the non-cooperative attitude of the numerically dominant non-tribal bureaucracy in the region on one hand and the lukewarm response from the tribal communities to the governmental inititiatives on the other. Charges and counter-charges regarding half-hearted executions of various Tribal Plans and programmes, diversions of resources meant for tribal welfare to other general purposes within the states were common. This not only created more misunderstanding, mistrust among the communities but also jeopardized any future hope of redemption in redeeming the ethnic identity divide in the region. These aspects and issues even though perceptible and known among many State Governments in the region were not officially discussed for obvious reasons. What was significant is that it affected the general attitude, behaviour pattern and response between the two sets of people.

Thus, from both perspectives of the upland communities and the lowland communities for different reasons in the beginning, the non-tribals feeling neglected and the tribals feeling cheated being clubbed with a socio-religious categorisation of people, the classification and categorisation of people as Scheduled Tribes in the Northeast somehow became a much-misunderstood legislation. In due course, by interplay of circumstances it morphed into one of the major contributory factors in ethnic identity divide in the region. Perhaps for the first time in the social, cultural and ethnic history of the Northeast, the people of the region saw themselves as two distinct sets of people, as tribals and non-tribals, differentiated and enforceable by law. Even though the years have passed, the feelings of resentment on both sides persist, jeopardizing the intended collaborative approach to regional planning and development. In short, the constitutional amendment sharpened the ethnic divide among the various communities of the Northeast, particularly between the uplanders (tribals) and the lowlanders (non-tribals).

An important observation in this connection is that the British while in India, in spite of all their professed empathies with the upland communities never formally made any official distinction between the two sets of people based on ethnicity, caste, creed or community in the Northeast. Even though distinctions were recognised, they did it subtly without in any manner obtrusively creating a rift between the two sets of people, at least officially. Thus even though the rudiments of the conceptual framework for evolving such an obvious distinction between the tribal and non-tribal groups were put in place in the form of the Inner Line Permit System and the categorisation of 'Excluded Area' and 'Partially Excluded Area' in the region, the British never considered the differences ubiquitous enough to warrant a legislative or constitutional amplification of this difference. The British instead created a 'living space' in the form of the 'exclusive' or 'excluded' areas for the upland communities so that these communities could live in a manner appropriate to their life-style un-interfered. Simultaneously with the lowland communities, the British cleverly entered into political alliances and military partnership on the ostensible ground of sharing political power. The British kept both sets of people happy by respecting their distinctive ethos and histories and pampering their egos.

Critically analysed the formalized introduction of the concept and the term 'Tribe' in the Indian Constitution as an instrument of social inclusion and change in the Northeast marks the beginning of a distinct phase in the ethnic identity history of the northeast region of India. It set in motion the formal polarization of the people of the Northeast between tribal and non-tribal population based on socio-ethno distinctions. Progressively, this distinction combined with and propelled by the obnoxious religious divide between the followers of Christianity and the Hindus on one hand and the tribal non-tribal divide on the other, created its own brand of identity politics. The combination of these factors marked the end of the homogeneous and pluralistic social fabric of the region and the beginning of political instability and uncertainty among the people of the region. It marks a major defining moment in the history of the inter-ethnic relationships and the politics of identity in the Northeast.

In retrospect, the Government of India could have avoided the problem in the Northeast by categorizing the population of the region based on various levels of poverty indices in addition to their ethnicities rather than purely based on their ethnicities alone. For instance, the upland tribal communities of the Northeast could have been formed as a separate category or group based on their distinct social, cultural history and background without bracketing them along with all the tribal communities in India or with the socio-religious categorisation of the Scheduled castes adopted for the rest of the country. Simultaneously, the large numbers of poor among the non-tribal communities of the region could have been provided with some special economic packages based on comparable levels of economic poverty indices in conformity with those accorded to the tribal communities. Such an approach could have prevented the misunderstandings created by the constitutional provisions between the upland communities and the poorer sections of the non-tribal population by keeping in view the peculiar and unique histories of these communities.

Given the already highly charged atmosphere following the religious 'divide' between Hindu non-tribal communities and the Christian tribal communities, the Constitutional enactment only reinforced and aggravated the ethnic divide by tenaciously introducing the polices of ethnic identity in the region. Thus, even though the inclusion of the upland communities of the region into the Scheduled Tribe category in the Constitution was a noble and desirable gesture, the seemingly 'partisan' manner of implementation in the Northeast was ill conceived. It created further rift and divided the people between the 'favoured' tribals and the not 'so-lucky' non-tribals. The effect still lingers on.

In conclusion, it is apparent that in the Northeast the inclusion of the upland communities into the 'scheduled tribe' categorization did not evoke the same kind of positive response as it did in the rest of the country initially. It had a mix response. The Constitutional enactment meant different things to the upland tribal communities on one hand and another to the lowland non-tribal communities. This mixed response is because even though the concept of categorizing of people based on their ethnicity, clan, caste or creed surreptitiously crept into the region after the coming of the two universal religions, Hinduism and Christianity in the Northeast, the distinction was never formalized. On the other hand, the Constitutional enactment by categorizing the various upland communities from the land-locked Northeast as Scheduled Tribes in a definitive way, legally and constitutionally divided the people of the region into two clear separate groups based on their ethnicity and all that goes with it. The categorization of the upland tribal communities of the Northeast and their inclusion as members of the Scheduled Tribes without any corresponding Government enactment for the amelioration of the economically poor members of the non-tribal communities in the Northeast gave rise to misunderstandings leading to the problems of ethnic divide in the Northeast region of India. The story of the Northeast would never be the same ever again.

Endnotes

1. Lalsangkima Pachuau, "*Tribal*" *Identity and Ethnic conflicts in North-East India: A Christian Response*.
2. As per the *Census of India 2001*, there are 140 major Schedule Tribes in the Northeastern States including Sikkim, out of 573 in the whole of India. The state wise breakup is 20 in Arunachal Pradesh, 23 in Assam, 29 in Manipur, 17 in Meghalaya, 14 in Mizoram, 16 in Nagaland, 2 in Sikkim and 19 in Tripura. As against the total National Scheduled Tribe population constituting 8.22 percent, 26.93 percent out of this are in the Northeast including Sikkim. In terms of State wise breakup the number of Scheduled Tribes in Arunachal Pradesh is 64.22 percent, Assam 12.41 percent, Manipur 34.20 percent, Meghalaya 85.94 percent, Mizoram 94.46 percent, Nagaland 89.15 percent, Sikkim 20.60 percent and Tripura 31.05 percent.
3. B.B.Kumar, *The Tribe Caste Continuum*, 1999, Kumar points out the possible source of the confusion created by the distinction in Hindustani language and usage of the two terms.

CHAPTER - 8

OTHER DETERMINANTS OF IDENTITY FORMATIONS

There are several factors responsible for the rise of assertive ethnic identity politics in the Northeastern region, which eventually split the region, particularly erstwhile State of Assam into many separate political entities based on tribal and non-tribal ethnic identity. Five of these are discussed and analysed in this Chapter. The first of these, which made a distinctive impact and was responsible for religious and ethnic 'tribal' 'non-tribal' divide, and perhaps the most misconstrued is the 'supposed' link of the kingdoms of Manipur and Assam with the Aryan Indic civilization based on the references made in the Mahabharata. This deemed 'link' largely a 'construct' without any historical basis, provided the non-tribal Hindus an air of superiority over the upland tribal communities in the region. This is deviously responsible for the misunderstandings between the upland tribal and the lowland non-tribal communities leading to the calamitous social polarization between the two set of communities in the region.

The second and one of the principle reason for the rise of ethno-nationalistic aspirations among the various ethnic groups in the region as compared to other regions in the country was the disparaging tendency to view the northeastern region primarily as an anthropological preserve of indigenous people, a 'Human Zoo', comprising of non-descript backward communities. The Government of India unintentionally and unconsciously followed this view left behind by British and other foreign anthropologists, scholars, social scientists of cataloging the people of the Northeast region into predetermined slots of anthropological backwardness. Part of the problem of the Government of India arose **due** *to the dearth of a* *clear policy prescription to deal with the tribal problems of the Northeast immediately following independence. This situation was further compounded by the different interpretations given to the tribal welfare policies enunciated by Nehru and Verrier Elwin, two important individuals instrumental in the formulation of tribal welfare policies in post independent India. These confusions left behind a trail of adverse consequences. Because of the mismatch between expectations and the actual implementation of programmes and schemes mainly due to the failure to understand the subtle nuances and differences between tribal communities of Northeast India from those living in the other parts of the country, tribal policies of the Government was misunderstood by the upland tribal communities from the region as undermining their interests. Conjoined to this unsatisfactory situation was the nagging legacy of British Northeast Frontier policies with regard to the unclear special status for the upland communities. All these made the ethnic identity issue in the region highly volatile.*

The third factor responsible for the rise of ethnic identity politics in the region was the introduction of Bengali as the administrative language by the British-India Government in pre-independent Assam, then encompassing the whole of the Northeast excluding Manipur and Tripura. This policy not only hurt Assamese sentiments, but also paved the way for the rise of assertive Assamese identity. The politics of language in Assam had an adverse cascading effect on everyone in the region, especially among the many minor constituent ethnic groups mainly comprising of tribal communities both living in the hills and plains of erstwhile Assam. Because of the belligerent nature the course the language politics took in Assam, it unfortunately became one of the main causes leading to the political disintegration of Assam into several states. The political fragmentation of Assam ultimately led to the dismantling of the once economically viable state of Assam, which in turn is adversely affecting the overall growth and development of the region as a whole. The reasons and consequences behind the balkanization of Assam and its consequences, form the fourth factor being analysed.

Last but significant, as an example in understanding the reasons behind the rising divisive ethnic identity politics in the Northeast is the example of the Bodos, the Plain Tribals of Assam who have sought a separate political space of their own. This problem which arose due to the tendency of the Assamese, representing the dominant ethnic group, to dominate and neglect the smaller ethnic groups in the valley areas of the State , especially the 'plain-tribals', the autochthonous of Assam is analysed. This retaliatory reactions from the Plain tribal communities of Assam; the Bodos, in spite of their being an integral and intrinsic part of Assam's long cherished history is perhaps the saddest story of all, since it consummately sums up the changing nature of the ethnic identity divide in a region bereaved of such distinctions as tribals and non-tribals.

These five issues and problems in the Northeast are discussed.

1. Under the Shadows of the Mahabharata

"What is truth? Said jesting Pilate, and would not stay for an answer", Sir Francis Bacon wrote in one of his well-known essays on 'Truth' in the 16th Century ADE. Pontius Pilate, the Roman Prefect or Governor of Judaea between 26 and 36 ADE, also known in history as the V Roman Procurator of Judaea made this remark ostensibly after washing his hands in the traditional Roman gesture publicly approving the crucifixion of Christ. Pope in the same essay also wrote extolling both the virtues of truth and its sobrieties stating, *"Truth may perhaps come to the price of a pearl that showeth best by day; but it will not rise to the price of a diamond, or carbuncle, that showeth best in varied lights"*. What Pope meant was that a little mixture of 'untruth' to the 'truth' could make the 'truth' a little more interesting. More than two thousand years from the event, and four hundred years after Pope wrote his famous essay, we still do not have a final answer of what is 'truth'. The 'truth' about the connection of the Northeast, especially Kamrupa (Assam) and Manipur, mentioned in the great epic of Mahabharata[1], is similarly placed, an alchemy of imagination, myth and hearsay, emblematic of the 'supposed' Hindu connections of the region with Aryan Indic civilisation. This belief unfortunately sustained generations of people in the region but sent them on the wrong trajectory of civilisational connections.

The references found in the Mahabharata are one of the most baffling but significant association available between Northeast India with the Indic Aryan civilisational history. Hindus across the Northeast, particularly from Assam, Manipur and to some extent Tripura have extolled this link and connection, drawing inspirations and deriving mileage out of it. In fact, a theoretical connection between Hindu Aryan civilisations with Hindu Northeast India is drawn based on these references found in the ancient epic. The people of the Northeast, particularly the Hindus among them, have long cherished and extolled in it. Ironically, it is the same 'connection' and 'association', which has divided the upland tribal communities from the lowland Hindu non-tribal communities. Unfortunately, based on this connectivity with the Indic Aryan civilisation, the Hindus assumed an air of 'superiority' and racial 'arrogance' over their non-Hindu tribal counterparts in the region.

The analysis about this 'supposed connectivity' acquires importance, because it is one of the most significant contributory factors leading to the ethnic divide and social polarization among ethnic groups and communities in the Northeast. Because of this 'supposed connectivity', the lowland Hindu population in the region, not only abrogated and disowned their own anthropological historical pagan past but also severed the age-old affiliations and bond between them and the upland tribal communities. Much of the misunderstandings and social prejudices that have crept in the region between the non-Hindu tribal and Hindu non-tribal communities are due to this factor.

Conversely, putting the facts straight to remove all misgivings, both perceptible and otherwise, is considered desirable to put to rest the ongoing misunderstandings between the upland non-Hindu tribal people (now predominantly Christians) and the non-tribal Hindus. An objective critical assessment, by properly contextualising the issue, from the perspective of ethnic identity formation seems necessary and desirable. I have largely depended for the analysis on the translated versions of summaries of the epic undertaken by the well-known Indologist and historian Dr. R.C. Majumdar.

The Contents

Out of the five references made to Eastern India in the Mahabharata, the first and the most popular are the references made to Arjun and Chitrangada the epical princess of Manipur. The supposed, *"self-imposed exile of Arjuna"* (Adi-parva, 170) in Manipur is summed by Dr. R.C. Majumdar[2] in the following summary of the original version of the Adi-parva. *"Arjuna, during his exile, came down from the Himalayas and proceeded to the eastern region. In the course of his journey, he visited the holy places, temples and the hermitages of Anga, Vanga and Kalinga. He then passed by the Mahendra mountains to Manipur on the sea. After visiting the temples and the holy places of this country, he met its ruler Chitravahana, and married his daughter Chitrangada. He stayed there for three years and begot a son named Vabhruvahana, who became the king of Manipur"*. Dr. Majumdar refers to the various descriptions of the Digvijayas (Great triumphs) and other escapades of the Pandava brothers as given in the Mahabharata.

Pragjyotisha (erstwhile Assam) finds mention in the second reference. *"Having exacted tributes, various kinds of jewels and precious articles, he proceeded as far as Lauhitya or Brahmaputra river. Arjuna also conquered Pragjyotisha by defeating after a severe fight its king Bhagdatta supported by the Chinese and Kirata soldiers and also those living by the sea-shore"*. Dr. Majumdar raises several doubts especially on the question of whether the Manipur and Pragjyotisha referred to in the Mahabharata are actually the two states in the northeast region or not. Many scholars believe that the popular theory of the 'connection' is a hermeneutical manipulation through interpretations to somehow 'include' and 'fit' the northeastern states into the Aryan worldview for various reasons.

The earliest references of the eastward expansion of Aryan culture and influence mentioned in the Mahabharata and the Puranas come in the form of isolated references. In all these references, the term 'eastward' denotes the whole of Eastern India covering Bengal, Bihar, Orissa, Jharkhand and the whole of the Northeastern States along with Bangladesh. It is the vastness of the areas covered under the term 'eastward' that makes the task of identifying and precisely finding the locale of the ancient kingdoms associated with epic extremely difficult. The present Northeast region is only one of the many areas covered under the term 'eastward'. It provides scope for unending analysis, debates and interpretations.

The *Puranas* mentions the people from the eastern parts called Anga, Videha, Madguru (Monghyr), Antargiri-Vahirgiri, Suhma, Vanga, Pragjyotisha and Tamralipta. The Bhagavad Puranas (II.4.18) describes the Suhmas as a sinful tribe, along with the Kiratas, Yavanas, and Khasas. The Mahabharata mentions possible contacts with people beyond the Aryan influence while referring to Pragjyotisha, Mlechchhas living on the seacoast and the kings of hilly region like Paundraka, Vasudeva of Vanga and Kalinga. The episode pertaining to the marriage of Arjuna with Chitrangada the Manipuri princess also forms a part of this narrative.

Two events narrated in the epic that go against the possible connection with the Northeast, or the so-called 'associations' or 'connections', are analysed.

(1) Anga and Vanga, referred were people who were found 'beyond the Sadanira', which is around present Bihar and West Bengal or its vicinity, with Vanga being somewhere in the South of the estuary of the rivers Padma, Ganges and the Yamuna (as the Brahmaputra is called in Bangladesh). The Vangas and the Angas in the *Puranas* are described as people living beyond the river Sadanira (Probably the river Gandaki as per Dr. R.C. Majumdar). The immediate references of the travails of Arjuna thereafter progressing to Kalinga (Orissa) *"...by the Mahendra mountains to Manipur on the sea"*, only seem to suggest that the Manipur referred to in the Mahabharata in all probability is a place on the way to the sea or close to or *"on the sea"*. Present-day Manipur or Assam is nowhere near the sea, except for the large numbers of water bodies like lakes and rivers, including the mighty River Brahmaputra.

(2) The subsequent reference describes *"visiting the temples and holy places of this country"*, in Manipur. However, the visits to the temples appears unfounded because Hinduism, based on existing studies and scholarships on the subject came to Assam only between the 6th and the 14th, while the earliest references available about Hinduism in Manipur traces the contacts only from the 18th century ADE. It is important to note that Muni Ved Vyasa wrote the first version of the epic, and dates back to the 8th century BCE and other versions continued to appear until around the end of the reign of the Gupta dynasty in the 4th century ADE. Obviously, the Manipur referred to in the text of the epic could not be the present-day Manipur or Assam.

Analysing further, based on this most probable route that the Pandavas took it can be assumed that Arjun passed the thickly forested mountainous regions of the Chotanagpur areas of present Jharkhand (Mahandra Mountains), and then took a southward journey towards the sea where Kalinga (Orissa) is located. Given these facts the most probable routes that the Pandavas could take are the ones through Anga (South Bengal) and the Vanga country (North Bihar and West Bengal), where Hinduism or some form of it had probably been well established, when the various versions of the Mahabharata were written.

It is reasonable to accept this 'route' taken by the Pandavas for two reasons. (1) No land surface journey eastwards into the Northeast was possible at that time in history because of the Ganges, which Diodorus described *"is separated from further India by the greatest river in these parts for it has a breath of 30 stadia"*. (2) The Greek and Latin writers, particularly Diodorus, when referring to the two nations of Prasioi and Gangaridai (var-Gandaridai) describes the *"Ganges which is 30 stades broad, flows north to south forming the boundaries towards the east of Gandaridae"*. Dr. R.C.Majumdar thinks that the Ganges referred to by Diodorus probably is the river Padma (Bangladesh), the eastern most branch of Ganges and not the Bhagirathi or Hooghly, which is the western most branch of the mighty Ganges. Thus constrained by many physical barriers and topography, Arjun could not have gone beyond the Padma or Ganges in present-day Bangladesh. Logistically based on both the references Dr. Majumdar, considers that it is apparent that the Manipur of today could not be the one referred to in the text of the epic, since present-day Manipur is neither located on the sea nor is it anywhere near Kalinga, the present-day Orissa, which is referred intermittently throughout the text of the epic.

The next point of contradiction is the reference to Arjun's conquests. Dr. Majumdar translates the conquests as follows, *"... he proceeded as far as Lauhitya or Brahmaputra river. Arjun also conquered Pragjyotisha by defeating...king Bhagadatta..."*. The description is restricted to the fact that Arjun went up to the river Brahmaputra but does not say at which point or part of the Brahmaputra. This is important since the Brahmaputra enters the Bengal plain (present Bangladesh) after meandering through Assam, stretching from present day North Bengal, bordering Goalpara district in Assam across the whole of Bangladesh before entering the Bay of Bengal in the south and becoming part of the confluence of three mighty South Asian rivers. Crossing this mighty estuary is extremely difficult if not physically impossible even today without adequate means of appropriate river transport. It is therefore, not clear whether Arjuna's battle with king Bhagdatta of Pragjyotisha, who was *"living by the sea-shore"* and supported by the Chinese or the Kirata soldiers could be the ruler of Assam, since there is no sea close to Assam in any time of its known history. In fact, the recurring references to the sea in the epic in the context of king Bhagdatta of Pragjyotisha, and in the references made to Manipur in the Mahabharata makes one believe that the two kingdoms referred to in the epic must have been close to or abutting the sea.

References are also made to the ruler of Pragjyotisha, who participated in the celebrations of the Rajasuya-yajna that follow the Digvijayas (Great triumphs) achieved by Bhima and Arjun. In the narrative translated by Dr. Majumdar, the event and occasion is described giving details about the rulers who attended the yagna and those who *"made valuable presents, we find the names of Bhagdatta, ruler of Pragjyotisha, of great fame, attended by the Mlechchhas leaving on the sea coast and the kings of hilly region, and Paundraka Vasudeva of Vanga and Kalinga"*. Here also, the correct identity of king Bhagadutta of Pragjyotisha is not conclusively established. Dr. Majumdar therefore, points out that the only possible connection of the ruler of Pragjyotisha, Bhagadutta, which he could connect is probably to the references made to the mythological son of Narakara. The Nidhanpur copper plate of Bhaskarvarman of Assam 'refers' to the lineage of Bhagadutta with Narakara, but since conclusive proof are not found substantiating this connection, many scholars are skeptical about the connections of the ruler of Assam with king Narakara.

Dr. Majumdar also doubts this connection of Bhagadutta with Narakara, because the dynasty to which king Bhagadutta is associated is in the Northwestern frontier provinces of India, on the opposite direction of Pragjyotisha or Kamrupa. Dr. Majumdar makes the assertion based on the inscriptions found at Hatun in the Northwestern frontier, up the Gilgit River, which refers to one Paramabhattaraka Maharajadhiraja Paramesvara Patola-deva Sahi, who was born in the family of Bhagadutta[3]. Based on paleographic evidence, Dr. Majumdar places the reign of Paramabahttaraka Maharajadhiraja Paramesvara Patola-deva Sahi, in the 6th century A.D.E. and establishes the point that this ruler was a contemporary of King Bhaskaravarman of Kamrupa in *"whose record contains the first epigraphic (Nidhanpur copper plates) reference to Naraka and his son Bhagadatta"*. Dr. R.C. Majumdar[4] is therefore of the view that the ruler Bhagadutta of Pragjyotisha mentioned in the Mahabharata may not be the ruler of present-day Assam or Kamrupa or Pragjyotisha.

The third reference, made in the Bhagadutta-vamsa Sambhuta, is the military campaigns of Arjuna in connection with the Asvamedha sacrifice performed by Yudhishthira. Dr. R.C. Majumdar sums up these events as given in the original text of the epic as follows: *"...while protecting the horse, Arjuna had to fight strenuously for three days before he could defeat the great hero Vajradatta, son of Bhagdatta and ruler of Pragjyotisha. Arjuna then followed the horse to the Sindhu and defeated the assembled chiefs or rulers (Rajanah) who had ceased the sacrificial horse. The horse thus released wandered about in different countries and then entered Manipur. This resulted in a fight between Arjuna and his son Vabhruvahana, in the course of which Arjuna was defeated and killed. But his life was restored by Ulupi, the daughter of Naga king, whom Arjuna had married just before he had married Chitrangada, the mother of Vabhruvahana".*

The locations and descriptions of 'Sindhu' (Western India), and those of 'Manipur and 'Naga king' mentioned in the epic, if they are supposed to be where the present-day Manipur, Nagaland and Sindu are located, the movement or route taken by the Asvamedha (horse) appear logistically quite irrational and improbable. This is because given the physical distances involved, separating present day Manipur and Sind; in the two extremities of India, one in the east and the other in the west, it would be logistically impossible for the Asvamedha (horse) to traverse the entire distances involved physically. The inconsistency is obvious, since logically if Pragjyotisha is Kamrup or Assam of today, it should be adjoining Manipur, side by side to each other. Thus, logistically and logically, Arjun after defeating Vajradatta the son of Bhagadutta of Pragjyotisha (Assam) should have gone to Manipur of today, which is contiguous to Assam, rather than traverse back all the way to the west into Sindhu, which meant going all through the length of the country and thereafter trudge back to Manipur once again.

Pragjyotisha of Mahabharata: The other view

In contrast to the views reflected in the analysis made by Dr. R.C. Majumdar, there are other historians and scholars, mainly from the Northeast, who strongly advocate the 'connectivity' theory; one among them is Dr. (Mrs.) S.L. Baruah[5]. According to Dr. Baruah, Pragjyotisha in the times of the epic includes the whole of the northeastern region and far beyond its present boundaries. It included *"Koch-Behar, Jalpaiguri, Rangpur, Bogra, Mymensing, Decca (sic), Tripura, portions of Patna and probably portion of Nepal"* and *"According to most of the Puranas, the kingdom of Kamarupa extended up to the river Karatoya in the west and included Manipur,*

Jaintiya, Cachar, parts of Mymensing, Sylhet, Rangpur and portions of Nepal and Bhutan". "It appears therefore, that the kingdom of Pragjyotisha-Kamarupa covered the major portions of Eastern India". She concludes by quoting other well-known scholars of Assamese history, Dr. K.L.Barua and B.K.Barua[6]. Dr. K.L. Barua describes the possible extent of Pragjyotisha-Kamrupa *"...it is clear that Pragjyotisha or ancient Kamarupa was much larger kingdom than most of the other kingdoms mentioned in the Mahabharata and most of the sixteen Mahajanapadas existing during the time of Gautama Buddha"*. This theoretical assumption is based on the contents of the Kalika Purana, Yogini Tantra, and on B.K. Kakati's[7] references.

Based on the views and the work done by Dr. K.L. Barua and Dr. B.K. Barua, Dr. (Mrs.) S.L. Baruah provides an interesting explanation to the recurring reference to the 'sea' mentioned in the Mahabharata as *"...the Lauhitya (Lohita) Sagara"* because of its immense size and spread. *"This sea was the Lauhitya (Lohita) Sagara. It is almost certain that part of Sylhet, Mymensing and neighbouring lands were under water at least in the Epic age and the Brahmaputra fell into the Lauhitya Sagara taking a southern course round the Garo hills, as it does today".*

Additionally, according to Dr. Baruah, the references of Arjun's battle with Bhagadatta, ruler of Pragjyotisha, should mean that, *"The Varaha mountains mentioned in the Ramayana was the Assam Range and the sea lay to the south of the hills which was perhaps connected with the Bay of Bengal by the estuary of the Brahamaputra..."*. She further explains that the *"Kiratas meant the Mongoloid or Indo-Mongoloid people (the Bodos) and the Chinas (sic) probably stood for the Bhutanese and the Tibetans. The dwellers of the sea-coast were the people living in the marshy regions of Sylhet, Mymensing and Tripura".* Equally interesting is Dr. Mrs. Baruah's explanation that the 'sea' referred to in the context of ancient Pragjyotisha is actually the extended sea, which stretched from its current position as the estuary deep into the north covering present Sylhet, Mymensing and other areas around close to the foothills of Assam.

In spite of these assertions, the fact remains that much more evidences are required before we can arrive at a dispassionate conclusive proof about the connection. Suffice to say that from the available texts and manuscripts of the different versions of the epic, the various places, names and incidences mentioned in the epic are not the present places that appear to be connected or associated with the present-day Assam or Manipur in the Northeast. Conversely, the present-day names of Manipur and Pragjyotisha to Assam in the Northeast may actually be adoptions of the original names of the places mentioned in the epic instead.

Manipur of the Mahabharata

In the Mahabharata, there are many references to Manipur in various parts of the text. It is referred to as Manipura in some manuscripts, while in some, for instance in the critical edition of the Adiparva Mahabharata (Ch.77-78), it is referred to as Manalur. However, the co-relationship with present Manipur, like the case of Assam remains vague and shrouded in doubts. Based on the various facts available Dr. Majumdar does not rule out present-day Orissa being the Manipur, Manipura, or Manalur of the Mahabharata, because of the recurring reference to its location being 'on the sea'. Following this interpretation, many scholars believe that the Naga princess Ulupi, whom Arjun is supposed to have married before he proceeded to Manipur and married Chitrangada, could probably be a daughter of a Chieftain from the Chotanagpur hilly regions, a region which Arjun passed before reaching Kalinga(present Orissa), and 'Manalur'. Dr. Majumdar substantiates this assumption because the Aryans had a very intimate knowledge of South Bihar, West Bengal and East Pakistan (Bangladesh) in the days of Dharma-sutras. Logistically, the assumption seems quite logical and believable.

Dr. Majumdar bases his findings that Aryan's stronghold, especially the Guptas was in Bengal, which extended up to Bihar. Dr. Majumdar substantiates his conclusions based on the discoveries of several numerical inscriptions in the ruins of Mahasthan in Bogra District of erstwhile East Pakistan, Naokhali, and the Kushana coins from Murshidabad district in Bengal, the Susunia rock inscriptions in Bankura District written in Sanskrit in Brahmi letters, and in Prakrit in the Brahmi alphabet of the third century B.C. From these evidences, Dr. Majumdar concludes that Aryan civilisation and influence before the 4th century A.D., around the time when the Mahabharata was possibly written, extended to the whole of *"West Bengal and East Pakistan, excluding the hilly region in the North"*. On the basis of all these evidences, he observed "... *it would thus appear that while we have definite evidence of the Aryanisation of Bengal before the end of the 4th century B.C., we possess no such evidence of its advance further towards the east before the 4th century A.D".*

The Connection: Was there any?

It is evident that the 'supposed link' was a popular subject and theme among scholars and intellectuals and the people of the region alike since it has several implications and connotations involving religious, ethnological, historical and purely academic interests. Consequently, there are several divergent and often contradictory views on the subject; mainly because it was the main reference available, based on which Hindu Northeast India established its Indic Aryan connections. Given, the nature of the interest on the subject and divergent views, the best way is to accept the dispassionate observation and conclusion given by Sir Edward Gait, KCSI, CIE of the Indian Civil Service, (1863-1950) a distinguished British officer known for his understanding and knowledge of the Northeast. Sir Gait, in a footnote on the chapter on Manipur, in his well-known book, 'A History of Assam', first published in 1905, wrote about the possible association of Manipur with the Mahabharata. He wrote, *"The Manipur mentioned in the Mahabharat was the capital of Babhruvahana, king of Kalinga. It must therefore have been situated somewhere in the south of Orissa or north of Madras. Various sites in the tract have been suggested by Lassen, OP Pert and others. Its exact place is still uncertain, but there can be no doubt whatever, that it was nowhere near the place of the same name in Assam. It has already been mentioned that the people of Java have also adapted the Mahabharat to their own history and assigned local sites for the principal scenes. In the same way, the Chutiya kingdom of Upper Assam was called Vidarbha. Canbodia gets its name from a place in Upper India."* [8] (sic).

Objectively analysed, based on the various historical evidences and facts available, it is difficult to establish any authentic and reliable historical link between present-day Assam and Manipur with the kingdoms and places mentioned in the Mahabharata. Present-day Northeast, Assam and Manipur were never part of the world conceived by Vyasa in the epic, Mahabharata. Because, given the physical features and isolation of the region, especially at the time when the Mahabharata was first written by Rishi Ved Vyasa, it appears most improbable that the two states of Assam and Manipur that we know of today, are the ones mentioned in the epic in spite of all the scholarships available on the subject trying to justify the claims. On the other hand, historically analysed, connecting the present-day Northeastern states of Assam and Manipur to the epic are possibly subsequent interpretations made by the exponents of Hinduism and Hindu scholars around the sixth to the 18th century ADE when Hinduism was extending its reach into Northeast India.

In fact, this view is much more realistic, keeping in view the general trend to give Aryanised names to Assam and Manipur, commensurate with the growing influence of Hinduism in the region. It can also be assumed that the association with Assam or Kamrup or Pragjyotisha and Manipur were made much later long after the epics had been written. From this perspective, both Manipur and Pragjyotisha were probably Aryanised names either given by the rulers themselves or given by other rulers and scholars from outside the region after Hindunisation in an attempt to put Hinduism's stamp on the two kingdoms. For instance, the rulers of Manipur rechristened the kingdom's ancient pagan name several times by successive rulers. Just to name a few Konna (Langba) Chak, Kanglei Pungmayol, Kangleipak, Meitrabak etc and much more, were changed to Manipur, later when they became Hindus in the late 17th and early 18th century ADE. The analogy is similar to the present practices, where the North Eastern Frontier Agency (N.E.F.A), was changed to Arunachal, erstwhile Khasi and Jaintia Hills and the Garo Hills, was changed to Meghalaya after these districts and divisions became States in the Union.

The most realistic way is therefore to view the setting and the places mentioned in the epic as symbolic places rather than seek their historical, geographical, or regional connections. The themes in the epic are universal and timeless; these events in the epic could have happened anywhere in any period or place and need not be exactly the two states of Assam and Manipur. The places are representative, to be read and understood more in the metaphorical sense rather than view them from any historical corelationship. It is best to accept the inference that these two places, Assam and Manipur are symbolic representations of distant lands or places with the mystery associated, which every author of the epic is entitled to use in providing the much-needed physical setting of the events narrated. The relative merit of all epics is to provide to the readers a world they are familiar and at the same time have the mystery and romance associated in keeping the interest of the readers alive. The references to distant exotic places become essential prerequisites only to enhance the quality of storytelling in conveying the contents of the epic.

Epistemologically analysed as a theological text, since the canvas covered is so vast and profound in content, delving into the realms of philosophy and transcending beyond the visible world, the epic has adopted the simple medium of storytelling to convey the message and meanings contained in it, so that the illiterate readers can understand and appreciate the contents and the discourses. Additionally, devoid of the actual historical and geographical connotations, the content of the epic in its overarching philosophical contexts and contents are otherwise immensely complex and profound, which devoid of its physical settings would have been extremely difficult for the readers to understand. It is the ability of the author to provide a comprehensive overview of all that is great in the Aryan Hindu traditions and thoughts, but not necessarily Hindu exclusively in content or in its context, in a language, form and narration, which everyone can easily understand that makes the epic a great work of art. It is both a treatise and a comprehensive summation of the Aryan world-view perceived and told through the skill and simplicity of the author at his command.

Seen from the context of the Northeast, the people of the region, irrespective of their ethnicity or religious affiliations need to view the Mahabharata by Rishi Vyasa, for that matter the Ramayana by Rishi Valmiki as great immortal works of literature involving expansive discourses eulogising the essence and philosophy of life in its totality. The immense universal appeal of these epics lies in the immensity of the philosophical contents, which transcends from the purely Hindu world-view to the universal, and encompasses the discourse on the vast knowledge and philosophy of life in general. In other words, while these epics are not necessarily reflections of Hindu thoughts and philosophy, as many make out or think them to be, since the contents in essence are universal , its inherent strength lies in its appeal.

The fact that epics like the Ramayana or the Mahabharata, have universal appeal is established from the fact that there is a Mizo version of the epic Ramayana. This version is incorporated in the collection of Mizo and Non-Mizo Tales called "Mizo leh vai thon thu" by J. Shakespeare, the British Superintendent of Lushai Hills[9]. Many believe that the Mizo version of the Ramayana is a byproduct of the Buddhist version imbibed by the Mizos during their long sojourn across Burma and Southeast Asia[10], where Hinduism was flourishing, before they settled down at present day Mizoram. The great Epic has attracted the Mizos because of its philosophical content and discourses epitomized in the Bhagavad Geeta. The ideas contained in these epics, which are universal and infinite must have appealed to the Mizos senses of righteousness more than to the religious contents.

While therefore, the Mahabharata is epistemologically associated and connected with the northeast region with Pragjyotisha (Kamrup or Assam) and Manipur, both these associations and references are best considered as having been mentioned to as representative places; universal symbols of exotic distant lands, which 'exist' anywhere in the world. The freedom and flexibility to co-relate these places and peoples as readers of the epic would like to imagine or think, actually 'frees' the two places from its temporal and physical 'moors' or specificity of both time and space. In this sense both Assam and Manipur, the two names acquires a 'timelessness' quality that is relevant at all times. Perhaps it is better that these references to the two states in the Northeast are as such put in the context in which they appear devoid of trying to establish any connectivity with the present states of Assam and Manipur. The satisfaction should mainly come from the fact that as long as the teachings and contents of the epic is read, the names of the two states, Pragjyotisha and Manipur will always adorn its famous pages. It is best to desist from the temptation to bring in this great literary and philosophical work the controversy involving mundane worldly aspects of ethnicity and identity.

Given the above position, the basis on which the lowland Hindu communities in the Northeast articulated their Aryan connections and assumed an air of superiority over the upland tribal communities in the region is more in the nature of 'assumptions' rather than supported or established by the facts of history. The preponderant tendency of this 'assumption' passed down through the generations beginning with the Hindunisation of the region to the present, has greatly harmed inter-ethnic relations, and in a way introduced an undesirable clash between the Aryan Hindu way of life and the Chritianised upland Tribal communities and to some extent with the indigenous form and way of life. The genises of ethnic divide polarizing the societies in the sensitive region can be partly traced to this 'assumed' Aryan Indic connectivity.

Even though the assumed 'superiority' of the lowland ethnic groups has diminished over the years, the residual air of superiority complex and the associated prejudices, which once marked their conduct and relationship with the upland tribal communities, must be seen in the context of the unsubstantiated hypothesis on which the theory of Indic Aryan connections stand. Simultaneously, it would be desirable for the upland tribal communities of the Northeast, now mostly Christianised not to carry the prejudices and burdens of mistrust of the past and instead, focus on what can be done to restore the trust and bondings that once epitomized the Northeast. It is best to forget the past and look ahead to the future.

2. 'The National Park' or 'Human Zoo'

Historically speaking, the Northeastern societies by disposition always have been too insular and inward looking. This is primarily because of the insecurity arising out of the inherent fear of being overwhelmed by outsiders. This is understandable. It is however, the xenophobic predilections towards the other smaller sub-groups within the same ethnic group and communities or similarly placed ones, which is perplexing. Part of this phenomenon is explained by the fact that many of these communities, especially the upland tribal people, have lived isolated lives and not been exposed to the outside world as they were confined for centuries within their respective 'natural preserves' or habitats in the region. Barring a few pockets in erstwhile Assam, bordering present day Arunachal Pradesh, forming the rich Makum Areas where deposits of coal, oil and tea were discovered, the entire region was seen and treated by the British essentially as a large 'human preserve' in line with the views of British and European social scientists, working in the region. British administrative policies like the 'Inner Line Permit System', the 'Excluded Area' and the 'Partially Excluded Area' and through its policy of 'exclusivity' enforced this isolation further by preventing the mixing of the ethnic groups with each other.

In one way, this was desirable, since development in the modern sense of the term, would have serious socio-cultural ramifications on the upland tribal communities in the Northeast and would be repugnant to the social ethos and milieu of these communities in particular. Protection therefore meant prevention, which in turn meant, preservation. Successive reinforcements of this view however, not only led to the isolation of the people of the region from the national mainstream but also over a period undermined the potentialities of the people of these communities by making them social recluses. The trend and tendency in evolving a Northeastern tribal policy based primarily on available scholarships, observations and situations witnessed by European socio-anthropologists and British administrators when the tribal communities in the region were at their most primitive stages, is perhaps one of the reasons why the tribal policies are distractibly miscued.

Among the most preeminent and well-known anthropologists and social scientists based on whose experiences and knowledge the country has largely depended for its Northeast India tribal policies were Christoph von Furer-Haimendorf of German ancestory and Verrier Elwin a British, who advocated a protectionist's approach to tribal welfare. Christoph von Furer-Haimendorf served as a Special Officer on North East Frontier of the Government of India in 1944. He began his fieldwork in the Northeast among the Konyak tribe of the Nagas in the 1930s. Furer-Haimendorf eulogized the head hunting tribe of the Nagas in his famous book, 'The Naked Nagas'. His Konyak friends also popularly remember Haimendorf as "The White Headhunter". He also worked among the Apa Tanis, Nishis and the Adis in the 1950s in the North Eastern Frontier provinces, as revealed in his book, 'Himalayan Barbary'. Haimendorf worked all over India among various tribal communities, which included the Chenchus in the Deccan, the Konda or Hill Reddis in the then Orissa state. He subsequently moved over to Nepal where he undertook anthropological research among the Sherpas and researched in Western Nepal. After his retirement, he held a seat as professor for Anthropology at the University of London. Out of the two, Verrier Elwin played a much more prominent role in the formulation of tribal policies in India.

Verrier Elwin a British came to India in 1927[11] after leaving a position as a clerical don at Oxford. He met Mahatma Gandhiji through a Christian group, which was working with Gandhiji. He worked among the Gonds in Central India and married a Gond tribal woman in a tribal ceremony. Elwin became an Indian Citizen in 1954. He became the Anthropological Adviser to the Government of India under Prime Minister Nehru in the same year. In addition to the task of implementing all tribal welfare programmes, Elwin was placed in charge to look after the Northeast even though his main experiences were in Central India, having spent most of his early carrier there. Elwin's association with the Northeast as such began only after his appointment as the Anthropological Adviser. He did his primary work on the Northeast in NEFA (North East Frontier Agency) mainly, as an anthropologist and later wrote extensively on the Nagas.

Verrier Elwin played a very significant role in shaping the tribal policy of the country in general including the policies on the Northeast. It is from this perspective that the views of Verrier Elwin becomes important in understanding the various tribal policies of the Government of India especially those pertaining to the period immediately prior to and following India's independence. Verrier Elwin held two distinct views on the tribal policy, one before independence and another after independence.

In the pre-independence phase, according to Govinda Chandra Rath, Elwin held the view that *"...tribal history is rather a story of economic exploitation and cultural destruction by caste society"*[12] and hence advocated isolation of the tribal communities and societies. Rath elaborates, *"...isolation aims at conscious separation of the tribe from the political and economic mainstream..."*[13]. Rath attributes the perpetuation of the tribal culture and their unique life-style as the concept of the 'National Park', a policy of tribal welfare and appeasement, which principally advocate 'isolation' and 'protection' of the tribal communities by enforcing an exclusive zone where they would be undisturbed. Rath observes, *"The economic elements of Elwin's 'National Park' approach bear much similarity to the Gandhian idea of self-sufficiency of Indian villages. Being a follower of Gandhi, Elwin imbibed his conception of Gram Swaraj and reproduced it in his 'National Park' approach with the required modifications."*

In the post-independence phase and in the later part of his career during the 1950s and 1960s, Elwin however, changed his view. Falling in line with the integrative process in national identic formation, which Pandit Nehru very strongly advocated, Elwin changed his idea of 'isolation' just after independence. In 1951, Elwin wrote, *"I agree entirely with Dr. B.S. Guha who wrote in 1951: 'Complete isolation has never led to progress and advancement, but only to stagnation and death whether we look to lower animals or human beings'.* He wrote in his famous book, *A Philosophy for NEFA* in 1957, of the need *"...to bring the blessings and advantages of modern medicine, agriculture and education to tribes, without destroying the rare and precious values of tribal life"*[14].

In this second phase or the post independence period, the focus shifted to "assimilation" or "integration". This meant "... *integration, in contrast, is a respectful merger with the mainstream, staking a claim to an equal share of power and resources as other citizens. It is important to note that Elwin resorted to the approach for integration at the particular time when Nehru was engaged in giving a final shape to the Second Five Year Plan"*[15]. Elwin was compelled to make such a change because after independence, many geographically specific welfare programmes and other measures specifically for the tribal population of the country were introduced and he was enthused by the process of national integration and efforts made by Nehru in building a new India. Elwin became sensitive to the political realty of India through Nehru's influence.

Seen in retrospect, Nehru and Elwin held different views on the semantics involved in the definition of tribes, their understanding of tribal history and differed in their approach to tribal development and welfare in the initial years of their association. According to Nehru, the problem of the tribals was an 'integration-related difference', not based on facts but placed on *"a wrong footing"* by the colonial powers and *"purposefully segregated the tribes from Indian society and projected them as different from mainstream civilization"*. On the other hand, Elwin in the first phase of his association with the tribals, the pre-independence phase, *"when India was under British rule"*[16], held the view that tribal history was *"a story of exploitation and cultural destruction by caste society"*, a view, he shared with the colonial powers. Hence, Elwin, in the pre-independence phase, pursued an 'isolationist' approach, largely advocating the need to keep the tribal communities away from contact with the mainstream communities. Nehru on the other hand, did not subscribe to the 'isolationist' policy of keeping the tribal communities away from mainstream developments and changes, and hence did not agree with the views and policies of the British.

Much of what followed in our national policy for the Tribals in the period immediately following independence, was governed by Elwin's compromised and modified views, which Elwin calls the 'middle path'; a compromise between his pre-independence and the post-independence views, a direct consequence and result of Nehru's influence on Elwin. According to Elwin, the 'middle path' was meant to approach *"...the historical development of the tribal life and culture with respect and the people themselves in a spirit of affection and identification that eliminates any possibility of superiority. It would not ignore the past, but would build upon it. It would bring the best things of the modern world to the tribes, but in such a way that they will not destroy the traditional way of life, but will activate and develop all that is good in it."*[17] It was a balancing approach between his two views, by moderation and equanimity that would ensure both 'protection' and 'integration or assimilation' in dealing with tribal communities and evolving appropriate policies to bring them into national mainstream. Nehru's daughter and Prime Minister Indira Gandhi followed this policy.

Confusion Galore

Critically viewed the post-independence view and approach of Elwin to tribal welfare was much more 'liberal' keeping in mind the need to 'integrate' the tribal communities across India into the mainstream of Indian life, through what Elwin called the 'middle path'. It was pan-Indian in outlook and approach, essentially focusing on development and growth. In this connection, Elwin did not evolve or formulate any separate or specific set of approach for the tribal communities of the Northeast in particular, even though he undertook anthropological studies of specific groups in the NEFA (North East Frontier Agency). In other words, Elwin dealt the tribal issues and problems generically for the whole country, rather than on regional basis.

Given the fact that the issues and problems of the tribal communities in the Northeast have always been different from the rest of the country, a distinct and different policy prescription was required for the Northeast. For instance, as discussed in the proceeding Chapter, the categorisation of the upland communities of the Northeast as Scheduled Tribes along with other tribal communities in India were resented by the upland communities in the region because they consider themselves a distinct group living a different lifestyle and hence were not part of the Hindu socio-religious categorisation of people. It is precisely because of such issues, the tendency to generalise and the inability to understand the distinctive nuances and attributes of tribal lifestyle and their way of thinking in the Northeast that the problems of tribal welfare management in post independent India for the Northeast occurred. There was considerable dissatisfaction and consternations in the Northeast in general and in Government of India because of the failure to find the appropriate approach in dealing with tribal issues of the Northeast.

The post-independence views of Elwin, largely influenced by Nehru's thinking could not effectively achieve the desired result or create the desired impact in the Northeast, unlike the successes in other parts of India. This was because the tribal communities in the Northeast of India were not only distinct but were reluctant to be part of the 'integrative processes', a condition, which was the main basis of the Nehruvian tribal policy in post-independent India. The tribal communities of the Northeast were hesitant and reluctant to be assimilated into the national mainstream, since they felt that it was an indirect way of getting them entrapped into the Indo-Aryan Hindu socio-cultural ethos and way of life. The luke-warm response to the 'integrative processes', was largely due to the differences in perceptions of the ethnic, social, and cultural value systems between the people of the Northeast from the rest of the country. It was a clash of socio-cultural value systems. In the process, much of the enunciated policy prescriptions available and introduced as tribal policy, which were applicable to all tribal communities in the country, remained largely ineffective and inappropriate for the Northeast.

Unfortunately, it was around this time that the region also witnessed ethnic identity assertions in the form of insurgencies, causing serious law and order problems. In the ensuing disruptive phase, the tribal problems and issues, including inter-ethnic problems and other issues of the Northeast got enmeshed with the various law and order problems of the region. These unfortunate developments combined with the Chinese incursions in 1962 in the border areas of the region, shifted and diverted the attention of the Government from the phase of governance for development to one of addressing immediate security concerns in the Northeast. The emerging situation made tribal policy in the Northeast much more complicated and confusing.

Thus, in 1964 when both Elwin and Nehru died, Government's policies for the entire Northeast including tribal policies were in disarray and entangled in confabulations. In other words, an adverse interpolation and overlapping of the two views and opinions of Nehru and Elwin, particularly the pre, and post–independence views of Elwin took place and became the available prescriptions for evolving a tribal welfare programme by the Centre. The confused juxtapositioning of the two approaches to the tribal policies in the country, one of 'exclusion' or 'isolation', the other of 'inclusion', denoting the pre, and the post-independence phases of Elwin's approaches to tribal welfare programme were subjected to various interpretations and misapplications. What followed was an indiscriminate application of the two approaches, without factoring in the unique features of tribal life and the special needs of the Northeast. The all-India schemes and projects meant for tribal welfare and development therefore, had serious problems of inappropriateness in the region because of the indiscriminate use and application of Elwin's two approaches to tribal welfare in the Northeast. Consequently, while various tribal welfare schemes and programmes worked well in large parts of the country, in the Northeast, the capricious nature and inappropriateness of these welfare measures, which include several important schemes, projects and programmes failed to provide the much-intended relief.

Consequently, many policy decisions including welfare programmes took the form of extending the 'inclusive' or 'integrative' approach in an area or region where 'exclusion' or 'isolation' would have been much more effective. Conversely, what ought to have been effective by adopting the 'exclusion' approach was implemented as the 'inclusive' approach to tribal policies and welfare. This adoption of the tribal welfare and development measures, without understanding and appreciating or factoring in the unique tribal ethos and sensibilities of the Northeast by policy makers was a major flaw in the conceptualisation and implementation of post-independence tribal policies of the Government of India in the Northeast. Moreover, the various tribal communities from the Northeast saw the introduction of the common tribal welfare programmes meant for the whole country on them, as attempts at trivialisation of their unique tribal customs, ethos and institutions. The prevalent subconscious fear of losing their identity by being trapped into the welfare programmes meant for socio-religious based castes and communities were reinforced by the consequences of the misapplication of the two approaches of tribal welfare and development attributed to Elwin. Implementation of Tribal welfare programmes meant for all the tribal population of the country in the Northeast therefore sharpened the divide between the upland tribal communities of the Northeast and the rest of India.

The tribal welfare programmes of the Government of India in the Northeast therefore, did not make the desirable impact, in spite of all the good intentions of the Government. Because of these factors, the feeling of the people of the region in general and the tribal population in particular, that they were a neglected lot, unfortunately become a major rallying point for various ethnic groups. This contributed in galvanizing local opinions against the Centre and became a popular rallying point for inciting parochial and ethno nationalistic feelings in the region. The tribal welfare policy of the Government of India in the region somehow became a source of discontent and misgivings, which distanced the tribal communities of the Northeast from the rest of India. In a nutshell tribal policy based on the Nehruvian model and the compromised 'middle path' enunciated by Verrier Elwin, which formed the conceptual basis for the formulation of the policy meant for the whole country, was wrongly applied in the Northeast.

3. The Politics of Language in Assam

One of the most important contributory factors leading to the balkanization of Assam (the Northeast) into several states, was the politics of language. Like religion, language exacerbates and entices, divides and also unites people; essentially juxtapositioning of contradictions depending on its usage and application. The politics of language, because of its inherent connections to the politics of identity unfortunately carries within it the seeds of communal disharmony and hatred. In a physically compact region like the Northeast, composed of large numbers of heterogeneous ethnicities with divergent and distinctive social and cultural histories, the problems posed by language like religion, becomes extremely complex.

In this background the impression and belief that the Assamese wanted to impose the Assamese language on the various ethnic groups and other constituent members of the erstwhile state of Assam is true to a certain extent. However, mere impressions do not reflect or explain adequately the circumstances and reasons behind this vilificatory adage given to the politics of language in Assam. This issue is much more complex then how it is often analysed or interpreted in the context and history of ethnic identity relations in erstwhile Assam prior to the formation of Nagaland in 1963. Had it not been for the politics of language, which became one of the main causes and reasons leading to the balkanization of Assam, even though was inevitable, the ethnic groups could have parted ways in a much more friendlier manner with much less bitterness than it did. Conversely, the story of ethnic relations in the Northeast would have been different.

The genesis of the problem began when the British approached the issue of language in Assam rather simplistically and casually, by arrogantly introducing Bengali in the region, unmindful of its consequences and impact on the Assamese population as an imperial power would. On the face of it, this fact may appear paradoxical and preponderous, since it was the British as a foreign power, especially the Christian missionaries who popularised and encouraged the use of Assamese and other local vernaculars and dialects of the region. The Christian missionaries resurrected many local vernacular formats as part of the proselytisation efforts to teach the Bible and other holy scriptures to the many small ethnic groups in the region. In Assam, for example the American Baptist was the first group of Christian Missionaries to use the 'Assamese-Sibsagar' dialect in 1813 for ecumenical purposes. They were also the first to introduce Assamese prose in 1819. Bani Kanta Kakati in his well known book on the history of the formation of the Assamese language wrote in 1941; *"The Missionaries made Sibsagar in Eastern Assam the centre of their activities and used the dialect of Sibsagar for their literary purposes"*[18]. The missionaries also started a printing press in 1836 in Sibsagar and in 1848 started a monthly periodical called 'Arunodai'. Nathan Brown compiled the first Assamese Grammar, while M. Bronson published the first Assamese-English dictionary in 1867.

The British did not consider Assamese as a language but treated it as a dialect, less important than Bengali. The first consolidation of the Assamese language began when the Arundoy School of the Assamese language formed in 1846, subsequently it was changed over scientifically to the Jonaki School of Assamese language in 1889 when Laxminath Bezbarua started the Assamese journal 'Jonaki'. The first modern Assamese dictionary 'Hemkosh' was published in 1890. Rajanikanta Bordoloi published the first Assamese novel 'Mirijiyori' in 1894. It was once again American missionaries like Nathan Brown, Oliver Cortrer, Miles Bronchon, and Choybus Barker all foreigners, who intervened and reinstated the Assamese language to its preeminent legitimate position as the Official Language of Assam on 8 April 1873. Until then, Bengali was the official vernacular language of Assam and *"even primary education being taught in that medium"*[19].

Popular resentment against the imposition of Bengali as the official language in Assam started for the first time by Gunaviram Barua and others in 1836. It was the first middle class Assamese's reaction and response against the marginalisation of the Assamese language, an expression of their steadfast desire to maintain their unique culture, ethos and above all their identity. This protest against imposition of Bengali language in Assam was the bellwether to several other popular uprisings against British policies in Assam. It marks a distinct phase in the history of assertive Assamese identity. The first of these uprising took place at Phulbari on 17 September 1861 under the banner of "Raijmal" or Peoples' Court, which then spread to Patidarrang, Nalbari, Lachima, Barama, Bajali, Khetri and Upor Barbhag. Several other upheavals also occurred in Rangia in 1893 and the last recorded one occurred at Patharughat in 1894.

The reaction against the introduction of the Bengali language came out in the open because it was one of the many decisions in a long series of similar decisions taken by the British directly affecting and hurting Assamese sentiments and interests. The growing resentments and anger against the British began ever since the British made Assam a part of the British Empire after the signing of the Yandawoo Treaty in 1826 at the end of the First Anglo-Burmese war, followed by the formal annexation and control in 1838 by dethroning the Ahom king Purandar Singha. Further, as part of the aggressive British policy to exploit the rich natural resources of Assam, especially tea, hydrocarbon and other minerals, large tracts of arable lands were taken from the local landholders by restricting their holdings to only one hundred acres under the infamous "The Waste Land Regulation". Simultaneously, the British introduced two land revenue rates, one for the local landowners and another for the British companies. The rates levied on the Assamese landowners were much higher than the rates levied on British companies.

Set therefore against this backdrop, the imposition of the Bengali language was literarily the last straw on the camel's back. This decision by the British became a clear threat to Assamese society, culture and their way of life and above all to their identity. Many Assamese intellectuals felt that it was the beginning of the denigration of the Assamese people and consequently of their culture and ethos. This decision to enforce Bengali as the administrative language brought all the diverse sub-ethnic groups of the Assamese community and interestingly all Assamese-speaking people under one single platform against the British. The sense of insecurity of their own future in the land of their birth disturbed the Assamese greatly and instilled a great sense of apprehension about their future. In addition, the British companies brought in large numbers of Bengali support staff and labourers from other regions of British India for the tea and mining industries overlooking the local Assamese. The fear was real and the alienation of the Assamese complete.

The calamitous impact of the provisions of the 'Partition of Bengal', which followed later in 1905, dividing Bengal into the Eastern and the Western halves even though short lived, was considered as the first step in this direction. The Assamese felt that the slow but sure process of dismantling Assam politically and Assamese ethos in general was on. Even though the 'Partition' was intended to effectively counterbalance the increasing aggressive posturing of the dominant Bengali Hindus on the Western half of Bengal by creating a counter-balancing region in the form of a new Bengali speaking Muslim dominated Eastern half, Assam unfortunately was made part of the Bengali speaking Muslim dominated Eastern half. As a result, Assam administratively became part of the Bengali speaking Muslim dominated and poorer eastern half of Bengal. In effect, the 'partition of Bengal' meant that Assam would be part of essentially a Bengali dominated region jeopardizing interests of the Assamese and the entire future as a race in spite of having their own distinctive ethos, character and history.

This inclusion of Assam as part of the Eastern half of divided Bengal additionally meant opening out the vast fertile and mineral rich valleys of Assam to the multitude of land-starved Bengali speaking Muslim population of Bengal. What began as a trickle eventually became a flood and soon the local Assamese population became a minority in many of the districts in Assam. The alarm bells were sounded in 1931, when the Census Superintendent, C. S. Mullen in the Census Report of 1931 made this observation. *"Probably the most important event in the province during the last 25 years-an event, moreover, which seems likely to alter permanently the whole future of Assam and to destroy more surely than did the Burmese invaders of 1820 the whole structure of Assamese culture and civilisation-has been the invasion of hordes of land-hungry Bengali immigrants, mostly Muslims from the districts of Eastern Bengal and in Particular Mymensingh".*

The subsequent influx and continued dominance of the Bengalis over the local Assamese population during the British rule in the Eastern region was so overwhelming, that in February 1946, Lord Pethic Lawrence, the then Secretary of State for India, actually proposed the inclusion of the whole of the Northeast India to be part of East Pakistan after the partition of India. The views of the British India Government on Assam's future was subsequently summed up when the Cabinet Mission on May 16, 1946 made the British government's intention clear by recommending that Assam and Bengal be combined to form one composite division with a provincial constitution. The proposed restructuring was based on the premise that Assam had a close affinity with Bengal, implying Bengali language, ethos and culture and that separation from Bengal was undesirable. Assam was, in the perceptions of the British, overwhelmingly Bengali in character, Bengali dominated and predominantly a Bengali speaking region. The inherent sub-conscious fear of every Assamese that the British essentially considered them a part of the larger Bengali sensibility and ethos became a reality. It is a different matter that the plan was abandoned because of the serious opposition mounted by Gopinath Bordoloi, who with the support of Mahatma Gandhi vehemently fought against such a move. It is said that at one stage Gandhi told the Assam Congressmen to leave the party in protest against such move to make Assam a part of East Pakistan, assuring and reinforcing in no unclear terms that Assam had a different history, culture, social values and an identity of its own. The inerrant British policy on Assam suffered because of their wrong perceptions that Assam and Assamese ethos and culture composed of other minor indigenous people, was quintessentially an extension of Bengali culture and sensibility.

The disparaging perception of the Assamese language and the people of Assam by the British hurt Assamese sentiments and angered intellectuals in many ways than one. The British in their usual administrative 'no-nonsense' style steam-rolled Assamese feelings by ignoring them. It was the over-bearing dominance accorded to Bengali identity, language and culture by the British, by negating Assamese identity and sensibilities that aggressive posturing by the Assamese against Bengali came about. The anger and malice that the average Assamese has against the constant influx of illegal Bengali migrants from across the borders into Assam, has as such a much deeper connotation and background than what is often dubbed as the xenophobic predisposition of the Assamese against all Bengalis.

The anger and animosity is a summation of all the historical denial of the legitimate status to Assamese language, and marginalization of the Assamese as an ethnic group. It was this threat to their identity that gave rise to the xenophobic attitude of the people of Assam. In due course, the simmering anger over the years found expression in the form of regional political parties and organizations during the later part of the 20th century, which seized political power from the all-powerful Congress party. Thus while the regional parties like the AGP (Ahom Gana Parishad) led by the All Assam Students Union emerged as the democratically recognised political façade of Assamese hurt sentiments and feelings, the militant wing like the ULFA (United Liberation Front of Assam) was the violent manifestation of the assertive Assamese ethnic identity. The popular response and support enjoyed by the regional political parties like the AGP, which in a way reflected Assamese anger, helped the AGP to wrest political power from the entrenched Congress party in Assam during this phase. This rise of the AGP as a regional political power reflects the out burst of the dormant Assamese anger that began with the imposition of Bengali language over Assamese by the British. From the available evidences, it is clear that Assamese anger was directed against the imposition of Bengali, an injustice indirectly undermining the Assamese as an ethnic group by the British.

The imposition of Bengali as the official language, the induction of large numbers of Bengali officials and other groups of people into Assam, the Partition of Bengal all combined to intensify the feelings of insecurity among the Assamese. The threat was clearly on the impending danger of the obliteration of the Assamese as an ethnic group and by deduction, a threat to its ethos and sensibilities. Given this background, what the continued unchecked influx of illegal Bengali immigrants from across the international borders into the few arable valley areas of Assam meant to the average Assamese who depended for their livelihood on the narrow arable tract of land in the Assam valley need to be appreciated and understood. The combination of these factors made the usage of Assamese, as a language became a rallying point for the Assamese.

The preoccupation of the Assamese with the politics of language is as such the outpouring of the pent-up feelings, which had been suppressed ever since the British denied to it its legitimate place as the official language of erstwhile Assam. The issue of Assamese as a language was evocative and provocative enough to use it as a political weapon to assert Assamese ethnic identity. My understanding is that the Assamese preoccupation with Assamese as a language in its historical perspective is a self-assuring act, an assurance to themselves of their existence as a separate identifiable ethnic group more than an assertion of their identity over other ethnic group or community. It is certainly not a deliberate act of trying to belittle or denigrate other languages or dialect in Assam.

An important aspect that needs to be noted consequently, is that the politics of language in Assam arose not so much as to assert or impose the Assamese language on other autochthons in the region, as much as directed at protecting and defending Assamese identity itself. Seen from this historical perspective, it is clear that Assamese preoccupation with its language began essentially as an expression of its anguish and anger at marginalisation of the Assamese as a community by the British over a long period. Therefore, the misunderstanding among the various smaller ethnic groups in erstwhile Assam that the Assamese were out to impose Assamese language on them and thereby marginalize or trivialize them is not entirely true. I believe that the misgivings and impressions are the results of unintended collateral adverse consequences unconsciously inflicted on the native autochthons by the Assamese in their attempt to thwart and prevent further dilution of Assamese ethos and culture by the overwhelming unchecked inflow of illegal Bengali migrants into its shrinking territories. Assamese preoccupation with Assamese as a language is consequently, not a blatant attempt at imposition of Assamese language on the reluctant autochthons in the region as often made out by many, as much as to reassure themselves of unique and distinctive ethnic identity.

Unfortunately, for the region, the impression and misunderstanding that the Assamese were out to impose themselves over other ethnic groups, through the wide spread use of Assamese language only added to the discomfiture of the tribal leaders in erstwhile Assam. The politics of language snowballed into a major issue based on which demand for separate tribal states came to be justified. Perhaps a proper understanding and contexualisation of the issues involved could have prevented the political division of the state on ethnic lines. And if not, at least the parting would have been less acrimonious, less painful and not jeopardised the future relationships between the new states and Assam to enable them to work together in a spirit of partnership and cooperation as a region for development and progress.

4. Reorganisation of Assam: The Empty-Nest syndrome

One of the advantages enjoyed by erstwhile-undivided Assam, prior to its balkanization was that it was a viable economic entity, unlike the present economically 'divided' Northeast. It could retain this economic homogeneity because all the ethnic communities whithin it were politically together as a single state. This unique position came about essentially because Assam, predominantly covering the rich valley formed by the river Brahmaputra runs from east to the west and acts as a natural communication corridor for the entire region. Because of this strategic location, Guwahati its principle city became the centre of trade and commerce in British India. The British conferred this authoritative status on the people of Assam further by bringing all the territories in the entire region including parts of present Bangladesh into what was known as the Assam Province. The strong objections raised by the various leaders of Assam, especially Gopinath Bordoloi when its status as a separate identifiable region in British India was threatened when Assam was made a part of the eastern half of Bengal at the Partition of Bengal, also led to confer upon it an overarching role and dominance in the region.

However, by far the most important single phenomenon, which compelled Assam and the Assamese to dominate the affairs of the region, was the extensive use of Assamese language as the main *lingua franca* by almost all the ethnic groups in the region, leaving out Manipur and Tripura. Both consciously and sub-consciously by the given set of circumstances, Assam and Assamese language began to slowly dominate other ethnic groups. Even in terms of population Assamese speaking population comprising of non-tribal and tribal population was far larger than all the different languages spoken in the region. The dominance is significant because as against a total number of 1,652 different mother tongue recorded in the Census of India approximately 420 of these are from the Northeast alone. Even though the numbers of the members speaking different languages may be small the fact that Assamese as a link language was able to bridge the 'divide' is in itself significant. The Assamese knew this fact quite well. It is therefore not surprising that when the 'Reorganisation of the States' in India took place in 1956, Assamese language as the main spoken language enabled Assam to retain its territorial integrity. From the Assamese point of view, the Assamese language performed a very important task in the preservation of erstwhile Assam territorially, politically and economically.

The inference is that Assam without the numerical advantages of the various ethnic groups speaking Assamese in the region could not have been able to retain its territorial hold during the 'Reorganisation of States' during 1956. The role played by Assamese language, even though only spoken by most of the ethnic groups in erstwhile Assam, was significant in many respects. In this context, the illegal Bengali Muslims immigrant from Bengal[20] who settled in Assam and had learnt the Assamese language actually helped in boosting and enhancing the numbers of Assamese-speaking population during the survey undertaken at the time of the reorganisation. The fact is that Assamese language was in one sense the cementing force of the various ethnic and sub-ethnic groups in erstwhile Assam.

The attempt at the political consolidation of Assam territorially based on the widespread use of Assamese language by the indigenous groups like the Bodos, Kacharis and others, who speak Assamese and often considered part of the Assamese society is however, resented by these smaller ethnic groups. Whether this assimilation takes place by coercion or voluntarily, is a matter of debate. In fact, one of the main grouse of the Bodos against the Assamese is that these absorptions by first converting the Bodos into Hindus and then absorbing them into the Assamese society help in increasing the Assamese population at the expense of the Bodo population. Additionally, the Bodos also feel that their extensive assimilation into Assamese society would marginalize the Bodo as an ethnic group and eventually create internal dissension and social turmoil within the Bodos themselves.

The Bodos, Kacharis, like the Nagas, Mizos, Khasis, Jaintias, Garos and other numerically smaller ethnic groups and other non-Assamese communities did not understand properly the fact that the focus and emphasis on projecting all of them as Assamese speaking communities was essentially to retain the territorial integrity of Assam and not directed to marginalize or belittle any one of them. Like every other upland tribal community, the plains-tribals also mistook the Assamese intention in including them as 'Assamese' during the linguistic survey undertaken to determine the territorial jurisdiction of Assam as a state in 1956.

Objectively analysed, in the overall perspective most political analysts and commentators see the basis and logic adopted by Assam in projecting the extensive use of Assamese to hold together its territory during the reorganisation of states in 1956 as administratively sound, politically prudent and geo-politically and economically a practical move. The main problem arose when doubts and suspicions began to surface that this move was intended to establish Assamese hegemony and dominance politically over the various smaller groups especially the upland tribal communities. Conditioned by neglect developmentally, primarily arising out of the topography of the areas the upland tribal communities occupied, many of the tribal communities began to nurture their own aspirations as distinct ethnic groups. The various ethnic groups as such saw the whole issue as an Assamese-centric politically motivated move at their cost, an attempt at undermining their ethnicities and jeopardizing their future interests. In due course, because of the ongoing feeling of being neglected and the rising trend of ethno-nationalistic aspirations among many of these ethnic groups, the demand for either autonomy or complete segregation from Assam administratively was a foregone conclusion. Once this justifiable ethno-political aspiration overtook the leadership among the tribal communities in the region, every conceivable issue tended to take a political bias and colouring. The initiative and move to explain and reassure the various ethnic Assamese speaking tribal communities even though was made, failed because these were either too late or its fervour could not match the rising political expectations among these groups. The developments were however, economically disastrous for the region.

Seen in perspective it was clear that the intended consolidation of Assam territorially by using the Assamese language as the basis of holding all the different ethnic groups together politically would not succeed in perpetuity. This is because the mere speaking of a language does not necessarily abrogate, negate, or can forever suppress a person's loyalties and affiliations to one's ethnic identity or community. A person can subscribe one's mother tongue as Assamese as an example, and yet not be an Assamese both by birth and by intent. This aspect is established in the format of the questionaire in the Census of India, which shows that a person can be a Bengali by birth and yet can indicate that his or her mother tongue as Assamese. There is therefore, no guarantee of establishing a person's correct ethnic identity or loyalty merely based on the language spoken by him or her. Additionally, the chances of any illegal immigrant anywhere in Assam declaring that Assamese is *not* his or her mother tongue would be extremely rare for fear of either being deported as an alien or socially marginalised for all times to come.

The festering politics of language undercurrent in the polity of Assam became its soft underbelly. It was clear that the attempt at territorial consolidation of erstwhile Assam by leveraging and justifying the claim based on the extensive use of Assamese language would work in two ways. It enabled Assam to retain its territories during the Reorganization of States in 1956 on one hand, while on the other, it introduced the seeds of its own balkanization and dismemberment. The reorganization of erstwhile Assam into several States and Union Territories was inevitable. In short, the feeling among the various ethnic groups that erstwhile Assam was repugnant to their development and progress foreclosed the possible political options. The situation was ripe for the various non-Assamese ethnic groups to make the issue of Assamese language the rallying point for demand of separate political spaces of their own. Thus, ironically, what was meant as an instrument for enforcing unity actually became the cause for disunity.

In this politically surcharged atmosphere one of the major consequences nobody could foresee was the likely adverse economic impact that would fall on the region because of the impending political reorganization of Assam. The very fact that Assam by its size and locational advantages held the key to the economic success of the constituent States and the region somehow failed to draw the attention of the various leaders of the region of the new aspiring states during this phase. The politics of ethnic identity aspirations would prove to be too strong an influence to keep the various ethnic groups economically together within erstwhile Assam. This phase in the history of the Northeast was the beginning of the end of the composite and unified economic entity that Assam once was. Economically and developmentally, this would prove disastrous in the long run for the whole region.

The unfortunate fallout of the reorganization of erstwhile Assam, which followed consequently, was that it set in motion the internalization of the politics of ethnic divide in the region. This led to the implosion of the ethnic identity politics in the region adversely affecting and jeopardizing economic partnership and cooperation among the newly formed states in the region with Assam. The idea of regional planning, which was considered as a way out of the impending economic disaster the region was heading into was as such doomed to fail from the start. It was a sad end to the once composite, multicultured and economically homogeneous state of Assam.

The politics of ethnic identity, which eventually led to the balkanization of erstwhile Assam was a foregone conclusion given the set of circumstances. However, it is the acrimonious nature of the protracted negotiations followed by the bitterness and unpleasant exchanges, which made the 'parting' a 'lose lose' situation for all concened. The 'parting' left a trail of anger, misgivings and above all set in motion 'mistrust' between the new states and Assam. The Assamese felt upset at the turn of events, which made them not only saddened but also felt slighted. They reacted with a series of indifferent acts and responses, both political and perhaps most damaging economically. Many believe the response was reflective of the psychological state of mind often called the 'empty-nest syndrome', often attributed to a stage in the life of women when they primarily feel lost when grown up children leave home for new pastures of their own. Assam became after the reorganization a 'stand-alone' state economically to the detriment of the region.

5. The Politics of Identity: The Plain Tribals of Assam

The Bodos are the original inhabitants of Assam, the autochthons ruling most part of what was Assam during the medieval period much before the Ahoms. They are categorised as Scheduled Tribes under the Indian Constitution, and euphemistically known as the 'plains tribal'. The Bodos are tribal communities who have settled in the valleys of Assam, in contrast to other tribal communities who reside in the hills and mountainous areas of the state. The Bodos are the largest of the group sub-divided into a number of sub-tribes having many clans and sub-clans. Some of them are the Basumatari, Sargwari, Musahari, Sibigri, Narjari, Doimari, Gayari, Brahmari and a number of other smaller sub-classifications. The Dimasa, Madani, Mech form a separate group. While the Saraniya, Rajbangsi also known as Koch, Chutiya, Moran, Tippera, Mahalia, Dhimal, Solaimiya and Phulgaria and other smaller indigenous groups do not consider themselves as Kacharis. Most of these subgroups have converted themselves to Hinduism. The Lalung, Rabha, Garo, Hajong have isolated themselves from the parental ethnic group and have their own identity. Some of them under one Kalicharan Brahmachari started a Vedic movement and adopted a new faith in 1907[21]. The Mech occupy areas in Western Assam, the Bodos in central Assam, the Dimasa and Hojai in the north of the Cachar Hills and the

Sonowal and Thengal occupy the eastern part of the Brahmaputra. All these groups occupy the eight districts of Dhubri, Kokrajhar, Bongaigaon, Barpetta, Nalbari, Kamrupa, Darrang and Sonitpur, on the north bank of the Brahmaputra in Assam. The total area covered by the eight districts is approximately 35 per cent of the total area of Assam.

The Kacharis once constituted one of the important kingdoms in the region with Dimapur (now in Nagaland) as its capital. The Kacharis presented a separate memorandum to the Simon Commission when it visited Shillong in 1936 highlighting the fact that even though they had a rich historical past the British neglected them. Anthropologically, the Kacharis, Bodos and the Meiteis of Manipur belong to the same racial stock of people. From the traces of the few remnants of the kingdom, especially their beliefs in the cult of fertility and animism[22] Dr. J.H.Hutton and A.J. Moffatt Mills found a close affinity between the Nagas and the Kachari cultures.

Historically the cause of the ethnic divide between the Bodos, the other affiliated smaller tribes euphemistically known as the 'Plain's tribal' and the Assamese was historical since the Bodos and others always consider themselves as the original habitants of Assam. However, because of the dominance of the Ahom rulers the Bodos lost much of its importance in the subsequent history of the state. The simmering signs of discontent and first sign of rebellion among the Bodos, Kacharis, Karbis, Dimasas and other indigenous groups in Assam, began due to the prolonged marginalization of these communities by the Government of Assam and Assamese in general. A possible explanation of the growing acrimony between the Assamese and the Bodos in general and with the Government of Assam was the general impression and feeling of being overwhelmed by Assamese ethos and culture. The feeling arose partly from the growing tendency among a few intellectuals and leaders in Assam to impose Assamese ethos and sensibility on all the ethnic groups in Assam. Unfortunately, the fact that the various smaller ethnic groups in Assam did not subscribe to this idea did not register adequately among the Assamese.

Seen from this perspective, the attitude of the Bodos and other affiliated tribes and sub-tribes towards the Assamese was more or less in line with the general feeling of neglect that every tribal community both large and small felt in Assam as well as in other states, which had a mixed population of tribal and non-tribal population. This feeling of marginalization politically and otherwise as such was not an exception only in the case of the Bodos alone. One of the reasons for this neglect was the preoccupation of the Assamese with the problems of the massive demographic changes taking place in Assam due to the influx of large illegal Bengali migrants from Bengal immediately preceding and following the independence of the country. The fact that these illegal immigrants predominantly occupied Bodo lands added to the complexity of the problem. The Assamese and the Government of Assam failed to see the brewing signs of discontent from the tribal communities living in the valleys and plains of Assam.

Objectively analysed, many factors are responsible for the anger and resentment against Assamese dominance in Assam by the Bodos and other smaller ethnic groups. However, what precipitated the impending crises were the growing pattern of ethnic identic assertions of the tribal communities in the whole of Northeast against the age-old hegemony of the majority lowland non-tribal communities in general. Bellwethered by the Nagas and followed by the Mizos, the voice of dissent, thereafter revolt and finally the demand for autonomy and independence became a popular slogan and movement in the entire region. The Government's response to these demands by according statehoods and providing various financial and economic largesse only encouraged the various ethnic groups like the Bodos to make similar demands in the hope of carving out a separate political future for themselves or at least obtain special economic packages as part of the appeasement policy or peace deal that invariably follow such confrontations. The special status accorded to the tribal groups in the North East under the Sixth Schedule of the Constitution, the encouragements to form local self-governments in the shape of the Autonomous Councils, Autonomous Hill District Councils and other traditional and local institutions whetted the political appetite of these ethnic groups including the Bodos and other Plain tribes of Assam.

The other major factor for the Bodo-Assamese-disconnect was the continued unchecked influx of illegal immigrants from erstwhile East Pakistan into the Bodos domiciled areas comprising of the eight districts of Dhubri, Kokrajhar, Bongaigaon, Barpetta, Nalbari, Kamrupa, Darrang and Sonitpur, on the north bank of the Brahmaputra. The unabated inflow of immigrants into western Assam from erstwhile East Pakistan, which started by the British as part of the policy to people the vast tracts of lands occupied by the Bodos, which the British considered as 'waste lands', defied all punitive actions taken by the post-independent Government of Assam to prevent the situation. These influxes became a source of constant friction and acrimony between the Bodos and the immigrants. The Bodos and the Kacharis who bore the brunt of the illegal migrations much more severely than the Assamese dominated areas felt that the Government of Assam was not taking adequate steps to protect them and prevent the illegal immigrants from occupying their lands forcibly. The fundamental issue of control over land, an important aspect of Bodo economy and livelihood came to take centre stage. This threat to their livelihood and insecurities to their lives ignited the already pent-up anger among the various Bodo groups. They used the opportunity to galvanize, consolidate their position as an ethnic group, and assert for their rights and identity like every other ethnic group in the Northeast.

In addition, the Bodo, Kacharis and other ethnic groups saw the hegemonic conceptualisation of a 'nation-province' conceived by the Assamese intelligentsia covertly, without taking them into confidence or without their tacit understanding as typical Assamese arrogance, a demonstration of the 'big-brother' attitude. The failure to recognise these growing resentments among these ethnic groups were Assam's undoing. Gurudas Das surmises the inevitable situation, *"...the incongruity between the Assamese aspirations to make Assam a 'nation-province' and the polyethnic population composition has long been a persistent source of ethnic conflicts"*[23]. The concept of a 'nation-state' comprising all the divergent ethnic groups under the Assamese was unfortunately a view and approach not shared by many of the smaller ethnic communities of Assam. The rising tide was clearly against Assam's dominance in the Northeast region.

It was clear that the post-independence preoccupation of many of the indigenous ethnic groups in the Northeast was one of assertion, consolidation and reconceptualisation of their ethnic identities. Assertive ethnic identity and demand for separate territorial spaces was therefore central to the idea of reconstruction and consolidation of their respective ethnic identities. The immediate requirements of each of these communities is what Thomas Hylland Eriksen described as the *"...trimming and shaping, the past to fit present needs, inventing traditions where no organic traditions exist, or are adequate, to ensure a sense of continuity with the past"*[24]. The case of the Bodos is only one such example to illustrate the growing preoccupation among the various tribals in the region with their respective ethnic identities irrespective of whether they were from the upland hill areas or the plains in the Northeast. The problem was part of the general trend symptomatic of the phase in the ethnic identity history of the Northeast.

The inevitable 'disconnect' between the Plains tribals of Assam and the Assamese was therefore a foregone conclusion. The only way for the Assamese to amicably settle and resolve the demands of the various upland tribal ethnic groups was either to allow these groups form their own separate political spaces by letting go large areas of its territories by redrawing its existing political boundaries, or alternatively abandon the idea of the 'nation-province' inadvertently conceived. Even though various attempts were made to prevent the divide between the Plains tribal communities and the Assamese by well-wishers from both sides, the impending 'divide' could not be avoided. In the end, Assam had to forego both territories as well as the idea of a nation-province. Conferment of adequate autonomy to these groups within Assam and thereby preserve the territorial integrity of the state was another option, which in many respects has worked well in a few cases so far. However, from whichever angle one looks at the post-independent political scenario of erstwhile Assam, the growing ethnic divide among the various ethnic groups not only affected the character of the once socio-politically homogeneous region but had its adverse consequences on the question of economic viability of the entire region.

The 'divide', or wedge between the Assamese and the Plains tribal communities of Assam especially with the Bodos hurt the sentiments of the Assamese. This was because the 'parting' changed the history of Assam, its rich legacy by diluting the rich tapestry of its composite culture and ethos. Today in many ways than one Assam remains a divided house, trying to come to terms with itself like elsewhere in the region. In this connection, the Assamese need not feel sad by these developments since in many ways, the politics of ethnic assertive phase of the Bodos, the autochthons of erstwhile Assam is part of the long process of ethnic consolidation of people and communities taking place in the Northeast, searching for their roots and identities like anyone else across the world. The division of Assam even though politically inevitable, the revolt of the Bodos, the autochthons of the state is distinct from the others in many ways than one. This is because the Bodos and Its affiliated sub-tribes form an intrinsic constituent ethnic group in the long glorious history of undivided Assam, and because of which they have a special position and status. Their 'revolt' as such forms perhaps the saddest part of the ethnic identity history of Assam.

Endnotes

1. The *Mahabharata* is the longest epic covering a text of 100,000 two-line stanzas written in Sanskrit. It is in the Indian context neither an epic, in the sense of its multifarious applications, as opposed to the preeminence normally accorded to the central hero in an epic. Nor, does it have an iconic status of the Bible as an example. It is a synthesis of both, a little of each, it is neither an epic nor has the weight of the religiosity of the Bible. It is religious but not holy; it is human and yet has superhuman connotations. It is approximately eight times as long as Homer's Iliad and the Odyssey put together and 12 times as long as the Bible.

   To say that the work is a story about a great war is an over simplification. It dates back to 300 BCE and 300 ADE and the setting of the events relate to a period set in 5000 BCE (Before Common Era). Its significance lies in its sweeping presentation of vision of the cosmos and humanity, divinity and in essence the universality of all that encompasses human knowledge. The *Mahabharata* itself says,

   "Whatever found herein may also be found in other sources,

   Whatever is not found herein does not matter."

   It is divided into 18 Parvas (Chapters or books) concerning the 18-day war among 18 armies with the first ten books (Adi, Sabha, Vana, Virata, Udyoga, Bhishma, Drona, Karna, Shalya, and Sauptika) containing the war. The remaining eight comprising the Stri, Shanti, Anushashana, Ashvamedhika, Ashramavasika, Mausala, Mahaprasthanika and Swargarohana forming the residuary Parvas. Rishi Vyasa authored it but exist in many forms, genres, languages and versions for over two thousand years, including a Southeast Asia version. The *Mahabharata* and Valmiki's *Ramayana* are the two most important epics forming the essence of "Hindu" culture of India.

2. Dr. Ramesh Chandra Majumdar, M.A. Ph. D, Bharata-tattva-Bhaskara the eminent historian and scholar. Quotes are from his Memorial lecture '*Expansion of the Aryan Culture in Eastern India*', delivered in the Atombapu Sarma Memorial Lectures of 1966-67 at Imphal on 15 and 16 November 1966. Taken from the compilations of the lectures by the Atombapu Research Centre, Imphal, p-13 and14.

3. Bharatiya Vidya Cf, Bombay, June 1945, *Bhagadatta-vamsa Sambhuta*, p.112.
4. Dr. Ramesh Chandra Majumdar, ibid.
5. Dr. Mrs. S.L. Baruah, *A Comprehensive History of Assam.*
6. Dr. K.L. Barua *Early History of Kamarupa*, 1966 and B.K.Barua; *A Cultural History of Assam*, 1951.
7. Bani Kanta Kakati, *Assamese, its Formation and Development*, 1941.
8. Sir Edward Gait, *A History of Assam*, Chapter XII, footnote on page 270.
9. Dr. Sangkima, *Essays on the History of the Mizos*; Chapter 22, Impact of Ramayana upon Mizos.
10. Lalruanga: Ramayana leh Zofate, *Ramayana and Mizos*, 1997 p-135.
11. All quotes from 11 to 17 are from Verrier Elwin, Philanthropologist: Selected writings, compiled by Nari Rustomji, from different Chapters, and from Tribal Development in India; The Cotemporary Debate, edited by Govinda Chandra Rath.
12. ibid.
13. Ibid.
14. ibid.
15. ibid.
16. ibid.
17. ibid.
18. Bani Kanta Kakati, *Assamese, its Formation and Development*, 1941.
19. B.G. Verghese, p-26.
20. Gurudas Das, Probable Options. *Cementing the Faultlines in Assam*, http//www. Satp.org/.
21. B.G. Verghese, ibid, p-61.
22. Dr. Mrs. S.L. Baruah, ibid.
23. Gurudas Das, Probable Options, *Cementing the Faultlines in Assam*, ibid.
24. Thomas Hylland Eriksen. *The Nature of Ethnicity in the Project of Migration.*

CHAPTER - 9

The Future: Looking Ahead

The book has so far identified the various causes responsible for the preoccupation of the people of the Northeast with their respective ethnic identities. The disturbing feature of this preoccupation is that it has not only divided the region on ethnic lines but has also jeopardized the economic development of the Northeast as a region. An interesting aspect of this acrimonious relationship, as observed in the preceding Chapters, is the 'assumed' notions of dissimilarities mostly based on hearsays. In other words, the differences are far more imagined than real. Moreover, these 'differences' were 'imposed' by the circumstances of history on the people and hence are not of their making. Perspectively viewed, as such in the context of the available studies on the theories of ethnic identity formations, the anthropological histories of the various ethnic groups and especially because of the geophysical constraints and political isolation of the region, the present acrimonious ethnic 'divide' and disconnect appear rather naïve and ironical. In a region behest with several problems, the various ethnic groups instead of coming together and trying to overcome these handicaps through cooperation and partnership, are unmindfully working at cross-purposes and often against each other. In short, given the preponderance of the overwhelming need for peace, understanding and empathy among the constituent ethnic groups of the Northeast for development and progress of the region, the present scenario is to say the least, self-effacing and self-destructive.

Simultaneously, the Government of India also needs to change its approach in dealing with the various problems confronting the region. The general tendency to look at the problems of the region essentially from the Law and order, and security perspectives need to change. It need not be the only focus area of concern in dealing with the region. The time is long overdue to look at the various problems of the region essentially as problems arising out of economic deprivation, underdevelopment and poverty. It implies that the perpetual on-going debate, of whether peace should 'come' first, before development, or vice versa, a debate the Government has been involved ad nauseam, should now cease. The nagging fear in New Delhi that increase inflow of funds in the region, as part of the various development projects, programmes and schemes can further fuel insurgencies and hence the consequential need to restrict the flow of funds for development, only can end up into a much more vicious cycle of chaos and mayhem.

Understandably, from New Delhi's perspective, since the present law and order situation in the region nullifies the development efforts in the region, its preoccupation with law and order is understandable. However, this cannot be at the cost of development and economic progress of the region. The fact that security, especially national security, is a concern of every Indian and cannot be the concern of the Central government alone must be realised by government. However, sharing of responsibilities can only come about if the trust and confidence between the public, the stake-holders and the Government at the Centre and in the Northeast is created. There is a caveat though, underdevelopment and poverty, the two core issues, which are the root causes of all the problems in the region, must also be simultaneously addressed on top most priority.

The Government of India is at the right junction and time of history to take the process forward. Positioned as it is on the cross road of economic changes ushered in by the globalization process, a phenomenon in which the country is increasingly getting integrated into, the Government of India can make the Northeast an integral part of this process. Because unless the Northeastern states are made to find a place and its moorings at this time of India's economic transformation and change, a rare opportunity would have been lost to the country to retrieve the region from the clutches of mayhem and chaos.

Simultaneously such a move forward is possible only if the stakeholders, the people and state governments plan and develop the whole region together as one single economic bloc. This will put the energies and resources of all the constituent member states together so that the required synergy for planned development collectively as a region can be achieved. The present tendency of the constituent states in the region to position themselves as individual political entities, while politically correct and justified, however, given the precarious stages of economic development, compounded by the topography of the region, the state-wise segmented approach to development is economically unviable and financially imprudent.

This Chapter and the next, the penultimate part of the book examines this approach in the context of the globalization process sweeping across the country. These Chapters postulate that in a fast changing world of economic priorities and constantly evolving paradigms of investment decisions, where the decisions across the world has shifted to non-state players, the Northeast region must gear-up to adjust itself to confront the new challanges ahead. The various options and alternatives available for directionally changing and reorienting the focus and approach to achieve this goal are discussed.

This part of the book critically examines the reasons why if institutions like the European Union, which is a partnership of sovereign nations of a whole continent can work together for the economic progress and development as a single economic group and achieve results, why the Northeastern states of one country cannot work together as a single economic bloc in a similar manner. The role, functions of existing institutions like the North Eastern Council, especially various difficulties it faces in effectively discharging its responsibilities as a regional planning body is analysed.

Economic development and the moral imperative to change

The twin problems of underdevelopment and economic poverty in the Northeast are partly due to inaccessibility of the region arising out of the geo-political isolation at the time of Partition of the country in 1947 and partly due to the topography of the region. To these, is the added problem arising out of the post-independent political balkanization of the erstwhile economically viable state of Assam into several states. Devoid of these factors, the Northeast has all the prerequisite attributes and potential for development and progress like any other part of the country. It required the determined adventurous exploits of the British pioneers to exploit the rich natural resources of the region to make it into one of the most economically important regions in the whole of the British occupied territories in India in spite of all the physical impediments as far back as the early 19th century.

Amelendu Guha sums up the historical perspective of Assam's venture into economic development succinctly. *"The period from 1826 to 1873 was one of transition of Assam's pre-capitalist economy into its colonial phase. British capital penetrated the economy and started building an infrastructure to sustain exotic capitalistic set-up."* The tea industry grew from 2,311 acres in 1841 to about 8,000 acres by 1859[1] in Assam. By 1872 tea plantations covered more than 56,000 acres and by 1901 it was 3,38,000 acres. The production of tea increased from 12 million lbs to 134 million lbs during the same period. *"The Assam Company-first joint-stock company of India to be incorporated with limited liabilities under the Act of Parliament in August 1845 was started in 1839."*[2]. British interests thereafter extended to oil, forestry and various minerals of Assam. The first Indian oil refinery was started in Digboi in Assam more than one hundred years ago. All equipments for the first oil refinery in the region came into the remote eastern Assam through the river Brahmaputra.

Historically examined, economic development began in the Northeast after the British came to the region. The British established the first commercial contacts through the East India Company with the rulers of Assam. Economic planning and development, in the economic sense is a post-independence phenomenon, which is yet to find its proper moorings in the region. Economic development and especially industrial and commercial development as such historically, remains in the Northeast essentially an Assam oriented phenomenon. One of the reasons for the Assam-centric development of the region is the accessibility of Assam through the riverine routes through the Bengal Plains along the Brahamaputra, the Surma and other major tributaries of these rivers.

The two determinants of industrialisation and commercialization of the Northeast are accessibility and the other is the rich natural resources of the region. Accessibility into the region historically was restricted, except into the valley areas of Assam through the riverine routes. Emotional and sentimental reasonings apart, objectively analysed other constituent states do not have the locational advantages geographically that Assam has. In other words, the composite state of erstwhile Assam, that to only in the valley areas before reorganisation of the Northeast, then constituting most of the present Northeast 'region' leaving out the two princely states of

Manipur and Tripura, was the only State where industrialization was possible.

The reorganisation of states in the region, starting in 1963 when Nagaland became a state and followed by the formation of the other states in 1972-73, resulting in the political dismemberment of Assam was a major setback economically for the entire region. While the reorganisation is the culmination of a very long-felt desirable and politically needed solution to meet the aspirations of the various ethnic groups in the region, in purely economic and financial terms, the reorganisation was a disaster. It created several political units without the cohesive economic infrastructure capable of developing on their own steam. It simultaneously dismantled the composite nature of the economy of the region irrevocably. The Northeast region today comprises of ethno-politically desirable consensual units (States), but economically and developmentally, a cluster of unviable states, which is not helping either the region as a whole or any of the states in particular. The precarious financial health of the constituent states of the Northeast reflects the adverse financial and economic ramifications of the reorganisation of states in the region.

One of the major conditions, in fact the *sine qua non* based on which States were organised and formed in India in 1956 is their financial viability. However, the geo-political compulsions were so overwhelmingly in favour of giving the Nagas a constitutional identity within the Union in the form of a separate state of their own, that both the financial and economic viability issues were overlooked and Nagaland made into a separate state within the Union in 1963. In spite of vehement objections from the Finance Ministry and the Planning Commission, the objections were overruled. The grant of statehood to Nagaland not only became a precedent, but also meant the abrogation of the principle of financial and economic viability as a prerequisite for the formation of states in India. It was a major departure. The present precarious financial conditions of all the eight States, including the state of Sikkim, which is historically an 'inductee State' into the region and is comparatively and marginally better than the other seven States, all depend almost entirely on the largesse of the Centre for their survival. All the eight states in the Northeast are a financial liability to the country.

As per a World Bank Report[3], the fiscal indicators for the Special category states, which include all the states of the Northeast for 2001/02, reveal that the 'Own revenue' of these States was 5.9 per cent of the GDP. On the other hand, the Central Government's transfers were to the tune of 19.7 per cent of the GDP. The Debt stock of the Special Category States was 39.4 per cent. Further as against the 'Own revenue' of only 5.9 per cent of the GDP, the expenditure was 31.5 per cent of the GDP. The average Central assistance to the various States and Union territory in the Northeast was 85 per cent for Arunachal Pradesh, 51 per cent for Assam, 80 per cent for Manipur, 70 per cent for Meghalaya, 72 per cent for Mizoram, 80 per cent for Nagaland and 70 per cent for Tripura. The Central Government provided an average of a little over 70 per cent of the money available in these seven States and Union Territory. These states therefore depend largely on devolution of funds by the Central Government. The World Bank report also observed that Nagaland has an outstanding debt stock of more than 80 per cent of the GSDP in 2003/04 according to the state's own budget estimates. Overall, other states have "*similar levels of deficits and debt stocks*". Where these monies go is another dimension of the problem, which is not being analysed.

The fact remains that the reorganization of states by creating new states in the region in 1971-72 was not only detrimental to the economic progress and development of the region as a whole, but proved a major financial burden on the Central exchequer. The Vijay Kelkar headed Thirteenth Finance Commission, which submitted its recommendations and findings in 2009-2010 has recommended a grant of an amount of Rs. 51, 800 crores (Non-plan Revenue Deficit Grant) to help bridge non-plan revenue deficits in the country after post devolution Non-Plan Revenue Deficits have been tabulated. Excluding Himachal Pradesh, Jammu and Kashmir, whose shares are Rs. 23825 crores the remaining Rs. 27975 crores is the share of the Six Northeastern states. Even the two Northeastern states of Assam and Sikkim which have been left out has a Pre-Devolution Non-Plan Revenue Deficit of Rs. 7149 crores and Rs. 248 crores respectively. After the transfer and devolution of central funds, Assam and Sikkim have been able to muster a Post-Devolution Non-Plan Revenue Surplus of Rs. 422 crores and Rs. 65 crores respectively. All these only show the prevailing conditions of the finances of the states in the region and the total dependence on the Centre to meet their respective non-plan revenue expenditures.

The Financial Viability

The developing trend of the precarious financial situation and the economic downturn of Assam, epitomizes the prevailing precarious financial health and economic conditions of all the states in the region. The Human Development Report 2003 of Assam, prepared by the State's Planning and Development Department provides an insight into the prevalent problems faced by the state, which in a way is indicative of the general trend in the region. The per capita income of state as per the HDI (Human Development Index) Report of Assam reveals a disturbing trend; *"At independence, Assam's per capita income was only marginally less than the national average. In 1988, the average per capita income for the country was over 108 times that of Assam.... The state's per capita income in 1950-51 was 4.1 per cent higher than the national average; by 1980-81 the state's per capita income was 27 per cent lower than the national average; and by 1998-99, the gap had widened to 45.5 per cent".* The Report further states that, *"...two issues that have certainly been exceptional in the duration of their existence, the intensity of their occurrence and the extent of their impact are"* the *"... severe fiscal stress...the mismatch between the resources needed to provide basic services, maintain assets, promote growth and development and create infrastructure and the resources available to the state..."*[4].

If one considers the fact that at the time of independence erstwhile Assam was one of the most prosperous states in the country, which ranked higher than most economically advanced states of today, it reflects the general downward trend in Assam's economic condition over the years since its political balkanization. Over and above, the other factor that is a perennial source of financial burden on the States and the Central Government is the huge amounts of money spent on enforcing and administering the law and order problems in the region. For instance for every kilometer of road built in the region, almost double of that amount is required to ensure the safety and security of the people involved in the execution of the road. M. S. Prabhakara attributes the *"severe financial stress"* therefore on the additional costs burden imposed on both the government at the Centre and the States due to *"decades of unrest, agitation, and at a later stage by insurgency"*[5]. An analysis of the percentages of expenditure of the insurgency infested states in the country, particularly the Northeastern states, including the state of

J&K, will indicate that bulk of the states resources, including funds received as Central assistance in the form of grants and loans mainly endup as administrative expenses and meeting other overheads. Conversely, in per capita terms most of the insurgency-infested states are able to spend much less on the various welfare and social sectors.

The inference is therefore obvious; it is the ethnic assertions leading to the political division of Assam into many separate small political units by dismantling the economically viable state of Assam, which is one of the main causes of the retarded growth and underdevelopment of Assam and the other states of the region. The dismantling of the economically viable State of Assam, with Guwahati as the main commercial and economic hub, in a way disbanded the composite nature of the economy of the region. The other States in the region in the absence of an important trading centre like Guwahati, lack the basic infrastructural access required for trade links with the rest of the country. Even movements of products meant for local consumption within the region suffer due to the number of checks at the borders between states enforced by each of the constituent states. This political barrier, more man-made than physical, divides the region into several disjointed economic units, which affects trade and commerce between states within the region. Such a situation for a region already badly handicapped by its topography and lack of adequate infrastructure is to say the least, economically disastrous.

Additionally, because of the numerous disjointed pockets of economic units in the region, which are politically co-terminus with State boundaries, large pockets and areas of underdevelopment have sprung up along the border areas between states due to a phenomenon, which for want of any appropriate definition I call the *'negative border areas syndrome'*. The 'negative border areas syndrome', in short NBAS, is the general tendency of states, and within states the districts, the subdivisions etc, to neglect these peripheral border areas that tend to develop into a 'no man's' land as they fall beyond the focus and attention of the state Governments or their respective administrative sub-structures and sub-divisions. These areas breed their own peculiar problems in the region arising of neglect by neighbouring and adjoining states or their respective districts authorities as the case may be. These areas end up as pockets of highly discontent and grudging populations in the border areas of the states in the region, which given the prevailing law and order situation becomes the ideal breeding ground for various subversive and illegal activities.

Similarly, regional oriented projects initiated by the central government require the consent of several state governments in the region, which takes a much longer time to receive the consent from the respective states. Since the new states individually and separately has neither the wherewithal nor the expertise required in scrutinizing these large-scale projects, execution and completion of large-scale interstate developmental projects eventually end up with both time and cost over-runs invariably. The series of revised estimates that follow, the procedures of financial reappraisals of these projects and the constraints imposed by the climate of the region (workable months are essentially limited from September to March when the region is free from the monsoons) all combine to make every project in the region financially unviable. The much-hyped leakages of funds due to the pernicious links and nexus between insurgencies, political parties, contractors and bureaucrats are some of the additional problems of the region. It needs to be added however, that the issue of insurgency in the region is often used as bargaining points for seeking additional central funds or as excuses and explanations for either not completing the projects on time or to explain away cost and times overruns.

To address these special problems such as the one required to regulate the free movement of goods and services within the region or ensure the timely coordination and completion of large-scale inter-state projects of national and regional importance a centralized coordinating agency is a crying need for the region like the Northeast. For want of a coordinating central authourity to facilitate the movements of goods in and out of the region or for planning and executing interstate projects by a centralized regional body, the economic development and progress of the region has suffered over the years.

The prevailing situation is ironical because the fact that there exist several ways out of the predicament even though known is for reasons other than economics not formally acknowledged. Part of the problem lie within the region itself. For instance, even though the States in the region are aware of the preeminence of Assam historically, and locationally Guwahati specifically, as the only trading and commercial centre and outlet for the region, yet no one State is willing to accord this preeminent status to Guwahati for fear of political backlash or fallout in the respective states. This reluctance to accept the economic reality, simply because, no state is willing to relinquish or make compromise on their respective importance as a State, essentially a psychological inhibition, remains a major constraint in the economic progress and development of the region. The prevailing resultant disconnect and the disjointed underdevelopment of the region appear rather naïve and short sighted especially because of the tremendous potentiality the states in the region possesses as a single economic bloc in the context of the likely cascading benefits the globalization process taking place in the country can provide.

The discomfiture of the states are understandable given the fact that each state in line with their newfound identity and political freedom, plan and undertake developmental programmes in consonance with their own sets of priorities and goals. However, unfortunately even though politically each state is in the best position to plan and undertake projects and schemes based on their own priorities, the disengagement between the states in the region in the sphere of economic development adversely offsets the gains that the overall developments of the region could have provided to the states. In this unfortunate situation regional planning and development is the biggest casualty. The end-result is the disjointed, retarded and sluggish growth and development of the region mainly created by attitudes rather than by the facts of developmental logic. The question is can this thinking, predilection and situation be allowed to continue or something needs to be done?

The consequences of the 'disengagement' between States is affecting not only large national or interstate projects involving two or more states in the region, but also incapacitates the states from fully exploiting and using the benefits that can come from these large national and interstate projects and schemes. This is because the primary focus and emphasis of development and investments in the given set of circumstances in these states are primarily the localized small schemes and projects, which does not provide the much-needed collateral benefits the neighbouring states in a region like the Northeast urgently require. The net result is that huge investments neither generate the expected returns in monetary terms nor provide the much-needed socio-economic benefits for which it was planned. Considering the fact, that it is precisely regions like the Northeast, which require planning for development at the regional level more than any region in India, that the absence of an authoritative apex-coordinating agency, duly recognised and accepted by the States is severely felt. The void left by Assam in the form of a unified economic entity to the region before the reorganisation of states in the Northeast needs filling up as soon as possible.

There are many other issues and reasons in addition, strong enough as to why a collective approach to regional planning and development for the Northeast is necessary. Some of these factors are internal while others are external. Among the internal factors, the problems of endemic ethnic identity divide analysed in the earlier Chapters is of serious concern. Arising out of this factor, a few are largely psychological inhibitions, the hangover of past prejudices, a few imagined fears, while some are obvious signs of despondency and lack of will-power of the leaders and people of the region to overcome them. The preponderance of the impending changes in the external economic environment created by globalization and the consequential adverse affects on the region due to the likely shift of investments to the more prosperous regions in the country, are the other major concerns of the people of the region. These are analysed in brief in the context of why regional cooperation among the States in the Northeast, in spite of their political standoff is necessary to overcome these impending problems in the days to come.

Insurgencies and regional cooperation

Stephen Thel[6], quotes German sociologist Gunnar Heinsohn who once wrote *"...that nations with an oversupply of frustrated young men (a "youth bulge") are more prone to violence"*. This amply describes the present plight and fate of the Northeast region, with its 'oversupply' of young 'educated' youths as compared to any region in the country. Having registered some of the highest literary-rates in the country, the abundance of young educated energetic minds and restless body, confined and cut away from the rest of the country, the region has become the breeding ground for insurgencies and various types of anti-national activities; a refuge for the 'betrayed' youths. Ever since the independence of the country, the region has not seen many days of peace and quiet. These youths are the legacies of the impounded history of the region. Today the Northeast region is synonymous with insurgency and underdevelopment.

Critically viewed, however, if one looks at the law and order problems in the country, the problem is not the privilege or monopoly of the Northeast alone since these problems exist in some form or the other in other parts of the country, albeit lesser in magnitude and intensity. The trajectory and cycle of violence has its own rhythm of ebb and flow in the region like everywhere else. It is however, the national hypocrisy and the prejudice that in spite of the prevalence of such incidences taking place elsewhere in the country, the Northeast and Jammu and Kashmir alone are hyphenated to a pariah status because of a few such occurrences. In the process, a vicious cycle of mistrust and fear entraps the thinking of the average Indian about the people and of the region. This affects development because of the prevailing atmosphere and impression about the region. Badgered both ways, as such from the chaos inflicted by insurgencies on one hand, and the lack of investments from other sources than government, adequate development and progress in comparative terms with the performance indices in the rest of country eludes the region. This affects the people psychologically, who in turn blame the Government of neglect and discrimination. A vicious blame-game perpetrates between the people of the region and the central government benefiting no one.

What then is the future for the Northeast region given the present situation of law and order? Histories of insurgencies in the world, gives three distinct stages of its evolution and denouement. These are the (a) ideological stage; (b) the execution or operational stage; and (c) the denouement stage. The history of the surviving major secessionist insurgency movements, the Nagas, Meiteis and the Assamese, have gone through the first two stages but the elusive denouement do not seen to be anywhere near at hand. The demand for political independence, which was the initial demand, seems to have somewhat petered down to reasonable demands for autonomy and self-governance within India. For instance, the Nagas in spite of all the public posturing they may take realises the difficulty the Government of India has in giving complete autonomy, not to talk of independence to it. Even the reconciliatory demands made by the NSCN (IM) for a spatially larger political entity encompassing territories from its neighbours, Manipur, Assam and Arunachal Pradesh seem quite elusive, since none of the affected states is willing to part with the territories claimed by the NSCN (IM). In short, given the nature of the situation, the problems of law and order confronting the region are bound to persist for some time to come in one form or the other since these problems are inextricably tied down with many other issues, which refuses to fade away. The question is what does the region do until then, especially for its growth and economic development?

One is contextually aware of these issues and problems, which is bad is to say the obvious. Nevertheless, there are positive signs and indications that these can soon change. The new hope comes from the expectation that the region will imbibe the positive effects of an economically resurgent new India and be part of the changes taking place. These are visible, cognitively discernable in the form of economic successes the country has demonstrated in recent times to the world by becoming one of the fastest growing economies in the world today. This success story will hopefully, also percolate to the troubled region. This is a positive sign, a development, which can provide the desired hope among the young troubled minds in the region. The perceptible and palpable sign is evident from the desire and determination of the people of the region to be part of the 'change story' the country is witnessing.

Some of the most obvious positive signs about the region is the fact that in spite of all the rumblings and the chaos, democracy and democratic institutions have functioned most admirably amidst the most trying circumstances and prevailing law and order situations in the Northeast. The various elections to the State Assemblies and the Parliament are held as per schedule, at regular intervals without any major disruptions. The sub-functionaries of the democratic system, the traditional and local institutions, like the District Councils, Tribal Councils, Village Councils and the Panchayat system function satisfactorily and have in fact, evolved and reified into new forms in conformity and keeping in tune with the changing times. Similarly, the State Government machineries in spite of the various problems of geographical isolation and physical handicaps have largely been able to deliver what is best possible in the given scenario, in some cases with aplomb and in style. Peace at least permeates on the surface officially, even though they are fragile, marked by occasional outburst of 'madness', which in a situation like the one in the region is bound to occur. The threat to life and property remain, and the problems of accusations and denials on violations of human rights persist, yet there are signs and hope that all these are passing phases of a young democratic country in which the Northeast is just a part of it.

The ethical dimension of development

The underlying emphasis in the above analysis is the fact that in spite of the ongoing law and order problems, basic tenants of democracy prevail in the region, in fact in many instances much better than in many parts of the country. From this perspective alone, the region deservedly needs to be given its legitimate share of development funds and other inputs devoid of the grudging tenor often echoed by New Delhi due to the fear and apprehension of these funds being siphoned off to the insurgent groups.

In highlighting the above facts, the basic and fundamental principle of ethics in democracy comes into play. In this, the Central Government's role comes into sharp focus, since it entails the ethics of fairplay and equity in enforcing that the fruits of welfare economics are equitably distributed across the country. Ethics of economics here means the 'fairness' involved in the dispensation of developmental largesse to the states of the country in general, and with specific reference to region like the Northeast. In this regard, one is compelled to refer to the basic and fundamental premises of Amartya Sen of *"...how descriptive economics, prognosis, and policy can be improved by making more room for welfare economics in the determination of individual and group behaviour; and how the study of ethics can, in turn, benefit from a closer contact with economics"*[7]. Ethics in economics in the context of the Northeast, does not merely denote or imply the monetary and financial aspect, it encompasses the much more fundamental moral obligation that the country owes to the region for politically isolating it insensitively from the rest of the country at the time of independence. This is because as pointed in an earlier context, the isolation of the region is a man-made tragedy, which destroyed the spirit of the people of the region from within. Fairness means equitable justice to rectify the wrongs done in history by addressing the issue of 'dealing' with development of the region from the ethical perspective in procedure and as a principle of governance and not merely as an act of charity.

Devoid of this ethical perspective, all efforts become mere routine redressal mechanisms of Government towards some disgruntled people in the periphery of the country's remote borders and frontiers. This 'human touch', the core and essence of welfare economics, must prevail in the thinking of the country in re-connecting to the people of the region, to touch their hearts to restore faith and trust in the Government at the centre. This implies that financial assistance to the region should be allocated out of sincere concern for the people of the region, rather than dictated by the patronizing arrogance of power, a behaviour pattern, which is one of the main causes of the psychological 'divide' between the Central Government and the people of the region, for that matter between the people of the Northeast and the rest of the country.

In the parlance of the Northeastern psyche, 'money' is not everything, but sincerity, feelings and respect, not necessarily in that order, matter immensely. Perhaps understanding this aspect of the Northeastern psyche by the policy makers at the Centre is crucial in successfully planning and implementing its various schemes and projects in the region. What is also important, in the ultimate analysis is that the Government is ethically bound to discharge its obligation to a community of 'wronged people' who in spite of all the travesty of unkind history has upheld the country's democratic traditions and institutions exceptionally well ever since the unfair physical isolation at Partition. There is a special moral responsibility due from every Indian because of this 'unfair' dispensation to the people of the region. Healing requires understanding and empathy devoid of the patronizing attitude, the understanding of which is sorely lacking while dealing with the people of the region. If the people of India can appreciate and understand this aspect of the Northeast psyche, many issues and problems would automatically get resolved on their own and prevent similar problems from occurring. This is the only appropriate self-correcting mechanism to bridge the divide between the people of the Northeast and the rest of India.

The World Commission formed by the United Nations in a far reaching conclusion, expressed similar sentiments, high lighting the 'fairness' involved in development, in the context of globalization on the peripheral economies of the world. The World Commission on the Social Dimension of Globalization in its report, 'A fair globalization: Creating opportunities for all', under the co-Chairmanship of President Mkapa of the United Republic of Tanzania and President Halonen of Finland, which examined the issues was released on 24th February 2004. The findings of the Commission are relevant and significant for the world and especially for people and economies in the peripheral regions of India, like the Northeast. The Commission has placed 'equitable fairness' and 'availability of opportunity' as the main issue to be addressed in the context of the impact of globalization on the underdeveloped and developing countries across the world. The report spells out 'fairness' both of 'decent work practices' and also of providing 'opportunities' as the main plank on which Globalization can succeed in the true sense of the term. The World Commission observed; *"Much has been done to facilitate global finance, trade, and investments, but very little to reinforce local communities and local markets where people live and want to stay if given the opportunity. The livelihoods of many families throughout the world are under serious stress and social policies must respond to their needs and aspirations...There cannot be successful globalization without successful 'localization'"*[8]. The operative word 'fairness' or 'Fair globalization' implies the principle that the international community must apply in the globalization process so that economic benefits also accrue to the rural and peripheral regions of the world. The ILO (International Labour Organization) has taken up these concerns as part of the follow up action.

It is in the context of these developments across the world and in the country, especially given the locational and historical disadvantages imposed on the region by the country's history that the need to address the problems of underdevelopment of the region and eradication of poverty must be addressed emphatically from the angle of justiciable economic 'fairness' and 'equity'. It is only fair therefore, that at this juncture of the country's development history, especially because India is a major player in the process of globalization, that the Northeast region must be made a part of this globalization process. Frittering away this opportunity will be extremely costly in the end.

Given these set of conditions, unless there is a paradigm shift and change in thinking among the regional leadership and by those who matter in the Centre, to make the Northeast region part of the globalization process the country is involved in, the Northeast region will lose out as it always was in the past. It will be an opportunity gone waste. This requires a change in thinking by the Centre by going beyond the positional expressions of concerns and tendencies to see nothing beyond the law and order perspective. There is a need to seriously look at the Northeast from the fact that it is what it is today because of the political isolation after independence and that consequential affects are not necessarily the makings of the people of the region, but a situation thrust upon it historically. Justice, especially economic justice means fairness to even out the asymmetry imposed on the region by the politics of the division of the country.

Similarly, a change of heart of all people and governments in the region is required if they have to redeem the situation and regain the lost opportunities for growth and development in the past. The prescription, therefore, is that the States in the region must resolve and overcome their political differences and other inhibitions and instead work together as a region based on mutually agreed economic programmes to face the challenges confronting the region in the globalized world order. The Centre must facilitate this coming together of minds and intentions.

The 'Initiatives of Change', a diverse, global network committed to built trust across the world's divide based in Caux with its main office in Geneva, which has a 'Special Consultative Status with the Economic and Social Council' of the United Nations (ECOSOC) and a participatory Status at the Council of Europe in Strasbourg defines human security as follows. *"Human security depends not just on freedom from conflict and the threat of terrorism. It also lies in meeting basic human needs for shelter, food and work, health and education-and a sense of self-worth. For millions these needs are far from being met. In a world of plenty, poverty and injustice persist."* The 'Initiative of Changes' believes that these challenges can be met by adhering to the issues through the *"core values of honesty and integrity, purity of heart and motive, selflessness and courage, love for people- and forgiveness. Such values, lived out, along with fresh inspiration found through times of silent reflection, enable each of us to make a difference. They help us to address the root causes of insecurity and sustain hope for the future."* The Northeast region of the country is in need of such a prescription.

The Global Dimension

L. Friedman describes the 'new-world' as the 'Flat World'[9], a world that had *"started to get smaller and flatter...one that would transform education, infrastructure, and governance in a much more profound manner"*. The corridors of knowledge-information and access to data capable of transforming the world almost immediately are now easily accessible and available to everyone. The politically and spatially defined contoured world of yesterdays has morphed into an unrecognizable entity, where the importance of the politically contrived national boundaries has blurred, if not totally become irrelevant. The rapidity, with which the world is amalgamating as one large economic entity, expropriates and marginalises existing political concepts of nation states.

The phenomenon is so overwhelmingly overpowering that nation-states are losing their omnificence, their prerogative and freedom to determine investment decisions or independently make economic policies, since often decisions are made outside national boundaries and governments far beyond their jurisdiction and control. It is this dismantling of the decision making process, marked by the distinctive shift from the domain of Government to non-state players that make regions like the Northeast highly vulnerable to neglect and commensurate decay. Niall Johnson, Director of the Commonwealth Parliamentary Association (CPA) sums up the emerging need for interdependence among nations in a conference held in Bangalore on 14 May 2006, where 42 participants from 15 countries took part. Nial Johnson observed, *"States are now integrating and it is essential for them to address problems together. We must work together, across borders, because we can no longer resolve issues inside borders. In short we must learn to pool our sovereignty".* Indeed the inter-dependency across the world is a reality.

Similarly, since market-forces will decide the precise nature of goods and services to be produced and provided, based on cost efficiencies of the production bases, goods and services need no longer come from within one country and can instead come from far away production centres at much cheaper prices. The present trend of protectionism, employed for sustaining and encouraging domestic production centres, irrespective of cost considerations, can no longer be the determinant factor for sustaining unviable industries. Production bases, which are no longer competitive will automatically die a natural death because they have to go through a regime of rigorous tests of choices and preferences of the consumers even if the subsidized product find their way into the markets. National brand loyalties to products identified with a country based on sentimental attachments, which in many cases once sustained economies of a country, will no longer have much relevance. It is the market forces, which will decide on the product-mix. In short, the world is now so intricately connected and integrated in many ways than one that it forecloses the freedom to 'choose'.

The humble beginning of the IT industry in Bangalore is one example. *"Information technology services served as the Trojan horse through which globalization entered Indian economy and gained acceptance..."* observed Nandan Nilekani. Nilekani further extols the impact, *"The success of our domestic IT firms led to a dawning sense across Indian industry that we were in a position of almost unique strength in the international economy."*[10] These remarks from a remarkable man emphatically exemplified by the various BPOs (business process outsourcing) or KPOs (knowledge process outsourcing) in Bangalore speak volumes of the inherent strength and resilience of the Indian economy. Many could not have imagined some thirty years ago seeing Mr. Narayan Murthy and Nandan Nilekani in Bangalore, that one day the two gentlemen would contribute to the dominance of the Indian IT industry in the world.

Global needs rather than domestic, dictate the character of business in the IT sector. From merely "answering calls" in the BPOs and account keeping, the KPOs have got into the field of *"highly intellectual knowledge-oriented sectors like equity analysis for US mutual funds, advise mega foreign banks on Indian credit card sector and even prepare mortgage industry market reports for Fortune 500 company"*[11]. The scenario of interdependence and interlink globally for instance is so structured that a strike in Bangalore by the BPOs and KPOs can actually cripple the working of many of the civic institutions and bodies in the United States, United Kingdom etc. The reach of the BPOs and the KPOs is worldwide. The institutionalized new regime of interdependence and co-operations among countries however, also means new challenges for regions like the Northeast. Question is, can the people of the Northeast then live in their own-cocooned world as they did in the past?

Catapult, as India is, as a role model nation among the developing countries in its growing influence internationally, its commensurate responsibilities within the country increases substantially. One recollects what Lee Kuan Hue erstwhile Prime Minister of Singapore remarked while acknowledging India's new role as an economic leader among the international community of nations, particularly in the Asian context when he remarked during his visit to India in 2006 that the Asian economy is moving ahead on the two wheels of India and China. From an 'indifferent and sluggish' economy often compared to the elephant in a pejorative sense of the term, in comparison to the aggressive South East

Asian 'tiger economies' in its neighbourhood, today India boosts of as the second fastest growing economy in the world next only to China. India is also in terms of the PPP, (Purchasing Power Parity principle) the fourth largest economy in the world only next to the USA, China and Japan. In the Information Technology sector, India has become an indispensable destination, literally placed in an unassailable position. India hopes to become the fastest growing economy by 2015-16. The image of India as an elephant is back, but this time it is in the positive sense of the metaphor, implying that it is out in the world to claim its rightful place. In this given scenario, does the Northeast provide the kind of destination that foreign and private investors look for? The fact of the matter is that the Northeast is hardly in a position to be capable of competing with other regions of the country to be a preferred destination for attracting domestic or external investments, especially if it remains what it is.

These changes taking place in the country have a profound impact and implication for the peripheral regions like the Northeast, which has so far depended largely only on the largesse of the Government. With the shift of investments decisions from the domain of governments to non-state players, the future of the region appear bleak. In fact, whatever little is flowing in as private investments will also end as reverse outflows from the region to other regions with better investment opportunities outside the region. These are serious concerns, a growing gnawing apprehension and fear in the region and across the world, that globalization may not be fair to many of the fringe societies like the Northeast since the benefits of globalization may not percolate down to these societies, unless some drastic measures are undertaken. The apprehensions and fears are real. The changing parameters of investments decisions largely based on economic considerations and financial viability will certainly without any doubt whatsoever, relegate the region to a pariah status, unless the Central Government ensures either substantial flow of funds or enables the creation of the desired climate for private investments to flow into the region. It is under this shadow of fear and vulnerability created by the affects of globalization, which is the cause of serious concern among the people of the Northeast region.

Terms like 'globalization', 'development' and 'progress' are not *mere "...theft of language, the technique of usurping words and deploying them like weapons, of using them to mask intent and to mean exactly the opposite of what they have traditionally meant",* for people in the Northeast. Neither do these 'usurpations' mean as Arundhati Roy brilliantly sums up the new phase of human civilisation and its reckoning, as the *"most strategic victories of the tsars of the new dispensation"*[12]. For the people of the Northeast, these are not mere inventives from the arsenal of the English dictionary; they mean most importantly, opportunities for a new beginning somehow long denied and which has eluded them by the given circumstances of merciless history. Simultaneously the globalizing process is also an overwhelmingly overpowering prospect of an uncertain future for the people and the region, especially when they are not the decision-makers of their own destinies. Nothing could be more disturbing and distressing than this situation at this critical juncture of the region's history. It is an opportunity as much as it is also an impending disaster waiting to happen, a threat to their future and the region, economically, developmentally and in the long term politically. People in the country, the Governments in the Centre and in the Northeast must guard against these possibilities and find ways to overcome and face this emerging scenario.

Globalization and Northeast

In all these analyses there is one alternate view, however, which many may consider miscued, but certainly a distinct one, quite different from many other possibilities. This is to see the changing scenario in the globalizing process as a 'God-sent' opportunity for the region like the Northeast. This hopeful and optimistic note arises from two factors.

First is the fact that the tenor of globalization in India is unique in its own way, a blend of 'compulsions' and made out of deliberate 'choice'. It is 'Compulsion' because it had no option but to change the tenor of development, given the sluggish performance of the economy under the legacy of the socialistic pattern of development in the country since independence. It is by 'Choice', because instinctively the native Indian trait to be cautious, articulate this 'choice' keeping in view the large numbers of poor that outnumber the rich and the size of the country. For India, welfare economics and economic planning meant the preponderance towards addressing the needs of the majority of the population, a conscious reaffirmation of its democratic values and principles. Consequently, the process of globalization in India, which had to factor in this requirement, evolved its own style and genre. The distinctive feature of Indian globalization process is therefore in a way the equi-distancing from the two extremes of too much dependence "on foreign finance" or too much dependence "on exports". Arvind Subramanian[13] describes the Indian version of globalization as one, which *"...followed a strategy that can be called 'Goldilocks globalization' relying neither too much on foreign finance nor too much on exports'"*. It is this inherent flexibility inbuilt in the Indian economy; the ability to forge and evolve its own brand of development economics on its own terms, by means of careful calibrations that enables it to continue with the existing pattern and model of welfare economics.

India's approach to the globalization process and assimilation into it is as such unique, because it suggests circumstantial progression and convergence, a fusion of two thought processes compelled by circumstances of the changing external economic requirements and articulated by the domestic needs of the country. To a certain extent, therefore destiny has made the choice for India. The Indian model of globalization that ensued incorporates and reflects the inherent flexibility to accommodate the needs of the globalization processes and at the same time has the built-in resilience to adequately absorb the internal domestic needs that a country of India's background needs. The Indian globalization process is successful, therefore, in many ways than one in its own way.

The second factor, which is a blessing for the Northeast in the short term in the context of the fast globalization process in the country, is that the region is unlikely to be one of the favoured destinations for investments by any major foreign or domestic private investors in the scale and volume-taking place elsewhere in the country. This is because, the whole country, especially the favorably placed states and regions are available to the new Czars of the industrialized global world to choose for investments, which on a comparative scale places the Northeastern states nowhere near most of them. However, for the region on the positive side, as the more favorably and advantageously placed States and regions begin to attract private and foreign direct investments (FDI), it also means conversely that these favorably placed States will be depending much less on the Central Government for funds hereafter.

To put it differently, the Centre will not be under any obligation or compulsion to continue to dole out financial largesse to these well-to-do states, at least not to the extent of what it is now at present, as these states would have been able to mobilize adequate resources to finance their development activities on their own. This implies that the Central Government can make this share of funds and amounts, which would have otherwise gone to these States, available to underdeveloped regions like the Northeast. Even though this would mean much more dependence of the Northeast region on the Centre, this would provide the much needed additional resources into the region to catch-up in development with the rest of the country. The much talked about idea of the region becoming the 'arrow-head' of the country for trade and commerce with the Southeast Asian economies by fully exploiting its strategic location, which is in the tri-junction of East Asia, South East Asia and South Asia can become a distinct possibility.

For regions like the Northeast, this means well for the future. It implies that it will be possible to continue to avail financial support from the Centre, and gear itself up to create the necessary infrastructures to attract potential investors into the region. Simultaneously, ingrained in this hypothesis is the assumption that there exist well-defined planned strategies to create the kind of conducive environment required to attract private capital and investments in the region in the mean time. This opportunity, which the changed scenario in the country presents as such, can provide the region with both finances and time to prepare itself to be capable of joining the big-league States and even compete with them. There is a caveat however, that this is possible provided the States in the region respond positively and undertake the onerous responsibility to work in conjunction by supporting each other rather than at cross-purposes.

In the overall analyses, to take advantage of the opportunity that globalization can provide to the Northeast region and also to counter the threats posed by the globalization process sweeping the country, a much more efficacious way and means for achieving these objectives is required. It also postulates that the role and responsibilities of the people and the Governments in the region changes and increases dramatically. As stakeholders, all the member states of the region, must rethink and learn to consider themselves as constituent members of a single economic bloc without in any manner diluting or disturbing the existing political setup and administrative arrangements. Given the prevailing disjointed nature of planning and development of the region, which are more State centric rather than regional, a much more cohesive and efficacious process of regional partnership among the constituent states is called for. From this perspective, there is an urgent need to overcome the unfortunate prevailing atmosphere of mistrust and acrimonious equations among the states in the region. In the context of the prevailing gloomy sentiments and feeling of hopelessness, even this expectancy and hope of making the Northeast an economic hub in the days to come is by itself certainly a most welcome change. The role and responsibilities the Central Government in making this possible only means added responsibility for it.

The *Hindu* on March 10, 2010 reported that Ratan Tata while addressing a joint press conference with the Assam Chief Minister Shri Tarun Gogoi on 9th of March 2010 at Guwahati after the first meeting of the Assam Investment Advisory Board remarked, *"All of us run successful business in the other parts of India. But I must say that there are tremendous opportunities in Assam too, and that the potential of the state has not received attention for a long time. A new Assam is here. We are drawn by the opportunities and the challenges here. We are here by choice"*. Unilever President M.S. Baga, Videocon Chairman V.N. Dhoot, Eveready Industries Chairman B.N. Khaitan, HSBC CEO Naina Kidwai, O.P. Bhatt Chairman of State Bank of India, former Indian Ambassador to the United States Ronen Sen, attended the conference among others. The future for the region does not seem to be so bleak.

Solution: Regional Economic Partnership

It is apparent from the foregoing arguments made so far that the most conspicuous missing link in the development process in the Northeast is the lack of cooperation and partnership among the member states of the region. It is evident that development of the Northeast region is badly in need of a viable regional planning and development process, to synergise the efforts made by the states separately and independently. The region has to do away with the fastidious nature of its present disjointed approach to planning, which are essentially assortments of individual state plans that do not fit into a homogeneous comprehensive regional plan. This calls for a regionally inclusive planning process for the region, which is participative, open, consensual and formulated within an integrated economic grouping reflecting the general will and priorities of the region, without in any manner disturbing the federal spirit of the

Constitution and in which the various state plans form an inherent part.

The situation is ironical especially in spite of having institutions like the North Eastern Council (NEC), an important, well-conceptualised institution but badly in need of a clear direction and purpose to be able to play its legitimate role. In fact, an institution like the NEC is essential for a region like the Northeast not only for development purposes alone but also to bring all the diverse ethnic groups on a common platform to work in tandem to resolve the various problems together as a region. Institution like the NEC has a legacy, a regional relevance, a presence and commands respect. It is this inbuilt strength, sub serving the purpose of bringing about the coordinated planning for development among the constituent member states of the region, which makes the continuation of the NEC indispensible. The Administrative Reforms Commission under Veerapa Moily has brought out the reasons and justifications for its continued role as the regional planning body. A new way of invigorating and reifying the NEC to enable it to perform its legitimate role of infusing and bring about the much needed partnership and cooperation among the states in the region is required. This, however, requires segregating and distinguishing 'people' from the 'problem'. In other words, problems and issues of development for all people in the region, irrespective of their ethnic identities, must take precedence while undertaking interstate developmental projects and schemes. This is not going to be easy.

It is also imperative and important that this partnership among the States of the region is recognised as a concept and idea to infuse the principles of inclusive growth of all states on a regional basis for economic development primarily, without in any manner impinging on the either the political autonomy or the Constitutional status of the states. The 'interests' of the region as a whole and the country at large, must guide and be the sole basis of this cooperation and partnership among the constituent member states, rather than be guided by the 'stated positions' of the individual states. This rearticulation of thinking and approach is required because development of the individual states and their priorities is concomitant with the developments of the region; both are mutually dependent on the other, and certainly not mutually exclusive to the other. It is in this context that the region must gear up to work as a single economic entity, while retaining their respective separate political identities and histories.

Collateral success in development programmes of the Government and private investments is possible only when the region becomes attractive as an investment destination collectively and acts as a region. This is because of the nature of the geography in which the states are located, in close physical proximity to each other and especially also because they all have to depend on the few rudimentary infrastructural support available in the region. Appreciation of this qualificatory provision is necessary because most of the states individually and separately, simply do not have the means or posses adequate infrastructure, the basic essential pre-requisites required to induce or attract private investments.

Given the nature of the investment climate and environment in the country, therefore, it would be wise for all the states in the Northeast to work in conjunction and in tandem so that the rudimentary infrastructural requirements are put in place on a regional basis. To achieve this cooperation and partnership they need to go back into their roots, rediscover their innate cooperative strength through the reification the common shared anthropological, social and cultural histories of their traditional age-old ties and bonds, and use it for development purposes through partnership and cooperation. Such cooperation and partnership among the states is possible inspite of the political constraints because economic progress and development neither negates ethic identities nor undermines their respective political status. On the contrary, economic development supplements the political efforts in resolving various problems confronted by the states.

In fact, for a region like the Northeast because of the similar nature of its composite history, cultures and confronted by almost identical socio-economic problems, confined within a hostile physical territory, many of the problems and issues faced by the states can be much better resolved collectively as a region rather than separately or as individual states. In other words, it means that development and economic well-being of the people can be attained and law and order and all related issues easily overcome if they are dealt collectively as a region through a composite solution-solving platform. The political parties in the region themselves must appreciate that the nature and tenor of their success in developing their respective states to a large extent is dependent on how much they succeed in developing the region as a whole.

The European Union as a model

To achieve this objective the workable concept immediately available, as a model for the Northeast to consider, is the European Union, the transnational economic forum and association of European nations. The Union transcends ethnic and national political boundaries by bringing all the collateral countries of Europe as a common market known as European Common Market under a Constitution. The European Union is the most successful and visible form of the concept of an economic union and partnership among nations.

The concept of 'jointness', in the areas of trade and commerce economic partnership is not unknown to the region as several models in international relations exists. Within the Asian regional context itself, there are a number of such partnerships, in which India is a party. The ASEAN Forum, the BRYMEK (Brahmaputra-Yangtze-Mekong) economic region, the BCIM (Bangladesh, Southwest China, Northeast India, Myanmar) also known as the track-II Kumming Initiative, BIMSTEC (Bangladesh, India, Myanmar, Sri Lanka and Thailand), the South Asian Development Quadrangle (Nepal, Bhutan, Bangladesh and Eastern and Northeastern India), and SAFTA among the South Asian countries are some examples of the consensual economic forums of Asian and South East Asian countries for achieving collateral benefits in economic and trade.

The significance and importance of the Asian intra-regional trade agreements lies in the fact that out of the total trade in the region, more than half of this is accounted by trade among the constituent members. A discussion for the introduction of a common currency for facilitating intra-regional trade within the Asian context is the next step towards, which the Asian Development Bank is working on for an ACU (Asian Currency Unit). In October 2009, Prime Minister Manmohan Singh speaking in Hua Hin (Thailand) in the fourth East Asian Summit (EAS) impressed the participative countries of the Summit to agree to the idea of economic integration of the region to forge the Asian Economic Community. Dr. Manmohan described the integration process as an 'act of foresight'. The inference is that if such economic 'jointness' can succeed on a transnational basis why can such a concept not succeed within a region in one country?

In this context, the working of the European Union requires examination. Article I-1 sums the main conceptual framework on which the European Union is based upon. The primary objectives of the European Union are given in its Constitution. (All highlights in the form of italics are mine.)

"1. Reflecting the will of the citizens and States of Europe to build a common future, this Constitution establishes the European Union, on which the Member States confer competences to attain objectives they have in common. The Union shall coordinate the policies by which the Member States aim to achieve these objectives, and shall exercise on a community basis the competence they confer on it."

"2. The Union shall be open to all European States which respect its values and are committed to promoting them together."

Article 1-3; "1. The Union's aim is to *promote peace, its values* and the *well-being of its peoples*".

"2. The Union shall offer its citizen an area of freedom, security and justice *without internal frontiers*, and an *internal market where competition is free and undistorted*".

"3. The Union shall work for a sustainable development of Europe based on *balanced economic growth* and price stability, a highly competitive social market economy, *aiming at full employment* and *social progress*, and a high level of *protection and improvement of the quality of the environment*. It shall promote scientific and technological advance."

"It shall *combat social exclusion and discrimination*, and *shall promote social justice and protection, equality between women and men*, solidarity between *generations* and *protection of the rights of the child*".

"It shall promote *economic, social and territorial cohesion*, and solidarity among Member States. It shall *respect its rich cultural and linguistic diversity,* and shall ensure that Europe's *cultural heritage is safeguarded and enhanced.*"

The two main principals, governing the working of the European Union, which are relevent and important to the Northeastern states and the ones that can be adopted to moderate and guide the states in their functioning as a collective econoimic group are the two principles of 'Subsidiarity' and 'Proportionality'. The principle of

'Subsidiarity' means that the Union has the power to act only when *"...proposed action cannot be sufficiently achieved by the Member States...by reason of the scale or effects of the proposed action, be either better achieved at Union level."* The principle of 'Proportionality' restricts the power of the Union, which *"...shall not exceed what is necessary to achieve the objectives of the Constitution"*.

Besides the Union has the competence and jurisdiction encompassing almost all fields and areas of interests, which include common foreign and security policy (Article i-16); a) Health; b) industry; c) culture; d) tourism; e) education, youth, sport and vocational training; f) civil protection and g) administrative cooperation. From (Article i-17), however in the areas of Exclusive competence there are five areas. Out of these five, three are of relevance in the context of the Northeast. (a) Customs union; (b) establishing of the competition Rules necessary for functioning of the internal market; and (e) common commercial policy. The other remaining two pertain to c) Monetary policy and d) conservation of marine biology resources.

The concept of 'jointness' as defined in the Constitution of the European Union (Article I-11, 3 of the European Constitution), cover those areas of activities, which *"cannot be sufficiently achieved by the Member States...but can rather, by reason of the scale or effects of the proposed action, be better achieved at"*. Conceptually, the parameters of the roles assigned permit the member countries in the European Union to constitute a common forum by evolving a single agenda for social, economic and commercial endeavors cutting across the political divide.

The Northeastern states can similarely work together through partnership and cooperation to achiev common economic goals and in the process bring about social cohesion by bridging the ethnic devide in the region. The role and activities in the developmental areas will primarily focus on determining and undertaking (1) interstate projects, which the member states cannot individually or separately pursue or are not in a position to undertake without the cooperation or help from other state or states for various reasons of either scale, geography, effects or costs. (2) The power of the common authority dealing with the economic zone should be limited only to the extent of achieving the common agreed project or programmes and nothing beyond. It of course goes without mentioning that the exercise of both these powers by the common authority shall be with the specific approval of the Government of India and shall be carried out under its supervision directly or through its appointed agency.

Is there a contradiction and paradox in the proposition of asking the member states of the region to relinquish part of their constitutional freedom to choose and implement developmental projects and programmes on one hand, while simultaneously accepting the principle of ensuring full political powers to the State on the other? The answer to this question is a counter question. Can the States retain their undisputed authority and position devoid of development? Alternatively and more pertinently, can the States or for that matter any State in the region undertake any large-scale project or scheme without involving another, given the nature of the topography and the present levels of infrastructure available in the region? An objective and honest answer is discernibly found in the sizes of the states, their available inbuilt capacity, the limited infrastructure, the topography and the histories of their industrialization. All the states have to necessarily depend on each other and work together.

What is required therefore, is an objective and long-term view in dealing with the various problems of development in the region. One is ofcourse aware of the pernicious essumption and inherrent fears of the states and the people that regionalisation of projects and schemes could dilute their authority and importance as political entities representing deffent ethnic identities, which many of them consider as vital. Eventhough this is largely unfounded, this apprehension remains a major obstacle to progress, partnership and regional cooperation.

Viewed from this perspective, it is important for people of the region to realise that planning and undertaking interstate development projects jointly together as a region does not in any manner dilute or rob one's ethnicity or ethnic identity. This is because as Sudhir and Katharina observes a person's ethnicity or ethnic identity is not *"...a garment that can be put on or taken off according to the weather outside; it is not 'fluid', but marked by a sense of continuity and sameness irrespective of where the person finds himself during the course of his life"*[14]. Further Sudhir and Katharina attribute this intrinsic value of ethnic identity to the fact that *"...the possibilities of 'fluid' and changing identities in adulthood are rather limited"*. This is also because one does not have the freedom to choose our ethnic identities, since the choice has already been predetermined and imposed on us at the time of our birth, being born as a Kannadiga, Tamilian or Punjabi etc. Even though the option to make a change in name or affiliations later in life is possible, but the inherent organic ethnic identity, as distinct from his or her acquired identities, still remains and is incapable of being changed. In other words, irrespective of the changes in the external embellishments, identities, especially ethnic identities do not and cannot change given the fact that it is intrinsically genetic and organic and quintessentially an inextricable part of one's persona.

In this connection understanding, the importance and significance of the two principles of 'Subsidiarity' and 'Proportionality', the two principles governing the working and functioning of the European Union can help in easing the troubled minds and reduce the insecurities and doubts in the minds of the various ethnicities and states in the region. The European Union is essentially an 'enabling' institution for specific tasks jointly agreed upon and nothing beyond it. Properly contextualised and understood, the two principles governing the functioning of the European Union imply calibrated restrictivity and specificity of its activities. These two principles form the basis of relationships and equations among the member countries. Understanding this aspect would help in appreciating the proposed idea of a joint economic union for the Northeast. These two provisions in its Constitution make the European Union a good example and model for adoption for the economic partnership among the States of the Northeast without in any manner diluting the constitutional federal structure of the country or changing the constitutional positions of the states.

In short, the sub-text of the proposition is that economic partnership and cooperation among the constituent member states of the Northeast is not at the cost of one's ethnic identity or a threat to the authorities of the states, or for that matter to the unity of the country. In effect, a result oriented successful implementation of large development projects and schemes through such collaborative efforts, as demonstrated in the past between the states and the Centre, which help in poverty eradication and reduce underdevelopment, can only enhance the qualitative successful index o f the states and the Central government. What is important is that the preponderous affiliations to one's ethnic identities even though important should not detract the states from undertaking the economic development of their respective states as part of the comprehensive development of the region as one single economic entity, since the results that ensue through such collective efforts, can and will certainly benefits each one of them.

In the ultimate analysis, development and poverty eradication for the people of the region, irrespective of their ethnicities and affiliations must be made the paramount objective and consideration in this partnership among the states. This is essentially because ethnic identities are organic and inherent attributes and are not imperative to changes depending on one's moods or mental predilections. Conjoined in this ineluctable conclusion is the fact that all other 'issues' and 'needs', including perpetuation of one's ethnic identity can succeed only as collateral and consequential benefits after poverty and underdevelopment are eradicated and overcome in the region. The inverse logic and approach would be a disaster. If this proposition is appreciated, it would not be difficult to realize why it is important to understand that the states, which were formed, based on ethnic identities are only a means to an end and not the end in itself. The underlining sobering realization that the main responsibility and objective for the states in the region and the *raison d'etre* for their formation is essentially to eradicate poverty and under development from the lives of the people over whom the respective governments pontificate will make both the government and the people of the states sadly realize that their present preoccupation with their respective ethnic identities may need not after all be the main priority of concern.

This realization should sensitize the people of the region the immidiate need to relegate their preoccupations with ethnic identities to lesser slot of importance by shifting their energies and efforts to bring about mutual trust to achieve poverty eradication and overcome underdevelopment in the region. Economic redemption, peace, development and progress, not neccesarily in that order of priority, are all conjoined appellatives, which are only achivable if the states and the people in the region join hands through economic partnership and cooperation. Through such a partnership and understanding the ethnic faultlines formed over the years can be re-cemented.

Endnotes

1. Amelendu Guha, *Planter Raj to Swaraj*, ICHR, New Delhi, 1977. p-7, 16, 17, 20 and 28.
2. Amelendu Guha, ibid, p-7.
3. *World Bank Report, 2001-2002*; State Fiscal Reforms in India, Progress and Prospect, p-89. Annex 1.
4. *HDI Report* (Human Development Index of Assam) *2003*.
5. M.S. Prabhakara, Fruits of unrest; *Frontline*, May 5, 2006.
6. Stephen Thel, The Youth Bulge and the coming Rebel Defeats, quotes German sociologist Gunnar Heinsohn *"...that nations with an oversupply of frustrated young men (a "youth bulge") are more prone to violence"*. *NEWSWEEK*, June 15, 2009, p-8.
7. John M. Leitche; Foreward to Amartya Sen's *On Ethics and Economics*.
8. *A Fair Globalization; The Role of the ILO, 2004*, p-5.
9. Thomas L. '*The World Is Flat: A Brief history of the twenty first Century*'. p-400.
10. Nandan Nilekani, *Imagining India, Ideas for the New Century*, Home and the World, p-133.
11. V. Kulkarni, Brickwork India, p-6, Simply Bangalore, *India Today*, March 2007.
12. Arundhati Roy, Democracy's Failing Light; '*Outlook*', 13 July 2009 issue, p-18.
13. Arvind Subramanian, India's Goldilocks Globalization, World View; *Newsweek* June 15, 2009, p-5, Subramanian is a senior fellow at the Peterson Institute for International Economics.
14. Sudhir Kakar and Katharina Kakar; *The Indians: Portrait of a People*.

CHAPTER - 10

North Eastern Council

The idea of a 'partnership' and 'cooperation' among the Northeastern states, especially based on a foreign model; the European Union, might ring alarm bells in the Central government. This is obvious, given the prevailing geo-political environment in the region. However, the idea is not new. As far back as 1972, the North Eastern Council (NEC) a regional planning body was formed by an Act of Parliament. Historically, however, even though an institution for regional partnership among the Northeastern states exists, somehow, it has not been able to function to its fullest potential or its efficacy adequately tested. Part of the problem for this is the unclear mandate and lukewarm support given to it by the Government of India and the states.

The role of the NEC and the need for partnership and cooperation among states for a region like the Northeast is not only to formulate plans for the region, which is the primary function but is also necessary because the growing ethnic divide of people in the Northeast must somehow be overcome. In fact, it is institutions like the NEC, which can built bridges between the various ethnic groups now synonymous with states by making them work together as a region. The growing ethnic divide in the region is one of the most worrisome aspects of the polity of the Northeast, which the Government at the Centre has not paid the kind of attention it deserves. This phenomenon is in many ways the root cause of all the problems of the region, especially in the areas of development and progress. The problem is like an ulcer that is eating into the development energies of the constituent states in the region. The Centre by its ambivalent attitude and disregard to this growing menace of ethnic divide is only waiting for a major implosion to take place. Seen from this perspective the Government of India by undermining the role of the NEC is not helping in resolving the problem but instead is creating more problems for the region.

It is precisely to shift the emphasis to this neglected area of concern and address the growing 'divide' between people in the region, that role of regional institutions like the NEC is being redefined and analysed. In fact, at this time when its role can be utilised most effectively and fruitfully, especially in the post-liberalisation and globalised regime, its detractors are instead questioning its credibility and relevance. This doubt puts the ambitious 'Look East Policy' (LEP) and the projections made in the 'The Vision 2020 Statement', at jeopardy. The role of NEC, the problem it faces in performing its legitimate role as the regional planning body and also act as the pivotal catalytic institution capable of bridging the ethnic divide by bringing all the ethnic groups (States) of the region together is reassessed in the penultimate Chapter. The Chapter looks critically at the issues involved and pleads for strengthening the NEC as an instrument of change for the region.

North Eastern Council (NEC)

The history of the North Eastern Council is a long one. Its beginning goes back into the time when attempts to prevent the political balkanization and fragmentation of Assam into several political units had begun to falter in the early 1950s. The Pataskar Commission constituted to find a way out to retain the economic homogeneity and viability of the Northeastern region by preventing the fragmentation of Assam was not successful in its mission. The balkanization of erstwhile Assam created tribal dominated States of Nagaland, Meghalaya and Mizoram. Even though the reorganisation of Assam was a foregone conclusion having become politically inevitable, given the dynamics of the ethno-political situation in the region, there were hopes of preventing it. However, in purely economic terms, the reorganisation was an economic disaster for the region. Many leaders of the region knew the consequences and understood the implications but could not prevent the calamitus economic balkanization of the region. It is in this scenario that the NEC was setup as an institution to preserve the economic homogeneity and thereby the financial viability of the states in the region.

In fact, historically, attempts were made earlier in the past to bring the various ethnic groups in the Northeast together and forge a closer relation between the plain and upland communities in the region after the independence of the country under the sagacious leadership of political leader like Nichol Roy. *"In the first week of November 1947, at Nichol-Roy's initiative a hills-plains (unity) week was held in Shillong. About 450 delegates from the Naga, Lushai, Garo, Manipur and Jowai hills and Tirap, Sadiya and Balipara Frontier Tracts attended the conference"*[1]. The attempt however did not succeed.

These attempts failed for many reasons, but primarily due to the continued preponderance of ethnic political aspirations, religious differences, and above all the growing disenchantment with the slow development and economic progress of the upland areas of erstwhile Assam. The geomorphological distinction of people and communities into 'tribal' and the 'non-tribal', reinforced by the ensuing psychological 'divide', was too overpowering and too strongly entrenched to be easily overcome. The anger and resentment of the tribal ethnic groups led to pointing out minutiae ethnic, social and cultural differences and distinctions between tribal and non-tribal ethnic groups unabashedly rather than attempting to find homogeneities among the various autochthons and people of the region. The feeling of neglect by the constituent upland tribal ethnic groups in Assam crystalised into demands for separate tribal based states. The prospect of retaining Assam as one single political entity began to diminish overtime and the end finally began with the formation of Nagaland in 1963.

The Government of India realized the significance of the impending division of Assam would cause to the economy of the region. To overcome the problems the NEC was conceived as an institution to retain a semblance of the economic unity among the new States to ensure their respective economic viability. Initially, when the NEC was setup in 1972 it was constituted as an advisory body comprising of all the Governors and Chief Ministers of the region. In 2002, by an amendment of the Act the NEC was made into a statutory Planning Body for the eight states of the region, including Sikkim.

In addition to its role as a regional planning body dealing with development matters of the region, the NEC could discuss law and order problems of the region on the lines of the Zonal Councils setup for other regions of the country. Such an arrangement was considered necessary, so that while each state was free, to undertake developmental programs independently with their own priorities, and within the resources available to them, regional interests that affect and concern more than one state were to be dealt by the NEC. The NEC was to correlate the aspiring demands of the new states with the regional perspective plans so that it can bring development through cooperation and partnership among the states.

However, the prevailing sentiments of the various new states at that time immediately following the reorganisation in 1972 was one of suspicion and doubt about the veracity and intentions of the Government of India in setting up the NEC. They were not very favorably inclined to accept the role of the NEC as most of them saw it as an institution especially setup by the Central government to impose its authority and *diktat* on them indirectly. Further, in 1972 the NEC was statutorily only an 'advisory' body, without the mandatory authority to be the regional planning authority. This curtailed its effective functioning as a planning body for the region.

In addition to the above drawbacks, there was considerable confusion regarding the provisions in the NEC Act, which empower it to discuss and review law and order matters of the region. This responsibility, assigned to it primarily because the Home Ministry, a regulatory Ministry meant for ensuring security, law and order in the country administratively controlled the NEC was seen by the new states as an infringement on their powers as a state, since law and order was a state subject. The role of the NEC therefore appeared confusing and unclear since it projected itself as an omnibus institution neither strictly as a developmental body nor as a law and order regulatory authority.

In the process, the states did not take the NEC seriously and instead began to evolve their own developmental plans inspite of the NEC being designated as the regional planning body. Thus, a formal administrative edifice came into being without the conceptual clarity of its role to enthuse the kind of response and acceptance necessary for its success from the constituent member states of the region. The states in the meantime in keeping with their new found political powers drifted away from each other into separate political silos identifying more and more with their respective ethnicities and forgetting in the process the importance and significance of regional partnership for an economically fragile region like the Northeast. Plans for development became fractured and development a mere conglomerate of disjointed small unviable projects and schemes. The notion and idea of regional economic partnership and cooperation began to wane. Consequently, the NEC lacked the soul or the spirit required for success. In addition, the status and functioning of the NEC was further diluted with the creation of the new Department for the Development of the North Eastern Region (DoNER), which eventually was converted into a separate Ministry.

New Role of NEC

Over the years, there has been a major perceptible attitudinal change about the role of NEC among the political leaders of the region and the Government of India. Almost all political leaders of the various States have tacitly realized the significance and importance of regional cooperation and partnership as an efficacious instrument for faster development of their respective states and of the region, even though this fact is not openly admitted. The setting up of the Department (later a Ministry) for the Development of the North Eastern Region (DoNER), the conceptualization of the Look East Policy (LEP) and the formulation of the Vision 2020 Document are some of the major changes and initiatives taken by the Centre that had a salutary effect on the role of NEC within the Northeast. More importantly, the growing menace of ethnic divide, residual fallout of the ethnic aspirations among various ethnicities for their own political spaces, which precariously places the sensitive issue of how to bridge the growing ethnic divide among the various ethnicities in the Northeast, places the role of institutions like the NEC on a new pedestal once again.

However, in the course of the long years after the Reorganisation of States since 1972, due to the ongoing political tussle among the States arising out of the ethno-political division and fragmentation of the region, the importance of regional planning process, has greatly suffered. This has in turn undermined the importance and the significance of NEC, the regional planning body advrsely affecting in the process, the overall development of the economically unviable region as the Northeast. Subsumed in this observation is the reality that the growing ethnic divide can hinder the planned economic development of the region. The fact that institution like the NEC can play an important and positive role at this stage, by becoming not only the planning authority of the region for which it is constitutionally mandated, but also can be a change-agent and built bridges across the ethnic divide has been recognized. More importantly, given the predominantly state-specific oriented development projects undertaken by the states and their failures to achieve the desired results, there is a growing feeling among the States to evolve a new strategy and approach to development in the respective States. The commensurate political sagacity and the wisdom of the leaders from the region, conspicuous in their style of functioning and in their relations with the Centre amply demonstrate these changes. Thus while the initial suspicions and apprehensions of the central government's intentions in setting up the NEC have changed among the political leaders in the region, simultaneously, New Delhi has also realized and endorsed the loyalties of the people of the region, whom they consider and believe have adhered to the democratic principles like all other constituent members of democratic India. There is a renewed air of expectancy and hope for the development of the region.

To enable the region to undertake a much more efficacious planned development of the region, the Government of India must however clearly spell out the specific role of the NEC and simultaneously provide to it the required delegation of authority in clear and unambiguous terms. Such a clear mandate along with the necessary administrative government orders, appropriately empowering it with the specific terms and conditions are necessary if the States in the region are to take the NEC seriously and consider it as their regional planning body. This also postulates that all the State governments in the region will agree to cooperate and work together in partnership in the area of economic development for the region as a whole through mutual trust and cooperation.

Finance or Cooperation?

The insatiable needs of finances, considered as the main obstacle to the economic progress and development of the region by the member States on one hand, and the simultaneous assertions by the Government of India that adequate finances are allocated to the Northeast region is a never-ending debate. However, as per the data released by the Reserve Bank of India on state finances for 2009-2010 all the eight member states of the NEC (including Sikkim the eighth Member of the NEC) were given a total grant and loans of Rs. 29,084 crores or approximately 44 percent of their total combined expenditure. Comparatively, this is less than the grants given to the Jammu and Kashmir, which received Rs. 13,252 crores or approximately 50-60 percent of the state's total expenditure. This is in spite of the fact that Jammu and Kashmir's population constitutes only about 1 percent of India's total population while that of the eight Northeastern states constitute 3.8 percent as per the 2001 Census. The other states which received the next highest grants and loans after the eight Northeastern states is Orissa, Rs. 7,258 crores or 22 percent, West Bengal Rs. 6,210 crores or 9 percent, followed by Haryana at Rs. 2,269 crores or 7 percent. These figures are against the total grants released to all states during 2009-2010, amounting to a total of Rs. 1,68,683 crores.

As per the Vision 2020 Statement released by the Prime Minister in 2008 the approximate requirement of funds is about Rs. 13 lakh crores until 2020 if the Northeast has to catch-up with the average growth rates with the rest of the states in the country. The Vision 2020 indicates that if the country's GDP grows at around 8 to 9 percent per year at 2006-07 prices, till the end of the XIII Five Year Plan (2017-18 to 2019-20) at 2006-07 prices, the national average per capita GDP is expected to grow between 7.51 percent to 7.80 percent. For the Northeast region to attain the national average growth of anywhere between 7.51 to 7.80 percent, the average GSDP of the states in the region have to grow at a staggering rate of 10.00 percent in the XI Plan, 13.67 percent in the XII Plan, and around 16.37 percent in the XIII Plan. The average growth rate required is 12.95 percent in GSDP terms or the region has to grow at an average of 11.64 percent[2] in per capita terms. The region, in short has still a long way before it can even reach the normative economic performance indices in the country. To achieve these percentages on a rough estimate, the approximate funds required to achieve the average growth rate of 12.95 percent in GSDP terms or at 11.64 percent in per capita terms is Rs. 13 lakh crores in approximately 13 years, until the penultimate year of Vision 2020, or approximately Rs. one lakh crore per annum. The amount required is staggering for an economy of the size of Northeast India.

On a rough calculation, the funds can be mobilised by factoring both government and private sources of investments. The total Plan Resources of the Centre during the Tenth Plan was Rs. 21,56,571 or approximately 21,57,000 crores. While the States' resources was Rs. 14,88,147 or 14,88,200 crores, a total of Rs. 36,44,718 or 36,45,000 crores. This is approximating about Rs.7,28,940 per financial year during the Five Year Plan period. As per present norms, at the mandatory 10 percent of the Gross Budgetary Support (GBS) of 49 Ministries to be spent on the Northeastern region, excluding Ministries with less than Rs. 10 crores budget, is about Rs. 2,21,500 crores (CS&T) per year in the Tenth Plan. Ten percent of this amount is approximately Rs. 22,150 crores per year. This does not include the additional funds available from Ministries like Defence, Space and other departments and Public Sector Undertakings involving the Oil, Power Generation, Coal, the Airport Authority of India (AAI) and other sectors, all of which have considerable presence and stake in the Northeast, and also excludes the unspent balances of funds from the NLCPR over the years. This amount will increase with every Five Years Plan period. Further, additional investments in the region from the private sector are expected. Thus, a substantial portion of funds required can be mobilized by 2020.

From the above facts, it is amply clear that the real hindrance to the development of the Northeast is not the shortages of funds, but other problems, which have nothing to do with finances. Some of these are its inability to absorb and utilise such large volumes of funds due to capacity constraints mainly arising from the problems associated with inadequate infrastructural support to sustain and undertake large number of projects simultaneously. In addition, the climate of the region acts as a major hindrance. Over and above these factors, there are the capricious invectives of the state-agencies' failure to prevent the alleged siphoning of scarce government funds and resources by the various insurgent and underground groups, which inhibit the Central Government from freely providing unencumbered funds to the region.

The lingering problems of insurgencies in the rgion, an important and significant problem of the growing menace of ethnic-divide, is adversely affecting the development of the region. This problem of the growing intolerance among states of each other on various issues, has not only polarized the region completely on ethnic lines, but is adversely affecting development in general across the region. The Centre by its ambivalent attitude and disregard to the growing problems of ethnic divide in the region and simultaneously undermining the role of institutions like the NEC is only playing into the hands of its detractors.

To overcome these problems, institution like the NEC located in the region can deal with the myriad problems of the region much better. Tackling the various problems of the Northeast require the continuous presence and monitoring by an institution like the NEC. This is however, easier said than done, because even though an institution like the NEC exists in the region the powers and authority given to it remain as vague and amorphous as ever. This is adversely affecting the working of the NEC as a regional planning and developmental body. Part of the problem is the undefined relationship and equation with the various government institutions but primarily with the Planning Commission and DoNER; institutions whose active participation, contributions based on clearly defined equation are vital for its effective functioning. Because of the unclear equations and undefined working relations between these important institutions, the efficacy and importance of the NEC as a regional planning body has suffered in recent years. In the process, planning for the Northeast, as a region even today remains a highly hyphenated concept; a clubbing of various state plans. In the ultimate, this and various other unstructured equations with other governmental institutions, both in the Centre and in the states makes the NEC ineffective. The NEC's main USP (unique selling point) of being a time tested central institution for almost forty long years located in the region has been lost in administrative ad-hocism for a long time.

Present Status of the NEC

Set against this background, in spite of the unclear verdict on its role and inherent contradictions, the NEC still retains its relevance and conceptual framework based on which it was modeled even today. The NEC, one has to remember represents symbolically to the people of the Northeast, in a strange but peculiar way, the general goodwill and desire of the people of India to see and ensure progress and development of the region. The people of the region in turn see the NEC as their own institution, in spite of the critical views about its lackluster performances from its detractors. Most importantly, the people of the region see it as their change agent.

It is in this sense, an institution 'owned' and 'managed' by the people of the region. This perception of the NEC by the people of the region is important psychologically because rightly or wrongly, they feel that they have a say in the various developments taking place in the region through the NEC. Seen from this point of view, for the efficient management of its affairs adequately empowering the NEC is justified on this single consideration alone. Conversely, any dilution of the authority of the NEC would be seen as undermining the interest and needs of the people of the region and hence not in the interest of the Central Government. It would send out a wrong message.

and become the change agent for the Northeast by being the region's social catalytic converter.

Given this background, if NEC is to play an effective role and ensure the comprehensive development of the region, it has to segregate 'people' from the 'problem'. This is not going to be easy; since it implies that, all decisions important to the region must be solely based on the 'interests' of the region as a whole, rather than be guided by the 'stated positions' of the individual States. In other words, regional interests must determine major investment and other decisions that affect all the members of the NEC while ensuring fairplay and equanimity in the allocations of the resources and the sharing of commensurate benefits that accrue out of the investments made to the region and to the states. This collective approach to development of the Northeast as a region is possible and desirable to overcome the disjointed development of the region, which in turn adversely affects the developments of the states.

However, one of the factors, which come in the way of developing such a partnership among the States in the Northeast, which indirectly means bringing the various ethnic groups of the region together on one platform is the psychological inhibition and apprehension this creates among a few opinion makers in New Delhi who believe that setting up of such a body could fuel regionalism and encourage secessionist tendencies, even after sixty years of independence. Nothing could be more far from the truth. There is a general apprehension about the very mention of the word, regionalism, since it has several adverse conotations. This is understandable generally in the Indian context. However, in the context of the Northeast such an apprehension is indicative of the basic lack of understanding of the problems confronting the region. In this sense, such apprehensions arise primarily because of the tendency to view the region primarily from the security, law and order problems devoid of the region's potentials for development. It is a view in which every Northeast Indian is a sulking enemy within the country. This thinking needs to change as preposterous and unfounded, because the perpetuation of this mindset and attitude smack of mistrust of the people of the Northeast and more dangerously, denigrates the whole region as anti-national. While such assumptions had their validity in the aftermath of the geo-political turmoil in the past, things have changed over the years in the security environment in the region, which is now largely peaceful and where more and more people are realizing the futility of the various disruptive fissiparous tendencies in the region.

Mercifully, such views are however changing and the saner elements in New Delhi are now taking a much more proactive developmental approach to overcome the problems of the Northeast and have begun to view the people of the region from a perspective and appropriate context quite different from the views held by a minority few in recent times. It is important to understand that even though the role assigned to the NEC and the approach it adopts smacks of 'regionalism', for a region like the Northeast, given the topography, financial health, sizes and spatial spread of these states such an approach is inevitable.

In the context of the Northeast, the notion or idea of 'regionalism' has an economic connotation, rather then political, either pejoratively or otherwise in any sense of the term. Regionalism is not a dirty word, if seen from the prospect of economic partnership among the states in the Northeast as such. Regionalism in the Northeast, the collective sum of all ethnicities capable of working together is a compelling, therapeutic mechanism a phraseology, which is necessary for adoption to overcome both economic backwardness and the problems of ethnic divide that impede development in the region. It is used in the positive, constructive and affirmative sense of the term to bring about economic partnership among the diverse governments and people of the region.

One of the other reasons why New Delhi and the rest of India find difficulties in dealing with the people of the region as a whole, besides socio-cultural and other differences that exist, is the inability to change the old stereotyped views about the region. One such view is to look at the Northeast as a national liability rather than consider the region as an asset to the country. The earlier New Delhi and the rest of India changes this view and perceives the Northeast region as an asset to the country, a potential economic hub and 'arrow head', for inroads into the South East Asian economies, capable of contributing to national interests and not merely a sensitive border region strategically located, the better it would be for the country and the region.

This observation is necessary, because there is apparently a thinking going around in New Delhi, reinforced by Yojna Bhawan; the

Planning Commission that the idea of the NEC is outdated and irrelevant, especially when there is the Planning Commission, an apex body for the overall planning for the country including the Northeast, and the Ministry of DoNER. What is most often forgotten in this thinking is the ineluctable fact that the NEC is not merely an inanimate institution, an economic planning and development body, but an institution quite capable and appropriately placed to bring the various ethnicities (States) to work closer together. This aspect as observed earlier is good enough reason to ensure not only its existence but is also a strong enough justification to empower it appropriately by defining its role much more clearly and definitively than it is at present.

To enable the NEC, therefore, to discharge its primary role as the planning body of the region, and also as the unifying catalyst to bring all the ethnicities together to work in a much more congenial and cooperative environment several constraints in the form of the ambiguous nature of its status, position and equation with other institutions and organisations need to be looked into on priority. Some of these are (1) the role and equation of the NEC as the regional planning body and its equation with the Planning Commission remains undefined. (2) The overlap of jurisdiction and control of the areas of work between the Ministry of the Development of the North Eastern Region (DoNER) and the NEC, especially the delineations of specific areas of responsibilities are confusing to the member states. (3) Empowering NEC to priotise to address the problems of inadiquate infrastructure arising out of the physical isolation and topography of the region.

Clarity on these issues are necessary since the emerging investment environment in the country is changing fast for the better and which warrants a much more proactive role for the NEC. Some of these positive developments are, (1) the cascading effect of economic development taking place in the country hopefully percolate down to the peripheral North Eastern States. (2) The formulation of the 'look east policy' (LEP) of the Government of India recognizes the pivotal role the North Eastern States can play in becoming the 'arrow head' for the country in its attempt to make inroads into the South East Asian economies. (3) The political maturity and confidence attained by the constituent States of the region over the last thirty-nine years of their existence. All these factors give the region the much-needed psychological fillip to be much more proactive in pursuing economic goals and objectives collectively as a region. Given these set of favorable conditions the time is most appropriate to allow the NEC to play its constitutional role unequivocally.

The Planning Commission and NEC

One of the most exasperating situation for the NEC as a planning body is the undefined working equation between it and the Planning Commission. The existing disconnect between NEC and the Planning Commission is one area, which needs immediate attention. This aspect of the equation and relationship of the NEC with the Planning Commission on one hand and with the Ministry of DoNER on the other is often raised and debated. The comparative difference between the Planning Commission and the NEC is obvious. While the former is the apex planning body for the country, the later is the regional counterpart. More importantly, the NEC is region specific and is located in the midst of people for whom it plans. On the other hand, the Planning Commission is physically located in New Delhi and is too big and amorphous an institution to deal with the specificities unique to the region and hence far withdrawn both physically and psychologically from the people of the region. Visibly and perceptibly for the people of the region this is an important and vital difference between the Planning Commission and the NEC.

The Planning Commission was setup in the year 1950 through a Government resolution, whereas North Eastern Council was setup by an Act of Parliament in 1971. Yet, the Planning Commission by virtue of being the apex planning authority in the country is the ultimate authority responsible for the entire planning process and as such, institutions like the NEC are subordinate to it. Given the preeminent position of the Planning Commission, which has a unique position it cannot be overlooked or dispensed even though it is not a statutory body backed by legislation as the NEC.

Part of the inhibition of empowering the NEC adequately, which prevents it from functioning effectively as the regional planning body is the general impression that the roles of the Planning Commission and that of the NEC overlap. This aspect has been amply made clear in various documents of the Government, one of which is the Revitalisation Report on the NEC. The Revitalisation Report headed by Shri. P.P. Srivastav, a sitting Member of the NEC at para 8.1 points out that there are no such overlaps of functions. *"Thus functionally, NEC is intended to play the role in respect of the planning for the North Eastern Region that is similar to what the Planning Commission does in respect of the planning for the nation as a whole. The Planning Commission scrutinizes and finalises the Plan size of States and allocates Plan funds among them accordingly, but does not implement any Projects/Schemes directly. NEC on its part not only formulates the Regional Plan but also allocates/ releases."* In addition, unlike the Planning Commission the NEC is additionally expected to *"review, from time to time, the implementation of the projects and schemes included in the regional plan and recommend measures for effecting co-ordination among the Governments of the States concerned in the matter of implementation of such projects and schemes."*, as spelled out in Section 4 (3) (a), (b) of the NEC Act.

Surprisingly, neither in the original NEC Act of 1971-72 nor in its amendment, the Act of 2002 spells out its working equation as the regional planning body vis-à-vis the Planning Commission. Neither there is any administrative order in this connection nor any subsequent clarification issued for operationalising the statutory role of NEC as the regional planning body. The functional relationship and equation between NEC and the Planning Commission remain undefined, unclear and as vague as ever. Thus, even though the North Eastern Council is on paper the statutory Planning Body for the entire Northeast its functions and powers remain essentially unclear.

Given the comparative position, the Planning Commission holds as the primer planning authority in India, it is obvious that NEC should not and cannot function outside the ambit of the Planning Commission. However, simultaneously the Planning Commission cannot ignore the role of the NEC especially because of its immense potentiality as a regional planning body located and working amidst the people of the region. The NEC has the ability and potential to contribute (if allowed) positively to planning and development of the entire region. Considering the special and unique nature of the region, its peculiar history and particularly the need to coordinate the development activities of the States, the NEC can play a complimentary role to the Planning Commission. It can provide the required regional perspective to the planning process and effectively facilitate the Planning Commission in consonance with National priorities and Plan objectives for a balanced regional development. Thus, without transgressing the jurisdiction of the Planning

Commission, NEC can undertake planning for all inter-State and regional specific schemes in the North East keeping in view the development needs of the region under the overall supervision and aegis of the Planning Commission.

One of the main reasons therefore, why the NEC has not been able to establish its bona-fides and prove its credentials and effectiveness as the Regional planning body is the absence of a clear Central Government directive or order defining and delineating the precise nature of the equation between the NEC and the Planning Commission. The only link at present between NEC and the Planning Commission is that a Member of the Planning Commission is one of the Members of the NEC and the remaining two Members of the NEC are invited to be present during the plan discussion involving the Northeastern states including Sikkim once a year. This inconsequential role in turn makes the NEC appear a redundant institution in the perceptions of the member states of the NEC.

DoNER and NEC

The Department for the Development of the Northeastern Region, (DoNER), was created based on the recommendations of the S. P. Shukla Commission[3], which was submitted to the Government of India on March 7, 1997. The idea and concept of the Non Lapsable Central Pool of Resources (NLCPR) was introduced soon thereafter in 1998. It stipulates that the various ministries and departments in the Government of India place the unspent balances of 10% mandatory provision meant for the Northeastern states in a special non-lapsable central pool account, which could be spent in the Northeast in the subsequent year or thereafter. The responsibility of supervising this task was given to the new department, which was set up in the Ministry of Home Affairs (MHA) known as the Department for the Development of the Northeastern Region or DoNER. The NEC came under the control of this new department in September 2001. However, since the Ministry of Home Affairs was essentially dealing with the law and order problems, and with the government's attempt to shift the emphasis to development of the region converted the Department into a new Ministry on 27 May 2004 by delinking the working of DoNER from the Home Ministry. The new Ministry for the development of the Northeast region or DoNER became the administrative Ministry for NEC.

Prior to this in 2002, the role and function of the NEC had changed. From a mere advisory planning body it became the statutory planning body for the Northeast region under the amended Act. The NEC however, remains essentially a Council of the eight Governors, the Chief Ministers of the Member states along with three nominated Members. The NEC is as such distinct from a government department or a Ministry. The NEC is a legal entity in its own right discharging its legitimate functions assigned to it by an Act of Parliament. The functional equation and relationship of the NEC with Ministry for the Development of the Northeastern Region (DoNER) is best seen from this comparative perspective.

The creation of the department, later the ministry however, confused the member states of the NEC, which also included the state of Sikkim as the eighth member subsequent to the amendment of the NEC Act in 2002. Part of the confusion lies in the fact that the Minister in charge of the Ministry of DoNER also simultaneously functions as the Chairman of the NEC. More significantly, there is an overlap in the functions and responsibilities of the Ministry of DoNER with that of the NEC since both are essentially development functionaries of the Government. The workings of the NEC and DoNER as such suffered in the course of the unclear and vague mandate given to the two wings of the Government. The situation remains unclear.

Further, even after the NEC discontinued to be administratively controlled by the Ministry of Home Affairs the NEC was still made to continue to review and discuss law and order problems of the region. By the amendment in 2002, a Security Advisor was appointed. The ambivalence lies in the fact that the Ministry of DoNER had nothing to do with law and order issues being dealt by NEC. This meant that NEC had to interact with the Ministry of Home Affairs directly, since law and order was handled and supervised by the Ministry of Home Affairs. Therefore, technically the NEC was controlled administratively primarily by DoNER but was in a way answerable to the Ministry of Home Affairs for law and order issues. The dual control was confusing, so much so that law and order issue, supposedly, to be discussed by the NEC was mostly never discussed in the Council. The Administrative Reforms Commission headed by Shri Veerapa Moily aware of the lacunae has after examining all these aspects, recommended the abolition of the Ministry of DoNER, and revert to the situation as it was prior to 2002, and transfer the control of NEC to the Ministry of Home Affairs. The Commission's recommendations have yet to be accepted by the Government.

The Revitalisation Committee headed by P.P. Srivastav has examined the distinction and roles of NEC and DoNER in some detail. The Committee in its report defines the equation of the NEC with DoNER in the following manner. *"As a statutory body established by the Union Government under a Central law and in terms of the Government of India (Allocation of Business) Rules, 2001, NEC is, undoubtedly, formally answerable to the Union Government only through DoNER...Formally speaking, therefore, Ministry of DoNER is the parent Ministry for NEC."* The observation is significant since it means that the DoNER was not a substitute for NEC, but was to function as the administrative Ministry to undertake the focused attention of the Northeast. DoNER was to provide support from the Centre by interfacing with other Ministries to enable NEC to function effectively in the region. The Ministry of DoNER exists because it is the administrative controlling Ministry, through which NEC is answerable to the Parliament. The NEC is neither a Ministry nor a Government department. A clear jurisdictional delineation of the roles exists. Yet on several occasions there are attempts from both the NEC and DoNER to intrude into each other's roles inadvertently and unconsciously or as it occurs often due to the confusion.

In the area of functional relationship of the NEC with the DoNER, the Revitalisation Committee observed in Para 8.3, the following. *"The primary consideration is the fact that NEC is located in the Region and embodies the quintessence of knowledge and wisdom of and about the NER, the needs of the area and the people. DoNER is the focal point in the GOI mandated to ensure that all central investments are given the regional orientation to become relevant to NER and yield the desired results. The relationship should be such that NEC is perceived as DoNER in NER and DoNER is seen as NEC in the Centre. The role of DoNER, the nodal point in the Union Government for the NER and that of NEC, which is the collectivity of the political and administrative leadership of the Region, has to be complimentary, being partners in a common endeavour. "*

The Revitalisation Committee further adds in Para 8.4. *"It is clear that such relationship between DoNER and NEC cannot be prescribed by Rules that can at best only define the legal and procedural parameters. It has to be developed by healthy conventions. The NEC should be treated as a sensitive field formation, located amidst the people and responsive to their sensitivities, apprehensions and aspirations, frustrations and hopes of realizing their full potential. Hence, the considered views and proposals of the NEC must be given the highest regard. In case there is any difference in the perspectives between the two, they must be sorted out with due deference to the Regional perceptions."*

Much of the confusion occurs due to misconception and misinterpretation of the roles assigned to the DoNER and the NEC. Smt. Indira Gandhi while inaugurating the NEC in 1972 made the position and role of the NEC very clear when she said, *"It is not a super Government. It does not abridge the power of the States & UTs in any manner whatsoever. It is not an extension of the Union Government..."* It is only when this aspect of the NEC in the overall context of its role and special position in the Northeast is understood and appreciated that the equation and relationship between NEC and DoNER and other Government institutions can be worked out.

Manishanker Aiyer, former Minister for DoNER and Chairman of NEC, defines the role and relationship in diplomatic terms. *"DoNER is the ambassador of the NEC in the Delhi durbar, while NEC is the ambassador of DoNER in the Northeast"*. This definition of DoNER as NEC's representative in Delhi, amplifies the need for DoNER to facilitate the effective functioning of the NEC by providing the necessary supportive role required by it at the Centre and act as its interface. Importantly DoNER should concentrate and ensure that the various line Ministries in the Government of India spent their 10% budget on the Northeastern states annually over and above the funds available as NLCPR as mandated. However, in spite of the role-play of NEC and DoNER eruditely defined by Shri. Manishanker Aiyer, the fact still remains that there is a total overlap of functions and duties between the NEC and DoNER. The confusion still persists.

It is evident from the foregoing facts that the functions of both DoNER and NEC overlap leading to duplication of work. The Ministry of DoNER not only functions as the administrative Ministry, but also usurps and assumes the role of a field organisation, which NEC should legitimately perform. In short, the primary role of DoNER is to look after the NEC as the administrative Ministry and importantly interface with the states in the region through NEC instead of undermining the role of NEC and engaging itself in a proxy turf-war. The dual control exercised by both the NEC and DoNER on the member States not only confuses the states but also has undermined the respective roles of both DoNER and NEC. This greatly affects and undermines the working and functioning, especially of the NEC as a regional planning body. In the ultimate, this situation only leads to disjointed and segmented planning process, which ultimately ends in underdevelopment of the region and that too at tremendous opportunity costs due to time and cost overruns.

The Logic to the Future

The present-segmented efforts at economic development undertaken by the constituent states are at best, only tinkering with the peripherals rather than tackling or addressing the core and larger issues affacting the development of the Northeast. Many of these efforts are no doubt commendable, but in the context of the impending globalizing world, threshold to a new economic order, the stage is set for the region to think big and work in tandem to achieve the elusive economic development the region has been wanting. The existing disconnect between States and the commensurate fragmented policy prescription for development based on purely state-centric plans cannot produce the desired economic development of the region and consequently the states in turn. This segmented development, which is consequences of sectarian prejudices arising out of ethnic biases in areas of economic development activities, somehow needs to be overcome in the best interest of the region as a whole.

One of the simple examples of the adverse consequences of segmented state-oriented approach to planning and execution of programmes and schemes is the workings of the various horticulture departments in the region, which pursue almost identical programs and schemes. For instance, almost every State in the region has gone about investing large sums of money on various types of exportable exotic fruits, following the same techniques and methods. The consequences are a surfeit and a glut of these produce in the markets. The net result is loses, unnecessary wastage of scarce finances, resources, time and energy. All these takes place simply because there is no centralized planning body for the region to deal with such problems in the region. New Delhi is too far away for such planning and constant supervision. There are a number of such examples in the region, involving almost all the states.

The other examples are those of large-scale interstate projects, which cover or involve more than one member state, requiring the consent and agreement among beneficiary and affected states. The problems of undertaking highways and state roads, major river dams, hydroelectric projects, which are interstate in nature are areas and sectors where serious problems in planning and executions take place. Due to administrative bottlenecks and different political dispensations, many of these projects are languishing for want of a consensus either on its location, or due to the adverse consequences to one of the participatory states. The list is long. The obvious inference is that the region is badly in need of an institution to formulate a regional plan for the region to prevent such situations. Today development and consequently planning in the region remains highly State specific essentially driven by the politics of identity, rather than driven by the logic of sound economics and common sense. The future has to be different. Breaking out from the present cloistered individual approach to development requires courage and conviction.

In this context, the Reorganisation of states, which brought some peace in the region, fulfilling the long drawn demands of the various ethnic groups in the region to form their own states has since consolidated their respective positions. However, in its wake, other numerically smaller but distinctive ethnic groups are making similar demands for similar dispensations in the form of separate political units. The demands are numerous. Simultaneously, in the meantime, ethnic identity differences have sharpened due to the formation of physically demarketed ethnic identity based states, making the people unfortunately imperceptive to the adverse economic consequences on the region. In all these, each ethnic group is preoccupied with their respective long drawn process of identity consolidation and aggrandizement, which is unsettling many of the age-old ethnic equations and relationship in the region. Dispute over a few square kilometers of inhabitable lands, access to a few forests and a host of interstate related issues are all snowballing into serious law and order problems for the region. The growing ethnic divide not only hampers social and political relationships between states and the ethnic groups but also directly impinges on the quality of development of the region. Institutions like the NEC must be made to play a much more constructive role of the peacemaker among the various ethnic groups, now synonymous with the various state governments.

The Next Step

Given this preponderous dispensation of history and prevalent situation in the region where do the Northeastern communities of India fit in this tumultuous phase of Indian economic history today? Should they hold on to their age-old preoccupations with their ethnic insecurities and insist on preservation of their ethnic identities at the cost of development? In a fast changing world of globalization, where the concepts of Nations, States and other politically defined boundaries are fast losing their significance beyond a certain point and which are becoming less and less definitive, where does ethnicity and identities with which Northeasterners are preoccupied stand? Alternatively, is it time to introspect of where they stand developmentally in the fast changing world of today and prepare themselves to face the world unitedly as a single regional economic block, while simultaneously retaining their existing political ethnic identities as states without comprising their self-esteem? While many can only suggest answers to these vexed questions and as possible ways out of the present situation and predicament, the best answers and appropriate solutions to these questions perhaps can only came from the people of the region themselves.

Briefly, in a world of rapid changes propelled by economic compulsions the challenge for the people of the Northeast is indeed formidable, even to match or equal the growth rates most states in the country have attained. Given this situation, the need for collaborative approach to economic planning and development of the region to provide the necessary climate conducive for investments to potential investors, rather than be preoccupied with the issues and problems of ethnicity or identity, seems imperative and desirable. This however is possible with the caveat that the respective Governments in the region ensure that each ethnic group and State see each other as economic partners on their way to progress and development. Nothing could be more disastrous for the people and the region to subjugate their entire energy to the monomaniacal pursuit of identity however; important this is in their lives. If this partnership among the various ethnic identities is achieved consensually, there is a good chance for the region to come out of the situational entrapment the region is in at present.

To enable the change-over to this line of thinking, there is need to go beyond the stereotype view of looking only within the interests of the individual states as separate single economic entities and instead see themselves as part of a common economic bloc or entity. Transcending beyond the boundaries of one's ethnic identities and its physical correlates, the State, also means the ability to transpose the Northeast region in the larger economic Asian and Southeast Asian framework for its planning and development. To believe in this philosophy one has to refer to what B.G.Verghese[4] wrote. *"A border is not a dead end but marks a cultural, economic and environmental zone, a continuum divided by a political boundary. Culturally and ethnically, the Northeast is truly part of Southeast Asia. This logic should drive policy"*. It is in this context that the 'Look East Policy' (LEP) initiated by the Government of India has perhaps for the first time, recognised the potential of the Northeast. The 'Look East Policy' (LEP) has all the ingredients and potentiality to succeed where earlier efforts at economic development of the region have failed. For the States it is imperative to take a broader and holistic view of the region as a whole rather than seek economic and developmental solutions to the problems only from the restricted narrow confines and perspectives of individual States. The region can ill afford to lose this opportunity now at this time of India's developmental history. The people of the Northeast must ensure that the policy becomes a reality.

Conclusion

Way back in 1982 when the Asian Games was telecast live in colour across the country and in Northeast India, people in the Northeast region saw the grandeur and pomp of the opening ceremonies in their television for the first time like many across the country. I remember distinctly the remark of a young man in the streets of Imphal telling the other, of how happy and surprised he was to see the impressive opening ceremony of the Asian Games held at Delhi. The look on the young face told the story of a young 'rebellious' mind accepting perhaps unconsciously, the pride of being an Indian for the first time. It was a poignant sight, especially to see hopelessness turn to pride and hope, even if it was for only a few seconds. This is probably one of those rare moments in the history of the Northeast when a whole generation of young men and women possibly reaffirmed their faith and loyalties to the country.

People of the region see the changes taking place in the country both economically and developmentally and share with pride with the rest of the country. These inspire and motivate them to delink the unfortunate past and see into the future with hope. In a region starved of such small luxuries as pride in one's country, such departures are indeed welcome. It was a positive psychological reaffirmation and reinforcement demonstratively of what India is capable of doing. The present economic achievements of the country are no less inspiring, capable to transform and change the thinking of the young minds in the remote part of the country like the Northeast, because nothing succeeds like success, so goes the old saying. This is also true of the Northeast. People in the region need development and changes in their lives to bring them out of the morose and preoccupation with their ethnic identity.

Somewhere between then and now, the Northeastern region of India lost itself in the labyrinth and aftermath of the politics of religion, assertive identities, unfair Partition, political and economic isolation and unfairly condemned by the circumstances of insensitive history. The people in the region and the country must bestow what is due to the region so that the pains and loss of the past can be somewhat redeemed by legitimately exploiting its potentials to the fullest. I am hopeful of a rainbow; of hope, of joy, very different from the despondency and despair that the last generation of people has witnessed and seen in the region. Even though that generation of 'hopeful people' have gone and faded away, at least the new generation should be provided with the opportunity to smile and to hope. Peace, economic growth and development are the only 'mantras' that can change the future of the Northeast of India, because as Pavan Varma observes, like every Indian who is a *'pragmatic materialist"*[5], the average Northeast Indian too realizes the importance and essence of being a *'pragmatic materialist"*.

Endnotes

1. S. K. Chaube, *Hill Politics in the Northeast India*, p-81.
2. *Vision Document 2020*, pp7-9, Table 2 and 3.
3. The Commission rearticulated development strategies for the Northeast region.
4. B G Verghese, *India's Northeast Resurgent*, pp-442.
5. Pavan Varma: *Being Indian*, pp-96

Epilogue

Come gather 'round people wherever you roam
And admit that the waters around you have grown
And accept it that soon you'll be drenched to the bone.
If your time to you is worth savin'
Then you better start swimmin' or you'll sink like a stone
For the times they are a-changin'.

—**Bob Dylan**

India was an impossible concept once. That is what the world and the British thought, but they were wrong. It is still an impossible concept for many; an enigma, but in spite of its heterogeneous demure, it has proved that it is a workable nation. It has in the process, chalked out for itself a determined destiny to become the world's largest and one of the most successful democracies, which is on the way to become an economic superpower on its own terms. It withstood the onslaught of the ravages of time and history, and in spite of all the capriciousness and cynicism, not forgetting the disparaging appellatives the world had about it, India is a successful 'impossible concept', whatever the world may say.

Within this 'impossible concept', crested as it were, is another 'impossible concept', collectively known as the Northeast, euphemistically referred to as the 'Seven sisters'. In the seemingly impregnable mountainous terrain cradling some of the most beautiful valleys and mightiest of rivers, nature has crafted within its fold a small sanctuary, a little paradise. The region has a chequered history having one of the largest concentrations of diverse indigenous people forming a menagerie of people of diverse ethnicities and influences largely comprising of Mongoloid origin, from across Asia, who have made the region their home over the years.

Compelled partly by the compulsions of geography and partly by the ethnic composition, a rare confluence of societies and communities with different customs, social habits and cultural attributes evolved. All these ethnic groups conjoin in a symbiotic relationship of seven different states, united to form one single phenomenon like the rainbow with its seven colours. This symbiotic relation has been an integral part of the distinctive feature of the northeast region. The isolation and geo-morphological exclusivity of the region helped it to preserve the inherent purity of the social and cultural ethos, value systems and unique life-styles of the various communities in the region. In one way, this isolation also gave a sense of security, homogeneity and peace to the region. This was not too long ago. Sadly, this sense of security, homogeneity and peace did not last very long.

Just as fate ordains lives of ordinary individual human beings, it also destines the history of communities and regions. In the serenity of the excluded time zone, cut away from the rest of the world and governed by the native sense of justice and fairplay and respect for each other, except when provoked to retaliate in defence, people lived peaceful lives. Each community adhered to its own traditions, accepting life sculptured by the unfolding drama of pain and suffering, interspersed with the occasional smile and laughter that life entails.

However, somewhere, along this road of destiny, unknown to the people of the region, fate conjured and conspired to impose another story, a sad and tragic one. Because hidden behind these stories are the many exogenous influences that changed the lives of the vulnerable and susceptible friendly people of the Northeast. Compelled by circumstances of history and induced by these exogenous factors the politics of ethnic identity assumed ominously menacing proportions. In a haven of seemingly harmonious social and communal cohesiveness, life soon morphed into a cruel drama of tragedy and pain, de-establishing the ethnic equation, social and cultural homogeneity of the region, as ethnic identity politics found resonance among almost all the people across the region. Preoccupation with identity politics became the soft underbelly of the region. History of the region was never the same again. Somewhere at some time in the history of the region, calamitously, many things went horribly wrong.

Already condemned to desolation, underdevelopment and neglect through a series of unfair historical dispensations, the region acquired the ignominy of being one of the most backward and disturbed regions in the world, an appellative that meant a region full of disgruntled people of diverse ethnicities and affinities. Yet hidden behind all these is the smiling demure of the Northeast persona, a unique trait, with an obsessive emphasis of being nice to people. Unfortunately, this positive human attribute; their smiling demure, is most often mistaken for their naivety, simplicity and timidity. The sad part is many people take advantage of this.

The problems of ethnic identic assertions for decades, which gave rise to the law and order problems, have adversely affected the development and progress of the region. Resolutions of this problem still remain elusive and are a cause of major concern for the Governments at both the Centre and the states. Many sympathisers, well-wishers, policy makers have been grappling with this problem to find an amicable solution for the last few decades. In spite of few successes, which provide the occasional glimmer of hope, resolutions of the major issues and problems remain elusive. There is consequently a growing feeling of despondency and a general sense of indifference to the problems of the Northeast, conspicuous by the occasional cosmetic attention and exhibition of concern through half-hearted attempts at peace. This trend is disturbing. Attempt in this book was to take stock, have a relook and find new ways and methods beyond the tried, to overcome the problems posed by ethnic identity assertions, which is acting as a major obstacle to regional development.

I am conscious of the fact that the overview this book provides is too simplistic a cartography to capture all the individual hues and textures the many histories of the various heterogeneous groups and societies of the people of the region with the large brush strokes on a canvas as vast as it is in this book. Yet, the containerisation of the whole region and all the people in it as one single bloc, in spite of the various diverse ethnic groups, having different origins, socio-cultural diversities and religious beliefs, simplifies the process of explaining the region's unique place in the history of identity formation in the country. Further, given the 'distance', both physical and mental as the region and the people are from the rest of the country, such an overarching view is inevitable.

Given the existing fact that politically, altering the demarcated territories will not be easy except for a few marginal alterations and adjustments, reappraising and understanding the ethnic historical 'divide' in the region, in the perspective it should; socio-anthropologically as a region seems a logical corrollary. From this perspective, the historical and anthropological links long forgotten and often ignored are retraced so that the age-old ties and connections among the ethnic communities in the region can be reified. Appreciating their anthropological links, migratory histories and connections in the light of the new perspective can dramatically change attitudes and reduce the misunderstandings among the various ethnic groups in the region. This in turn can infuse a new equation in the relationship among the states and people of the region, which can then facilitate a new approach to regional development through cooperation and partnership and help in resolving various problems connected with the region.

In this context it is important to appreciate that the principle of 'jointness'; partnership and cooperation among the member states of the region is borne out of necessity rather than by choice, since the topography of the region the people occupy as their homes bind them together. The irreversible geo-political reality and the fact that the pain of poverty and want, cuts through the ethnic identity divide should make the people of the region ponder over the problems of ethnic divide and finds ways and means to overcome it. The signs are otherwise ominous and their futures bleak.

The imponderables of history are many, and yet human beings have overcome and effectively countered them and made destinies of their own choose and liking. I have faith in the inherent capability and the goodness of the people of the Northeast to 'overcome' the odds set by blind and insensitive destiny. I say this because; the reality that without planned economic development there cannot be true political power and that for a region like the Northeast without sincere partnership and cooperation among the constituent states of the region real economic development is a mere illusion. This realization must propel the leaders and every right-thinking person in the Northeast and in the country to act fast to neutralize the growing menace of ethnic divide in the Northeast, which threaten the whole development process in the region. Nothing is more beautiful than the hope and prospect of a prosperous and peaceful

Northeast where all the constituent communities and people live and work together to share the benefits of peace and prosperity.

Hope of a changeover requires change of attitude and approach. There are signs that this can be realised. May be in the not too distant future we may see a rainbow, a HOPE, when all seven states together in conjunction like the seven colours of the rainbow fillup the menacing dark sky of despair and hopelessness that engulfs the Northeastern today. The prospect looks promising and tempting.

At the end, therefore, even though I am unable to say what exactly the future holds for the people of the Northeast region, given the imponderables en-route, the faith that I share with many people from other parts of India for the region in this context is, to say the least, sincere and enduring. Perhaps, the book I hope will inspire at least a few people to start thinking and looking at the Northeast region of India with this new hope and perspective. If this optimism is shared, the objective of writing this book and the efforts that went with it would have been certainly worth the while.

Bob Dylan long ago in one of his famous songs, entitled '*The Times they Are A-Changin'*'; first released in 1964 sang of the predicaments facing mankind in the changing times and prognosticated the need for people to change their roles and attitude to live in the present. For now *"...that the waters around"* them *"...have grown ..."* it was time for them to learn to *'swim'* to survive and live in today's world. The first stanza; a part of this epochal song befittingly sums up the main theme and essence of this book. The people of the Northeast of India, irrespective of their ethnic identic affiliations must learn to adjust, respect and help each other to build a new economic order, so that all of them can swim through the tide of economic changes that is sweeping the world all around them. Or else, the people of the Northeast will be once again sadly left behind, drowned as they always have been. History need not be made to repeat once again, at least this time.

This song was sung long ago, when people of my age then shared the hopes and dreams for the people of the unfortunate Northeast with the rest of the country. It touched our hearts and stirred our minds then. Forty long years and more, after the song was first heard the true meaning and import of the song is now much clearer; it has now a deeper and much more profound meaning than it ever did.

This book through its pages, would have perhaps let the people of the country realise what changes are required in their way of thinking about the people and the Northeast, and for the people of the region, the changes required to be made in their attitudes and relationships with each other within the region, if they hope to find peace, development and progress in their midst. Because it is only then, that the future can truly be theirs for the asking. It will be time then to not only hope but also finally find the elusive fulfillment they have been hoping for so long. This is possible, because it is my sincere belief that as the country wakes up to the true potential of the Northeast region, the people and their leaders will respond positively and adequatly to the new dawn. Hope, they say is like the clouds, some pass by, while others bring rain. I hope for the latter. This hope lives on.

INDEX

In the context of regional partnership among the states, as a prefix, one of the major obstacles is the ethnic 'divide' prevalent in the region. This point is reiterated because of its significance and importance as a major problem affecting the development of the region. This is primarily because there is a direct link between the prevailing levels of underdevelopment, backwardness in the region and the nature of segmented individual state oriented planning and development process arising out of the ethnic divide in the region. An institution like the NEC is best placed to neutralize this unfortunate development by bringing the various states together on one platform as the statutory planning body for the region. In fact, even though the NEC's primary role is to plan and coordinate the execution of all the major and interstate development projects and schemes in the region, but along with the civil society the NEC can effectively play the role of a catalytic institution by bringing together the various ethnic groups (states) closer.

Conceptually one thing is clear, given the geo-political environment; the NEC remains one of the most important institutions created by the Government of India for the Northeast. The NEC today, even though made to appear to be a preposterous institution of contradictions, given the prevalent disposition of the Government of India towards it, is nevertheless the only institution in the Northeast, which has the right pedigree and capability to ensure the coordinated and planned development of the region through consensus among the states of the region. Perhaps, more significantly its potential role as a peacemaker of sorts, of bridging the ethnic divide in the region, a role not legally or administratively mandated, nevertheless significant from the perspective of the people of the Northeast, is what distinguished it from all other central institutions in the region. From this perspective, NEC occupies a unique and special position in the region.

Given this background of the needs of the region, economically and also ethno-politically, the NEC as such cannot be a mere 'appeasing institution', a symbol of empathy of the Government of India to placate the sentiments of the people of the Northeast region as was done in the past. The NEC has to be empowered in such a manner that it can act and function as an instrument of 'change' for the economic development and holistic betterment of the lives of the people of the Northeast region.

In short, if the NEC is provided with the necessary and appropriate support, authority and a clear direction, it is capable of not only fulfilling its mandated role as the regional planning body but also become the catalytic institution that is capable of reducing the growing ethnic divide. In one way, it can be said with a certain amount of conviction and experience that one of the reasons why the ethnic divide has increased in recent times in the Northeast is the undermining of the unifying role of the NEC in the region. In fact, it will not be too far out a statement to make that the biggest threat to peace and prosperity in the Northeast in the days ahead is most likely to come from the implosion arising out of the growing problems of ethnic divide in the region. The Central government by treating the NEC as a planning body and forgetting the fact that the role of the NEC can go far beyond the scripted text and that it can be made into an institution capable of bringing the warring ethnicities closer together, has failed to see the true worth of the NEC. The Central government needs to overcome such shortsightedness on its part and reassess the role of the NEC holistically by going much beyond mere invectives against it. In short, the NEC as an institution is what it is today primarily because the Central government has not only given to it a clear mandate or direction about its role and functioning over the years, but has also failed to realise its potential as a social catalyst capable of bridging the ethnic divide in the Northeast. The NEC was simply allowed to pursue its mandated role as a mere planning body, and that too without the mandatory administrative orders required for it to function effectively, forgetting in the process its true worth and value.

Thus, while respecting the political freedom and status of the various State Governments, the NEC as a regional planning body can play the role of an economic and social catalytic converter by breaking down psychological barriers of ethnic identities and forging an economic partnership among the constituent member States of the NEC. The role of the NEC should be similar to the role played by the European Union, which undertakes decisions collectively on economic and social issues that affects all the constituent member countries of Europe. The question that arises is if the concept and role of the European Union is efficacious enough and has worked well for the countries of Europe, there is no reason to doubt why the NEC with its Constitutional mandate behind it, should not be able to perform similar role as the regional planning body satisfactorily